A. J. Coates

The ethics of war

Manchester University Press

Manchester and New York

distributed exclusively in the USA by St. Martin's Press

Copyright © A. J. Coates 1997

Published by Manchester University Press,
Oxford Road, Manchester M13 9NR, UK
and Room 400, 175 Fifth Avenue, New York, NY 10010, USA

Distributed exclusively in the USA by
St. Martin's Press, Inc., 175 Fifth Avenue, New York,
NY 10010, USA

Distributed exclusively in Canada by
UBC Press, University of British Columbia, 6344 Memorial Road,
Vancouver, BC, Canada V6T 1Z2

British Library Cataloguing-in-Publication Data
A catalogue record is available from the British Library

Library of Congress Cataloging-in-Publication Data
Coates, A. J. (Anthony Joseph), 1940–
       The ethics of war / A. J. Coates.
           p.   cm.
       Includes bibliographical references (p.   ) and index.
       ISBN 0–7190–4045–0 (hardcover). — ISBN 0–7190–4046–9 (pbk.)
       1. War—Moral and ethical aspects.   2. Just war doctrine.
     I. Title
       U22.C5397   1997
       172′.42—dc21   97–5364

ISBN 0 7190 4045 0 *hardback*
     0 7190 4046 9 *paperback*

First published 1997
01 00 99 98 97   10 9 8 7 6 5 4 3 2 1

Typeset in Great Britain
by Northern Phototypesetting Co Ltd, Bolton
Printed in Great Britain
by Bell & Bain Ltd, Glasgow

Contents

Acknowledgements   *page* vi
Introduction   1

Part I: Images of war

1	*Realism*	17
2	*Militarism*	40
3	*Pacifism*	77
4	*The just war*	96

Part II: Principles and concepts of the just war

5	*Legitimate authority*	123
6	*Just cause*	146
7	*Proportionality and the recourse to war*	167
8	*Last resort*	189
9	*Proportionality and the conduct of war*	208
10	*Noncombatant immunity*	234
11	*Peacemaking*	273

Bibliography of works cited   295
Index   305

Acknowledgements

I am indebted to the staff at Manchester University Press for their efficient and friendly support throughout the preparation of this book. Richard Purslow's help with the conception and the planning of the book was essential. Dr Peter Moorehead Wright of the University of Wales (Aberystwyth) read part of the draft manuscript. His comments and suggestions were extremely helpful, though he must not be held responsiible for the use to which they were put. I am grateful to Pat Hicks and Ann Cade of the University of Reading, particularly for their help in finding a way through the maze of word-processing, and to David Phelps for his help in the preparation of the typescript for publication.

Above all I wish to thank Paula, my wife, for her constant support and encouragement, and John and Peter, my sons, for their patience and understanding.

Introduction

This is a book about the *ethics* of war, about war in its moral or normative aspect.[1] The central question that it addresses is how (if at all) moral reasoning might be brought to bear upon the activity of war. The very notion that morality may be applicable to such a destructive enterprise as war will strike some as bizarre, even perhaps as scandalous. The contrary assumption that war lies beyond any moral pale is not only a common one, but one that, particularly in the light of twentieth-century experience, often seems irresistible.[2] Nevertheless that assumption will be resisted here, even while the dangers of exaggerating the moral potential of war are underlined. The moral regulation or limitation of war, it will be argued, *is* possible, though it depends in great part upon keeping the moral impulse itself in check.

Though the book examines alternative conceptions of war, its central focus is on the just war tradition of thought.[3] This may seem an arbitrary narrowing of its subject-matter. The ethics of war is not after all exhausted by any single tradition. The just war tradition, however, is not simply one tradition among many – something that even its firmest critics acknowledge. One recent critic describes it as 'the dominant intellectual tradition of thought about the morality of war' (Norman 1995, p. 117). Another, while acknowledging that 'the ethics of war and international relations cannot be reduced in absolute terms to the just war tradition', suggests that 'this does represent its most important development' (Zolo 1997, p. 86 n. 4).[4] The fact is that this tradition has monopolised the moral debate about war, at least in the Western world.

In the theoretical sphere the tradition has been by far the most prolific in the development of an apparatus of specific moral principles and concepts by means of which the experience of war can be articulated and subjected to systematic moral investigation. The moral argument about war, though by no means confined to just war utterances, is more often than not conducted in just war terms, so that even opponents of the tradition remain in its debt, developing their own moral response to war largely in contention with just war thinking.[5] Moreover, given the extreme catholicity and internal variety of the tradition itself (a variety sometimes bordering on anarchy) the narrowing of focus is more apparent than real. The problems, issues, arguments, methods and concerns that an inclusive ethics of war might be expected to address fall well within the tradition's wide embrace.

The influence of the tradition has not been confined to the realm of moral theorizing. Just war principles and concepts have helped to shape (and have in turn been shaped by) international law in a decisive way. Its idiom has become the most popular moral idiom of war, an idiom frequently employed by those engaged either as practitioners of war or as media commentators upon it. This is not without its problems so far as the moral theory itself is concerned: the dangers of deliberate subversion or of unconscious distortion (of a moral 'highjacking') are real, and may account for much of the criticism levelled at the tradition.[6] In its popular and all too 'political' form the concept of a 'just war' is often stripped of its essential moral complexity and ambiguity, with the result that the idiom is made to serve an ideological or propagandist, that is, war-*enhancing* purpose. Transformed into a moral crusade, its critical and constraining function is lost and it becomes a prime catalyst of war.[7]

The argument of the book rests on no delusions about the moral grandeur of war of the kind that, though sometimes associated with a just war approach, are more aptly associated with militarism. To speak of a 'just war' in this context is not to stamp war (either in general or in particular) with the kind of unqualified moral seal of approval that serves to silence all further moral questioning. Far from it. The just war tradition is rooted in a sense of human moral fallibility and the conviction that any moral enterprise, especially one as unpromising as war, is always to a greater or a lesser extent flawed. Its initial moral presumption against war (evident in the moral hurdles with which it surrounds the recourse to war) stems from the recognition that *at best* war is an extremely blunt and imperfect instrument of justice. However 'just', no war is ever so pure or ever so untainted as to be entered into without grave moral misgivings, or to be conducted without continual moral scrutiny and anxiety, or to be concluded without a sense of moral failure and remorse.

That moral remorse is an appropriate response to a just war is disputed by critics of the tradition. Richard Norman, for example, argues that the understanding of war as an act of justice provides no grounds for remorse. Quite the reverse: the logical as well as actual response of those who see themselves engaged in a just war is moral triumphalism (Norman 1995, pp. 198–9).[8] Many objections take a similar form, and stem from the conviction that a just war approach, far from making things better, makes things worse, the frequency and ferocity of past wars often being attributable to the moral energy for war-making that so-called 'just wars' have generated and released.[9]

There is little doubt that, in practice, the association of moral triumphalism with a just war approach has sometimes been justified. *In its authentic form, however, the aim of just war thinking is not justification (and certainly not glorification) of war, but containment.* In introducing the topic of war Aquinas posed a question the negative form of which indicates the proper orientation of just war analysis: 'Is warfare always sinful?' (Sigmund 1988, p. 64); and the scepticism that should inform any just war analysis is evident in the prominent place given to right intention in this and other early formulations of just war principles (an emphasis that arose from the perception that even a just cause is more often than not simply a pretext for the advancement of other, often unjust, aims).[10] A just war is more a matter of preventing or curbing evil (one's own as well as that of an adversary) than it is of promoting good. The object is to retain some semblance of a moral hold upon an activity that constantly threatens moral dissolution. Of course the kind of control that morality may exert over war is always severely limited – much more limited than the moral control achievable in less extreme situations. Yet the conviction remains that some control is better than none, and that even in the barbaric realm of war morality can make a difference.

This 'negative' appraisal of war, which underlines its limited and fragile moral potential, ought to rule out not just the militaristic and enthusiastic embrace of war but also the complacent acceptance of war as a normal instrument of justice and a permanent feature of the international order. The tradition's alleged failure to do so constitutes its principal weakness in the opinion of some critics, particularly those of a pacifist or 'pacificist' persuasion, whose aim is the abolition of war.[11] The real problem, they argue, is not with the tradition's enthusiastic and occasional support for particular wars, but with its general and permanent moral endorsement of war. Even in its more restrained and apparently critical form the tradition ends up sustaining and strengthening the institution of war, its very attempt to subject war to moral regulation lending moral credibility and support to the activity. It has become one of the mainstays of the prevailing system of war, and a prime obstacle to the achievement of a real peace.

This is a serious criticism that strikes at the heart of the moral project in which the just war tradition consists. Like the critical attribution of militarism, it is a salutary criticism from which the tradition has much to learn. The realism on which the tradition sometimes prides itself is also a potential source of weakness, as well as one of its great strengths. Interpreted too conservatively the theory becomes less one of moral analysis and criticism than of moral propaganda, an ideological tool at the service of unscrupulous rulers. Preservation and constant renewal of its critical spirit is essential to the continuing health and vitality of the tradition. Its key concepts must be understood as *critical* concepts, not in the sense of being formed in disdainful regard for the 'facts' (a common enough form of criticism, but one that is fundamentally alien to the tradition), but in the sense of arising out of an awareness of the limits or inadequacies of existing practice. This applies not just to the concepts of war but, even more importantly, to the concepts of peace that the theory brings to its understanding of war. Exponents of the tradition must guard against the suppression or neglect of its more dynamic aspects. The radical overcoming of war (and not just its moral containment) should be an aspiration that the tradition shares with other more overtly pacific traditions of thought, and one that shapes and informs just war thinking.

The internal variety of the just war tradition makes its accurate assessment more difficult. Much criticism of the tradition appears to arise from an identification of the tradition as a whole with a particular and, in some key respects, unrepresentative or bastardized version of it. The criticisms of both Norman and Holmes, for example, rely heavily on the identification of the tradition with the work of Michael Walzer.[12] It is this, for example, that accounts for the prominence that Norman gives to the 'aggressor–defender' distinction[13] in his criticism of just war theory, or for the primacy given to national sovereignty and territorial integrity in his discussion of just cause (a primacy that clearly contradicts the universalist premiss of traditional just war thought); and this that accounts for Holmes's judgement that '*reason of state* begins to show itself in the guise of just war theory' (Holmes 1989, p. 170), a judgement that owes everything to Walzer's (and, it is alleged, O'Brien's) concept of 'supreme emergency'.[14]

That Walzer's work should be singled out in this way is not surprising given the prominent role it has played in the renewal of interest in just war thought. At the same time it is important to recognize that Walzer's study is, like any other, only one interpretation of the tradition and, moreover, one that often deals cavalierly with the classical tradition of just war thought. The criticisms that Norman and Holmes level at Walzer, therefore, are criticisms that are likely to emerge from within the just war tradition itself. His excessive 'realism', his reliance at key points in his analysis on utilitarian argumentation, his apparent willingness to sacrifice a fundamental just war norm like noncombatant immunity to military necessity, his preoccupation with national sovereignty and territorial integrity, his inclination to moral particularism are all out of step with mainstream just war thinking. From the latter viewpoint Walzer's work often looks more like a statement of the 'morality of states' than it does a statement of just war theory. Criticism of Walzer (however conclusive or convincing) is not therefore the same as criticism of just war theory.[15]

The perception that the just war approach has become an anachronism, that the reality that lent the tradition credibility and may once have established its relevance no longer exists, is another common source of criticism. One form of this criticism argues that the reality of modern war places it outside the scope of just war thinking. In some cases this judgement is driven by a preoccupation with the nuclear issue, so that it is the 'nuclear age' in which we are now seen to live that has made just war thinking irrelevant. This was the prevailing view of things throughout the period of the Cold War, and it had a damaging impact not just on just war thinking but on the ethics of war as a whole. The monopoly of the moral debate about war by the nuclear issue led to the extensive neglect of the moral investigation of conventional forms of warfare, despite the fact that these forms of war, including the more novel varieties of guerilla warfare and terrorism, continued to proliferate throughout the period in question.[16]

The relative neglect of the nuclear issue in the argument of this book (its focus anyway is less on specific forms of warfare than on principles and concepts of analysis) is, therefore, quite deliberate, and reflects the imbalance created by that earlier monopoly. The problems of conventional (that is actual war) are in some respects more pressing. Certainly, they can be and need to be addressed independently of the nuclear issue – something it was difficult to do during the period when the nuclear super-powers so often adopted the posture of war and when any recourse to war seemed to threaten escalation and nuclear anni-hilation. The end of the Cold War has allowed these problems to be given the moral consideration that their importance justifies.

The judgement that the just war is outmoded is not always driven by the thought of nuclear war and its apparent destruction of any ethical mould. Often it derives from the view that all modern war – whether nuclear or conventional – is by its nature 'total', and therefore beyond the just war or any other moral pale. This seems an exaggeration of the present state of things, though it rightly draws attention to certain aspects or tendencies of modern war that, morally speaking, are acutely problematic. However, far from demonstrating just war's redundancy, these developments suggest a need for the continued and urgent application of just war thinking, and for renewed resistance to the fatalistic acceptance of some forms of contemporary military strategy and practice.[17]

In the post-Cold War era the charge of anachronism often results from a focus, not on the new face of war, but on the changing face of international relations. In a global and pro-gressively cosmopolitan era, it is argued, just war thinking is out of place. Leaving aside the question of how well founded this ver-sion of the contemporary world is, the implication on which this criticism depends for its force, namely, that just war theory is essentially wedded to the 'states-system', is highly disputable. Given the tradition's emergence prior to that of the system of sov-ereign states this seems unlikely (though this is not to deny that *some* contemporary versions of just war theory may be unduly attached to the states-system). It will be argued within that the basic premiss of just war thinking is a universalist premiss that posits the existence of an order transcending states. To link the 'just war' to some form of moral particularism (which its interpretation as a 'states' theory would seem to imply) would make a nonsense of this version of just war theory. This is not to say, of course, that just war theory is antagonistic towards states or to the existence of a plurality of political communities – anything but. Just war theory is universalist without being cosmopolitan, and the universal order that it promotes is not without internal variety or differentiation. In this respect the just war tradition seems better equipped than most to respond to a world in which global interests and concerns appear increasingly to the fore.

The book is divided into two parts. The scope of Part I is much wider than that of Part II. The object of enquiry in Part I is the broad image or conception of war that the more detailed moral analysis of war pursued in Part II is seen to presuppose. The principal object of investigation here is not the precise form that the moral analysis of war takes but the much more general question of whether the attempt at the moral regulation of war is justified in the first place. With this in mind attention is directed not only to the just war conception but to rival images of war – realism, militarism, and pacifism – with which just war thinking must contend. Through a comparison with these alternative and vying conceptions the just war image may be brought into sharper focus and the formidable challenges (and threats) that these images of war represent may be exposed. The overall purpose is to investigate the proper nature and the limits of any attempt at the moral regulation of war, and identifying the obstacles and pitfalls in the way of such regulation is seen as crucial to the outcome.

In defining positions and in making comparisons simplification is apparent and deliberate. The abstract categories employed are in some respects misleadingly straightforward and unambiguous. The historical and contemporary phenomena to which they are intended to relate are more varied and complex, embracing subdivisions of opinion in some of which the image of war attributed to the general category can appear blurred. Not all realists, for example, take an amoral view of war, though it is primarily in those terms that realism is understood here. Where such concrete blurring of an ideal image occurs the gap between a just war approach and the image in question may begin to close. Nevertheless simplification serves a useful analytical purpose, since the sharper the focus the clearer conceptual differences (and practical outcomes) become. As Aron suggests: 'to distinguish between opposing concepts we must consider extreme cases' (Aron 1983, pp. 406–7).

These simpler images or conceptions of war are wider in definition and application than those that are sometimes encountered in the literature. In *Thinking About Peace and War*, for example, Martin Ceadel (1989) distinguishes five 'war-and-peace theories' (along with several subdivisions): militarism; crusading; defencism; pacific-ism; and pacifism. Though it makes no claims to be exhaustive (the distinctions are chosen on the grounds of their significance relative to the overall argument and with a particular analytical purpose in mind), this list is fuller than the one employed here. Ceadel's more specific and concrete classification enjoys the advantages that derive from more detailed investigation, and contributes much to an understanding of the literature of war. Its disadvantage is that it suppresses some important affinities that cut across more specific (and conventional) boundaries, affinities that are of practical as well as theoretical interest, since, if left unrecognized, they may threaten the moral regulation of war. Ceadel's narrow definition of militarism, for example, which largely equates it with fascism, obscures the covert militarist tendencies sometimes discernible even in the most overtly pacific images of war. By accepting the pacific credentials of a movement at face value – pacifism as the complete *antithesis* of militarism, for example – the way to the undermining of the moral limitation of war may be left open.

In Part II the principles and concepts of just war analysis are explored. The attention of the reader has been drawn already to the internal variety of the just war tradition. The point is worth reiterating. There is no definitive list of principles and concepts, much less a definitive interpretation of them. Even the basic distinction itself between just recourse (*ius ad bellum*) and just conduct (*ius in bello*) engenders internal controversy (as to the relative emphasis to be given to the different parts of the distinction, for example). Some lists of principles are longer than others.[18] Variability is most evident in the definition of the principles of just recourse, and what is included and what is left out here is often a good indication of the general orientation of the particular just war approach and of the manner in which just war theory is being interpreted. In the present case the list is a full one, but the discussion of two of the principles – *right intention* and *prospects of success* – is combined with the discussion of other principles (*just cause* and *proportionality* respectively). The reasons for this are partly organizational and partly conceptual. The latter consideration is paramount in the case of *prospects of success*, which seems less a principle in its own right than a corollary of *proportionality*. *Right intention* is a different matter, and might well have warranted independent discussion. Certainly its incorporation into the chapter on *just cause* is not a reflection of the relative unimportance attached to it by the author.[19]

As befits a form of *applied* ethics, the method adopted in Part II may be described fittingly as one of 'moral casuistry', though the term needs to be used with caution. The term and the method have attracted considerable moral opprobrium, often not without justification. The method is open to two principal forms of abuse. In some instances of its use the method is employed in an excessively deductive form, according to which the reference to cases is purely illustrative, the principles being already well established independent of experience and the study of cases contributing nothing to the fuller articulation and understanding of the principles themselves. When this occurs moral theory becomes more and more abstract, dogmatic, and out of touch with the moral reality that it seeks to shape and influence (a progression marked by increasing clashes between the moral theory and common moral intuitions).

What such 'moral deductivism' ignores is the *proper* dependence of moral theory upon moral practice or conduct. As Oakeshott has observed: 'Moral ideals are not, in the first place, the products of reflective thought, the verbal expressions of unrealized ideas, which are then translated ... into human behaviour; they are the products of human behaviour, of human practical activity, to which reflective thought gives subsequent, partial and abstract expression in words' (Oakeshott 1962, pp. 72–3). Both in its origins and in its continuing development the just war theory – like any moral theory – is linked to moral practice, and it is in the interest of sound moral reasoning that that link should be recognized and that it should remain a strong one.

In this 'experiential' method the reference to cases is never purely illustrative. Rather it is a way of articulating, testing and refining principles in the light of a moral experience shaped by changing social and historical circumstances. Of course the dangers of 'moral inductivism' are as real as those of 'moral deductivism'. Recognition of the dependence of moral theory upon moral practice may lead to the betrayal of moral principle or to the uncritical moral endorsement of a particular practice. As Oakeshott's defence of the creative interplay between theory and practice suggests: 'This view of the matter does not [and must not] deprive moral ideals of their power as critics of human habits' (Oakeshott 1962, p. 73). Nevertheless, the dangers of such a deprivation are real and need to be acknowledged and guarded against. The rejection of moral deductivism should not be interpreted as a plea for 'situation ethics' or for 'a morality without rules' that determines 'what is right by electing that course of action which offers the most beneficent consequences or greatest utility in each act, each particular situation' (Fletcher 1978, p. 421).

This 'casuistical' method accounts in large measure for the contentious nature of just war reasoning. A form of moral analysis that depends so explicitly on the interplay of theory and practice must, by it very nature, lead to some disagreement. Not only do just war theorists differ in their understanding of theoretical principles and concepts, but they differ in their interpretation of the facts on which the moral judgement of war is crucially dependent. There are, for example, just as many critics of the Gulf War among just war theorists as there are defenders of it. This divergence, though in some cases the result of theoretical dispute, arises in large measure from the contingent nature of the assessment and from the large number of imponderables that apply in this or any other war (the nature of the Iraqi threat, the efficacy of sanctions and diplomacy, the likely costs of military action, the sustainability of the coalition, and so on). There is nothing abnormal (much less anything scandalous) about such disagreement.

Finally, and perhaps most importantly, the method has an

advantage that may not be enjoyed by less empirically based theories: it keeps the reality – the horror – of war firmly in view. Thereby it inhibits that moral insensitivity that the preoccupation with a too theoretical or abstract model of war can engender. Moral theories of war need to guard against that 'callous complacency with which', according to Siegfried Sassoon (writing in 1917), 'the majority of those at home regard the continuance of agonies which they do not share, and which they have not sufficient imagination to realize' (quoted in Graves 1960, p. 214). The more remote or abstract the reality of war becomes the less reliable (and the more glib) its moral assessment becomes. For those happily denied the direct and personal experience of war the imaginative realization of war for which Sassoon and others plead becomes an essential part of the moral understanding of war. Those who seek that understanding do well to remember the words of Wilfrid Owen:

> But cursed are dullards whom no cannon stuns,
> That they should be as stones.
> Wretched are they, and mean
> With paucity that never was simplicity.
> By choice they made themselves immune
> To pity and whatever moans in man
> Before the last sea and the hapless stars;
> Whatever mourns when many leave these shores;
> Whatever shares
> The eternal reciprocity of tears.'

(Wilfrid Owen, *Insensibility*)[20]

Notes

1 The specific and practical focus of the book needs to be emphasized. There is no attempt to engage 'meta-ethical' issues or even to consider the general principles and concepts that apply to all 'normative' ethics. This is an exercise in applied ethics. As such, the argument is conducted at a much lower and more concrete level than is the case in other more fundamental and ambitious forms of ethical study.

2 'Never think', Hemingway wrote, 'that war, no matter how necessary, nor how justified, is not a crime' (quoted in Fussell 1991, p. 25).

3 The book is an *interpretation* of the just war tradition, not a history

or a summary of it. Though historical references may occur from time to time, no attempt will be made to trace the course of its development. Similarly, while the attention of the reader may be drawn on occasions to the present (often contentious) state of just war thinking, no attempt will be made to examine current just war thinking in any full and systematic way. The aim is not to give an account of the tradition so much as to use its resources to develop a moral understanding of war. As an interpretation of the tradition it will of course contain a strongly subjective (even perhaps idiosyncratic) element. As befits any tradition, but particularly this one, there is no definitive or received version of it. Though the tradition is not without a certain identity, its theoretical expression and practical application comprehend an often bewildering variety of positions, many of which are not reconcilable. As a result any individual reading of the tradition is likely to be contentious to some extent, as much for supporters as for critics of the tradition.

4 Another, less critical, source claims 'that barring extreme positions such as Machiavelli's any departure from strict pacifism inevitably leads to an acceptance of those principles espoused by the theory of the just war' (Fernández-Santamaria 1977, p. 130).

5 This is is the case with Robert Holmes's *On War and Morality* (a defence of pacifism) and Richard Norman's *Ethics, Killing and War* (in which a 'pacificist' position is advanced). Both are sympathetic criticisms of the tradition that readily acknowledge indebtedness (e.g. see Norman 1995, p. 237).

6 Even well-informed and sympathetic criticism often seems to rely on the assimilation of the theory with a practice to which moral exception is justifiably taken. For example, in his criticism of just war theory, Richard Norman makes much of the fact that governments 'tend to assume that they have an automatic right of military resistance to any violation of national sovereignty ... [but] ... tend to regard armed resistance to internal oppression as much less justifiable' (Norman 1995, p. 156). This is probably true, but hardly constitutes criticism of a moral tradition that, typically, denies the state that automatic right and upholds the principle of a just revolution (see within, especially Chapter 5). The tradition cannot be held responsible for the malpractice of rulers (or the deficiencies of international law) when the malpractice in question is proscribed by the tradition itself. A misuse of the tradition is not an instance of its practice. It may be the case, however, that the reason for the assimilation stems from the particular statement of the tradition that Norman's criticism targets, one that is more closely identified with the practice in question than more traditional or orthodox formulations (see within).

7 Even so, perhaps the widespread use of the just war idiom is an indication of how closely related moral theory and moral practice are in

this instance. This may be regarded as one of the tradition's great strengths, and not just as a potential weakness. Just war thinking appears in step with basic moral intuitions about war.

8 In opposition to that moral triumphalism Norman cites Hemingway : 'I think that after the war there will have to be some great penance done for the killing' (Norman 1995, p. 199). What Hemingway alludes to here, however, is an ecclesiastical practice *shaped by just war thinking*.

9 See David Welch *Justice and the Genesis of War* (1993). Underlining the influence of the justice motive as a cause of war, Welch argues that without a 'global institutional structure' it will continue to be part of the problem rather than part of the solution.

10 Aquinas's scepticism is echoed by the seventeenth-century neo-Thomist thinker Suárez, who wrote, 'while a war is not *per se* evil, yet, because it may bring many misfortunes, it is one of those undertakings which are often ill done, and therefore it needs a good many conditions to make it just' (quoted in Hamilton 1963, p. 142).

11 Both Holmes and Norman argue along these lines.

12 The same is true of Zolo's criticism in *Cosmopolis*.

13 The moral inadequacy of this distinction is discussed in Chapter 6.

14 See Walzer 1992 and O'Brien 1981.

15 This distancing of the just war tradition from Walzer's position is not intended to belittle in any way the enormous contribution that his work (particularly *Just and Unjust Wars*) has made to a moral understanding of war and to the renewed emphasis on the moral regulation of war.

16 As Weigel argued at the time: 'Too exclusive a focus on the problem of nuclear weapons, their possession and use ... has led to a situation in which we lack sufficient moral clarity on those issues of the use of military force that are before us virtually every day' (Weigel 1987, p. 474).

17 Fussell voices that fatalism when he writes: 'Aerial bombing of civilians is now such a natural part of modern war that no one any longer would think of wasting time debating its morality, as some people did even so recently as the Second World War' (Fussell 1991, p. 20).

18 Aquinas lists only three [*legitimate authority, just cause and right intention*), though other principles (*proportionality*, for example) are implied in his further discussion of just war (*Summa Theologiae* II-II, Qu. 40, art. 1 and Qu. 64, art. 7). Later in the tradition additional principles were articulated or made explicit.

19 The author has discussed the principle at greater length in an article entitled 'The New World Order and the Ethics of War', in B. Holden (ed.) (1996), *The Ethical Dimensions of Global Change*.

20 Owen was killed by machine-gun fire a week before the Armistice that brought the First World War to an end.

Part I

Images of war

1

Realism

Realism resists the application of morality to war. Such resistance is typically part of a more general moral scepticism that is applied not just to the extreme circumstance of war but to international relations in general. The reason for this resistance is twofold. In the first place, it springs from the conviction that the reality in question is morally intractable, the dynamics of international relations and war being seen to confound most, if not all, attempts to apply an alien, moral structure to them. Secondly, and more urgently, it arises from the fear that the very attempt to impose a moral solution has tragic consequences. Not only does the attempt fail, it fails dangerously.

One of the most well-known and influential expositions of realism occurs in E. H. Carr's classic work *The Twenty Years' Crisis* (1981), first published in 1939. The point of origin of the book is a criticism of the assumptions that were seen by the author to have underpinned much of the foreign policy of the Western powers in the interwar period and to have lain behind such doomed initiatives as the League of Nations. In the book Carr argues that for all our sakes the realist perspective must come to inform (though not to monopolize) the conduct of international relations. Conversely, we require emancipation from a persistent 'utopianism' that distorts our understanding and corrupts our practice. Combating such utopianism is the declared objective of a book that was written 'with the deliberate aim of counteracting the glaring and dangerous defect of nearly all thinking, both academic and popular, about international politics in English-speaking countries from 1919 to 1939 – the almost total neglect of the factor of power' (Carr 1981, *Preface to Second Edition*). It is in the systematic neglect of the factor of power (to which a rationalistic faith in 'the compelling power of reason' gives rise) that 'utopianism' is seen principally to consist.

The meaning and the purpose of realism are revealed in this, its negative image. Without the antithetical notion of 'utopianism' (or of its synonyms 'moralism', 'idealism' and 'legalism') realism would be largely unintelligible. Realism is a reaction against the perceived and powerful tendency to apply, or to seek to apply, moral norms and prescriptions to the international domain with scant regard for the innumerable constraints that the realities and complexities of power impose. Utopianism has grossly inflated expectations about the world of international politics. Wedded to an abstract image of a just and perfect order, it concludes that the world at large must find its ideal constructs irresistible.

In utopianism or moralism two mutually reinforcing tendencies are seen at work. Firstly, the ends that are sought are invested with such compelling moral force or attraction that little thought needs to be given, and little thought is given, to the means of their attainment: 'The utopian, fixing his eyes on the future, thinks in terms of creative spontaneity' (Carr 1981, p. 11). Secondly, the moral puritanism associated with the self-conscious pursuit of lofty ideals breeds such contempt and hatred for the disorderly world of the present that it rules out the use of those imperfect and tainted instruments that normal diplomatic practice finds indispensable. From a utopian perspective a perfect end must be matched by perfect, morally unambiguous and unimpeachable, means. The 'instrumentality of evil' is a concept that is morally abhorrent to the utopian, but is central to most forms of realism.

'Utopianism', when applied to what realism portrays as the irredeemably hostile environment of international relations, is not simply false – it is dangerous. Blinded by its vision of a perfect world (or at the very least of a world that is just as amenable to moral regulation as the world of interpersonal relations), it ignores or treats with open contempt the intricate and delicate mechanisms whereby international order of an inferior but nonetheless real kind is sustained. Activated, perhaps, by the purest of motives, 'utopians' are seen to threaten the fragile construct in which an imperfect peace (the only peace on offer) is seen to consist. Their ostensibly (and always ostentatiously) 'moral' and 'pacific' interventions are thought to increase the likelihood both of war's occurrence and of its greater intensity and longer duration when it occurs.

The argument between realist and utopian is often acrimonious. The utopian claims the moral high ground, accusing the realist of moral duplicity and even of rank immorality, while the realist regards the utopian or moralist at best as a dangerous if well-intentioned fool, at worst as a self-indulgent hypocrite, more concerned with the preservation of a spurious moral purity than with the avoidance of conflict or the alleviation of human distress. The frequently voiced accusation of moral duplicity or double-dealing is something the realist has learned to live with, even perhaps to welcome. Since, according to realism, international relations are not amenable to moral determination, moral inconsistency is in this case not a vice but a virtue. The consistency realism does uphold lies in the persistent recognition of the possibilities and constraints of power and the continual striving to preserve that balance of forces that brings some semblance of order to an anarchic and, therefore, naturally bellicose world. If this results in 'moral duplicity', then so be it. The moral opprobrium that is heaped on the realist as a consequence is a price willingly paid for safeguarding the state's interest or, more broadly (and, morally speaking, perhaps more defensibly), for making the world a safer place.

This approach to international relations is much in evidence in an article about the Gulf War and its aftermath written by Henry Kissinger, the former US Secretary of State and one of the principal theorists and practitioners of realism in the period since the Second World War. While admiring some aspects of US policy in the Gulf, in particular the effective management of the allied coalition during the crisis, Kissinger regrets the creeping idealism that he detects in postwar presidential rhetoric about the creation of a new world order. In his view US foreign policy has suffered more than most from the affliction of idealism. He cites the former president and arch-idealist, Woodrow Wilson, who argued that peace depended 'not on a balance of power but on a community of power ... [in which] ... Nations agree that there shall be but one combination and that is the combination of all against the wrongdoer' (Kissinger 1991). As a moral aspiration, Kissinger suggests, this has a certain plausibility. Unfortunately, it runs counter to the real world.

Contrastingly, Kissinger defends the realist principle of the balance of power, a principle that, he notes, has attracted much criticism and hostility in American history because of its moral neutrality and in-built moral duplicity. The specific charge laid at the door of realism is admitted, but the consequent criticism is very firmly resisted. Winston Churchill's defence of the balance of power as a principle of foreign policy is quoted with unswerving approval:

> The policy of England [of opposing 'the strongest, most aggressive, most dominating' continental power] takes no account of which nation it is that seeks the overlordship of Europe. It is concerned solely with whoever is the strongest or the potentially dominating tyrant. It is a law of public policy which we are following, and not a mere expedient dictated by accidental circumstances, or likes and dislikes.[1]

The essential and permanent aim of such a policy, Kissinger argues, is to prevent domination – the hegemony of one power or of a group of powers – and to foster equilibrium. A foreign policy that has this as its prime objective 'knows few permanent enemies and few permanent friends'. Applied to the Gulf 'it would avoid branding Iraq as forever beyond the pale. Rather it would seek to balance rivalries as old as history by striving for an equilibrium between Iraq, Iran, Syria and other regional powers' (Kissinger 1991). What represents for some a damning indictment of US foreign policy – its readiness to make war against a state to which it had lent recent material as well as diplomatic support – is portrayed here as a mark of genuine statesmanship. Since the balance of power involves 'forces in constant flux', its maintenance demands continual adjustment to changing circumstances free of the constraints imposed by a moral purism.[2] Clearly, for Kissinger and other realists the accusation of moral duplicity is not at all unwelcome and is most unlikely to cause the moral anxiety or discomfort that, no doubt, it is intended to produce. The very different sensitivities and priorities of realism are captured in the robust remark sometimes attributed to Talleyrand (though perhaps more accurately attributed to Boulay de la Meurthe): 'This is worse than a crime, it is a blunder.'

In its purer forms, realism rejects the traditional subjection of politics to ethics and affirms, in particular, the radical autonomy of international politics. Morgenthau, for example, defends 'the autonomy of the political sphere against its subversion by other modes of thought' (Morgenthau 1973, p. 13). 'The political realist', he argues, '[though] not unaware of the existence and relevance of standards of thought other than political ones, ... cannot but subordinate these other standards to those of politics' (Morgenthau 1973, p. 11). Similarly, Schlesinger attacks those who 'regard foreign policy as a branch of ethics' (Lefever 1988, p. 27). 'Realists,' Carr suggests, 'hold that relations between states are governed solely by power and that morality plays no part in them' (Carr 1981, p. 153).

In some respects Carr's formulation is misleading (even as a characterization of 'pure' realism). If morality played no part at all in international relations, realism would lose much of its point. The issues are what part, or parts, *does* morality play and what part *should* it play in the conduct of international relations? In the first place, the realist recognizes that the idiom of politics (particularly in time of war) is commonly a moral idiom, and readily accepts that there is a place for moral or ideological appeals in the equation of power politics. Indeed, as Machiavelli argued long ago, moral rhetoric is one of the most potent weapons in the statesman's armoury, and the ability to convey the appearance of virtue is an indispensable part of the statesman's art. From this realist perspective, however, it is the political utility of morality which is paramount: morality plays, or ought to play, an important instrumental but always subordinate role.[3]

The problem arises for the realist when the moral appeal is regarded independently and is taken so seriously that it begins to undermine the powerbroking and diplomatic horsetrading in which international politics are seen to consist. Those who regard morality in this way intend that it should play the directing role in foreign policy. This cannot happen, the realist insists, because of the very nature or structure of international relations, which is resistant to such moral determination. However the attempt to apply morality is, unhappily, not without effect on international relations. The effect that it does have is quite contrary to the one that is intended by the moralist: such moral intervention, far from moderating or resolving conflict, has the effect of exacerbating it. International relations become more rather than less conflictual as a result of these well-intentioned but entirely misconceived moral initiatives. Real peace is placed in jeopardy by the foolhardy pursuit of a moral chimera.

For those who apply realist ways of thinking to international relations as a whole, the moral limitation of war, that is, of international relations *in extremis* is clearly ruled out: if international relations are thought to be morally indeterminable in times of peace, they will most certainly be so regarded in times of war. In fact realism strips war of its exceptional or abnormal status by affirming its continuity with politics and with that 'state of war' in which peace is seen largely to consist. It reaffirms the view classically enunciated by Clausewitz:

> We know, certainly, that War is only called forth through the political intercourse of Governments and Nations; but in general it is supposed that such intercourse is broken off by War, and that a totally different state of things ensues, subject to no laws but its own. We maintain, on the contrary, that War is nothing but a continuation of political intercourse, with a mixture of other means. (Clausewitz 1982, p. 402)

Though this view, in establishing a basic continuity between politics and war, has the effect of 'normalizing' war, it does not establish a case for easy or eager recourse to war. On the contrary, realists argue that the recognition of the thin dividing line between peace and war and of the fragile and artificial construct that is the state of peace makes realists less eager for war than idealists who assume a natural or normal, and therefore readily securable, condition of peace, of which war is taken to be the very antithesis. For the realist war, as the natural outcome of international relations, is a permanent threat and not a temporary aberration. Keeping it at bay is the principal aim and the great art of the statesman.

In the matter of *recourse* to war (the first broad area of concern so far as any ethics of war is concerned, and the one to which the just war category of *ius ad bellum* corresponds) realism argues that morality is a poor guide. The moralist is a man of extremes. Resisting war when he should embrace it and embracing it when he should resist it, his tendency is either to abhor war or to turn it into a moral crusade. The decision to go to war should be dictated not by the vagaries of moral sentiment but by pragmatic considerations of power and interest. Unfortunately, realists argue, the reverse often applies, particularly in the case of those wars of intervention that lend themselves more readily to a moral or altruistic interpretation. In Kissinger's view, for example, the disaster that befell America in Vietnam had its origin in 'a naive idealism that wanted to set right all the world's ills and believed American goodwill supplied its own efficacy' (Kissinger 1971, p. 230). As a result America found itself involved in a war that it 'knew neither how to win nor how to conclude' (Kissinger 1971, p. 232). Likewise, Schlesinger saw American involvement in Vietnam as 'a precise consequence of the belief that moral principles should govern decisions of foreign policy' (Lefever 1988, p. 37).[4]

Similar criticisms have been voiced of the more recent US intervention in Somalia, commenced in a spirit of high moral endeavour but ending, predictably, in abject failure and moral recrimination. In like manner, realists have persistently questioned the case for military intervention in Bosnia and have sought to unhitch foreign policy from the moral bandwagon rolling in favour of such intervention. Of course a realist case for intervention in Bosnia is possible; but typically it would appeal less to the humanitarian needs of the Muslim community than to the dangers of escalation and the threat to the regional balance of power. In other words, the case would be made (in reality if not in appearance) in terms of interests and power rather than justice and rights.

Characteristically, the realist resists the moral pressure to intervene in those cases in which the national interest is not clearly at stake and that are of such military and political complexity that the course and outcome of military intervention appears entirely unpredictable. In such frequently encountered circumstances the realist advises the kind of caution and restraint advocated by Clausewitz: 'No War is commenced, or, at least, no War should be commenced, if people acted wisely, without first seeking a reply to the question, What is to be attained by and in the same?' (Clausewitz 1982, p. 367). In a matter of such great consequence as war, Clausewitz argues, it is necessary 'not to take the first step without thinking what may be the last' (Clausewitz 1982, p. 374).

At the same time the realist's general understanding of international relations and ready acceptance of war as an instrument of policy means that in many instances the realist is quicker than others to see a need for war. Between the wars it was the realist, Churchill, who argued most vociferously against the policy of appeasement and who urged that steps be taken to curb the power of Germany before it was too late. The idea of a preventive war, of a small and limited conflict now to prevent a much more destructive conflict later, stems from the realist's perception of the essential role that war or the threat of war can play in the maintenance of that balance of power in which peace is seen largely to consist. By contrast, the moralistic approach to war veers uncontrollably between 'the sweeping moral rejection of international violence' and 'the helpless abandonment to its compulsions' (Kennan 1984, p. 90).

For the realist the *conduct* of war (the second main area of ethical concern, corresponding to the just war category of *ius in bello*) is, at least in principle, limitless. The pure logic of war dictates that it be fought without quarter and by all available means: 'War is an act of violence pushed to its utmost bounds', Clausewitz wrote (Clausewitz 1982, p. 103). In this area as in others the realist insists that the attempt to impose *moral* limits on a reality that is morally intractable is more likely to lead to an increase rather than a reduction in human suffering and misery (through the unnecessary prolongation of the war, for example). 'In such dangerous things as War', Clausewitz observed, 'the errors which proceed from a spirit of benevolence are the worst' (Clausewitz 1982, p.102). At the same time, the limitless or 'absolute' nature of war is applied by Clausewitz and other realists to war in its abstract or hypothetical form. In reality war often falls short of its absolute nature. While excluding the moral limitation of war, the realist accepts wholeheartedly the possibility and desirability of limitation of a non-moral kind, a form of limitation driven by pragmatic rather than moral considerations.

'Real' war is limited because of its *instrumental* nature and because it relies on political guidance to determine its objectives, objectives that if the realist has his way (and if morality and ideology are kept in check) are always specific and finite. 'A limited war', Kissinger argues,

> is fought for specific political objectives which, by their very existence, tend to establish a relationship between the force employed and the goal to be attained. It reflects an attempt to *affect* the opponent's will, not to *crush* it, to make the conditions to be imposed seem more attractive than continued resistance, to strive for specific goals and not for complete annihilation. (Kissinger 1957, p. 140)

Though refusing to rule out *any* use of force on *a priori* moral grounds, the realist is not inclined either to use disproportionate force or to prosecute a war beyond the point of diminishing political returns. For the realist war is not an end in itself but a means to something else. As long as it retains that instrumental and subordinate character it will remain limited (or at least defined) by the political ends that it is made to serve. Just as it was adjudged to be in a state's interests to go to war, so a point may be reached, well short of outright victory, when it is seen to be in its interests to cease hostilities and to negotiate a peace. Indeed as far as the realist is concerned war must be fought throughout its course with that possibility in mind, which is why it needs to be conducted with restraint and to remain subject at all times to political control. In short, the concept of war as 'an instrument of policy' itself implies limitation:

> Thus policy makes out of the all-overpowering element of War a mere instrument, changes the tremendous battle-sword, which should be lifted with both hands and the whole power of the body to strike once for all, into a light handy weapon, which is even sometimes nothing more than a rapier to exchange thrusts and feints and parries. (Clausewitz 1982, p. 403)

The idea of a limited war is not, therefore, as alien to the realist tradition as the theoretical espousal of 'absolute' war might at first suggest. In fact realists argue that a war fought in accordance with realist principles is much more likely to remain limited than one fought on overt moral grounds. A 'moral' war readily becomes a war fought without compromise, to which it is difficult to see any end short of the enemy's annihilation. The moral characterization or idealization of the conflict interferes with its 'normal' operation and places obstacles in the way of its limitation and termination. The more moral (or ideological) war becomes the more it approaches the state of total war: 'It is a curious thing, but it is true', writes Kennan,

> that the legalistic approach to world affairs, rooted as it unquestionably is in a desire to do away with war and violence, makes violence more enduring, more terrible, and more destructive to political stability than did the older motives of national interest. A war fought in the name of high moral principle finds no early end short of some total domination ... The legalistic approach to international problems is closely identified with the concept of total war and total victory, and the manifestations of the one spill over only too easily into the manifestations of the other. (Kennan 1984, p.101)[5]

Paradoxically, realism argues, the interest-led war favoured by realists is more moral, at least *in effect*, than the disinterested or altruistic war advocated by moralists. The limited (and thereby, perhaps, the moral) war is safer in the hands of realists than it is in the hands of moralists. In the end morality is better served by those who seem to disavow it than it is by those who trumpet it and who seek to carry all before it.

Though a realist approach may be applied to the business of war in its entirety, so that both the recourse to war and the conduct of war are seen to be beyond direct moral ordering or regulation, some forms of realism are less comprehensive. Not all realist accounts of war depend upon a realist version of international relations as a whole. For some, war represents a special case in a way that it does not for the more complete realist. It is no longer seen as the extension of the political or diplomatic process but as its complete reversal, involving the disruption of normal and morally determinable international relations. In this case, because the general conduct of international relations is seen as morally determinable, so too is the resort to war. The idea of just recourse is therefore admissible. A realist viewpoint, however, is applied to the conduct or prosecution of war, which, it is argued, must not be encumbered by internal moral constraints. In a just cause all available means of carrying the war to the enemy should be employed, not in any moralistic spirit of vengeance or retribution, but simply out of pragmatic necessity. What makes this a form of realism is the perception that in war no other course is possible: though the recourse to war is subject to moral determination, the activity of war itself is not a moral enterprise. Morality ends where war begins.

The bombing of German cities in the Second World War, for example, was defended by its architect, the head of Bomber Command, Air Marshal Harris, in terms such as these. The strategy was condemned by moral critics as a systematic violation of the principle of noncombatant immunity. Harris's defence lay partly in a reaffirmation of the justice of the Allies' cause and partly in a radical scepticism about the moral potentiality of war itself. The blame for the war and all its attendant suffering lay with those who had inflicted war on the world in the first place. No blame attached to the Allies for employing every means at their disposal to resist aggression and to defeat an unprincipled foe. Once begun, the horror of war was unavoidable, since there is no effective way of fighting war, particularly modern war, humanely, and attempts to do so cause more harm than good. Of a bombing policy that laid waste the principal cities of Germany he wrote: 'There was nothing to be ashamed of, except in the sense that everybody might be ashamed of the sort of thing that has to be done in every war, as of war itself' (Harris 1990, p. 58). Harris's words echo those of Sherman in the American Civil War: 'If the people raise a howl against my barbarity and cruelty, I will answer war is war ... War is cruelty, and you cannot refine it' (quoted in Veale 1968, p. 123).

For many who argue such a specific moral intractability of war the primary focus is on war in its modern form. According to this view the nature of war has been wholly and irrevocably transformed in modern times by a development that is as much political as it is military. Clausewitz was among the first to detect the change. In the aftermath of the French Revolution, he argued, war had come much closer to its pure or absolute form, ceasing to be the affair of monarchs and their mercenary armies and becoming an enterprise that engaged the energy and enthusiasm of an entire nation. The means employed in such a war were without limit, and its goal was nothing less than total victory. As to whether this represented the future of war Clausewitz refused to speculate, satisfying himself with the observation that 'bounds ... when once thrown down, are not easily built up again' (Clausewitz 1982, p. 387). In the opinion of many, however, that future was determined once and for all by the 'total' wars of the twentieth century. Henceforward, absolute war would cease to be a mainly hypothetical construct and become the dominant form of war. Modern war *is* total war: a war fought by all, with all, against all. As such it remains completely immune to all attempts at moral limitation.[6]

These realist perspectives, whether total or partial, reflect the preoccupations and concerns of theorists and policy-makers. There is another kind of war realism, a grassroots variety, that is rooted less in the experience of theoreticians, policy-makers and strategists than of those who do the actual fighting. Of course, if realism applies at strategic or command level, then it applies with equal if not greater force at the level of combat. It would be foolish as well as hypocritical to expect soldiers to fight morally when the strategic and tactical planning that determines where and how they will fight is indifferent to moral considerations. The primary responsibility for the manner in which a war is conducted must lie with the political and military leadership that lays down the policy, strategy and tactics of war. However, even when the deliberations of the leaders have been formed in the light of moral imperatives and with moral intent, the exigencies of combat itself are often seen to be such as to vitiate the moral conduct of war.

The argument is a powerful one, not least because it stems from the experience of war itself, expressing the moral powerlessness felt by those personally subjected to the cruel and seemingly irresistible logic of war. Philip Caputo, in his memoir of the Vietnam War, recalls how:

> Everything rotted and corroded quickly over there: bodies, boot leather, canvas, metal, morals ... We were fighting in the cruelest

kind of conflict, a people's war. It was no orderly campaign ... but a war for survival waged in a wilderness without rules or laws; a war in which each soldier fought for his own life and the lives of the men beside him, not caring who he killed in that personal cause or how many or in what manner and feeling only contempt for those who sought to impose on his savage struggle the mincing distinctions of civilized warfare – that code of battlefield ethics that attempted to humanize an essentially inhuman war. (Caputo 1978, p. 229)

Caputo applies his scepticism not just to Vietnam but to all guerilla war. Others, dismissive of the distinction between 'regular' and 'irregular' warfare, extend it further, to embrace all war. In this particular and most specific form of realism the unavoidable constraints of combat – especially in its modern form – are seen to rule out its moral conduct and to render any theory that seeks to subject it to moral regulation utopian or moralistic.

St Augustine, a major contributor to the just war tradition, argued that, despite the horror of war and the pain and suffering that soldiers inflict on one another, war can be fought without violating the law of charity: to fight without hatred and with compassion is a basic moral imperative. According to realism, however, the imperatives of combat are altogether different. In the first place, military training, or the preparation for combat, is designed to generate in the soldier feelings, dispositions, states of mind that undermine any moral capacity or inclination to fight 'justly' or compassionately, let alone 'lovingly'. The military trainee is to be divested of his civilian and pacific responses and turned into an efficient 'killing machine'. Not only is he to be taught how to kill, but the ardent desire to kill is to be implanted in him. In this way behaviour and attitudes that in peacetime would be regarded as beyond the pale become in war the moral or professional norm. As Field Marshal Montgomery advised: 'The troops must be brought to a state of wild enthusiasm before the operation begins ... They must enter the fight with the light of battle in their eyes and definitely wanting to kill the enemy' (Montgomery 1958, pp. 88–9).[7]

The nurturing of a homicidal disposition is one, perhaps indispensable, requirement of combat that is difficult to reconcile with the idea of a morally conducted war (and certainly with St

Augustine's image of the reluctant and compassionate warrior). Equally important, and equally problematic, is the practice of military discipline and the habitual acceptance of an authoritarian and hierarchical command structure. Whatever the military handbooks might say about the soldier's obligation to disobey 'unlawful orders', the specific disciplines of military training seem designed to elicit immediate and unquestioning obedience and to suppress the kind of critical reflection that moral assessment and moral conduct entail. The routines that appear so pointless to the civilian recruit – the endless drilling for example – teach individuals to obey instantly and to submerge their individual identities (and, arguably, thereby their moral identities) in the military unit to which they now belong. Despite appearances, there is nothing arbitrary or perverse about this. Militarily speaking, it is a rational response to the perceived demands of combat. Responses in battle must be both swift and cohesive. If they are not, the fighting unit loses all effectiveness and positions and lives are endangered. The kind of reflection that the moral conduct of war might be thought to entail may well appear a dangerous luxury.

The adoption of a group identity diminishes the sense of individual responsibility. This is not, however, the only way in which the cohesive nature of combat works against the moral conduct of war. The solidarity that members of the military unit experience as a result of shared danger and common suffering narrows their moral horizons at the same time as it deepens their moral sympathies. The sense of moral obligation that they feel towards one another may be strong enough to produce acts of astonishing self-sacrifice, but the more acutely felt the obligation to the group the weaker the sense of obligation to those outside it. Outrage at the death of a comrade in arms, for example, may unleash a blind hatred and bloodlust that makes a mockery of the laws of war. In *Goodbye To All That* Robert Graves compared his reaction to the death of a close mutual friend (in the trenches of the First World War) with that of Siegfried Sassoon: 'I felt David's death worse than any other since I had been in France, but it did not anger me as it did Siegfried. He was acting transport officer and every evening now, when he came up with the rations, went out on patrol looking for Germans to kill' (Graves

1960, p. 164). At the heart of all war, it seems, lies the moral paradox that Caputo observed in Vietnam: 'the comradeship that was the war's only redeeming quality caused some of its worst crimes' (Caputo 1978, p. xvii). It appears that the only 'moral' form of warfare is ruthlessly partisan and based on a moral particularism or collective egoism that habitually ignores the moral claims of an adversary.

War, this 'combat' realism argues, cannot be fought in a morally reflective way. Not only does moral reflection jeopardize the physical safety and military efficiency of the fighting unit, it disrupts the psychology of combat. The psychological pressures of warfare, already very considerable, would become intolerable if combatants were required to engage in constant moral self-criticism. The horrors of war and the moral ambiguity, to put it mildly, of so many acts of war mean that to survive a war, mentally as well as physically, all moral doubts and anxieties must be habitually suppressed.[8] The psychology of war militates against its moral conduct. The only way to remain sane – and militarily efficient – is through immersion in the activity of war and acceptance of its own compelling logic. If there is a time for moral reflection, and perhaps recrimination and remorse, it is after and not during war itself (when it is too late to influence the conduct of war).

The moral conduct of war is further inhibited by the calculation of risk that dominates the thinking of combatants and to which the instinct for survival naturally gives rise.[9] From the standpoint of the combat soldier the risks entailed by the moral conduct of war may well appear excessive. The moral principle of noncombatant immunity, for instance, requires that war be fought in a discriminating way. However, the attempt to differentiate combatant from noncombatant may in some, frequently encountered, circumstances so increase the dangers and risks of war as to rule out the principle's observance. Precision bombing, for example, may be morally superior to area bombing, but it may also make the bombing crew more vulnerable to attack; in a guerilla war, it is safer for a counterinsurgent force to operate 'free fire' zones than it is to attempt to identify an adversary who hides behind a civilian or noncombatant cover; in most battlefield situations, respecting the immunity of prisoners is likely to entail increased vulnerability; in urban and residential areas where military and civilian personnel are intermingled, giving warning of an attack allows the innocent to escape death, but inevitably yields the military advantage to a potential adversary.

Since the application of morality often entails greatly increased risks to life, it may seem that a moral war is also a heroic war. Most soldiers are not heroes and, arguably, we have no right to expect them to be. The only legitimate expectation, it seems, is that they fulfil the requirements of ordinary or common morality, not of an heroic morality. The problem is that in war ordinary morality becomes heroic by force of circumstances. To fulfil even the most basic requirements of common morality calls for a degree of moral heroism that, viewed realistically, must be quite exceptional. The morally conducted war is simply too costly. Once again, the realist argues, the sheer implausibility of the moral determination of war stands revealed. The attempt to apply morality to the domain of war is bound to fail (often disastrously). War *is* hell, and moral theorists delude themselves if they imagine it can be other than it is.

The realist understanding of war and international relations challenges the ethics of war in many respects. The nature and extent of that challenge (as of any response) must vary in accordance with the changing face of realism itself – something that a 'pure' and 'abstract' definition of realism is bound to neglect. The realist tradition, like any tradition, displays an internal variety that can be accounted for by a number of key variables, some of which (like the scope of realism or its sphere of application) have been identified already. The most important variable, however, so far as the ethics of war is concerned, is the nature and extent of realism's resistance to morality. Here degrees of realism are discernible, varying from an amoral realism that disclaims *any* moral intention or concern to a form of *moral* realism that approximates to just war thinking.

Realism of the amoral kind systematically suppresses the moral context of politics and war. Such realism may be either theoretical or practical in its orientation. Both forms claim to be morally neutral and detached (or 'value-free') in their approach, the one being concerned with description and explanation, the other with the identification and application of the technique or art of ruling, and both exhibiting at least a professional indifference to the ends that such knowledge or expertise is made to serve. This renunciation of the moral point of view may be partial or complete, depending on whether it forms part of a general moral agnosticism or whether it takes a more limited, even hypothetical, form (as in the case of the political practitioner who recognizes the claims of 'private' morality while banishing morality in a regulatory role from the domain of politics, or in that of the empirical scientist who attempts to suspend moral judgement for the purposes of scientific enquiry while acknowledging the force and relevance of morality outside the epistemological realm of science).[10]

Another form of realism, while still resisting the moral determination of politics (at least from time to time or in extreme circumstances), is far from indifferent to moral considerations. What it propounds is a moral paradox, whereby the achievement of political objectives necessitates the use of *immoral* means. What distinguishes this form of realism is its overt moral concern and the sense of moral unease or of moral tragedy with which it accepts the need for actions that other realists regard with equanimity. This form of realism recognizes the claims both of morality and politics, while affirming their potential irreconcilability and, at times, unavoidable conflict. Even normal politics are seen to be clothed in moral ambiguity, and in extreme emergencies no act, however wicked or immoral, can be excluded 'realistically'. Tragically (and, as it seems to critics, incoherently), the ruler may have a duty to act immorally, with all the moral anguish that entails.

Niebuhr's Christian and Protestant realism takes this form. The political order is seen as naturally resistant to morality, and the structure of power in which it consists as intrinsically flawed. Unlike the more purely moral domain of private life, 'the realm of politics is a twilight zone where ethical and technical issues meet'. It is impossible to act within that realm without incurring sin. Nevertheless, rulers have a duty so to act, while repenting of their actions and falling back ultimately on the mercy and redemptive power of God. This understanding of politics appears in a more secular guise in the thought of Hans Morgenthau, who argues that 'there is no escape from the evil of power' and that 'to know with despair that the political act is inevitably evil, and to act nonetheless, is moral courage' (Morgenthau 1946, p. 203). On this view the politician – and the soldier – are faced with hard choices or cruel necessities that, in the terms of one analysis, require that they 'stoically immolate their personal morality on the altar of the public good' (Evans and Ward 1956, p. 320).

Walzer, despite his explicit rejection of realism and insistence on the moral determination of war (cf. Walzer 1992, pp. 3–20 and *passim*), shares a similar, if less obtrusive, view. The moral determination of politics and war applies most but not all of the time. In the end the conflict and irreconcilability of values that are part and parcel of politics are inescapable. What, for example, does Walzer make of the ruler who orders the torture of a terrorist in order to discover the whereabouts of a bomb threatening the lives of the innocent?

> When he ordered the prisoner tortured, he committed a moral crime and he accepted a moral burden. Now he is a guilty man. His willingness to acknowledge and bear (and perhaps to repent and do penance for) his guilt is evidence, and it is the only evidence he can offer us, both that he is not too good for politics and that he is good enough. Here is the moral politician: it is by his dirty hands that we know him. If he were a moral man and nothing else, his hands would not be dirty; if he were a politician and nothing else, he would pretend that they were clean. (Cohen *et al.* 1974, pp. 69–70)

It is impossible, Walzer argues, to govern innocently: sooner or later the ruler will be required to override some basic moral principle in pursuit of a political good. As a ruler, he has a duty so to act, even though in doing so he incurs guilt and experiences moral anguish: 'It is easy to get one's hands dirty in politics, and it is often right to do so' (Cohen *et al.* 1974, p. 76).[11]

Here, then, is a form of realism that affirms the tragic but unresolvable opposition of morality and politics. One way in which realists of a different persuasion have sought to resolve that opposition is by giving morality itself a political form. In some cases this is achieved by the adoption of a moral particularism that gives absolute primacy to the state. State sovereignty and the national interest then become the rock on which universal moral principles founder. It is a position that finds expression in moderate as well as in extreme forms. Gilpin, for example, strongly dissociates himself from that 'amoralism [or 'vulgar' realism] ... which holds that the state is supreme and unbound by any ethical principles'. At the heart of his realism, he argues, lies 'a moral commitment' according to which 'states should pursue their *national interests*, not those of a particular dynasty or political party' (Keohane 1986, pp. 320–1). This moral commitment, however, while transcending internal or domestic factionalism, is conceived in exclusively political or statist terms. Here is a moral vision: but it is one in which the common good of the state is paramount, and in which a more general common good is not discernible. What such a version of realism presses are the claims of a *political* or republican morality that, ultimately (and notwithstanding qualifications about the 'moral' character of the 'national interest'), seems not to limit international relations decisively. In more extreme and less restrained versions of this position its corrosive moral implications are exposed, and the idea of a politics devoid of any moral limitation is openly proclaimed. There emerges what Maritain calls 'absolute Machiavellianism', in which '*boundless* injustice, *boundless* violence, *boundless* lying and immorality, are normal political means' (Evans and Ward 1956, p. 331).[12]

In its stronger form a 'political' morality may be regarded as the sole morality, applicable not only to the public domain but to the private domain as well (indeed, from the standpoint of this morality such a distinction is meaningless: the moral life is politically determined through and through; the citizen *is* the moral man). Machiavelli, for example, is sometimes credited with such a view, with the advocacy of a new and comprehensive republican morality, classically inspired and designed to replace the prevailing Christian ethical system, thereby overcoming the dualism inflicted on the body politic by the introduction of an apolitical Christian ethic.

In other forms of realism the claims made for a political morality are much less ambitious, and assume a moral dualism, a political *and* a private morality. The focus here is on the contextual difference of moral action as it occurs in the private and the public domains, a difference that is thought to be great enough to constitute two separate moral orders, each possessing its own distinctive structure and logic. The less complex area of private life and personal relations is seen to be ruled by a more exacting and restrictive morality than the permissive and minimalist morality that governs public life and that is the only practicable kind in such an intricate and technically demanding world. The moral prohibition of lying, for example, makes good sense in the context of personal relations, but no sense at all in affairs of state. Telling the truth is a moral luxury that politicians and diplomats can rarely afford. More than that, the fulfilment of their public duty will require them not only to conceal the truth but to suppress it and twist it constantly. This is not so much the violation of a single morality as the application of another and different morality, according to which the moral permissibility of any act is determined in the light of its foreseeable consequences rather than of its intrinsic quality. In this way what is morally impermissible in one sphere may become morally obligatory in the other.[13]

Finally, there is a type of realism that recognizes and gives priority to the varying circumstances in which the moral agent acts without drawing the conclusion that the public and private domains belong to two different moral orders. On the one hand, recognition of the peculiar moral demands and moral complexities of public life – considerable in the case of domestic politics, great in the case of international relations, immense in the case of war – leads to the rejection of that 'hypermoralism'[14] that attempts not only to apply the same moral principles to public life that it applies to private life, but that attempts to apply them in the same way and without regard to change of circumstance. On the other hand, the change of circumstance is not thought to be such as to warrant the espousal of moral dualism.

The source of that dualism is seen to lie as much in an exaggerated or hypermoral view of the private domain as in an unduly permissive moral characterization of the public domain. By taking an abstract and oversimple view of moral action within the private realm a gulf between 'private' and 'public' morality is opened up. Dualism can be avoided by recognizing that even in private life moral action is complex and conflictual, and that an individual may be required to sacrifice one value for the sake of another: it is not just politicians, for example, who encounter circumstances in which they seem to have a duty to 'lie' in order to avoid the perpetration of greater evil. As long as moral reasoning remains sensitive to the constraints that circumstances place upon *all* moral action then the transition from the private to the public domain will be marked by continuity rather than disruption (and the moral theorist will be better equipped to discern, however dimly, the moral lineaments of war).

It is true, then, that the realist tradition presents the ethics of war, and just war theory in particular, with a very considerable challenge. This is because for much of its history and for many of its exponents the chief concern of realism has been, and remains, to resist the moral determination of war either in whole or in part. An examination of the internal variety of the realist tradition suggests, however, that the divide separating it from the ethics of war is not as great as may appear at first sight. In the first place, a moral concern is not as alien to that tradition as it is sometimes thought to be. In fact some forms of realism are clearly driven by such a concern: it is for the sake of a better and certainly a safer world that the direct application of morality to international relations is resisted. Secondly, it seems clear that the tradition is not uniformly hostile to all attempts at the moral determination of war. What it opposes are 'utopian' or 'moralistic' approaches and, in principle at least, this is an opposition that it shares with the ethics of war. The bone of contention, of course, is the definition of 'moralism', and it is here that important differences can arise. Nevertheless, in identifying and criticising moralism realism makes a fundamental contribution to the moral understanding of war. In short, this is a tradition from which the ethics of war has at least as much to learn as it has to fear.

Notes

1 The quotation is adapted from Churchill's *The Second World War: Vol. 1, The Gathering Storm (Churchill, 1985)*, pp. 186–7. Morgenthau cites the same passage in *Politics Among Nations* (Morgenthau and Thompson 1985).

2 Cf. Kissinger 1982, p. 50.

3 The tendency for realism to reduce morality to ideology – that is to a factor of *power* – is evident in Tucker's assessment of just war theory: 'Modern just war doctrines share the fate of their predecessors in being scarcely distinguishable from mere ideologies the purpose of which is to provide a spurious justification for almost any use

of force' (Tucker 1960, p. 43).

4 For a very different reading of the Vietnam War confer Holmes's argument in *On War and Morality* (1989). Holmes contends that Vietnam, far from endorsing the realist case, was itself the product of realism: 'Vietnam ... was a war directed by dispassionate efficiency experts making calculated use of the best of modern technology and military science – precisely the opposite of the moralistic crusade that some realists would represent it as being once it failed ... that it was a product of the kind of foreign policy advocated by political realists is indisputable' (Holmes 1989, pp. 81–2).

5 Kennan cites the two world wars, arguing that in both the Western allies found it difficult to conclude an earlier and less destructive peace with Germany, one which stopped short of unconditional surrender, because of the way in which war had been turned into a moral crusade against an enemy branded as beyond the pale. For a cause so righteous and against an enemy so odious war had to be fought to its bitter and ruthless conclusion *regardless of consequences*. For a realist like Kennan that represents the ultimate heresy. However extreme the conflict, adversaries should be ready to deal with one another and to settle for less than total victory when it is in their interests so to do.

6 This is a view that realism shares with some forms of pacifism. More generally, of course, both realists and pacifists are moral sceptics so far as war is concerned, though scepticism yields a very different conclusion in the case of pacifism. See Chapter 3.

7 The CO of 50 Squadron of Bomber Command, engaged in the bombing offensive against Germany, urged all new crews 'to work up Hun-hate' (Hastings 1993, p. 143).

8 In the words of Leonard Cheshire, who played such a prominent part in the British bombing offensive against Germany in the Second World War: 'You couldn't afford to think too much about civilians ... you can't afford to let your mind dwell on casualties in war, whether they are the enemies or those of your own unit. Doubt, as well as fear, is something you have to hold at bay' (Cheshire 1991, p. 52).

9 See Graves 1960, p. 112.

10 The 'theoretical-scientific' approach is exemplified in the work of 'neo-realists' like Herz and Waltz (see Herz 1976 and Waltz 1979), while in the opinion of some commentators Machiavelli exemplifies the 'practical-scientific' approach. For those who interpret him in this way 'Machiavelli is a cold technician, ethically and politically uncommitted, an objective analyst of politics, a morally neutral scientist, who ... had no moral interest in the use made of his technical discoveries' (Berlin 1979, pp. 29–30). Ford, for whom 'Machiavelli develops the realist argument in its purest form', shares

this view: Machiavelli 'develops a new and amoral basis for the political community'; he 'casts himself in the role of doctor'; his 'realism represents a new and scientific approach to politics' (Nardin and Mapel 1992, pp. 64–6).

11 Walzer's recognition of the conflict of values that is such a prominent feature of politics, and especially of war, is shared by most contemporary moral theorists. What perhaps establishes Walzer's position as a form of realism (however exceptional and guarded) is the account that he gives of that conflict and of its resolution. At the end of the day his position seems incoherent, and there may even be doubts as to whether his is a moral account at all. How can there be a moral duty to act immorally? A more coherent moral – and non-realist – defence of the ruler's actions might employ some notion of proportionality to justify the act (the saving of innocent lives being seen as sufficient moral compensation for the disvalue embodied in the act of torture), as a result of which the act itself is no longer regarded as a moral evil. Alternatively, such justification might be rejected on the grounds that torture is an intrinsically immoral (or inherently disproportionate?) and, therefore, impermissible act. In either case the applicability of morality to the particular case is not in question. Contrastingly, Walzer, like Niebuhr and Morgenthau, seems to be arguing for the temporary suspension of morality on the grounds that some, if not all, political and military circumstances are morally indeterminable.

12 Whether Machiavelli himself held this view is disputed. In The Discourses (Bk. III, Ch. xli) Machiavelli seems to advocate it only in extreme situations (like Walzer perhaps) and not as a 'normal political means': 'When the entire safety of one's country is at stake, there should be no consideration of just or unjust, merciful or cruel, praiseworthy or disgraceful; on the contrary, putting aside every form of respect, that decision which will save her life and preserve her liberty must be followed completely' (Bondanella and Musa 1979, p. 411).

13 Cf. Hampshire 1978, esp. Chs 2 and 4.

14 The term is Maritain's. Cf. Evans and Ward 1956, p. 349.

2

Militarism

The concept of militarism must be neither too narrowly nor too broadly defined. The common understanding of militarism as 'the application to international relations of fascist assumptions' (Ceadel 1989, p. 21) needs to be resisted. Such a narrow identification confuses the species with the genus and seriously underestimates the diffusion and consequent influence of militarism. Ceadel's narrow definition, for example, yields the startling conclusion that 'the militarist has become extinct' (Ceadel 1989, p. 42). The militarist nature of fascism is indisputable; but militarism, more broadly but still coherently defined, can be seen to embrace much more than the fascist tradition. More importantly, it is in the interests of the moral understanding and moral limitation of war that the widespread distribution and continuing influence of militarist ideas and values should be recognized. Militarism is rife in the modern world, where its pervasive and multiform presence constantly threatens the moral regulation of war.

One of the great strengths of the pacifist tradition is its keen awareness of a common propensity or cultural bias in favour of war, upon which the war-maker is continually able to draw and with which any peacemaker has to contend. It is to this phenomenon, which first precipitates war and then dictates its ruthless prosecution, that the term militarism is applied here. The weakness of the pacifist understanding lies in its tendency to regard *any* defence of war and *any* resort to arms as manifestations of militarism. This association of all things military with militarism suppresses real and important distinctions and undermines any attempt to subject war to moral limitation.

The tendency narrowly to equate militarism with fascism owes much to the view that fascism is unique among approaches to war, firstly, in its affirmation of the primacy of war over peace and of martial values over civilian ones and, secondly, in its espousal of particularist rather than universalist values. The fascist accepts the ubiquity and necessity of war and accords it the central role in human development. War is a positive good (and not a lesser evil), something of intrinsic and unique value, worthy of being willed not as a regrettable means to some higher, external and pacific goal, but as an end in itself. As a result war is understood as a matter of first preference rather than of last resort, capable of delivering essential goods that are simply not reproducible by peaceful means. Underlying fascist militarism is a form of moral particularism that systematically excludes universal values and ruthlessly subordinates the good of humanity to the good of a particular race, state or nation.[1]

The application of the term 'militarism' to this way of thinking about war seems more than justified; but is this approach unique to fascism? The reversal of civilian and martial values and the upholding of an extreme moral particularism do occur in fascism; but they occur elsewhere too, as Benda observed in *The Treason of the Intellectuals*:

> The modern 'clerk' denounces the feeling of universalism, not only for the profit of the nation, but for that of a class. Our age has beheld moralists who have declared to the bourgeois world (or to the working classes) that far from trying to check the feeling of their differences from others and to feel conscious of their common human nature, they should on the contrary try to feel conscious of this difference in all its profundity and irreducibleness ... [The result of] this extolling of particularism by the 'clerks' ... [is that] ... humanity is heading for the greatest and most perfect war ever seen in the world, whether it is a war of nations, or a war of classes ... the hitherto unknown point of perfection attained by the spirit of hatred against what is 'different' among a group of men. (Benda 1969, pp. 91–2, 107, 183–4)

Failure to acknowledge the wider distribution of militarist ideas and tendencies stems largely from the fact that, unlike fascism, which openly parades its militarism, other forms of militarism are often covert, hiding their warlike nature behind a peaceful and humanitarian facade. The disguise proves most effective. Ceadel, for example, insists on the distinction between

'militarism' and 'crusading' (to which latter category revolutionary socialism is seen to belong) on the grounds that, unlike those
of the militarist, the crusader's values are 'civilized and universal'. It is the pacific and humanitarian intent of crusading, in its
varied forms, that separates it from militarism (or fascism),
despite a common acceptance of aggressive war: 'What distinguishes crusading is its essential altruism: it is undertaken for the
general good' (Ceadel 1989, p.44).

Is this point of difference decisive? Is it even a point of difference? As Ceadel himself acknowledges, fascism itself has *some*
conception of the general good: it is through war that human
progress comes about, and in fulfilling its historic destiny the fascist state serves not just itself but humanity at large. Moreover,
is fascism's understanding of the general good so very different
from the 'crusading' conception? The general good that 'crusading' affirms is *its own* conception and embodiment of the general
good, a conception that it seeks to impose on the rest of humanity by force. The readiness to equate the good of humanity with
the triumph of a particular community or set of values and to
advance that claim through war is common to both approaches.
In fact 'crusading universalism' is little different, either in theory
or in practice, from 'fascist particularism'. It is really a form of
imperialism: that is, of moral particularism masquerading as
moral universalism. In the end 'crusading' too stands for the victory of one particular moral community over all the others, and
the peace that it professes is dependent for its realization upon
the forcible elimination of difference.

The truth of the matter is that the crusader's 'altruism', by
which so much store is set, is not the enemy but the ally of militarism. It is precisely the 'altruistic' pursuit of warfare that generates militarism and that leads to the systematic undermining of
every limit placed upon war. 'He who plays the angel,' wrote
Aron, 'plays the beast' (Aron 1966, p. 609).[2] The characteristic
suspicion of morality that the realist displays is instigated in large
part by fear, a fear that arises from the conviction that to control
the horror which is war, to keep it within bounds, political or
pragmatic considerations must be allowed to dictate its course.
'The primacy of policy,' it is argued, 'permits the control of escalation, the avoidance of an explosion of animosity into passionate

and unrestricted brutality' (Aron 1966, p. 45). What can be seen to disturb the 'primacy of policy' is the intrusion of 'morality': it is the infusion of war with a higher, moral or transcendent, purpose which unleashes its full horror. The less 'political' and the more 'moral' or 'exalted' wars become the more 'total' or 'absolute' they become, until a point is reached when the 'political point of view' vanishes completely and only 'wars of life and death, from pure hatred' remain (Clausewitz 1982, p. 405). Tragically but predictably, the greater the moral investment in war, or the more 'altruistic' war becomes, the less moral or restrained it becomes: the higher the goal, the more intense the conflict.[3]

It is not simply the intensity with which such a war is fought, but the ease with which it is begun that demonstrates its militaristic nature. The hallmark of militarism is the lust for war.[4] Unlike the realist, who opts for war on pragmatic grounds, or the just war theorist, whose grudging acceptance of the moral permissibility of war stops well short of moral enthusiasm, the militarist *is* an enthusiast for war, a 'happy warrior' who shares none of the moral anxiety rightly associated with the just recourse to war. Religious fervour, ideological conviction, moral zeal undermine that deep reluctance to engage in war that is such an essential part of the just war disposition and that finds theoretical expression in those pragmatically based criteria of just recourse (*legitimate authority, proportionality, the prospects of success, last resort*) that are meant to temper the military ardour that the adoption of a just cause is inclined to arouse. Militarism sweeps aside these essential moral hurdles, allowing an unobstructed path to war.

In this broader sense militarism is *not* the monopoly of fascism or of the extreme Right. In the present context, as perhaps in most others, the conventional division of the political and ideological spectrum into Left and Right is thoroughly misleading, and serves more as an instrument of propaganda than of analysis.[5] What it ignores is what Left and Right have in common, namely that ideological understanding of war that is so central to modern militarism. Leftist militarism is effectively disguised by its much-vaunted espousal of pacific and humanitarian goals; but not too much significance should be attached to a concept of peace that dictates the prior annihilation of the adversary or to a concept of humanity so exclusive as to be terroristic in its practical implications. To satisfy the humanitarian pretensions of these movements millions have paid with their lives on revolutionary 'killing fields' throughout the world: eight million or more in the Soviet Union, one million in Cambodia, a similar number in Ethiopia, an untold number in China. The frequency with which such events have occurred, in countries having little in common other than allegiance to a particular ideology, is sufficient in itself to arouse scepticism about the pacific and humanitarian credentials of revolutionary socialism. It seems that the reign of terror is less an aberration or a practical distortion of the theory than its essential consequence, achieved not in spite of its humanitarian goals but rather because of them. As Burke observed of the practitioners of an earlier revolution: 'Their humanity is savage and brutal' (Burke 1969, p. 174). In fact, in their approach to war Left and Right have much in common – in theory as well as in practice.

It is the modern transformation of war into an ideological war (a war fought to vindicate a world-view), akin to the wars of religion that dominated and wrought such havoc in an earlier age, that generates militarism, quite irrespective of the specific ideological aims that war is made to serve. Even a 'centrist' ideology like Democracy, which prides itself on its moderation and pacific pedigree, can succumb to militarism by transforming war into an ideological crusade. As Winston Churchill foresaw in 1901: 'Democracy is more vindictive than cabinets [and] the wars of peoples will be more terrible than the wars of kings' (quoted in Grigg 1990, p. 27). It is not the specific form that an ideology takes that counts, but the ideological approach itself, the 'new style of politics'[6] to which the French Revolution is commonly thought to have given birth, a form of politics that was bound to be violent in its manifestations. As Burke's early characterization of the revolution argued, this was no ordinary uprising, but 'an armed doctrine' that, by its claim to a universal authority *and* a universal jurisdiction, was naturally inclined to the pursuit of missionary warfare. Faced with this approach, the choice confronting those unfortunate enough to encounter it has often been a stark one: Convert or Die. Viewed from this perspective, militarism is less the monopoly of one ideology than the common property of all ideologies, or at the very least a tendency to which all are naturally prone.

This ideological and secular version has become the dominant form of militarism in the modern (or at least the Western) world ever since religion ceased to function as a civil or political religion and ceased to be regarded as the basis of political legitimacy. With the separation of Church and State and the secularization of politics secular ideologies have come to perform the social, political and military functions once exercised by religion. Now ideological rather than religious orthodoxy has become the test of legitimacy and the cause of war. At the same time religious forms of militarism continue to exercise great influence in those parts of the contemporary world where secularization has met resistance and where the separation of religion and politics is regarded as alien or inimical to the life of the community in question. The sources of contemporary Islamic militarism, for example, are religious (as well as ideological),[7] and the same applies to other nationalist movements that define themselves predominantly in religious terms.

Whether in its fascist or its non-fascist forms, whether in its religious or its secular forms, militarism abolishes that moral threshold of war on the preservation of which the moral regulation of war crucially depends. In fact militarism establishes a predisposition to war or a moral bias in favour of war. The vision of war that it advances is free of that sense of moral ambiguity on which the moral limitation of war is so well founded. Its recourse to war is entirely without moral inhibition. The sense of mission that the religious or ideological understanding of war inspires provides an occasion of war independent of specific circumstance. The cause of war is not the perpetration of any specific injury or the posing of any particular threat, but the general offence and the general threat posed by the existence of the other. The very fact of otherness challenges the claim to a universal jurisdiction. In that sense the 'enemy' is an 'absolute' and 'existential' foe, one whose continued existence is incompatible with the vindication of the 'world-view' in question. As a result the aim of war is not the limited goal that would consist in the satisfaction of specific grievances, but the absolute goal of the removal of the other. As long as the other exists war will be necessary and peace will be attained only in a world from which the other has been excluded. Until universal or absolute supremacy has been achieved, or the 'world-view' vindicated, a state and occasion of war must persist.

Islamic fundamentalism, for example, posits a state of war between the 'house or sphere of Islam' (*dar al-Islam*) and the 'house or sphere of war' (*dar al-Harb*), a state which is terminable only by the universal political hegemony of Islam. Legitimate dominion has one true foundation – Islam – and the recognition of non-Islamic states on anything other than a temporary and pragmatic basis is impermissible.[8] This fundamentalist approach yields a starkly adversarial and conflictual view of the present state of humanity. The use of force to bring about the triumph of Islam is unambiguously and enthusiastically proclaimed. War is not a necessary evil, but a fundamental obligation or 'neglected duty'. Far from war posing a threat to religious observance, 'a religion without war is a crippled religion' (Ayatollah Khomeini), and jihad or holy war is the essence of Islam, as the fundamentalist understands it.[9]

This is a view of war encountered frequently enough in the Christian world. Just as the militant Muslim identifies the good of humanity with the universal triumph of the Islamic caliphate, so his Christian counterpart has often been tempted to identify it with the worldwide supremacy of a Christendom politically as well as spiritually conceived. In either case the legitimacy of alternative dominions, as well as the integrity and worth of alien cultures, have been denied in pursuit of a monistic and hegemonic universalism. For many (perhaps a majority) who took part in the Crusades, for example, the wars were fought to vindicate Christianity and to destroy infidelity rather than to remedy specific grievances or to achieve more defined objectives, while in the sixteenth century the Spanish conquest of the Americas was justified in similar terms, the infidelity of the Indians being regarded by some as just cause for war. In such instances Christianity was transformed into an imperial ideology and war came to be regarded as a religious vehicle. This religious understanding of war, once so common, has for long enjoyed at most a marginal existence in a modern and secular world; but secular substitutes have been in plentiful supply.

For German nationalists in 1914, for example, the approaching war was seen not simply as a military conflict between states fought for finite goals, but as a 'cultural war' of world-historical significance between the spiritual and heroic *Kultur* of Germany and the arid materialism of Western or Anglo-Saxon *Zivilization*..[10] This vision of war survived Germany's defeat and reached a new pitch of intensity in the Second World War. In no theatre of the war was this more evident than in the 'battle of ideologies' that marked the war in the east, in which the Germans cast themselves as defenders not just of German but of European (and by extension world) civilization against the 'red beast' threatening its destruction,[11] and the ideological, if not the racial, understanding of the conflict was reciprocated by the Soviet Union. For the Soviets the war against Germany was more than the defence of a state against an unjust and ruthless aggressor. They too saw it as the vindication of a 'world-view'. The long history of class conflict was now approaching its culmination. The climactic struggle was an absolute one between irreconcilable adversaries. On its resolution, and the subsequent elimination of classes, the good of humanity depended. The triumph of world communism (under the leadership of the Soviet Union) would bring 'pre-history' to a close and mark the dawn of history proper, an era of universal concord and real human emancipation. The Western and democratic states too were not immune to this way of thinking. For democrats of a more ideological and less pragmatic persuasion the vision of an embattled free world contending with evil forces intent on its destruction lay behind the elevated conception of a war to make the whole world safe for democracy. From his vantage point in the British embassy in Washington Isaiah Berlin described American understanding of the war as 'apocalyptic' and based on the assumption that America had 'a divine mission to save the world' (Fussell 1989, pp. 166–7). Similarly Churchill's war rhetoric tended constantly to the absolutization of the conflict: the Axis powers were one with the powers of darkness.

One of the reasons why wars of this kind are so much more destructive than more prosaic wars is that the religious or ideological conception of war turns every war into a 'civil' war. The war is always an internal as well as an external war, and the 'enemy within' is of as much, if not greater, concern than the

enemy without. To those Crusaders, for example, who saw themselves as engaged in an apocalyptic war against the Infidel it was
inconceivable that the Muslim should be attacked while the
greater Infidel in their midst – the Jew or Christ-killer – should
go unharmed. Yet despite his physical presence within the
boundaries of Christendom the Jew remained an external enemy,
an infidel. The fiercest religious wars of all were those waged not
against infidels but against heretics and apostates, those who
'attacked' the community from within and who thereby posed
the greatest threat. The most ruthless and extreme of all the crusades was arguably that waged against the Albigensians, while
the wars between Catholic and Protestant that afflicted Europe in
the sixteenth and seventeenth centuries seemed to Westlake,
writing in the late nineteenth century, 'the most terrible in
which the beast in man ever broke loose' (quoted in Morgenthau
1973, p. 241). Similarly with Islam, where the greatest hostility
and the severest treatment has often been reserved for its internal enemies, heretics and worst of all apostates, those who have
either watered down or rejected outright pure Islamic values in
favour of Western or secular ones. As one fundamentalist leader,
Abd Al-Salam Faraj, expressed it: 'To fight an enemy who is near
is more important than to fight an enemy who is far' (cited in
Rapoport 1990, p. 111).

It is not just religious militarism that guards the moral and
ideological purity of the community with such militant zeal. For
those cultural nationalists in Germany in 1914 the war was as
much a civil war as a war between Germany and her external
enemies. Germany herself was in need of purification, for she too
had succumbed, at least in part, to what Sombart called 'the
spirit of the trader'. The 'England within' needed to be defeated
and its alien values rooted out before Germany could be restored
to health and assume her historic role.[12] For Ernst Jünger (a
much-decorated veteran of the First World War and one of the
main spokesmen of the war generation in postwar Germany),
Germany's defeat was attributable to her internal corruption by
alien or 'bourgeois' influences. His aim was 'to witness the end
of the bourgeois age', and it was an aim which he proclaimed in
uncompromising fashion: 'everybody who feels differently must
be branded with the mark of the heretic and exterminated'

(quoted in Stirk 1969, p. 92). In Nazi Germany such conceptions of cultural integrity and purification gave way to the more basic and more exclusive notion of racial homogeneity and purification. The greatest threat to Germany was seen to lie in racial miscegenation. The racial basis of this ideology made it not only more exclusive but also more destructive in its implications: the 'enemy within' could no longer be converted and assimilated, but only physically exterminated.

The primacy of civil over interstate war, of internal over external war, is perhaps nowhere more evident than in the ideologies of the Left. In the language of the *Communist Manifesto* the proletariat must first settle its account with its own bourgeoisie before realizing its universal mission. In the ensuing 'proletarian war', as Lenin described it, all compromise with the class enemy must be ruled out. Of particular concern is the kind of internal opposition that the revolutionary movement itself is likely to encounter and, as in the historical archetype of modern revolutions, the French Revolution of 1789, the harshest treatment is reserved for those erstwhile colleagues who have begun to question revolutionary methods or who seem lacking in revolutionary zeal. The enemy within the revolutionary community is always the enemy from whom the revolution has the most to fear.

The external enemy, however, cannot be ignored. Here war is conceived in expansive terms. Given the sense of a historic and universal mission with which the community in question is imbued, the arena for these 'civil' wars is a worldwide one. The very presence of other communities based on values that are at variance with those of the chosen community poses a fundamental threat and constitutes, in itself, sufficient cause for war. The chosen community, with its universal pretensions, can brook no rival. Its integrity, let alone the fulfilment of its historic destiny, depends on the progressive elimination of its 'enemies'.

For those who view war in such exalted and uncompromising fashion war ceases to have the contingent and instrumental character ascribed to it by realist and just war theorist alike. The instrumentality of such a war is of a wholly non-specific kind, and gives to war itself a greatly enhanced value. As Aron has observed: 'the use of force with a view to such grandiose ends tends to become an end in itself' (Aron 1966, p. 593). Moreover, war itself is credited with a redemptive and transformative power whereby a new and better humanity is born and a new world created. In this way war acquires its own *intrinsic* value, a value far exceeding the instrumental value attached to it by realists and just war theorists.[13] For the militarist there are lessons to be learned in war that can be learned in no other way. The real object of war, its true gain, is the transformation of man and of the human condition – a transformation that can be seen to affect both the individual and the community.

In the first place individuals are thought to achieve a fulfilment in war that is denied them in peace. The enthusiasm of those who engage in a 'holy war', whether in its religious or secular manifestations, owes much to the belief in war as a source of personal, as well as collective, redemption. In religious forms of militarism this aspect of war has always been prominent: in both the Christian and the Islamic traditions, for example, death incurred in the prosecution of a war of religion has often been portrayed as a form of martyrdom meriting in itself an eternal reward. From medieval crusaders who regarded war as a salvific act to contemporary Islamic fundamentalists for whom jihad is, in Ayatollah Khomeini's words, 'the key to paradise', religion has provided strong spiritual incentives to engage in war,[14] and modern and secular versions of these ancient religious notions are very common. Those who are convinced that the war in which they are engaged has a revolutionary or historical significance can experience just as strong a sense of personal redemption or fulfilment, including even the assurance of immortality by securing a place in the collective memory of the state or of the revolutionary community which they claim to serve. In fact the incentive of immortalization is frequently invoked, as in the case of Patrick Pearse, the Irish nationalist and leader of the Easter Rising in 1916, who joyfully embraced the prospect of a glorious death ('to free me from my pain'). 'I care not,' he wrote, 'though I were to live but one day and one night provided my fame and my deeds live after me' (Dudley Edwards 1977, p. 344).[15]

The self-fulfilment and self-satisfaction that war generates derive in part from the religious or ideological significance attributed to it and from the resultant sense of participating in some grand design. It may be, however, that the experience of war itself comes to be prized for its own sake and not just for the great ends that it serves or promotes, for the excitement that is unique to war and in comparison with which pacific pursuits seem insipid. This understanding and experience of moral, psychological and emotional self-fulfilment enhances war and threatens its moral regulation. It transforms war from an instrumental into an expressive activity, and gives participants an incentive for engaging in it that is largely independent of specific cause and circumstance and is not susceptible to rational–instrumentalist argument or appeal. Of the anarchist Bakunin, for example, one historian has written: 'The revolutions in which he took part inspired him with an almost mystical exaltation ... the interludes of [revolutionary] action ... seem to have been sought not only as means to ends, but also as experiences in themselves, capable of raising him from the everyday life, which "corrupts our instinct and our will, and constricts our heart and our intelligence". Revolutionary action, in other words, was a personal liberation, and even a kind of catharsis, a moral purging' (Woodcock 1963, p. 139).[16]

Even when the cause is lost or won the intoxication with war may persist, driving the addict either to the suicidal prolongation of an existing war or to the search for new wars. Just as Bakunin scoured nineteenth-century Europe in search of revolutionary activity ('[breathing] through all my senses and through all my pores the intoxication of the revolutionary atmosphere': Woodcock 1963, p. 142) so Che Guevara roamed the New World in fulfilment of his revolutionary vocation. 'I was born in Argentina, I fought in Cuba, and I began to be a revolutionary in Guatemala', he wrote, and 'unredeemed America' was as much in need of his attention as Cuba, Guatemala, and Bolivia (and even Africa).[17] Given behaviour and motivation of this kind it is little wonder that some analysts have concluded that the activities of many 'belligerents' are simply not explicable in conventional terms. A student of contemporary terrorism, for example, has taken issue with the 'rationalist' explanation of terrorism, which starts from 'an assumption that the political violence is instrumental, a tactic to achieve the group's political goals, to help it achieve its cause'. His contrasting view, a view wholly in accord with the present argument, is that the violence is not instrumental but expressive, and that as such it is not amenable to the normal utilitarian logic of war. Therefore, it is not easily terminable: 'Terrorists whose only sense of significance comes from being terrorists cannot be forced to give up terrorism, for to do so would be to lose their very reason for being' (Post 1990, p. 38). The conclusion is reminiscent of Hegel's remark in *The Philosophy of Right* (with the case of the French revolutionaries who instigated the original Terror in mind): 'Only in destroying something does this negative will have a feeling of its own existence' (Hegel 1991, p. 38). Burke had anticipated Hegel's judgement. 'Something they must destroy', he wrote, 'or they seem to themselves to exist for no purpose' (Burke 1969, p. 147).

The transformation that war is thought to bring about in the life of the individual applies with equal if not greater force to the life of the community in the name of which and for the sake of which the war is being fought. For those of a militarist persuasion, war is the creator of community, an ethical force, the best form of practical education. The chosen community begins to realize its unity and to discover, or in some conceptions to rediscover, its true identity and purpose in and through the experience of war itself: war breathes life into the community.

This view of the socially creative power of war is a common one and, again, it is one that cuts across the religious and ideological divide. For the millennarian Christian sects of the medieval period the destruction of the forces of the Anti-Christ was at the same time an act of collective self-purification and an essential means of building the Community of the Elect: the blood-letting had a sacramental, redemptive and creative power so far as the chosen community was concerned.[18] The same is true of contemporary Islamic fundamentalism: jihad or holy war is as much a way of restoring the health and vigour of the Islamic community as it is of defeating the enemies of Islam. It was in this sense, for example, that Faraj, the leader of Al-Jihad or The Islamic Group of Egypt, understood jihad as 'the neglected duty': the neglect had led not only to Islam's external decline but to its internal and spiritual diminution.

Secular equivalents of this conception of war are rife, and they are common to Right and Left, embracing the modern revolutionary tradition as a whole. As Aron has observed: 'revolutionaries multiply acts of violence in order to forge their own community as much as to destroy the mixed community upon which they have declared war' (Aron 1966, p. 172). Pearse, for example, saw revolutionary war as a blood-sacrifice through which the Irish nation would come to a realization of its identity and historic mission,[19] while Jünger argued that the defeat of Germany in 1918 was also a victory. In 'the community of the trenches' Germany had learned a great lesson on which it must now build: a new man and a new social order had been forged in the crucible of war. Tellingly, Jünger thought that Bolshevik Russia had learned the same lesson and was putting it to work more effectively than Germany herself.

Jünger's assessment of the communal or socially creative nature of war is widely shared. It is at the heart of the fascist tradition as a whole, and is commonly recognized therein. The wider ideological distribution of this notion is, however, often overlooked. According to Mosse, for example, the Right's enthusiasm for the war was not shared by the Left, which 'had difficulty in coming to grips with this war experience', largely because 'its didactic and cosmopolitan heritage, as well as its pacifist traditions, proved the stronger' (Mosse 1987, p. 171). Such a commonly held view seems mistaken, allowing leftist opposition to war of a certain kind to obscure leftist enthusiasm for war of the approved kind. Though it is true that identification with the First World War (or with war in its 'bourgeois' and interstate form) was (and remains) difficult for the Left, this did not (and does not) apply to war in its revolutionary form (something that Lenin clearly acknowledged: 'Socialists cannot be against all war without ceasing to be socialists; they can never be against revolutionary wars').[20] In respect of that form of war the enthusiasm of the Left matches that of the Right, and 'the creative power of revolution' (as Lenin described it: 1965–70, Vol. 25, p. 488) is just as clearly and strongly affirmed.

For Marx and Engels the proletariat achieve class consciousness and the power of historic initiative in and through the experience of revolution ('there develops the universal character and the energy of the proletariat': 1975–90, Vol. 5, p. 88). The revolution is necessary 'not only because the *ruling* class cannot be overthrown in any other way but also because the class *overthrowing* it can only in a revolution succeed in ridding itself of all the muck of ages and become fitted to found society anew' (*ibid.*, Vol. 5, p. 53). In the midst of revolutionary violence the new social order can be glimpsed for the first time (a view that clearly informs Marx's and Engel's assessment of the Paris Commune), and later Marxists share the founding fathers' view of the creative and educative power of revolutionary war. 'At no other time', Lenin wrote, 'are the mass of the people in a position to come forward so actively as creators of a new social order as at a time of revolution' (cited in Churchich 1994, p. 245), a view that Fidel Castro expressed even more succinctly: 'Battle is the school of Marxism' (Thomas 1971, p. 1488).

According to Franz Fanon, the ideologue of the Algerian revolution and of liberation movements throughout the Third World, violence is a creative and indispensable force without which the native will never be truly free of the settler. In the act of killing the settler the native casts off his enslaved identity and realizes his true self: 'For the native', he wrote, 'life can only spring up again out of the rotting corpse of the settler' (Fanon 1967, p. 73). The 'positive and creative' effects of violence upon the communal life of a colonized and socially fragmented people are underlined: 'The practice of violence binds them together as a whole, since each individual forms a violent link in the great chain, a part of the great organism of violence' (Fanon 1967, p. 73). Fanon's view was endorsed by his intellectual and political ally, the Marxist–Existentialist philosopher Jean-Paul Sartre, not only in Sartre's laudatory preface to *The Wretched of the Earth* but elsewhere too. In his *Critique of Dialectical Reason* Sartre draws a distinction between two forms of human association: between a 'series' and a 'fused group'. The former, like a queue of people at a bus stop, lacks any real unity, and in it relations of 'alterity' or separation prevail. The latter constitutes a genuine community with a common identity and purpose, and its paradigm, according to Sartre, is the community forged in and by revolution.[21]

Across the religious and ideological divide the ethical power of war, its generation of a new man and a new order, are constantly celebrated. The intrinsic and exalted value that war is seen to possess as a consequence has the effect of lowering the moral threshold of war by undermining the moral and pragmatic limits with which more morally inhibited views of war have surrounded it. The criterion of *legitimate authority* is one such limitation on the recourse to war. Traditionally war has been defined as a public act, and the attempt has been made to outlaw private recourse to war. The exalted images of war under discussion wholly undermine this criterion. Those who are convinced of the grandeur, justice and historic importance of their cause have few inhibitions about resorting to violence even in the absence of public sanction or of popular support. Within the revolutionary tradition, for example, ideas of a *potential* community (at odds with an existing community imbued with a 'false consciousness' or subject to an alien political and cultural 'hegemony') are used to legitimize independent action by a revolutionary élite. Public or popular authorization can come later, as a result rather than as a precondition of war.

The criterion of *proportionality*, whereby prospective belligerents are required to weigh the potential benefits against the potential harms of war, suffers a similar fate. How can a war fought for such transcendent purposes ever be disproportionate? Millions of people, even a whole generation, can be sacrificed with perfect equanimity in the pursuit of a 'historic' objective. Khatayevich, one of the architects of the famine that the Soviet government used to subjugate the rural population, boasted of that policy's achievements: 'A ruthless struggle is going on between the peasantry and our regime. It's a struggle to the death. This year was a test of our strength and their endurance. It took a famine to show them who is master here. It has cost millions of lives, but the collective farm system is here to stay. We've won the war' (quoted in Conquest 1986, p. 261). The utopianism that inspires this form of war ensures that any calculation of proportionality will favour war. As perhaps the history of the twentieth century demonstrates, there is *no* price that is too high to pay for a war to end all wars.[22]

The criterion that obliges those who contemplate the possibility of war to judge the *prospects of success* goes the same way. From this heightened perspective 'success' in war often seems guaranteed. Even the prospect of certain military defeat can be readily entertained, and is certainly no reason for holding back. Pearse and the other leaders of the Easter Rising had little difficulty in resisting the arguments of MacNeill that the uprising was premature and was bound to fail, because 'failure' and 'success' were being measured by a different yardstick. Not only would the example of heroic self-sacrifice ensure the participants their place in history, but it might also acquire a certain symbolic value. The anarchists who terrorized French society in the 1880s and 1890s saw things similarly, practising 'the propaganda of the deed'. One of their number, Louis Chavès, wrote: 'You start with one to reach a hundred, as the saying goes. So I would like the glory of being the first to start.' Having explained himself, he went out to engineer his own symbolic death, first by shooting the Mother Superior of the convent where he had been employed as a gardener, and then by drawing the lethal fire of the police who came to arrest him (Woodcock 1963, p. 282). The sentiments and the practice were shared by Che Guevara: 'Wherever death may surprise us,' he wrote, 'let it be welcome, provided that this, our battle cry, may have reached some receptive ear and another hand may be extended to wield our weapons and other men be ready to intone the funeral dirge with the staccato singing of the machine-guns and new battle cries of war and victory' (Gerassi 1968, p. 424).

The final criterion of just recourse to war, *last resort*, is based on an assumption that runs directly counter to these militarist ways of thinking about war, namely, that it is always better to resolve conflict by peaceful means where such means are available. 'The mark of your militarist,' wrote Catherine Marshall,

> is that he would rather get what he wants by fighting than by any other way. He wants to force his enemy to yield, so that he may have him at his mercy and be able to impose what terms he chooses. ... I have heard socialists who were ardent pacifists on international questions, talk like this of class warfare. I have heard suffragists talk like this of the struggle for sexual equality. *They were all talking pure militarism* – they were all moved by the desire to dominate rather than to cooperate, to vanquish and humiliate the enemy rather than to convert him into a friend. (Marshall 1987, pp. 46–7)

The moral preference for a negotiated settlement that lies behind the criterion of last resort is not shared by the militarist. In fact the contrary moral preference applies. 'We are not fighting so that the enemy recognizes us and offers us something', declared a Lebanese fundamentalist. 'We are fighting to wipe out the enemy. We will not take the path of shame' (Taheri 1987, p. 8).[23]

Conciliation is rejected because the conflict is understood to be an absolute one: there can be no compromise and no reconciliation with an absolute enemy. The ends of war are not negotiable. The moral imperative of this kind of war is not to make peace with an enemy but to destroy him. The only way in which war might conceivably be avoided is through the total capitulation of the enemy; but even that solution is not without its drawbacks. While it might deliver the desired objective, it would deprive the militarist of the goods and satisfaction to be had only through the attainment of ends by violent means. In short, there is no political or pacific substitute for war.

This moral preference for war is shared by Right and Left. In Germany in 1914, for example, one of the main reasons why German nationalists embraced the war so enthusiastically was precisely because it marked 'the death of politics'; it was politics that had got Germany into the present morass, and war alone that could redeem her.[24] In Ireland a similar view was taken. The divide between the 'constitutional' and the 'physical force' parties was (and perhaps remains) a fundamental one. Among those of a militarist disposition the idea of a constitutional or bilateral solution to Ireland's problems was abhorrent. Pearse, for example, insisted that, for it to be real or authentic, Ireland's liberation must be an act of *self*-liberation. Freedom must be torn from the grasp of a harsh and unyielding oppressor.[25]

An insistence on the counterproductive, and even morally demeaning, nature of any political or pacific solution is evident in Marxist and communist thinking, and in its 'battle cry' that, 'The emancipation of the working class must be the work of the working class itself' (Marx and Engels, 1975–90, Vol. 45, p. 408).[26] The opposition of Marx and Engels to the conciliatory programme of social democrats was permanent and intense. Both criticized those 'conservative socialists' and 'bourgeois democrats' who repudiated the 'class struggle' and who pro-

moted the idea of 'class peace' ('We cannot possibly co-operate',
they wrote, 'with men who seek to eliminate that class struggle
from the movement': 1975–90, Vol. 45, p. 408). They and their
more faithful followers have argued that the interests of the proletariat and the bourgeoisie are antagonistic and irreconcilable,
and, therefore, that the essential conflict between these classes
ends in 'the inevitable life-and-death struggle' (1975–90, Vol.
45, p. 404), in the victory of the proletariat and the extinction
of the bourgeoisie. What is needed is not 'the smoothing over of
class antagonisms' but their exacerbation (as Marx argues in the
Address to the Communist League), and not just their exacerbation
but even their creation. Where peace or social unity exists that
unity must be destroyed in the interests of real progress. In an
address to the Central Executive Committee of the Soviet state in
1918, Sverdlov argued: 'We must place before ourselves most
seriously the problem of dividing the village by classes, of creating in it two opposite hostile camps, setting the poorest layers of
the population against the *kulak* elements. Only if we are able to
split the villages into two camps, to arouse there the same class
war as in the cities, only then will we achieve in the villages
what we have achieved in the cities' (cited in Conquest 1986,
p. 46). Far from resorting to war as a last resort when peaceful
remedies have been exhausted, the communist (like all true militarists) resorts to war as a matter of first and positive preference.[27] It is peace, not war, that stands in the way of progress.

The impact of militarism on the conduct of war (*ius in bello*) is
as calamitous as its impact on the recourse to war (*ius ad bellum*):
in both cases essential limits are swept away. Not only does militarism cultivate a disposition to war and a bias against peaceful
coexistence, it encourages belligerents to fight without compassion or restraint. The key moral principles that apply to the conduct of war – proportionality and noncombatant immunity –
both struggle to survive a war fought, typically, with reckless
enthusiasm and annihilatory intent.

The unlimited conduct of war that militarism encourages applies
not only to the ruthless treatment of an adversary but to the reckless manner in which combatants imbued with militarist ideas and
sentiments fight. The calculation of risk that structures the thinking of the ordinary belligerent, intent as he is upon personal sur-

vival, is absent from the militarist soldier's make-up. His often suicidal conduct of war defeats conventional military logic and leaves
those who fight in accordance with it at a distinct disadvantage.
The use of *kamikaze* units (or the Divine Wind Special Attack Force,
as they were known) in the Second World War illustrates the
point. In April–June 1945 in the course of the battle for Okinawa
the US fleet lost more than 20 warships sunk and 260 damaged
in *kamikaze* or suicide raids, in which 2,000 Japanese pilots were
expended. Japanese tactics left US sailors both terrified and
bemused. 'I just can't figure out how anybody can just commit suicide without feeling anything', one said. 'It's against human
nature. It's against the instinct of self-preservation, if you ask me'
(Feifer 1992, p. 200). It was an experience repeated in the Korean
War, where communist casualties exceeded UN casualties by four
to one, and where 'the huge "human waves" of Chinese Communist "volunteers" who poured against United Nations' firepower
were viewed with incredulity by the U.N. defenders' (Seabury and
Codevilla 1989, p. 120); and repeated again in the Lebanon,
where US marines were left defenceless against the suicide-bomb-
ings of a militarily insignificant but dedicated opponent.

What engenders such recklessness is often the enhanced value
that has been bestowed on war and, in particular, on death in
battle. In such cases soldiers may willingly, even joyously,
embrace certain death (this applies particularly to irregular warfare, participation in which is naturally more reliant on self-moti-
vation of that kind).[28] The reckless manner in which men fight
may, however, be less a matter of their own motivation than of
the relative indifference of their leaders to their suffering in the
face of the grandiose ends that the leadership has espoused.
Hitler's refusal to sanction the surrender of the remnants of the
Sixth Army at Stalingrad in 1943, for example, ran contrary to
the advice (and ultimately the practice) of his field commander,
von Paulus. It owed nothing to strategic considerations and
everything to ideological ones. 'Surrender is forbidden,' Hitler
replied to Paulus's request. 'Sixth Army will hold their positions
to the last man and the last round and by their heroic endurance
will make an unforgettable contribution toward the establishment of a defensive front and the salvation of the Western world'
(cf. Shirer 1964, p. 1110).[29]

Given his elevated conception of the aims of war, the militarist is easily persuaded of the necessity of great sacrifices. The kind of proportionality that applies to an 'apocalyptic' war is quite unlike that that applies to a war with more modest aims. In the former case a war that is limited in its scope and destructive force appears to lack symmetry: apocalyptic wars are expected to involve large-scale destruction, and the more destructive they become the more readily they lend themselves to an apocalyptic interpretation. In this respect their moral grandeur increases with the scale of their destruction.[30] Clearly such an understanding must undermine proportionality in its more conventional and restrictive moral sense: far from requiring economy in the use of force, militarism induces overkill.

Militarism poses as great a threat to the principle of noncombatant immunity as it does to the principle of proportionality. The ruthless and indiscriminate prosecution of war that it entails stems from its extreme moral particularism, which contradicts the fundamental unity and moral equality of belligerents on the habitual and mutual recognition of which the moral conduct of war ultimately depends. In a just war adversarial status is limited, and the state of war in which they find themselves is not allowed to obscure the common humanity of belligerents. The sense of belonging to one moral community of mankind encourages adversaries to treat one another with a basic respect and restraint even in the midst of war. In the case of militarism such moral inhibitions fall away: the enemy is an enemy in a total or absolute sense; all feelings of common humanity and all recognition of shared rights are suppressed. Outside the community of the elect rights and duties cease.

The consequences of being placed beyond the moral pale are terrible in the extreme, as the events that followed the fall of Jerusalem to the army of the First Crusade illustrate. Those events are described in a chronicle compiled by Raymond d'Aguiliers, the chaplain to one of the leaders of the crusade, the Count of Toulouse:

> Now that our men had possession of the walls and towers, wonderful sights were to be seen. Some of our men (and this was more merciful) cut off the heads of their enemies; others shot

them with arrows, so that they fell from the towers; others tortured them longer by casting them into the flames. Piles of heads, hands, and feet were to be seen in the streets of the city. It was necessary to pick one's way over the bodies of men and horses. But these were small matters compared to what happened at the Temple of Solomon. (Peters 1971, p. 214)

What happened was the indiscriminate slaughter of all the citizens – men, women and children – who had taken refuge in the temple. The atrocity evoked in the chronicler no sentiment of sympathy or remorse, no sorrowful reflection on the barbarity of war or on man's inhumanity to man. Instead his narrative continues in triumphalist vein without a hint of moral misgiving or anxiety: 'Indeed it was a just and splendid judgement of God that this place should be filled with the blood of the unbelievers, since it had suffered for so long from their blasphemies ... This day, I say, will be famous in all future ages, for it turned our labours and sorrows into joy and exaltation; this day, I say, marks the justification of all Christianity, the humiliation of paganism, and the renewal of our faith' (Peters 1971, p. 214). No doubt the excesses of the crusaders owed much to the sufferings they had undergone at the hands of the enemy before and during the siege; but the Jerusalem massacre was part of a pattern of behaviour persistent enough to appear systematic and preconceived. Another contemporary source relates how, after the battle of Antioch, 'when the Saracen women were found in their tents, the Franks did nothing evil to them except pierce their bellies with their lances' (Peters 1971, p. 64). After its capture the city of Barra was 'completely depopulated by the slaughter of its citizens', while in Marra the victors 'killed all the Saracens from the greatest to the least, and plundered all their substance' (Peters 1971, p. 69). And long before the crusading armies arrived in Asia Minor the Jewish communities of the Rhineland had discovered the high cost of religious and communal difference.

The process whereby the moral conduct of war is systematically[31] undermined seems clear: negative categorization of one kind or another dehumanizes the enemy or victim and suppresses those moral claims that are grounded in the membership of one community of mankind. The vulnerability of enemies who appear in inhuman form, or simply in such abstract form that they no longer have the capacity to arouse sympathy and therefore compassion in their attackers is extreme. 'What happens to the Russians, what happens to the Czechs, is a matter of utter indifference to me', Himmler told his SS Group Leaders. 'Whether or not 10,000 Russian women collapse from exhaustion while digging a tank ditch interests me only in so far as the tank ditch is completed for Germany ... We Germans, who are the only people in the world who have a decent attitude to animals, will also adopt a decent attitude to these human animals, but it is a crime against our own blood to worry about them and to bring them ideals' (quoted in Fest 1972, p. 177). Of course, the case is often worse than that (Himmler's indifference is feigned). In the conflictual view of the world that militarism imposes dehumanization typically takes the form of demonization. The militarist cannot remain indifferent to the fate of such enemies. Their annihilation becomes not just permissible but obligatory. An absolute enemy is an enemy without rights against whom total war must be waged. Extermination is the only fate worthy of the 'infidel', the 'AntiChrist', 'the Great Satan', the 'verminous Jew', the 'bourgeois', the 'Bolshevik', the 'Hun', the 'kulak', the 'untermensch'. In all its forms dehumanization or demonization of the enemy leads to the barbarization of war.

A comparison of Germany's conduct of the war in the West, against an adversary whose moral equality it in some sense acknowledged, with its conduct of the war in the East against an adversary it regarded as subhuman underlines the difference that negative categorization makes. In the West, for example, acts of looting, rape and murder perpetrated by German soldiers against the civilian population were treated, in the main, as criminal acts, and their perpetrators were punished accordingly by military tribunals. In the East not only did these acts go unpunished, but they were positively and systematically encouraged. Similarly, while in the West POWs were treated, again on the whole, relatively humanely, with the result that the majority survived the war, Soviet prisoners were subjected to a form of treatment that in its harshness and cruelty was virtually indistinguishable from a policy of extermination. It has been calculated that out of 5,700,000 prisoners captured by the Germans in the Russian campaign 3,300,000, or 57 per cent, died, some through immediate execution (either by the troops themselves or by the *Einsatzgruppen* or extermination squads that 'cleared up' behind the advancing army), others through starvation and general ill-treatment.[32]

The same process of negative categorization, along with its genocidal effect, has been much in evidence in communist practice, though here the categories involved have been socio-economic rather than racial. Of the treatment of the Russian peasantry by their communist rulers, Grosman recounts how

> ... the activists who helped the GPU [State Political Police] in the arrests and deportations ... 'had sold themselves on the idea that the so-called *kulaks* were pariahs, untouchables, vermin. ... They looked on the so-called *kulaks* as cattle, swine, loathsome, repulsive: they had no souls; they stank; they all had venereal diseases; they were the enemies of the people and exploited the labour of others ... And there was no pity for them ... In order to massacre them it was necessary to proclaim that kulaks are not human beings. Just as the Germans proclaimed that Jews are not human beings. Thus did Lenin and Stalin proclaim, kulaks are not human beings.' (quoted in Conquest 1986, p. 129)

Such absolute enmity abolishes the key distinction between combatant and noncombatant on which the principle of immunity from attack is based. Since the threat that the enemy is seen to pose is less military than 'existential', the object of annihilation is not just an opposing military force (there may not even be one, as the cases of the Jews or the *kulaks* illustrate) but an entire community. This is 'countervalue' warfare in its purest and most extreme form, and the enemy embraces all members of a chosen category regardless of age and gender, regardless of what they have or have not done, or of the physical or military threat that they pose. 'We are engaged in exterminating the bourgeoisie as a class,' a Cheka commander from Latvia is reported as saying. 'You need not prove that this or that man acted against the interests of Soviet power. The first thing you have to ask an arrested person is: To what class does he belong, where does he come from, what kind of education did he have, what is his occupation? These questions are to decide the fate of the accused. That is the quintessence of the Red Terror' (quoted in Fest 1974, p. 91).

In militarist thinking 'violence' is an elastic concept, and its elasticity lowers the threshold of counterviolence and enlarges the group against which it can be directed. In revolutionary socialism, for example, concepts of 'structural' or 'institutional' violence render those who live within, and who are seen to benefit from, such structures liable to attack. For those intent upon the liberation of a class or a nation 'violence' can be 'economic' or 'cultural' as well as physical or military.[33] To acquire the status of the 'enemy' it is not necessary to do *anything*, let alone to perform or to threaten to perform an overtly violent act. 'Your passivity,' Sartre wrote (echoing St Just),[34] 'serves only to place you in the ranks of the oppressors' (Fanon 1967, p. 21). In this kind of war there are no innocents and no neutrals, no place for the uncommitted: *all* are belligerents. 'Who are our enemies? Who are our friends?', Mao wrote (as if these categories were exhaustive), 'This is a question of the first importance for the revolution' (Mao Tse-tung 1967, p. 13). As Trotsky had insisted earlier, 'I know only two parties, the good and the evil citizens' (quoted in Deutscher 1954, p. 92).

Ruthlessness is reinforced by the ethic of hardness that is common to all forms of militarism and that supplants the ethic of compassion that is so essential to the moral conduct of war. According to Benda 'the extolling of harshness' is rife among modern 'clerks' or ideologues.[35] In this revised war ethic compassion is a sign of moral weakness rather than of strength. The test of virtue and of commitment to the cause is precisely the readiness to perform acts that go beyond the pale or that grossly offend conventional moral sensibilities. 'There is nothing which so much resembles virtue as a great crime', St Just declared (cited in Kedourie 1966, p. 18). Ironically but tellingly, it was St Just's humanitarian impulse that dictated his acts of inhumanity: 'the sacred love of the fatherland ... is so exclusive as to sacrifice everything to the public interest, without pity, without fear, without respect for humanity' (Kedourie 1966, p. 18). The mark of this ruthless humanitarianism is its lethal, but sadly all too frequent, combination of 'abstract' love with 'concrete' hate, that moral disposition that Dostoevsky had in mind when he wrote: 'I love humanity but ... the more I love humanity in general the less I love men in particular ... I become an enemy of people the moment they come close to me. But ... the more I hated men individually, the more ardent became my love for humanity at large (Dostoyevsky 1958, pp. 62–3).[36]

This reversal of values, whereby a vice is transformed into a virtue, and the readiness for excess is made the measure of moral strength and commitment, is widely shared. The Assassins practised it.[37] Bakunin recommends it: 'All the tender feelings of family life, of friendship, love, gratitude and even honour must be stifled in the revolutionary by a single cold passion for the revolutionary cause' (cited in O'Sullivan 1983, p. 67). Its result is that combatants are provided with a moral incentive to override the moral limits of war.[38] 'Sentimentality', wrote Lenin, 'is no less a crime than cowardice in war' (quoted in Kissinger 1971, p. 116). Himmler congratulated his fellow SS on the great work in which they were engaged: 'Most of you know what it means to see a hundred corpses lying together, five hundred, or a thousand. To have gone through this and yet – apart from a few exceptions, examples of human weakness – to have remained decent, this has made us hard. This is a glorious page in our history that has never been written and never shall be written' (cited in Fest, 1972, pp. 177–8). As Fest suggests (p. 183), 'the moral status of the SS rose with the number of its victims', and 'the desire, bred by the perverted image of the National Socialist ideal man, "to be described as harsh"... nipped doubt in the bud' (p. 427).[39]

The unlimited conduct of war that the militarist's understanding of war as total war dictates extends to the manner in which such war is concluded. This is a war that is fought neither to redress specific injuries nor to realize specific objectives, but that seeks a victory so uncompromising and complete that in its most consistent form it ends in the annihilation of an adversary or, at best, of an adversary's way of life. In such a war there is nothing by way of specific concession or restitution that an adversary can do to avoid or to terminate war. The satisfaction that militarism demands is unconditional surrender or total submission, and to settle for less would constitute betrayal of the cause for which the war has been fought. The idea that war can be conducted and end in mutual recognition and respect and in a negotiated or *bilateral* settlement is alien to this image of war. 'Victory or Death' is the necessary outcome of a war fought in accordance with militarist values.

Militarism, however, is not just a matter of the spirit and manner in which wars are fought and concluded. What convinces many that the fascist form of militarism is definitive is the perception that in fascism alone the triumph of war over peace and of military over civilian values is permanent and complete, so that even in times of 'peace' the dominance of war continues and the 'spirit of the uniform' pervades society. The good society *is* the 'war community', the 'armed state' of Hitler's dreams.[40] The perception is an accurate one, though (here as elsewhere) the exclusive attribution of this aspect of militarism to fascism seems mistaken.

The idea of the 'war community' has been alluded to already when discussing the ways in which militarists of various religious and ideological persuasion ascribe a socially creative power to war. Here the issue is the extent to which the war experience is definitive of the 'good society' as well as contributing to its emergence. Within the fascist tradition one of the most prominent exponents of this theme was Ernst Jünger, to whose work reference was made earlier. In the trenches of the First World War Jünger had glimpsed a new man and a new order. The war had not been unproductive, and it prefigured a new and healthy Germany. In the war the transcendence of that bourgeois order, to which Jünger fondly aspired, had begun. The supreme bourgeois values – security and privacy – had been shaken by the war with its 'community of the trenches'. The aim must be to make that 'front experience' permanent.

In Jünger's writings war in its modern 'industrial' form became the paradigm of the good society. The answer to the ills of peacetime lay in the 'total mobilization' of society, its revolutionary restructuring along military lines. The goal was underlined through the use of a military idiom, an idiom designed to break down the conventional (and normative) distinction between a state of war and a state of peace. Soldiers were described in industrial terms ('the day labourers of death' or 'workers in the lethal realm') and workers in military ones ('Every hand gripped on a machine suggests a shot will be fired, every completed work day is like a marching day of an individual in an army unit': quoted in Herf 1984, p. 90). In 'the wars of the workers' the soldier in the trenches and the worker in the factory are both combatants moved by the same spirit and serving the same purpose. Unlike the hated bourgeois, both accept the same disciplines and evince the same readiness for heroic self-sacrifice. Both soldier and worker live for the whole.

The new Germany will belong to the worker-soldier. Jünger's reticence about the details of that new order (like Marx's perhaps) was quite deliberate. His understanding of it, like his understanding of war itself, was not policy- or end-orientated. What he advocated was an activist regime that would retain the vitality and dynamism of war. The revolutionary experience was an end-in-itself, and the health and vigour of the national community would be maintained only if war or revolution was made permanent. An end-orientated conception of social order would lead inevitably to social stagnation and communal atrophy. Given these predilections, Jünger's admiration of the achievements of the Soviet Union, and of the 'positive and warlike will to power' of the Communists comes as no surprise, since in many fundamental respects his vision of the new order bore a striking resemblance to the theory as well as the practice of communism.

The 'dictatorship of the proletariat', as articulated by Marx and Engels as well as Lenin, is a concept with strong militarist connotations and a close affinity with Jünger's notion of 'total mobilization'. Drawing on the example of the Paris Commune – 'the glorious harbinger of a new society', according to Marx – all three attack the notion advanced by a variety of socialist thinkers that the revolutionary transformation of society can be achieved by the use of the existing state machine. The apparatus of the 'bourgeois' state must be 'smashed' and replaced by an entirely different kind of state. The principal difference lies in the way in which in the new proletarian state the distinction between state and society is broken down and the functions of the state are placed in the hands of the proletariat as a whole. Particular emphasis is placed by all three founding fathers on the proletarianization or socialization of military power (or on, what amounts to the same thing, the militarization of society), on 'the suppression of the standing army, and the substitution for it of the armed people' (Marx and Engels 1975–90, Vol. 22, p. 331).

In *The Tasks of the Proletariat in Our Revolution* , Lenin identifies the Paris Commune as a state which, in Engels's words, is 'no longer a state in the proper sense of the word', because it is 'one in which a standing army and police divorced from the people are *replaced* by the direct arming of the people themselves'. Lenin adds that 'it is *this feature* that constitutes the very essence of the Commune' (1965–70, Vol. 24, p. 68). In such a state, he argues elsewhere, 'order ... is maintained by the armed workers and peasants *themselves*, by the armed people *themselves*' (1965–70, Vol. 24, p. 39). The new state is achieved 'by *merging* the police force, the army and the bureaucracy with *the entire armed people* ... [In it] the proletariat must organise and arm all the poor, exploited sections of the population' (1965–70, Vol. 23, pp. 325–6; original emphasis throughout).

The purpose of such power and the manner of its deployment is unambiguous: the violent suppression of the bourgeoisie. The *dictatorial* nature of the proletarian state is certain. Marx and Engels, in the *Address of the Central Committee to the Communist League*, and Lenin, in *The State and Revolution*, leave no doubts on this score. The workers must strive for 'the most determined centralisation of power in the hands of the state authority' (Marx and Engels, 1975–90, Vol. 10, p. 285). They must resist 'the bourgeois endeavours to allay the storm, and must compel the democrats to carry out their present terrorist phrases', and 'far from opposing so-called excesses ... such instances must not only be tolerated but the lead in them must be taken' (*ibid.*, Vol. 10, p. 282). Engels, underlining that a 'revolution is certainly the most authoritarian thing there is', insists that 'the victorious party ... must maintain this rule by means of the terror which its arms inspire in the reactionaries' (*ibid.*, Vol. 23, p. 425). Lenin stresses the importance of 'establishing strict, iron discipline backed up by the state power of the armed workers' (1965–70, Vol. 25, p. 426). In the new order, where the enemies of the proletariat have not yet disappeared, 'control must ... be exercised not by a state of bureaucrats, but by a state of *armed workers* ' (*ibid.*, Vol. 25, p. 470), by a state in which 'the armed proletariat itself *may become the government*' (*ibid.*, Vol. 25, p. 489). In opposition to 'the renegade Kautsky', Lenin defends the violent and unrestrained nature of proletarian rule: 'The revolutionary dictatorship of the proletariat is rule won and maintained by the use of violence by the proletariat against the bourgeoisie, rule that is unrestricted by any laws' (*ibid.*, Vol. 28, p. 236).

In the light of guiding sentiments like these it is little wonder that the 'spirit of the uniform' has been displayed just as prominently in communist states as it has been in fascist ones.[41] The militarization of society, so evident in fact, is also a matter of fundamental principle. Still, this attribution to communism as well as to fascism of the defence of the 'war community' might seem unfounded, on the grounds perhaps that it confuses means with ends. It is true that, at least in theory, the dictatorship of the proletariat is a transitional stage towards the eventual 'withering away of the state' and the emergence of 'an association, in which the free development of each is the condition for the free development of all' (Marx and Engels 1975–90, Vol. 6, p. 506). The proletarian state was not itself the good or final society to which Marx, Engels or Lenin aspired. Therefore it might be thought wrong to describe it as a manifestation of militarism, or to associate revolutionary socialism with a militaristic creed like fascism. For militarists war and the 'war community' have an intrinsic, and not just an instrumental, value. In stark contrast, the value that Marxism-Leninism attaches to the dictatorship might be thought purely instrumental. Whatever militaristic features that transitional state possesses are to be wholly transcended in the classless society. There war ceases, true peace reigns, and the unity of mankind is realized.

The attempt to distance means from ends that this view entails is unconvincing. As has often been pointed out, the means are the end in the making,[42] and a peace that is attained through the annihilation of an adversary is not worth having. The real problem, however, with 'pacific' or 'humanitarian' forms of militarism, like communism, is not that evil means undermine a good end. Such an assessment is based on the false assumption that in these forms end and means *conflict*. This is far from being the case. In fact the reverse is true: end and means form one coherent whole. It is the end itself that dictates and fashions these violent means. It is precisely the conception of the end, that is, of 'peace', that is deficient and that leads by an inexorable logic to the systematic violation of the moral limits of war: peace and unity can be achieved only through the abolition of fundamental difference (whether that difference be 'class', 'race', 'state', 'nation', or 'religion'). The peace that communism, along with other secular and religious forms of militarism, upholds is the 'peace of the dead'. In short *this* humanitarianism and *this* universalism is a sham.

Notes

1 Cf. Ceadel 1989, Chapter 3.
2 Aron appears to be quoting Pascal: 'Man is neither angel nor beast, and unhappily whoever wants to act the angel, acts the beast ' (Pascal 1995, p. 128).
3 Clausewitz wrote, 'If policy is grand and powerful, so also will be the war, and this may be carried to the point at which war attains to its absolute form' (Clausewitz 1982, p. 403).
4 True militarism needs to be distinguished from that eager anticipation of war and fascination with things military commonly felt by the uninitiated. 'From time immemorial', wrote William James, 'wars have been, especially for noncombatants, the supremely thrilling excitement' (James 1924, p. 303). The romantic attraction that war may exert struggles to survive the encounter with the real horrors of war. Such fleeting enthusiasm does not pass the test of militarism. The true militarist finds himself at ease with the reality and not just with the prospect of fighting. His is an enthusiasm for war that is left unimpaired by its brutality and that even the prospect of military defeat fails to diminish.
5 On the general point see 'The History of Ideas and Guilt by Association' in Kedourie 1984, pp. 143–7.
6 Cf. Kedourie 1966, Ch. 1 and O'Sullivan 1983, Ch. 2. Both Kedourie's study of nationalism and O'Sullivan's study of fascism argue that militancy is not the prerogative of any particular ideology, but an intrinsic part of the new and ideological style of politics.
7 Contemporary Islamic fundamentalism is an amalgam of traditional and modern, indigenous and Western influences. Kedourie traces both sources of inspiration in a discussion of Islamic terrorism (cf. Kedourie 1987).
8 Lewis argues that according to classical Islamic jurists: 'The Muslim state ... may not ... recognize the permanent existence of another polity outside Islam. In time, all mankind must accept Islam or submit to Muslim rule. Meanwhile it is the duty of the Muslims to struggle until this is accomplished. The name of this duty is *jihad* ... one who performs it is called *mujahid*. ... The *jihad* was the holy war for Islam ... a perpetual duty, which will lapse only when all the

world is won for Islam' (Schacht and Bosworth 1974, p. 175). Subsequently, 'the duty of *jihad* was qualified and attenuated' and the classical juridical tradition disregarded, with the result that, particularly in modern times, *jihad* has been understood 'as a purely defensive obligation' and even 'as a purely moral struggle' (p. 176). This liberal and pacific intepretation is seen by fundamentalists as a betrayal of Islam.

9 See Taheri 1987, Hussain 1988 and Johnson and Kelsay 1990 (especially the article by Sonn, 'Irregular Warfare and Terrorism in Islam').

10 It was a view of war endorsed by contemporary Irish nationalists, who saw the revolutionary war against an imperial and materialistic England as a vindication of Irish 'idealism' as well as a struggle for independence.

11 The nature of the conflict was summarized by General Hoepner, the commander of Panzer Group 4, in the following directive to his troops:

> The war against the Soviet Union ... is the old struggle of the Germans against the Slavs, the defense of European culture against the Muscovite-Asiatic flood, the warding off of Jewish Bolshevism. This struggle must have as its aim the demolition of present Russia and must therefore be conducted with unprecedented severity. Both the planning and the execution of every battle must be dictated by an iron will to bring about a merciless, total annihilation of the enemy (cited in Bartov 1991, p. 129).

12 In a letter from the battlefields written in February 1915 Hitler expressed the hope 'that by the sacrifices and sufferings which many hundreds of thousands of us are undergoing daily, by the torrent of blood which is pouring out here day after day against an international world of enemies, not only Germany's enemies outside will be shattered, but also our inner internationalism. That would be worth more than all territorial gains' (cited in Fest 1974, p. 71).

13 This tendency whereby war is transformed from something of instrumental to something of intrinsic value is often overlooked in the case of non-fascist ideologies. Wilkinson, for example, regards Sartre's 'cult of violence' as a deviation from authentic or original Marxism, on the grounds that 'Marx viewed violence not as an end in itself but as a necessary means for achieving ultimate victory for the proletariat' (Wilkinson 1986, p. 76). This seems to be a great oversimplification, and one that hardly does justice to the creative power and transcendent properties attributed to revolutionary war by Marx and Marxists. Sartre's view seems not nearly as heretical as Wilkinson suggests.

14 In the tradition of the Assassins (who chose the dagger as their weapon as much to ensure their own capture and death as the death of their victims), the young suicide bombers of Hamas die in the firm

belief that as Islamic martyrs a glorious fate awaits them in the life hereafter, a life of untold riches lived in the company of 72 virgin brides. In pagan religions too death in battle was linked to conceptions of the after-life. The German tribes, for example, believed that warriors who fell in battle were rewarded by a life of endless combat: 'Each dawn they would awake, feed on mead and flesh provided by the sacred boar and goat, and then gird themselves once more for battle' (Aho 1981, pp. 23–4).

15 Pearse's brother Thomas also took part in the rising and was executed by the British along with his elder brother. In the poem that Pearse wrote just before the rising a mother finds consolation for the deaths of her two sons in the thought that 'the generations shall remember them, and call them blessed' (Dudley Edwards 1977, p. 263). It was Pearse's expression of sentiments like these that led the poet Yeats to observe: 'Pearse is a dangerous man; he has the vertigo of self-sacrifice' (Dudley Edwards 1977, p. 335). The evidence of Pearse's own writings as well as the testimony of those who knew him clearly indicates that for Pearse a principal part of the attraction of revolutionary action was the self-elevation and sense of self-fulfilment to which it was seen to give rise.

Pearse's sentiments are echoed by the Bolivian and Marxist revolutionary, Nestor Paz. Paz, the son of a Bolivian general, took part in the ELN campaign of 1970 against the Bolivian government and died of starvation in the course of that campaign (on the third anniversary of the death of Che Guevara who, along with Camillo Torres, served as his principal exemplar). He wrote in his journal: 'If I die I want my death to be full of meaning, to create waves of repercussion and reach other "receptive ears" who will struggle for the happiness of man' (Garcia and Eagleson 1975, p. 78). Elsewhere in the journal he wrote that, while not seeking death, 'In a vital way I'm even moving from the idea of "death" as a diminishment to the reality of "death" as fulness, and I am moving into a new dimension' (p. 58). Guevara himself is a prime example of someone for whom war, at least of the approved revolutionary kind, had much more than instrumental value. For him the revolutionary was 'the true priest of the reform', 'a guardian angel', 'the highest state of the human species'; and he too anticipated death with perfect equanimity.

16 The anarcho-syndicalist Georges Sorel viewed violence similarly: '[It] awakens in the depths of the soul a sentiment of the sublime'.

17 Guevara fought with the Kinshasa rebels in the Congo. He was not alone in his revolutionary migrations: among those who died with him in Bolivia were several members of the Central Committee of the Cuban Communist Party (Thomas 1971, p. 169).

18 See Cohn 1970.

19 In a funeral oration for O'Donovan Rossa he declared: 'Life springs from death, and from the graves of patriot men and women spring living nations' (quoted in Marreco 1967, pp. 190–1).

20 Elsewhere Lenin wrote: 'Socialists have always condemned wars between nations as barbarous and brutal. Our attitude towards war, however, is fundamentally different from that of the bourgeois pacifists [supporters and advocates of peace] and of the anarchists ... We regard civil wars, that is, wars waged by an oppressed class against the oppressor class, by slaves against the slaveholders, by serfs against landowners, and by wageworkers against the bourgeoisie, as fully legitimate, progressive and necessary.' Of course Lenin did not reject the goal of peace but insisted that, 'Whoever wants a lasting and democratic peace must stand for civil war against the governments and the bourgeoisie' ('Socialism and War' in Lenin, 1964–70, Vol. 21, p. 299).

21 Cf. Sartre 1976, esp. pp. 345f. With reference to the French Revolution and 'the revolutionary *praxis* of a group', Sartre wrote: 'Everyone reacted in a new way: not as an individual, nor as an Other, but as an individual incarnation of the common person' (Sartre 1976, p. 357).

22 In similar vein to Khatayevich, Che Guevara stated: 'We must proceed along the path of liberation, even if that costs millions of atomic victims' (quoted in Thomas 1971, p. 1470). 'How close', he mused, 'could we look into a bright future should two, three or many Vietnams flourish throughout the world with their share of deaths and their immense tragedies ... [with] imperialism impelled to disperse its forces under the sudden attack and the increasing hatred of all peoples of the world' (Gerassi 1968, p. 423). Mao's understanding of proportionality was just as inflationary. In a reported conversation with Nehru he declared: 'The atom bomb is nothing to be afraid of. China has many people. They cannot be bombed out of existence. If someone else can drop an atomic bomb, I can too. The deaths of ten or twenty million people is nothing to be afraid of' (Li 1994, p. 125). In a speech delivered in Moscow in 1957 he expressed a willingness to lose 300 million people: 'Even if China lost half its population, the country would suffer no great loss. We could produce more people' (Li 1994, p. 125).

23 As Taheri explains, the 'path of shame' is frequently employed in fundamentalist literature to refer to any negotiated settlement.

24 Cf. Ringer 1990, pp. 180ff.

25 The theme is a common one in nationalist literature. Fanon, for example, takes a similar view in *The Wretched of the Earth*.

26 In *The Pedagogy of the Oppressed* (a book informed by Marxist concepts and one that has had widespread influence, particularly on the

thinking of liberation theologians in Latin America and elsewhere)
Paolo Freire writes: 'Freedom is acquired by conquest, not by gift'
(Freire 1972, p. 31).

27 'This unforced choice, this fond election of evil' is how Burke
describes this attitude to revolution (Burke 1969, p. 127).

28 Courage is a virtue according to most moral traditions, including the
just war tradition; but in the case of militarism the value of courage
is so grossly inflated that it leads not only to the undermining of
other essential military virtues such as sympathy and compassion,
but to the suppression of that healthy regard for personal survival
on which the limited and measured conduct of war is often crucially
dependent.

29 About 140,000 German soldiers died at Stalingrad. Hitler was
incensed by the surrender of the survivors. 'How can they be so cowardly?' he asked. 'What is life? Life is the Nation. The individual must
die anyway. Beyond the life of the individual is the Nation. But how
can anyone be afraid of this moment of death, with which he can
free himself from this misery, if his duty doesn't chain him to this
Vale of Tears' (Shirer 1964, p. 1113).

30 Long before the outbreak of war Hitler declared: 'We must be prepared for the hardest struggles that a nation has ever had to face.
Only through this test of endurance can we become ripe for the
dominion to which we are called. It will be my duty to carry on this
war *regardless of losses*. The sacrifice of lives will be immense ... Cities
will become heaps of ruins; noble monuments of architecture will
disappear forever. This time our sacred soil will not be spared. But I
am not afraid of this' (quoted in Fest 1972, p. 87; added emphasis).
Of the Hebraic, Muslim, and Christian holy wars 'fought between the
absolutely righteous and the equally absolute incarnation of Evil', as
Aho argues, 'the ferocity of the violence in [such a] war must reflect
the enormity of the crime against God and man' (Aho 1981, p. 151).

31 The systematic nature of this process serves to distinguish it from a
tendency that is discernible in all wars. No doubt killing in any war
is made easier by exaggerating the differences between belligerents.

32 Cf. Bartov 1991, pp. 69–71 and p. 83 (the theme of dehumanization
and barbarization runs through Bartov's illuminating studies of
German military thinking and practice in the Second World War).
The policy of extermination was applied in its most explicit and organized form to the Jews. The ideological basis of the policy lay in Nazi
conceptions of a racial inequality so extreme as to undermine all
humanitarian considerations. In Nazi thinking the Jew was the arch-
enemy, the ultimate adversary and embodiment of evil, whose bane-
ful and insidious influence was everywhere to be found: hence the
constant merging in National Socialist propaganda of Bolshevik and

Jew, of the political and racial adversary, and the characterization of Bolshevism as 'Jewish Bolshevism'. The Bolshevik threat was part of the Jewish threat. In the words of the battle slogan of VII Army Corps: 'Behind the flood of the red mob grins the face of the Jew' (cited in Bartov 1985, p. 95). The Jew was the universal foe on whose total destruction human as well as German progress depended. The Jew was completely beyond, not only redemption or assimilation, but even preservation in the form of enslavement (the fate assigned to the Slavs). In this respect, as well as in its systematic nature and official authorization, the Nazi Holocaust was quite unlike that 'First [Christian] Holocaust' that accompanied the First Crusade: conversion was no longer held out as an alternative to death.

33 'The infidels had no need to attack us with their armies', Ayatollah Fazl-Allah Mahalati declared. 'The West captured the imagination of large sections of our people. And that conquest was far more disastrous for Islam than any loss of territory. It is not for the loss of Andalusia that we ought to weep every evening – although that remains a bleeding wound. Far graver is the loss of large sections of our youth to Western ideology, dress, music and food' (quoted in Taheri 1987, p. 13). It is this perception that inspires terror campaigns like that of the Qutbists in Egypt against cultural targets; these have included acid attacks on unveiled women, beheadings of the 'enemies of Islam' in the villages, the sacking of wine shops and restaurants, arson attacks on girls' schools, and the desecration of Coptic churches (cf. Taheri 1987).

34 St Just's version reads: 'Even the indifferent are to be punished, all who are *passive* in the Republic (cited in O'Sullivan 1983, p. 49).

35 He wrote: 'They proclaim the moral nobility of harshness and the ignominy of charity ... pity is depreciated, not to the benefit of inhumanity, but to the benefit of humanity *guided by reason* ... It seems to me that the modern "clerks" have created in so-called cultivated society a positive *Romanticism of harshness*' (Benda 1969, pp. 140–3).

36 Perhaps it is in this light that Che Guevara's words are to be understood: 'Let me say, with the risk of appearing ridiculous, that the true revolutionary is guided by strong feelings of love. It is impossible to think of an authentic revolutionary without this quality ... Our vanguard revolutionaries must *idealize* their love for the people ... They cannot descend, with small doses of daily affection, to the terrain where ordinary men put their love into practice' (Gerassi 1968, p. 398, emphasis added).

37 'To demonstrate commitment sufficiently profound to earn remission of all sins, the assassin violated what were considered his most cher-

ished bonds or personal feelings and struck victims in intimate encounters. Umayr ibn 'Adi, for example, the first assassin, killed his kinswoman (a poet who mocked Muhammed) "asleep with her children about her. The youngest, still at the breast, lay asleep in her arms"' (Rapoport 1990, pp. 124–5).

38 Of the Final Solution Fest writes: 'It was the appeal to idealism, to the readiness for self-sacrifice to a historic mission, and the perpetually reawakened devotion to a utopian world which placed at the regime's disposal those forces without whose willingness to serve, self-discipline and sense of duty neither the proportions nor the cold perfectionism of the extermination system would have been possible' (Fest 1972, p. 416).

39 The same test of political and moral authenticity was employed by the FLN in the Algerian war of independence. New recruits were required to demonstrate their commitment to the cause by carrying out some atrocity.

40 Cf. Nolte 1969, pp. 526–7.

41 Robert Nisbet, for whom the idea that militarism is a fascist monopoly is clearly preposterous, argues: 'It was realized very early in Soviet Russia that the work of militarizing society, through incessant exposure of the people to military symbols ... could not help but generate all-important processes of unification. Workers in the factories and the fields were called industrial soldiers, fully in keeping with the *Communist Manifesto*'s reference to "establishment of industrial armies"... Stalin's ... total militarization of Russia ... was no more, actually, than the fruition of the hated Trotsky's design ... More recently, we have seen the unification of the military and revolutionary communities in China under Mao Tse-tung [according to his 'principles of revolutionary militarism'] ... It would be hard to find a government anywhere in history which used the symbols, incentives, and disciplines of the military more widely and concertedly than that of China during the past two decades. Whether in industry, government, education, agriculture, or any other major sector of Chinese society, from the highest level of authority down to the smallest village council, the role of the military has been ubiquitous and for the most part decisive' (Nisbet 1974, pp. 88–9).

42 See, for example, Jacques Maritain's argument in *Man and the State*. Maritain writes there: 'means must be proportioned and appropriate to the end, since they are *ways to the end* and, so to speak, the end itself in its very process of coming into existence' (Maritain 1954, p. 50).

3

Pacifism

Pacifism harms and benefits the just war tradition in about equal measure. Its blanket condemnation of all things military (in some cases more presumed than real) disrupts the kind of moral regulation of war to which just war theorists aspire: war is considered to be beyond the reach of morality. At the same time it assists the just war project by its general insistence on the subordination of war to peace and by its creative and constructive understanding of peace and peacemaking. In fact pacifists and just war theorists share similar aspirations: the eschatological goal of a world without war structures the thinking of both, though its prospects and the manner of its achievement are conceived in radically different ways. In many respects the two traditions contest the same ground; which is why, perhaps, some of the fiercest critics of just war theory are to be found within the pacifist camp. Some of those critics have even arrived at pacifism via a just war route and, like many converts, appear determined to root out the error that they once entertained or the vice in which they once indulged. There is little doubt that pacifism presents the just war tradition with a formidable challenge. Any effective response must begin with an analysis of pacifism itself and a recognition of the internal variety of what is often very loosely identified as the 'pacifist' tradition.

In the present context 'pacifism' stands for 'the moral renunciation of war'. It is the *moral* renunciation of war that is in question. The rejection of war can rest on a number of grounds – not all of them moral. A realist, while having no moral objections to war, may for purely pragmatic or prudential reasons urge its renunciation. A small state that adopts a position of permanent neutrality in the face of the overwhelming military power of its neighbours may do so from a desire to escape the vagaries and ravages of war rather than from any moral anxiety about the activity of war itself. The same may apply to a state that dismantles its own defences (thereby avoiding the costs of defence and some at least of the risks of war) while relying on the defensive umbrella that the proximity of a powerful and friendly neighbour provides. It is in its *moral* opposition to war that the distinctive challenge of pacifism consists.

Secondly, the focus of the present discussion must be on the pacifist response to *war*. There are forms and aspects of pacifism that are not central to the discussion simply because they do not include or imply opposition to war. This is the case with 'private' or 'personal' pacifism, which disavows the use of force in defence of self while permitting, and even demanding, its employment in defence of the state. St Augustine, for example, is thought to have understood Christ's message of non-resistance as a counsel of perfection applicable to the individual in his personal life, but not to the soldier while acting in his public capacity as defender of the state or political community. 'As to killing another in order to defend one's own life,' he wrote, 'I do not approve of this, unless one happen to be a soldier or public functionary acting, not for himself, but in defence of others or of the city in which he resides, if he act according to the commission lawfully given him, and in the manner becoming his office' (quoted in Deane 1963, p. 312). In this case the right of private self-defence is denied, or its exercise at least discouraged, while the right and the duty of public defence is affirmed. Its acceptance of the moral permissibility of war clearly disqualifies this kind of pacifism as a form of war pacifism and, as St Augustine himself demonstrates, private or personal pacifism can sit easily with the adoption of a just war approach.[1]

Even where the renunciation of war rests on moral grounds, the nature and extent of that renunciation allows a number of important distinctions to be drawn. For one version of pacifism there are no conceivable circumstances in which war is morally permissible. The moral prohibition of war is an absolute one. Other forms of 'pacifism' are more selective, prohibiting war in some circumstances but not in others. This 'contingent' form of pacifism accepts the moral permissibility of war, at least in principle; and, even when the circumstances in which war becomes permissible are very narrowly drawn, such acceptance is perhaps sufficient to disqualify this as a form of pacifism in the strict sense. Contingent pacifism itself, however, may be seen to rest on diverse grounds and to involve very different degrees of opposition to war; and while some forms of contingent pacifism are indistinguishable from a just war approach, some are *virtually* indistinguishable from 'absolute' pacifism or pacifism proper.

In its least pacifist form 'contingent' pacifism may simply amount to the judgement that, while war remains licit in principle, this *particular* war is not. Much of the conscientious objection to the Vietnam War, for example, took this selective form. Those who had condoned the employment of American arms against Nazi Germany, or even more recently, against North Korea, felt unable to do likewise in the case of Vietnam. The moral misgivings that some entertained not just about the conduct of the war but, more fundamentally, about the American recourse to war in the first place were such as to engender not merely moral criticism of some aspects of the war but total opposition to it. Though its 'totality' may give this position the appearance of pacifism, such a description is inappropriate. When the objection to war is as specific as this and when no attempt is being made to develop a more general argument against war any talk of 'pacifism' seems out of place.

In itself this particular form of 'contingent pacifism' poses the just war tradition few, if any, problems. It may amount to no more than an application of just war criteria, in the light of which the moral deficiencies of a particular war are revealed. However, in some instances there is a tendency for the specific objection to widen into more general opposition. Such widening took place among those who participated in the anti-Vietnam War lobby: what began as a rejection of US involvement in Vietnam grew into a more radical opposition to war. It appears that when conscientious objection takes a political or mass and not just an individual form it can often transcend its limited origins and generate much broader moral scepticism and opposition. In some cases this may be because genuine pacifists conceal their total opposition to war beneath the veil of selective opposition for political reasons and in order to attract non-pacifist support.[2] In other cases, however, a process of genuine conversion may be at work: as opposition gathers momentum the people involved become more and more convinced that the problem is not simply *this* war but war itself.[3]

To begin with at least, the conclusion may not be as sweeping as that. Some forms of contingent pacifism admit the theoretical and even the historical possibility of the moral determination of war, but entertain such serious and extensive moral reservations about *modern* warfare, either in certain aspects or in its totality, as to virtually rule out any moral recourse to war by contemporary states. Here the view is taken that the transformation of the nature of war has made its moral determination less plausible. The just war has either become or is close to becoming an anachronism.

Again, the argument takes various forms, generating degrees of opposition to war. In some cases the objection may be restricted to a specific form of modern warfare, such as nuclear (or biological) war, which is seen as intrinsically evil and therefore morally impermissible. The absolute prohibition on these forms of warfare rests on the judgement that they are unavoidably 'total'. The enormous destructive potential of the weaponry means that recourse to war in these cases necessarily violates the principle of proportionality. Moreover, since the weapons are unavoidably indiscriminate in their effects they cannot be used without massive and systematic violation of the principle of non-combatant immunity. The immorality of use may be seen to exclude the morality of possession, so that even as part of a defensive and deterrent strategy the production and deployment of such weapons is seen as morally indefensible.

'Nuclear pacifism', if it remains simply that, hardly merits the description, since the moral denial of nuclear war may be accompanied by the moral acceptance of conventional war. The moral objection to nuclear war, however, may generate more widespread opposition to war through a process of linkage. For example, during the period of the Cold War, the perceived danger that a conventional war might develop into a nuclear war, given the bipolar and conflictual nature of international relations, was thought sufficient to rule out just recourse to conventional arms, even by non-nuclear states, and even though conventional war itself was not regarded as intrinsically immoral. Though in the circumstances that were thought to prevail at the time the net effect of this position was the comprehensive moral prohibition of war, its logic would seem to entail that in changed circumstances, say in the absence of nuclear weapons, or even perhaps in a multipolar world infused with the spirit of *détente*, conventional war would be readmitted to the moral fold.[4]

A more thoroughgoing opponent of conventional war would reject it absolutely and not just because of its perceived connection with another form of warfare. In this case the distinction between nuclear or biological and conventional war is thought to be morally insignificant. It is modern war itself, quite irrespective of its particular mode, that has destroyed the moral possibilities of war. Its 'strategic' and, it is argued, necessarily 'total' form is seen as intrinsically evil, violating, as on this view it unavoidably does, such key moral principles of war as proportionality and noncombatant immunity.Nuclear war simply takes to an extreme a trend that was already established well before the advent of nuclear or atomic weapons: the mass slaughter in the trenches of the First World War and the obliteration bombing of the Second World War, for example, were enough to convince some that the age of the just war had ended.

Some have even been led to doubt whether such an age ever really existed. The era of 'total war' has opened the eyes of many to what are seen to be the inherent deficiencies of the just war approach. For a long time, it is argued, these deficiencies went unnoticed because the limited capabilities of war gave the theory some credibility. From this perspective it is not pacifism but just war theory that appears (hopelessly) contingent: contingent upon a time when the physical and political limits of war made its moral limitation appear feasible. Moral theorists were misled into thinking that war could be subject to moral regulation by the fact that war in a pre-modern era was, militarily and politically speaking, inclined to be limited. That illusion has been shattered once and for all. Just war theory is not even out of date. Right from the start it misperceived the nature of war, confusing objective or factual limitations with moral potential, and ignoring the inherent tendency of all war to sacrifice morality to political and military expediency.[5]

The less specific and the more general 'contingent' pacifism's criticism of war becomes the more problems it creates for just war thinking, until, at the end of this spectrum of opposition to war, 'contingent' pacifism merges with 'absolute' pacifism. At this point the contradiction between the two traditions stands in open and clear relief; but, perhaps, it is the genesis of absolute *out of* contingent pacifism that presents the just war tradition with its most formidable challenge, for it often seems that this is a form of pacifism arrived at through the pursuit of just war logic itself.[6]

Pacifism in its pure or 'absolute' form shares with realism a deep moral scepticism about war. Both deny that war can ever be subject to moral limitation. Moreover, both regard the attempt so to subject war as dangerous or counterproductive, increasing rather than decreasing the likelihood of war, adding to its ferocity, and obscuring the moral degradation and corruption that war inevitably brings about. This coming-together of pacifist and realist perspectives is evident in the writings of Tolstoy, one of the greatest of modern pacifists (not least because his pacifism grew out of his own experience of war and his deep insight into its nature).[7] On the eve of the battle of Borodino Prince Andrew reflects upon the nature of war and concludes that the interests of peace would be better served if wars were fought without moral pretence:

> They talk to us of the rules of war, of chivalry, of flags of truce, of mercy to the unfortunate, and so on. It's all rubbish ... If there was none of this magnanimity in war, we should go to war only when it was worth while going to certain death, as now ... War is not courtesy but the most horrible thing in life; and we ought to understand that, and not play at war. (Tolstoy 1991, pp. 830–1)

For an absolute pacifist, as Tolstoy himself eventually became, the constraints of war are such as to eliminate entirely the opportunity for right conduct: to conduct a war morally is impossible. For such a pacifist the distinction between just and unjust war is wholly without foundation. Quite simply the 'just war' is a self-contradictory notion. War cannot be anything other than a moral obscenity, to which avoidance is the only proper response.

This, of course, is where the realist parts company with the pacifist. However hellish war may be, it remains, for the realist, an indispensable instrument of policy: recognition of its moral impermeability must not lead to its renunciation. The pacifist response is foolhardy in the extreme, and a very clear instance of the moralism against which realism inveighs.

From the pacifist perspective, however, war appears as a morally corrupting and therefore wholly unacceptable enterprise. Its nature and imperatives are such that it leads to the deadening of moral sensitivity and the erosion of moral responsibility. In war individuals are able to perform with equanimity actions that in peacetime would fill them with moral revulsion. This phenomenon is one of the most striking and most commonly observed features of warfare. George Orwell, for example, prefaces his wartime essay *England Your England* with the following reflection:

> As I write, highly civilised human beings are flying overhead trying to kill me. They do not feel any enmity against me as an individual, nor I against them. They are 'only doing their duty', as the saying goes. Most of them, I have no doubt, are kind-hearted law-abiding men who would never dream of committing murder in private life. On the other hand, if one of them succeeds in blowing me to pieces with a well-placed bomb, he will never sleep any the worse for it. He is serving his country, which has the power to absolve him from evil. (Orwell 1962, p. 63)

The phenomenon itself may not be in dispute, though its interpretation and the conclusion to be drawn from it often are. For a thinker like Saint Augustine, who believes in the possible legitimacy of war, its impersonal or 'public' nature is one of its moral strengths, enabling combatants to fight and even to kill one another without personal animosity or hatred, even without violating the unconditional law of charity. For the pacifist, however, a contrary lesson is drawn. It is its impersonal or abstract nature that makes war so *de*-moralizing, by enabling participants to overcome with consummate ease the moral scruples that their actions might otherwise provoke. 'It cannot be said,' Tolstoy wrote in *The Kingdom of God Is Within You*, 'that they [soldiers] are devoid of the conscience which should forbid them to do these things ... it does exist in them, but it is kept dormant' (Tolstoy 1894, p. 336).

The desensitizing nature of war is a major theme of Tolstoy's essay. In it he identifies those aspects of war that in his view undermine morality. The adoption of belligerent status requires, but also, psychologically, empowers, the individual to override common moral sentiments and prejudices, so that 'troops ... slaughter thousands without a vestige of remorse'(p. 333). Role-playing leads to moral evasion. In his new identity as 'soldier' the individual ceases to be bound by the duties that apply to 'ordinary men'. Furthermore, the collective nature of war, whereby the individual operates as a tiny cog in the great war-machine, erodes the sense of moral responsibility: 'When such deeds are committed, there are so many instigators, participants, and abettors that no single individual feels himself morally responsible' (p. 326).[8] The process of erosion is reinforced by the organizational and hierarchical structure of armies, by the chain of command and the habits of discipline and obedience to orders that military training is designed to instil. The entire military (and political) culture, Tolstoy argues, is such that throughout it is the participant's 'irresponsibility [which] remains intact' (p. 328) with the result that 'there is no crime too hideous for those who form part of the government and the army to commit' (p. 323).

The development of modern warfare has, in the opinion of contemporary pacifists, greatly accelerated the trends that Tolstoy discerned in the nineteenth century. If Tolstoy, who died four years before the outbreak of the First World War, thought nineteenth-century warfare morally impoverishing, what would he have made of the twentieth-century version, in which the impersonal and total nature of war has been taken to such extremes? The undermining of the sense of individual responsibility, a problem in any war, is seen to be greatly magnified by war in its modern and 'industrial' form, where the soldier, like the worker, has become 'an appendage of the machine'. The American pacifist James Douglass, for example, argues that there exists an inverse relationship between the humanity of war and its technological sophistication: the more technological war becomes the less direct and therefore less human the relation of combatant to combatant. 'In modern war,' he writes, 'it is by no means certain that the warrior will ever experience that moment of truth when war reveals its killing nature through a sudden insight into the enemy's humanity ... what is becoming more and more common with the perfection of military technology, is the warrior's failure to have any confrontation whatsoever with the enemy' (Douglass 1968, p. 245). As the 'killing-distance' between the soldier and the enemy increases, so the moral perception of the act of killing diminishes: an adversary who is never seen can be killed with equanimity.[9]

The 'absolute' pacifist's renunciation of war may be one that is free-standing or one that forms part of a more complete renunciation. The focus of the discussion so far has been on anti-war pacifism, and for some pacifists the objection is precisely to war; not all violence (perhaps it would be more exact to speak of force or coercion in these instances) is morally impermissible. There is room here for the idea of the legitimate use of force in cases of self-defence, for example, or in the sanctions needed to uphold the civil law. The objection is to war itself, the right of self-defence and of legal enforcement being conceded.

Such a partial form of pacifism is vulnerable to the criticism, commonly levelled against it, that it is inconsistent to deny the state the right to war while allowing the state itself, in its internal jurisdiction, the right of legal coercion and the individual the right of self-defence. The just war theorist Elizabeth Anscombe, for example, argues that there is a logical and moral continuum embracing self-defence, law enforcement and war, and that 'only if it is in itself evil violently to coerce resistant wills, can the exercise of coercive power [including the extreme case of war] by rulers be bad as such' (Anscombe 1981, p. 51).[10]

What the 'war pacifist' is forced to dispute, therefore, are the analogies frequently drawn by moral apologists of war, like Anscombe, between war and self-defence and war and legal enforcement. Accordingly, the case of war is seen to be fundamentally unlike either self-defence or legal enforcement, so that neither concept can be used to give legitimacy or moral respectability to war. The analogy with self-defence, it is argued, breaks down in the face of the impersonal and collective nature of war and of the fact that most of the killing, particularly in modern warfare, is done by those who are in no immediate personal danger. Similarly, the analogy of legal enforcement is regarded as inapplicable given the excessively violent or uncontrolled nature of war and the partial ends that it serves. Within the political community the rule of law prevails and coercion is the exception rather than the norm, and in those cases where it is necessary to uphold the law the use of force is strictly limited, controlled and impartial. All of this is seen to have very little bearing on the mayhem that is war, wherein the laws remain forever silent.[11]

There are, however, pacifists of a more radical and total persuasion who accept the criticism (while resisting its conclusion) and for whom 'war pacifism' does not go far enough. Such 'total' pacifism refuses to regard the violence of war as a special case. *All* forms of violence – and here the key distinction so far as the ethics of war is concerned between violence and force is systematically suppressed – are morally impermissible. It is always wrong to answer violence with violence. What is rightly denied the state in its external relations must not be permitted it in its internal relations, and what is denied the state – the right of self-defence – must not be permitted the individual.

The American pacifist and leader of the New England Non-Resistance Society William Lloyd Garrison (whose son corresponded with Tolstoy) was a pacifist of this total persuasion. He registered his opposition to all wars, whether offensive or defensive, to all preparations for war and to all military appropriations, and, since 'laws are enforced virtually at the point of the bayonet', to all participation in the legal and political system. He wrote 'that if a nation has no right to defend itself against foreign enemies, or to punish its invaders, no individual possesses that right in his own case. The unit cannot be of greater importance than the aggregate. If one man may take life, to obtain or defend his rights, the same licence must necessarily be granted to communities, states and nations. If *he* may use a dagger or a pistol, *they* may employ cannon, bombshells, land and naval forces'(quoted in Tolstoy 1894, p. 6). To prevent the moral slippage that occurs once the right of self-defence or of legal coercion has been conceded, pacifism must be total rather than restricted to the case of war. Some form of anarchism would appear to be the logical conclusion of so universal a form of pacifism, since from this radical perspective the state constitutes a form of institutionalized violence and a source of moral corruption. Tolstoy agreed. 'All governments are in equal measure good and evil', he wrote. 'The best ideal is anarchy' (quoted in Woodcock 1963, p. 207).[12]

This reference to an ideal brings to the fore the positive side of pacifism, something that can easily be ignored given the characteristic and prevailing emphasis on its negative aspect, that is, its *denial* of war and its policy of *non*-violence. The negative aspect is real and fundamental. Since violence is seen by 'absolute' pacifists as an intrinsic moral evil, it must be rejected at whatever cost. The idea that violent means can serve or promote moral and pacific ends, in any circumstances, is rejected. Violence is seen to corrupt all who resort to it (including those who use it only to counter the violence of others) and to destroy every moral endeavour. 'It has the capacity to turn whoever uses it into the likeness of the oppressor' (Wink 1990, p. 105). Though in this absolute form the objection to the use of violence is not based on a consideration of its consequences, even from the standpoint of consequences counterviolence is thought to be unjustified and invariably counterproductive, giving rise to an escalation or 'spiral of violence' that deepens the situation of conflict and makes the prospect of a real peace ever more distant. Conversely and more positively, however, non-violence is seen as a good-in-itself, and not simply as a rejection of something else. The pacifist regards non-violent action in much the same way that the militarist regards war – as an expressive rather than instrumental activity with the power to transform man and the world. In this more morally ambitious form pacifism is chosen as a way of life and a positive good, not simply as a means of avoiding moral contamination.

For Christian pacifists, for example, the renunciation of all forms of violence is seen at the same time as the affirmation of the ethic of love that is at the heart of the Christian religion. It is regarded as a fundamental requirement or primary norm, not simply as a counsel of perfection to be applied in practice only to a clerical élite: 'Non-violence is not an option for Christians. It is the essence of the gospel' (Wink 1990, p. 106). Violence leads inevitably to the denial of love and the loss of Christian authenticity – and in the view of pacifists authenticity has often been absent in the history of Christianity. The ascendancy that for much of that history the just war tradition has enjoyed constitutes for them a betrayal of Christian principles ('The whole discussion of "just" wars is sub-Christian': Wink 1990, p. 112). By becoming embroiled with the empire or state the Church forsook its original pacifism and became tainted with militarist attitudes and values at odds with its true mission. 'The way of life revealed in Jesus Christ,' Douglass writes, 'is contradicted by the just war doctrine, which has traditionally dictated that the Christian's relationship to the warring state be one of obedient homicide' (Douglass 1968, p. 182). The Christian way of life is a pacifist way of life, and it is as a way of life that pacifism is to be understood.

Just as pacifists resist the negative characterization of pacifism, so they reject the passivity often attributed to it. Pacifism is not about the mere avoidance of the evil that is violence, but about the replacement of evil with good, about the positive overcoming of violence. There is more to the Quaker understanding of pacifism, for example, than the simple avoidance of violence: the right and effective response to violence is not to meet evil with evil, but 'to *answer* that of God in every man,' to set 'the aggravating part' aside and to seek out the divine, the good, the loving element that exists in all men. According to Ghandi, to act violently is to assume a position of moral infallibility that suppresses the 'truth' of the other. The search for, and recognition of, that truth precludes the use of violence against him or her. This attitude of dynamic openness is fundamentally conciliatory. It is non-violence (in this active sense), not violence, that is truly disarming.

Pacifist activism takes different forms. It may be understood as a response on the part of individuals involving an interior or spiritual conversion and the cultivation of non-violent or loving relationships with others. In so far as a social remedy to the problem of violence is advanced at all by this form of pacifism it will be seen to lie in the nurturing and dissemination of pacifist values and the gradual extension of the network of transformed relations throughout society. For other pacifists the problem of war and violence calls for a much more collective and systematic response. Gandhi, for example, argued: 'That non-violence which only an individual can use is not of much use in terms of society' (Mukherjee 1993, p. 102).[13] The active pacifism of a Ghandi or a Martin Luther King demands engagement and contention with the 'violent' society and its oppressive institutions (not, as some traditional forms of pacifism have recommended, withdrawal from the wider social world and the formation of independent pacifist communities). Their version of pacifism was 'political', even 'militant' in conception.[14] It is not, of course, necessary to see these forms of pacifism as alternatives: in many cases interior conversion and the conversion of structures are seen as equally necessary and mutually reinforcing. Nevertheless, the weakness to which the tradition has been prone is its tendency to emphasize one version at the expense of the other.

In the past most criticisms of pacifism have been based on its perceived failure to address the question of means. Much recent pacifist literature can be seen as a response to the realist charge that pacifism is a utopian doctrine that in moralistic fashion ignores the constraints that the real world of power relations – the world as it is, and not the world as pacifists would like it to be or even perhaps as it ought to be – places upon human action. Increasingly, pacifists have addressed themselves to the question of instrumentalities. This may be a sign of the way in which the tradition has 'come in from the cold' and of the extent to which modern pacifism is indebted to more 'realistic' non-pacifist traditions. Converts from those traditions have been less ready to settle for an 'aspirational' pacifism, and have been much more sensitive to realist questioning than those of a more fundamentalist and isolationist persuasion.

Pacifists have responded to criticism by questioning the assumptions that are seen to underpin an 'abstract' realism. The pacifist tactic has been to turn the realist criticism against itself: for example, by describing realist principles as 'utopian', as in Häring's reference to 'the utopian dream that peace can be preserved through increase of armament and mutual threat of annihilation' (Häring 1986, p. 87); or as founded in illlusion or ideology, as in his references to 'the illusion that wars are unavoidable' and 'the ideology that wars are necessary' (p. 33). The reason why pacifism is regarded as 'unrealistic' is often because war is seen as something rooted in human nature, and therefore something that is ineradicable. The concept of human nature that this understanding implies, so it is argued, is one that ignores the developmental or historical dimension of man's existence.[15] In the interests of a greater *realism* human nature should be viewed, not as a static, unchanging entity, but as a social and historical phenomenon. If humanity is 'warlike', this tells us more about the social and historical environment in which it has been brought up than it does about a 'human nature' abstractly and statically conceived.

A pacifist who takes this view will accept that a propensity to war is generally discernible, both now and in the past. That propensity, however, is seen as the product of a social and historical reality that is not unchangeable. War may be something rooted in human nature (and therefore something more than a purely contingent event); but only in the sense of a human nature fashioned and produced by the existing 'war system'. From this perspective the object or strategy of pacifism must be the transformation of the 'structures of violence' that induce violent behaviour at both a domestic and an international level. The real task of peacemaking is not to bring about the temporary cessation of hostilities or to restore the status quo, but to achieve the genuine pacification of society and the transformation of a militarist culture into a pacific one.[16]

It is argued by contemporary pacifists[17] that over many centuries of historical development societies have been transformed into systems of war that are geared socially, economically and politically to the maintenance and often to the glorification of war. The 'garrison state' is the historical norm rather than the exception. Contemporary society is deeply committed to war and 'in countless ways nonmilitary institutions and practices serve military ends' (Holmes 1989, p. 268). Large and key sectors of a modern economy, for example, are either directly involved in or dependent upon the defence and armaments industries. As a result there are millions of people who have a vested interest in the perpetuation and even expansion of the business of war. The educational system too, formally and informally, cultivates a disposition to war. From the earliest age children – particularly male children – are imbued with military values. In both secular and religious circles language is dominated by a military idiom and imagery. In such varied and mutually reinforcing ways our social institutions secure a central place for war and ensure its widespread and ready acceptance. The roots of war lie deep within our culture.

To remedy this state of affairs a substantial programme of pacification measures is required, which must involve the radical transformation of institutions, beliefs and practices, a reconstituting of society (not just a conversion of isolated individuals to pacifist ways, leaving the system intact). Reconstitution would involve among other things a conversion to a peace economy. The present dependence of the economy on the war industry is such that the social and economic costs of conversion would be very considerable, at least in the short term. The process would need to be a gradual one; and to be fair, as well as politically viable, it would require the use of public funds and subsidies to cushion the harmful effects of mass unemployment and to develop alternative and peaceful forms of economic activity. This economic reform would go hand in hand with attempts to demilitarize the culture, so that the present hegemony of martial values would eventually be replaced by one of pacific values.

As far as defence itself is concerned contemporary pacifists are keen to rebut the charge that their policies would leave the state defenceless. They argue the efficacy of non-violent defence and the potential of mass involvement. Theirs is a form of pacifism that does not ignore or neglect the issue of power, but argues that the demilitarized or disarmed state is not in fact powerless. The basis of *all* power, even that of a tyrant, is understood to be consensual. Ultimately, the wielder of power is dependent on those over whom it is wielded. The powerful rely fundamentally on the cooperation of the seemingly powerless. Without that cooperation they are ultimately rendered powerless. In other words, non-violent resistance, with its techniques of non-cooperation and civil disobedience, is itself a form of power. If citizens refuse to obey laws or decrees, if administrators and police refuse to execute and enforce them, if workers refuse their labour, if children are withdrawn from school, and so on, the result is 'the dissolution of power'. The basic assumption behind this policy of non-violent defence is that if the people refuse to cooperate, in sufficient numbers and for a sufficient length of time, the country will become ungovernable and the government will be forced to capitulate.

Advocates of this strategy stress that its success would depend upon the careful marshalling and application of resources. As much planning and thought needs to go into these measures as at present goes into more conventional and military forms of defence. Organization and training of a high order would be required. The training, while taking a very different form (its emphasis, for example, would be on 'deliberate self-suffering, not a deliberate injuring of the supposed wrong-doer': Mukherjee 1993, p. 96) would need to be every bit as rigorous and technical as military training. Given its non-violent nature, it would embrace not just those of military age but the vast majority of the population, female as well as male and old as well as young.

Pacifists recognize that unilateral disarmament and the adoption of non-violent defence policies may not be sufficient to deter or repel an invader, but argue that they would present an occupying force with such enormous logistical problems as to undermine its will and to make it think twice about future invasions. The underlying assumption on which the strategy rests is that an occupation cannot succeed without collaboration. There is no military solution to widespread and sustained non-collaboration. Of course pacifists recognize that mass resistance is likely to involve widespread suffering and loss of life arising from economic disruption and the retaliatory measures of the occupying force; but they question whether the harm inflicted would be any greater than that inflicted by war, especially by war in its total and even nuclear form. Why, pacifists ask, are militarists so eager to discount the loss of life in the case of war, but so reluctant to do so in the case of non-violent strategies? In their view the likelihood is that there will be fewer casualties in non-violent than in violent forms of defence. One author, for example, compares India under the British with Algeria under the French, the huge loss of life in the Algerian war of liberation being contrasted with the minimal losses in India.[18] The reason for this discrepancy is seen to lie in the non-violent form of resistance adopted by the indigenous population of India, though alternative and less supportive interpretations are of course available.[19] Even where non-violence fails (for example, in Czechoslovakia in

1968), it is argued that it fails less disastrously than violence (Hungary in 1956). Non-violent resistance exacts a heavy price; but so too does war. Both require a readiness for self-sacrifice. The crucial difference is that non-violent resistance does not require the readiness to kill.

There seems little doubt that pacifism, at least in some of its various guises, presents the just war tradition with one of its greatest challenges. The two traditions have much in common both in their genesis and in their general orientation. Given such affinity the rivalry between them is understandable, and it has often been intense, and at times even bitter. In recent years especially, the just war tradition has sometimes seemed about to collapse into pacifism. In the much longer term, perhaps, that collapse will seem like the just war tradition's natural fulfilment and completion. For the foreseeable future, however, the two traditions seem set to continue along their separate though often parallel paths.

Notes

1 The distinction between 'private' pacifism and 'public' war is often thought to be crucial to the assessment of the morality of war, particularly among Christian thinkers. The effect of the distinction is to underline the 'other-regarding' nature of just war: what justifies war is not the defence of self, but the defence of others. In this way a just war can be seen as an expression rather than as a denial of the law of charity. A good example of this way of thinking occurs in a published interview with Leonard Cheshire, a convert to Catholicism and founder of the Cheshire homes for the disabled, who was awarded the Victoria Cross for his exploits with Bomber Command in the Second World War: 'If it's myself who is being attacked, it may be a counsel of perfection that I turn the other cheek and allow myself to be killed but if the aggressor is killing someone else, or worse still, a whole group of others, then it cannot be a counsel of perfection for me to refrain from going to their defence ... my clear duty in charity is to defend the victims' (Cheshire 1991, pp. 72–3).

2 The American pacifist Gordon Zahn, for example, appears to adopt this tactic in his attack on the Gulf War (see Zahn 1991).

3 Thomas Merton's pacifism seems to have emerged in this way.

4 Something like this seems to have occurred, the end of the Cold War leading at least in some circles to the moral rehabilitation of war. See my article 'The New World Order and the Ethics of War' in Holden 1996.

5 Zahn writes: 'It is time to file the Just War theory away in the same

drawer that hides the flat-earth theory' (Zahn 1983, p. 130).

6 The moral theologian Bernard Häring, for example, writes: 'During the past sixteen hundred years the theory of "just war" intended to keep war and warfare within narrow limits whenever there was no chance of avoiding it. There was a strong emphasis on the proportionality between hoped-for benefits and damage, and on the exemption of non-combatant civil populations. Under the present military situation these conditions cannot and will never be observed. Taking as basis the best Christian tradition on "just war", we come to the same conclusion as that of another Christian tradition: the tradition of pacifism' (Häring 1986, p. 81); and again, 'At this crossroad of human history the whole of mankind should become "pacifist" and ban any option for war' (p. 65).

7 As an artillery officer in the Russian army Tolstoy served in the Crimean War. An account of his experiences is contained in *The Sebastopol Sketches* (1986), and a fascination with war and things military informs the great novels, especially *War and Peace* (1991).

8 Tolstoy's view of war is reminiscent of Burke's view of democracy. Burke argued that since 'the share of infamy that is likely to fall to the lot of each individual in public acts, is small indeed ... a perfect democracy is therefore the most shameless thing in the world ... [and therefore] the most fearless' (Burke 1969, p. 191).

9 'The pacifist's problem,' Ryan (a pacifist himself) writes, 'is that he cannot create, or does not wish to create, the necessary distance between himself and another to make the act of killing possible' (Ryan 1983, p. 521). Of course it is at least conceivable that technological advance leads to the moral improvement of war rather than its moral diminution. Hegel adopts this position in *The Philosophy of Right* with regard to the invention of the gun (Hegel 1991, p. 365). More recently, similar assessments have been made of laser-guided missiles and non-lethal weapons.

10 It is a view endorsed, however reluctantly, by Erasmus (at least in his later writings): 'No one could doubt Erasmus's genuine hatred of war ... [but], as Erasmus confesses, to accept the lawfulness of the magistrate's sword necessarily implies acceptance of the prince's; and from there on there is no stopping' (Fernández-Santamaria 1977, p. 144; see also Fernández-Santamaria 1973).

11 For a fuller (critical) discussion of the analogy see Teichman 1986, Ch. 5.

12 Tolstoy's denunciation of the state grew more vehement as he advanced in years: 'I regard all governments ... as intricate institutions, sanctified by tradition and custom, for the purpose of committing by force and with impunity the most revolting crimes. And I think that the effort of those who wish to improve our social life

should be directed towards the liberation of themselves from *national governments*, whose evil, and above all, whose futility, is in our time becoming more and more apparent' (Woodcock 1963, pp. 209–10). According to Woodcock, Tolstoy did not describe himself as an anarchist because, while accepting the goal of anarchism, he rejected its characteristic employment of violent means, proposing instead non-violent resistance as the only means consistent with the end of a non-violent society (pp. 206–19).

13 Häring expresses a similar view: 'It would be unrealistic to dream that good interpersonal relationships automatically change social conditions ... We have to fight constantly against the "sin of the world", which embodies itself in institutions, processes, structures, social conflicts, and in a confused public opinion' (Häring 1986, pp. 82–3).

14 'Non-violence in its dynamic condition', wrote Gandhi, 'means conscious suffering. It does not mean meek submission to the will of the evil-doer, but it means putting one's whole soul against the will of the tyrant' (Mukherjee 1993, p. 100). He was at pains to dissociate the version of civil resistance that he upheld – satyagraha (the 'non-violence of the strong') – from the idea and the practice of 'passive resistance' ('the non-violence of the weak'). He underlined its activist nature by the frequent use of a military idiom, likening the civil resisters to 'an army subject to all the discipline of a soldier' (p. 146). This 'army of satyagrahis' was engaged in a 'holy war', and the *ahimsa* that it was required to practise 'calls forth the greatest courage ... [and] is the most soldierly of a soldier's virtues' (p. 96).

15 'For the "realist",' Régamey writes, 'what is "natural" cannot be overcome, for he treats as fixed, limits that in fact the nature of man should constantly be trying to extend.' He cites Aldous Huxley with approval: 'The malleability of human nature is such that there is no reason why, if we so desire and set to work in the right way, we should not rid ourselves of war as we have freed ourselves from the weary necessity of committing a *crime passionel* every time a wife, mistress or female relative gets herself seduced' (Régamey 1966, p. 57–8). Häring agrees, citing Von Weizsacker to the effect that 'changes similar to liberation from war have happened in the course of history: for instance, the victory over the deeply rooted and strongly ideologized system of slavery' (Häring 1986, p. 90).

16 Here the emphasis is less on changes to the international system than on changes to domestic sytems. The former are seen as dependent on the latter. Attempts to change the international system in advance of the required domestic revolution are often seen as futile.

17 See, for example, Holmes's *On War and Morality* (1989) and *Non-Violence in Theory and Practice* (1990), Sharp's *The Politics of Nonviolent Action* (1973) and Douglass's *The Non-violent Cross* (1968).

18 Wink 1990.
19 The case of India is frequently cited by pacifists as a demonstration
   of the power and efficacy of non-violence. Häring too, for example,
   suggests that 'the reason nonviolence worked in the cases of Gandhi
   and Martin Luther King is because it was an authentic expression of
   profound spirituality' (Häring 1986, p. 107). Such an assessment
   appears either naive or tendentious, discounting as it does other
   important factors, not the least of which is the nature of the adversary. It is difficult to see non-violence meeting with the same
   response against a more ruthless opponent as Bertrand Russell,
   despite his own pacifist leanings, acknowledges retrospectively: 'I
   had allowed a larger sphere to the method of non-resistance – or,
   rather, non-violent resistance – than later experience seemed to warrant. It certainly has an important sphere; as against the British in
   India, Gandhi led it to triumph. *But it depends upon the existence of
   certain virtues in those against whom it is employed.* When Indians lay
   down on railways and challenged the authorities to crush them
   under trains, the British found such cruelty intolerable. But the Nazis
   had no scruples in analogous situations. The doctrine which Tolstoy
   preached with great persuasive force, that the holders of power could
   be morally regenerated if met by non-resistance, was obviously
   untrue in Germany after 1933. Clearly Tolstoy was right only when
   the holders of power were not ruthless beyond a point, and clearly
   the Nazis went beyond this point' (Russell 1978, p. 431; added
   emphasis).

4

The just war

The image of war that just war analysis presupposes is the object of inquiry in this chapter: not the specific just war principles and analytical concepts to be examined later, but the general conception of war that underpins that complex moral apparatus. How does this image of war compare with the contending approaches outlined previously, with realism, militarism and pacifism? Where does just war thinking fit in this conceptual spectrum of war? Of the four different images of war considered here the just war image is the only one to uphold the moral limitation of war clearly and consistently. In opposition to the amoral and wholly pragmatic approach of the 'pure' realist, the just war theorist insists on the moral determination of war where that is possible, and on the moral renunciation of war where it is not. In opposition to the militarist, the just war theorist consistently affirms the moral primacy of peace over war, resisting the cult of violence and the drift into total war to which militarism in both its open and covert forms is prone. In opposition to the pacifist, the just war theorist resists the blanket moral condemnation of war and of all things military, affirming the potential moral instrumentality of war and the virtues of an imperfect and often precarious peace. These are fundamental and important differences; yet it would be mistaken to see the various comparisons in purely negative terms, since what they reveal is affinity, and in some cases even indebtedness, as well as opposition. In the contrasts and the affinities that exist between it and each of the contrasting approaches to war the just war tradition's own distinctive image of war is more clearly revealed.

The first image of war examined was Realism. In its strongest or purest form realism involves the total renunciation of the moral point of view and the denial of the moral limitation of war both in theory and in practice. The realist regards the attempt to apply moral criteria to the business of war, or even to international relations in general, as misplaced and even downright dangerous. Any moral determination of war is dismissed under the blanket condemnation of 'moralism' (or 'idealism'). For the realist all attempts to subject war to moral limitation are utopian and, through their neglect of harsh and abiding realities, put at risk the delicate and necessarily imperfect balance in which international order consists. The idea of a *moral realism* is a contradiction in terms.

Moral realism, on the other hand, is what the just war tradition purports to be about. Unlike the realist, the just war theorist insists on the moral determination of war. In just war analysis this moral determination of war is divided into two distinct though closely related parts, one dealing with the question of recourse to war (*ius ad bellum*) and the other dealing with the subsequent conduct of war (*ius in bello*). A realist perspective can be applied to both, with the result that neither the recourse to war nor the conduct of war are seen as fit objects of moral enquiry. In more partial or limited forms of realism moral considerations are applied to the question of recourse, but not to the actual conduct of war: in such a case *whether or not* to fight is acknowledged to be a moral question, involving among other things the consideration of just cause, but *how* to fight is a purely technical issue to be decided by military and political criteria free from moral restraint. In this partial or limited form of realism a morality of ends is applied to war, but not a morality of means. In opposition to both forms of realism the just war tradition upholds the moral determination of both the recourse to war and the conduct of war: the *ius ad bellum* and the *ius in bello* carry equal weight and authority in that tradition.

Viewed from a just war standpoint, realism is too inclined to see war as an extension of politics: an understanding that establishes the normality of war. Where the realist sees a continuum of politics and war, the just war theorist sees a radical disruption; and where the realist recognizes only pragmatic necessity, the just war theorist contemplates a moral tragedy. The realist's typical understanding of international politics as a state of war, in which states enter into relations with one another as particular entities subject to no higher law than that of their own individual welfare or national interest, makes of actual war a normal and expected occurrence.[1] Realism upholds a form of moral particularism, less extreme than militarism no doubt, but no less exclusive in its concentration on the moral claims of a particular state. The universalist perspective, underpinning just war analysis, of an international community embracing all states and establishing mutual rights and obligations is here suppressed. The state has duties only to itself. Even if the state's own conception of its duties demands respect for other states, this unilateral conception of duty leaves the way open for the total or unlimited prosecution of war.

The realist has few universalist aspirations, and an exaggerated emphasis on state sovereignty with its concomitant principle of non-intervention impedes the kind of moral ordering of international relations favoured by the just war theorist. About the claims advanced on behalf of the so-called 'international community' realism is characteristically sceptical. From a just war standpoint that scepticism often seems well founded. An aspiration is not, after all, the same as a reality. Yet aspirations *are* important, and without them the conduct of war and international relations must become distorted. The realist's view of the international order seems too conservative or quietistic judged by just war standards. The overriding emphasis on order leads to the neglect of justice. The preoccupation with the preservation of a fragile and uneasy peace is allowed to curtail the search for a more lasting and just settlement. The static and morally neutral conception of a state of equilibrium based on a balance of power leads to a 'management' view of international relations rather than the more appropriate one, so far as just war thinking is concerned, of their moral improvement and dynamic transformation.

It would, however, be a grave error to see the relation between the two traditions in purely negative and conflictual terms: realism and the just war tradition have much in common, and there are aspects of realism that are essential to moral insight and analysis. In the first place, both traditions, while finding a place for war, affirm its instrumental and subordinate nature. Neither view war as a primary or expressive activity, or as an end in itself without need of external justification. Both see it as acceptable only as a means to the securing of political ends, and of ends that (at least typically, if not exclusively, in the case of realism) are specific and finite rather than general and transcendent. Similarly, and in large measure consequentially, both traditions uphold a concept of limited war, though the realist's limitation of war on purely pragmatic grounds is too permissive and too insecure to satisfy the just war analyst. The primacy of policy and the instrumental nature of war only ensure limitation if policy itself remains limited. As realists like Clausewitz have recognized, there is an inevitable proportion between the ends that war is made to serve and the manner in which it is conducted, and the grander the object of war the more total or unlimited its conduct (hence the willingness of Clausewitz and other realists to accept 'absolute' or total war, at least in principle and despite their obvious preference for a more limited or 'real' war). The realist conception of the subordination of war to politics does not rule out, though it certainly does not encourage, its aggrandizement; and in an age dominated for long periods by an ideological style of politics it has sometimes led in practice to total war. In contradistinction, the just war can never be total.

The congruity between the two traditions is in part methodological. As one just war theorist has observed: 'The question of whether this or that use of force is morally justifiable is not simply a moral question. It depends on a whole complex of political causes and effects, a set of facts' (Vann 1939, p. 28). Moral judgements ought not to be made, though (sadly) in practice they often are made, abstractly or independently of the facts. The application of just war principles is not a one-way process: it is a question, not just of bringing the principles to bear upon the facts, but of bringing the relevant facts to bear upon the principles. The process of moral reasoning (of moral casuistry in the best and non-pejorative sense) is as much inductive as it is deductive. 'The moralist', John Courtney Murray wrote, 'can give no answer at all to the *quaestio iuris* until the *quaestio facti* has been answered.' The need, he argued, was of 'a far more vigorous cultivation of politico-moral science' (Murray 1960, p. 272).

This acknowledgement of empirical dependence is evident in the very criteria that just war theory employs in its analysis of war, criteria that cannot be applied in practice without reference to the facts and without the exercise of political and military judgement. When, for example, does the point of 'last resort', which just war theory lays down as one of the conditions of just recourse, occur? When have peaceful or diplomatic means of settling a dispute been *effectively* exhausted? Thinking of the events that preceded the outbreak of war in 1939, for example, at what point did Britain's continued search for a diplomatic solution and the consequent refusal to countenance war begin to imperil rather than to secure or promote peace? These are questions of a political or strategic rather than a moral nature; and yet they are questions on which moral judgement crucially depends.

Similarly, however just the cause of war, to have recourse to war with little hope of a successful outcome is thought by just war theorists to be unjustified. Yet the prospects of success, like the question of last resort, are determinable only by reference to the facts and by consideration of expert opinion. A moral judgement that, driven solely by the purity of its vision and the strength of its conviction or sentiment, simply ignores the 'facts' is not worth very much, and may well do untold damage. On that both realism and just war theory are in fact agreed. The realist attack on *moralism* for its self-indulgent neglect of the facts and its failure to acknowledge the realities and the constraints of power finds support within the just war tradition. 'Political hypermoralism,' wrote Maritain, 'is not better than political amoralism and ... in the last analysis it answers the very purpose of political cynicism' (Maritain 1954, p. 56). Like realism, just war theory acknowledges the dangers attendant upon the attempt to subject war to morality. To keep war within moral bounds the moral impulse itself needs to be kept in check. Where realism is seen to err, however, is in regarding all moral analysis of war as moralistic. While resisting the moral scepticism of the realist, the just war theorist accepts that the ethics of war must be informed by a realist perspective. What the just war tradition upholds is precisely a form of *moral realism*.

Just as the interests of morality dictate an infusion of realism, so the interests of realism dictate an infusion of morality. The amoral conception of reality is a false conception of reality. Any account of international relations that seeks to exclude morality is an *unrealistic* account of international relations. This applies even to the extreme case of war, which is fully intelligible only as a human, and therefore a moral, activity, informed by values and purposes. Realists might be prepared to acknowledge the moral character of war in this very general or 'anthropological' sense (a significant enough admission, since its effect is to open up the moral debate about war); but what they are particularly keen to dispute is the role and efficacy of moral principles when they are applied to the unyielding world of international politics and war. As far as the realist is concerned, there is always something epiphenomenal about morality's presence here. According to just war theorists, this is seriously to underestimate the power and efficacy of morality.

There are perhaps two main reasons for this underestimation, the first of which lies in a too literal understanding of the way in which morality 'works'. The assumption here is that morality is effective only when moral agents are acting in perfect conformity with moral principle. The realist, observing, correctly, that such conformity is a rarity, particularly in the field of international relations and war, concludes, wrongly, that morality is without effect. As a result he is inclined to dispense with those moral principles that appear ineffectual and out of reach (the principle of noncombatant immunity is perhaps a good example), and to replace them with principles that are more in accord with the 'facts'. Over time this substitution would have the effect of transforming the moral culture within which all moral agents necessarily act. In the course of this transformation the category of acts that are considered to be morally impermissible would contract and the category of permissible acts would expand (the targeting of noncombatants, for example, would be transferred from the former to the latter category). In this way moral restraints would be relaxed. Acts that formerly met with public disapproval and were performed with a bad conscience would now be performed without public censure and without moral inhibition. The certainty is that the incidence of such acts would then greatly increase. In other words, the cultural or educative role of morality would have proved decisive: morality would have made, as it always has made, the difference.[2]

The impact of the moral community or culture on the decision-making processes of politics and war appears much greater than realists are inclined to acknowledge, and the more open and democratic the state in which political and military leaders operate (and the more susceptible they are to political pressure as a consequence) the greater its potential influence. In the Gulf War the power of domestic, as well as international, public opinion seemed real enough. The attempt to fight the war discriminately and to limit the amount of 'collateral damage' during the bombing of strategic targets in Iraq owed more to political and moral considerations than it did to strictly military ones. Public opinion at home and abroad would not have stood for a policy of 'area bombing' of the kind practised regularly in the Second World War. Likewise, the war itself was brought to an earlier conclusion than some strategists would have liked, or thought prudent, largely because of such political and moral influences. The moral revulsion widely felt at the events at Mutla Ridge made a continuation of the war politically infeasible. Similarly, the investment by the government of the United States in the development of 'non-lethal' and laser-guided weaponry, which might allow wars to be fought in a less destructive and more discriminating way (that is, in effect if not in intention, in a more morally acceptable way), owes much to the perception that in the future American citizens are unlikely to tolerate the 'total' wars of the past. Even if this intolerance is more 'material' than 'moral' in its motivation, the case still suggests that in the long as well as the short term military policy is susceptible to shifts in the public's perception of what is and what is not morally acceptable. The just war attempt to influence the moral climate of war, therefore, seems anything but futile.

The second reason for the realist's underestimation of the efficacy of morality lies in his confusion of morality with moralism. The realist makes the mistake of assuming that the demands that morality makes upon international relations and war are exaggerated or inflated demands that by their nature can never be satisfied. There is no reason, however, why a moral theory or system should be incapable of recognizing the distinctive requirements of international relations and war. The just war theory claims to do just that. In doing so it brings within the boundaries of moral acceptability forms of behaviour that the realist may have assumed to be beyond the reach of morality. In just war theory, for example, there is no blanket condemnation of the modern practice of 'strategic bombing'. In certain circumstances and subject to certain conditions, such bombing can be carried out without violating fundamental moral principles, like the principle of noncombatant immunity.[3] As Maritain argued, 'Many rules of political life, which the pessimists of Machiavellianism usurp to the benefit of immorality, are in reality ethically grounded' (Evans and Ward 1956, p. 349).[4] Once this is recognized the yawning gulf that was thought to separate the conduct of international relations and war from morality begins to narrow.

The relation between just war theory and realism, therefore, is a highly ambivalent one. Realism is both the friend and the enemy of the just war tradition. There are aspects of realism that are simply not reconcilable with the ethics of war, just as there are other aspects from which the ethics of war has much to learn. The task so far as just war theory is concerned is to discern one from the other and to find the right balance between rejection and acceptance. In the opinion of some critics that balance has been lost (if it ever existed), and just war theory has become so indebted to realism as to have become virtually indistinguishable from it; just war theorists have become more 'realist' than the realists. 'Their actual prescriptions,' writes one such critic, 'in fact, differ little from those of political realists, and apart from the underlying rationales they provide for them it would be difficult to tell them apart. If anything, the just war theorists may be more hardline than political realists' (Holmes 1989, p. 163). Though there *is* cause for concern, these criticisms seem greatly exaggerated and, being mainly of pacifist inspiration, they reflect more fundamental disagreements about the moral determinability of war. Though it is not without its dangers, the just war project of an ethics of war informed by *moral realism* seems worthwhile and well conceived.

The second image of war examined was Militarism. From a just war standpoint the militarist's assessment of war is much too generous. What militarism, at least in its purest form, does is to overturn that primacy of peace over war that is at the centre of just war thinking, war being seen no longer as the instrument of an imperfect peace but as a way of escaping or transcending a disordered world. Instead of viewing war simply as a means to an external end, as just war theory requires, the militarist is inclined to regard war as an end in itself, as something of intrinsic value, as an expressive rather than instrumental activity in which human beings achieve an authenticity and moral perfection denied them outside war.

Similarly, the unilateral and triumphalist manner in which the militarist is inclined to regard and therefore to conduct war (totally and ruthlessly, systematically suppressing the common humanity, basic moral equality and rights of an adversary) is at odds with the just war approach. While the militarist demonizes, or at least categorizes and dehumanizes, the enemy in such a way as to facilitate his destruction or annihilation, a just belligerent seeks to preserve the image of an adversary's humanity and to respect his rights, employing economy and discrimination in the use of force against him. The ethic of hardness that militarism propagates, which makes a virtue out of the ruthless prosecution of war and the eradication of natural sympathy, contradicts the ethic of compassion that just war theory seeks to promote. The militarist's war is a war without compromise, a war fought to the death, which has as its sole aim total and unilateral victory. The only peace militarism recognizes is the peace of the dead or of unconditional surrender. The peace to which a just war is directed, on the other hand, is one that upholds the rights of all combatants, of the vanquished as well as of the victors, and that is concluded in a generous and forgiving spirit with the ultimate reconciliation of adversaries in mind.

Just war theory rejects the moral enthusiasm for war that militarism commonly exhibits. In the first place, moral enthusiasm seems entirely out of place given the enormous cost of war in human suffering. What the prospect of such suffering should engender is not enthusiasm but extreme reluctance – at most grudging acceptance of a necessary evil. Secondly, moral enthusiasm arises only from a gross oversimplification of the moral reality of war that disregards the moral ambiguity and complexity of war and reduces it to a struggle between the forces of Darkness and Light. Thirdly, the greater the enthusiasm for war the easier the recourse to war and the more uninhibited its prosecution become. In short, moral enthusiasm undermines the attempt to impose moral limits upon war.

Militarism must be a matter of very considerable and pressing concern to the just war tradition, not only because of the threat that it poses to the moral limitation of war, but also because of the tradition's own proven vulnerability to militarism. That vulnerability arises from the very attempt to subject war to moral considerations. Though the realist's blanket condemnation of morality is unfounded, the realist rightly sees in the moral impulse itself a potential threat to the limitation of war. Paradoxically, the moral limitation of war is dependent upon keeping the moral impulse itself in check. There have been occasions when the just war tradition itself has yielded to the excess of moralism, with catastrophic moral consequences. In such instances the moral pragmatism and restraint that is at the heart of the approach has been engulfed by the sheer intensity of moral or religious conviction and sentiment. Such a process of moral derailment was evident in the case of the First Crusade, and it may be instructive to chart its course.

The Crusade was proclaimed by Pope Urban II at the Council of Clermont in 1095. The idea of war promulgated by the pope broke in several key respects with the traditional understanding of war. The earlier attitude of the Church to war had been marked by deep moral ambiguity, and the prevailing image of any war, just as well as unjust, was a negative one. Clerics, for example, were forbidden to fight any war, and laymen were obliged to do penance before readmission to full communion after fighting even a just or a defensive war. This grudging moral acceptance of war was wholly transformed by the crusading movement.

The aims of the Crusade as set out by the pope did not depart from traditional guidelines. The war that he urged on Christendom was a defensive and limited war, its main objectives being the defence of Christian communities in the East and the recovery of Christian territories. Though the belligerents in the war would be divided by religion, this was not conceived by the pope as a cause of war. A war of religion, a missionary war fought to eradicate infidelity and to vindicate Christianity, was not what he envisaged. The official aim of the war was not the annihilation or forcible conversion of the infidel, but the defence of the faithful. Yet, though the pope did not conceive of the crusade as a war of religion in the strictest and fullest sense, he clearly did think of it as a war with a religious character and, therefore, as a war with a difference.

In a society where war for private gain was rife, the crusade was portrayed by Urban as a spiritual and redemptive form of war. 'Now, let those,' he declared, 'who until recently acted as plunderers, be soldiers of Christ; now let those, who formerly contended against brothers and relations, rightly fight barbarians; now, let those who recently were hired for a few pieces of silver, win their eternal reward' (Peters 1971, p. 31). The crusade was presented as a morally superior form of warfare, fought not for material gain or worldly glory but for a divine purpose and with divine assistance. This was God's work, 'not a carnal but a spiritual war' (as a contemporary manuscript, the *Gesta Francorum* (Hill 1962, p. 37), describes it), a form of armed pilgrimage. The pope understood the crusade as a kind of lay apostolate or a lay alternative to monastic life, embracing some of the monastic virtues and subject to some of the same disciplines. The crusader was required to take a vow and to adopt the symbol of the Cross, and his participation was thought to bring important spiritual benefits, including the remission of past sins, if accompanied by interior conversion and the renunciation of sinful practices. Taking part in the crusade was seen as an act of love, the emphasis of which lay less on killing than on the sacrifice of self in the service of God and of others. To those who died in battle and in this spirit an aura of martyrdom was attached: the crusade was no mere earthly enterprise, but a path to salvation and eternal bliss.

This moral enhancement of war undermined its traditional and predominantly negative image. By establishing the sacred character of the war Urban gave to the war itself an intrinsic and expressive value, far outstripping the instrumental value attached to it by the limited and specific aims for which it was officially being fought. In doing so he gave potential recruits a huge incentive to engage in war – an incentive they had never previously possessed. The aims of the war may have been limited to the liberation of occupied territories and the defence of Christian communities; but its transcendent attributes undermined the caution and restraint implicit in its more limited and modest aims. The pope's sanctification of the war swept aside all moral reluctance to engage in war, assuaged all moral anxiety, resolved all moral doubts, released all moral inhibitions. 'But now O mighty soldiers, O men of war,' declared St Bernard (in the course of preaching the Second Crusade), 'you have *a cause for which you can fight without danger to your souls*; a cause in which to conquer is glorious and for which to die is gain' (added emphasis).

The religious and moral enthusiam for war generated by the proclamation of the crusade was quick to bear fruit. As the first crusaders passed through the Rhineland en route to the East, in the late spring of 1096, they turned with fury on the Jewish communities of the Rhineland towns. The Jews of Mainz, for example, took refuge in the bishop's palace as the crusading army neared the town. The fate that befell them there is described in a contemporary chronicle:

> Emico and the rest of his band held a council and, after sunrise, attacked the Jews in the hall with arrows and lances. Breaking the bolts and doors, they killed the Jews, about seven hundred in number, who in vain resisted the force and attack of so many thousands. They killed the women, also, and with their swords pierced tender children of whatever age and sex ... From this cruel slaughter of the Jews a few escaped; and a few because of fear, rather than because of love of the Christian faith, were baptized. (Peters 1971, p. 103)

The massacre at Mainz was no isolated occurrence. Similar atrocities were perpetrated at Neuss, Cologne, Trier, Metz, Worms, Speyer, Altenahr, Kerpen, Wevelinghofen, Kanten, and Regensburg.[5] Though the perpetrators were an unruly and ill-disciplined mob, acting without official sanction and at times in the teeth of official opposition, they were motivated by more than material gain or simple bloodlust, as their singling out of the Jews

and their readiness to spare those who accepted baptism demonstrate.

In line with its general teaching, which excluded infidelity as
a cause of war and forbade the practice of missionary warfare or
forcible conversion, the leadership of the Church did not conceive
the crusade as a war of religion; but that was how it was understood by many of the crusaders themselves. 'When Pope Urban
II summoned the chivalry of Christendom to the Crusade,' writes
Cohn,

> he released in the masses hopes and hatreds which were to
> express themselves in ways quite alien to the aims of the papal
> policy ... Although Pope and princes might intend a campaign
> with limited objectives, in reality the campaign tended constantly
> to become what the common people wanted it to be: a war to
> exterminate 'the sons of whores', 'the race of Cain', as King Tafur
> [the leader of the poor or vagabond corps] called the Moslems.
> (Cohn 1070, pp. 61 and 67)

In the popular mind the crusade was first and foremost a war
against the infidel, a war waged on account of infidelity and not
on account of any specific crimes or injuries inflicted by Muslims
against Christians. Accordingly, it was inconceivable that the
war should be waged against the infidel in the East while ignoring the presence within Christendom itself of that far greater infidel, the Jew.

The popular distortion of papal teaching extended also to the
spiritual benefits of the crusade and the manner of their achievement. The pope urged participants to embrace the penitential disciplines of a pilgrimage, and the spiritual benefits were
conditional upon an interior and spiritual conversion. For many
crusaders, however, the act of fighting itself was thought sufficient to merit the spiritual reward, with the result that they felt
free to conduct the war with greater ferocity and less compassion. While in the papal view the value of fighting had more to
do with the readiness to suffer rather than to inflict pain, to die
rather than to kill, in the popular version the emphasis was
reversed ('who kills a Jew has all his sins forgiven').[6] The result
was that, far from limiting and purifying war, the crusade sanctified war's worst excesses: 'Situations were created which con-

firmed to the fighting men that the values of their marauding lives were, indeed, approved in a Christian context. The satisfactions of their calling, the delight in berserk slaughter, the rape of loot, the gorging of appetites in times of plenty, heroic victory and death, were repeatedly recorded as marks of divine grace' (Blake 1970, p. 21).

Much popular thinking took an apocalyptic form: the crusades heralded the advent of the AntiChrist and of the climactic battle between the forces of Darkness and Light that would lead to the new Millennium and the reign of Christ and his Saints. The earthly city readily being confused with the heavenly, the location of these events was thought to be Jerusalem, so that what many anticipated as they fought their way to that city was a final and terrible conflict that would determine mankind's destiny. In this cosmic struggle the crusaders identified themselves as the soldiers of Christ contending with a satanic horde, and the coming of the Kingdom was made dependent upon the extermination of that demonic adversary in whatever form (Muslim or Jew) it assumed.[7]

The crusade exacted a heavy price, morally as well as physically. The First Holocaust, as the Rhineland pogroms have been called, and the infamous Jerusalem Massacre (to which reference was made in an earlier chapter) were representative of the general manner in which the war was fought. At least part of the reason for this seems clear. In its official conception the crusade stayed within reach at least of a just (and limited) war tradition broadly defined. It rested, however, on the extreme margins of that tradition, at the point at which it is always in danger of collapsing into militarism. Through the boundless moral energy and enthusiasm for war that it inevitably generated, the crusade bred a fanatical militancy for which the moderate and compassionate use of force became an anathema. The words of St Bernard are the key to the process whereby the moral limitation of war is undermined from within the just war tradition itself. The die was cast as soon as people became convinced that they had 'a cause for which you can fight without danger to your souls'. The record of the crusades strongly suggests that the holier war becomes in its conception the more likely it is to breach those moral defences with which, for the most part, the just war tradition has sought to confine it.

The third image of war examined was Pacifism. The debate between the pacifist tradition and the just war tradition has often been a heated one. The intense rivalry to which the relationship has frequently given rise is a measure of how much the two traditions have in common. This common heritage consists of shared concerns and aspirations, even of common principles and concepts; and it ensures not just an occasional or partial meeting of minds, but even complete convergence at certain points along the spectra of opinion in which the two traditions, in their internal variety, can be seen to consist: 'contingent' or 'moderate' pacifism is almost indistinguishable from 'radical' just war theory. This merging and blurring of the two traditions, though not without value and significance, is of less theoretical interest since it obscures the distinctive nature of the two approaches to the problem of war. What is at issue between the traditions only becomes evident if we compare them in their purer forms.

In its pure, or absolute, form pacifism rejects the fundamental premiss of all just war reasoning. The true pacifist sees war as an intrinsically immoral enterprise, wholly resistant to all attempts at its moral regulation. For such a pacifist war is a moral abomination that deserves nothing but outright condemnation and complete rejection, and the idea that war might be used for a moral purpose is obscene. The just war tradition, by contrast, does affirm the potential moral instrumentality of war, and rejects the idea that the physical evil that is war is always and everywhere a moral evil. The blanket condemnation of war is ruled out. The central distinction of just war theory between just and unjust wars evidently implies that war is not to be understood in that indiscriminate way.

The precise nature of the just war claim needs to be underlined if the true difference between the traditions is to be understood. According to the just war tradition war is morally justifiable, not just theoretically or in principle, but also in *fact*. The addition seems essential, since there are those of a pacifist persuasion who would accept the theoretical claim while disputing its practical relevance. Someone who accepts the hypothetical moral regulation of war, but who rejects the moral determinability of actual wars (in other words, someone who accepts that, *if* war were to be fought in accordance with just war principles, it would be justified, but who insists that no actual war has ever, or could ever, meet these moral requirements) is adopting a pacifist rather than a just war stance. The just war claim is made in respect of real war, and not of war in some purely hypothetical sense.

The pacifist (not unlike the realist in this regard) argues that, despite the best efforts of just war theorists and their supporters, war is bound to remain morally indeterminable. This does not mean that the pacifist, any more than the realist, is inclined to regard their activities with indifference; for, far from subjecting war to moral constraints, these futile attempts at moral regulation are seen to have entirely the opposite effect, strengthening war by the moral gloss that they put on it. The just war tradition's vain attempts at the moral criticism and regulation of war have led, in the opinion of pacifists, to the nurturing and expansion of war, and the history of that tradition, pathetic if it were not so tragic, is one long tale of accommodation to the state and to its bellicose activities.

This is a moral theory in the service of the state. Pacifists point, for example, to the just war criterion of *legitimate authority* and to the wholly conservative or pragmatic way in which it is invariably applied, one that has the effect of suppressing moral criticism before it has a chance to form. The issue of just recourse is left safely in the hands of the state or of the expert political and military class, while those who are not privy to the affairs of state are absolved from any responsibility. In this way, pacifists argue (not without justification in some cases, it must be said) the initiation and prosecution of even the most blatantly unjust war meets with little moral opposition. The contemporary pacifist, Gordon Zahn, for example, cites the case of Nazi Germany and the Catholic bishops who, despite being schooled in just war theory, felt able to give the regime the benefit of almost every doubt (advising heroic dissenters like Franz Jäggerstätter that service in the Wehrmacht was morally permissible).[8] Yet the real test of just war theory is not whether it can be used against an enemy state (as the Allies were eager to do), but whether it can be used against one's own state (and in this respect the Allies as well as the Germans displayed a marked reluctance).

Pacifists argue that this long process of accommodation to the state and to war must stop. There is no moral half-way house of the kind that the just war theorist seeks to inhabit. The real moral choice so far as war is concerned lies between acceptance and rejection. What Christian pacifists proclaim, for example, is the *prophetic* role of Christianity, a role that just war theory is seen either to ignore or to relegate to the domain of interpersonal relations. The just war theorist is not only *in* the world, he is in fact *of* it as well, one of its staunchest defenders and most effective advocates. In its authentic form Christianity should be at war with the 'world', contending with it and seeking to transform it. The 'utopianism' of pacifism, which critics identify as its central weakness, should be regarded as its greatest strength. The inherent realism and conservatism of the just war tradition is profoundly unchristian.

Viewed from a just war standpoint the fear of accommodation is in part well founded and in part the product of pacifism's false premiss. Within the just war tradition itself the threat of an excessive realism – a realism that sacrifices morality to the dictates of war – is recognized, and generates an intense and ongoing debate. In the view of *internal* critics there are some forms of just war theorizing that *are* too accommodating and too permissive. This is seen to be so with those moral approaches to war of a purely utilitarian or consequentialist kind, according to which the morality of an act or category of acts is to be determined solely with reference to its consequences. Nagel voices a common suspicion when he suggests that, 'any means can in principle be justified if it leads to a sufficently worthy end' (Cohen 1974, p. 7). The adoption of a purely utilitarian or consequentialist morality of war is seen to lead to the erosion of basic moral norms (like the principle of noncombatant immunity) and to the emergence of a position that is virtually indistinguishable from realism. 'All too often', Cohen writes, 'these special moralities sanction unlimited violence as a political means ... There is little to choose between the view that international conduct is exempt from moral assessment and the view that it is governed by a morality which sanctions and even encourages the most objectionable practices of international life' (Beitz *et al.* 1985, p. 5). The application of a morality of conse-

quences to international relations and war is always in danger
of collapsing into realism, with moral considerations, at least in
more extreme circumstances, invariably yielding to so-called
military or political necessity. Therefore the just war tradition,
in some if not in all of its variants, resists the drift towards moral
consequentialism. Keeping consequential reasoning in check is
seen as a condition of the moral limitation of war. This is not to
say, however, that the examination and assessment of the consequences of a proposed course of action play no part in the
moral analysis of war. Given the prominence of the criterion of
proportionality in just war thinking consequential considerations are clearly central to the process. What must be opposed
is their monopoly of the argument.[9]

The just war tradition's recognition of its own vulnerability to
realism (as well as to militarism), and the acceptance that some
of its variants may be too submissive and accommodating to war,
are still very far from an acceptance of the general and much
more sweeping criticism levelled at the tradition by pacifists. In
a just war view that criticism rests on a false premiss. For the
true pacifist *any* attempt at the moral determination of war is
bound to be seen as an act of accommodation and a moral
betrayal, because war in all its manifestations is thought to be
beyond any moral pale. What pacifism lacks in just war eyes is
a morality of power that would enable it to recognize the legal
and moral instrumentality of war. Its studied neglect of any distinction between 'force' and 'violence', and its indiscriminate
application of the latter term to every use of coercive force, preclude such recognition.[10] While 'violence' has a negative moral
connotation, implying the absence of law and morality, the more
neutral 'force' may imply a legal and moral context of use. In the
just war tradition war, in its normative sense, is understood as a
case, albeit an extreme case, of law enforcement, and the rule of
law in both the international and the domestic spheres is seen to
rest ultimately on the readiness to exercise coercive power. War,
in this critical sense, is always an instrument of law, a rule-gov-
erned, institutional activity, and not a condition of utter lawless-
ness in which all legal and moral constraints cease to apply. The
moral dualism and Manichaean tendencies that pacifism appears
to exhibit impede such moral recognition of power, and produce

a deep hostility to institutions, particularly the more coercive institutions like war, that just war theorists regard as essential constituents of human society (at least in its present state). Similarly, pacifism's apparent preoccupation with utopian or eschatological conceptions of peace leads to the moral undervaluing and systematic neglect of those imperfect but still valuable arrangements and instruments that make up the *pax terrena*. In this way the alleged otherworldliness and destructive simplicity of pacifism's moral vision of the world is seen to do grave disservice to the cause of morality and peace.

Though pacifist and just war theorist disagree about the intrinsic moral nature of war, the argument between them is in part a dispute about consequences. The pacifist contention that just war attempts at the moral determination of war have the effect of endorsing and encouraging war is turned around by the just war theorist. The pacifist claim that there can be no moral determination of war simply confirms what the amoral realist has argued all along, and the outright moral rejection of war would lead not to its abolition but to its uninhibited pursuit. In the view of the just war theorist pacifism, like realism, underestimates the moral influence that can be, and often is, brought to bear upon war (not directly perhaps but indirectly, through the nurturing of a more moral climate or culture of war). If that moral influence were to be withdrawn, war would become even more hellish than it already is.

From a just war view pacifist neglect of the structures of power and authority on which domestic and international politics are based threatens a fragile peace, the securing of which is often dependent on the use or the threat of use of armed force. A policy of appeasement, which pacifism would appear to encourage, is no guarantee of peace (certainly not of a just peace) and often seems to have done more to promote war than to prevent it; while the alternative defence strategies of non-violent resistance appear largely unconvincing (cases of apparent success owing more to the self-imposed restraint of the adversary than the efficacy of the method).[11]

Doubts arise not just about the utility or efficacy of the pacifist strategy, but also about its moral consistency. The moral claim of the strategy rests on the assumption that non-violent resistance is non-coercive, that here is a morally superior form of action that is not part of a culture or cycle of violence. That assumption seems unfounded. As one critic argues:

> Even though your action is non-violent, its first consequence must be to place you and your opponents in a state of war. For your opponents now have only the same sort of choice that an army has: that of allowing you to continue occupying the heights you have moved on to, or of applying force – dynamic, active, violent force – to throw you back off them. Your opponents cannot now uphold the laws which they value without the use of such violence. And to fail to uphold them is to capitulate to you ... In terms of its practical impact, therefore, your tactic is basically a military one rather than a morally persuasive one – or even a political one. (Prosch 1965, pp. 104–5)

Not only does non-violent resistance invite a violent response from an opponent; it also produces – in some cases even deliberately engineers – circumstances in which those of a more militant and less sensitive disposition can realize their violent ambitions.[12] In such circumstances it seems either naive or hypocritical to parade one's pacific and non-violent credentials while ignoring the key role that has been played in the unleashing of the cycle of violence.

The differences between the two traditions, therefore, run deeply; and yet they have much in common. Both affirm the moral primacy of peace over war. For the just war theorist, war is justified solely as an instrument of peace. St Augustine, writing when the tradition was in its infancy, expressed this primacy in a letter written to a friend and soldier who was anxious to know whether the military life was reconcilable with the Christian calling: 'Peace', he wrote, 'should be the object of your desire ... peace is not sought in order to the kindling of war, but war is waged in order that peace may be obtained. Therefore, even in waging war, cherish the spirit of the peacemaker' (quoted in Deane 1963, p. 159). For the pacifist, of course, this strategy is misplaced, and the pacific and moral instrumentality of war is denied. However, the *end* affirmed by both traditions is peace, and for both the conclusion of peace is seen to involve the transcendence of war.

Though no doubt pacifists would strongly resist the comparison, the pacifist theme of 'answering' finds more than just an echo in just war teaching about the need for a bilateral approach to war and for the restrained and sympathetic treatment of a potential or actual adversary that just recourse and just conduct both require. Fighting injustice should never preclude the recognition of an opponent's rights (and even interests), nor the admission of one's own moral complicity in war. What Thomas Merton attributed to the pacifist strategy of non-violence seems just as attributable to a war fought in accordance with just war principles: 'Non-violent action is a way of insisting on one's just rights without violating the rights of anyone else ... The whole strength of non-violence depends on this absolute respect for the rights even of an otherwise unjust oppressor' (Régamey 1966, p. 12).

The just war tradition is more catholic in its understanding of peace than the pacifist tradition, recognizing far more readily than pacifism the virtues of an inferior and imperfect settlement. It does not, however, confuse the mere absence of war with peace in its fullest sense, and the complacent acceptance of the permanence and inevitability of war is alien to it. Both traditions employ the idea of 'peace' in a creative and dynamic (even 'utopian' and 'eschatological') sense, and both give moral primacy to peace in that final and complete sense. The agenda of peacemaking is, therefore, for both traditions a very full one, involving a work of reconstruction and active reconciliation aimed at the elimination of the sources of conflict and division and the radical overcoming of war. Though the just war tradition upholds the moral status and worth of the existing and very imperfect order, it is the vision of a world without war that informs and guides just war thinking about war.

Notes

1 See Hegel *Philosophy of Right*, paragraphs 333–40. It is in the light of Hegel's conception of international relations as a technical state of war that we should read his matter-of-fact conclusion that, 'if no agreement can be reached between particular wills, conflicts between states can be settled only by *war*' (Hegel 1991, p. 36).
2 See Maritain's discussion of the impact of Machiavelli and 'Machiavellianism' in Evans and Ward 1956, pp. 319ff.
3 See Chapter 10.

4 Elsewhere Maritain wrote: 'Machiavelli, like many great pessimists, had a somewhat rough and elementary idea of moral science, plainly disregarding its realist, experimental, and existential
character, and lifting up to heaven, or rather up to the clouds, an
altogether naïve morality which obviously cannot be practised by
the sad yet really living and labouring inhabitants of this earth.
The man of ethics appears to him as a feeble-minded and disarmed
victim, occasionally noxious, of the beautiful rules of some Pla-
tonic and separate world of perfection ... Accordingly, *what he calls
vice and evil, and considers to be contrary to virtue and morality, may
sometimes be only the authentically moral behaviour of a just man
engaged in the complexities of human life and of true ethics*' (Evans
and Ward 1956, pp. 323–4; added emphasis). Cohen argues along
similar lines: 'some of the actions which simple moralists con-
demn as immoral and realists defend as, nevertheless, politically
necessary are in fact defensible on more complicated moral
grounds' (Beitz *et al.* 1985, p. 21). According to Cohen the realist
'view [like that of the naive moralist] fails to provide an adequate
account of moral conflict and lacks an adequate understanding of
moral tragedy' (p. 10).
5 Synan 1965, p. 74.
6 Quoted in Ruether 1975, p. 206.
7 See Cohn 1970.
8 Zahn 1962 and 1964.
9 See the criticism of moral consequentialism in Finnis, Boyle and
Grisez (1988).
10 In this context Arendt's warning about the indiscriminate use of
such key terms of poltical analysis as 'power', strength', 'force',
'authority', and 'violence' seems apposite. 'To use them as synonyms,' she wrote, 'not only indicates a certain deafness to linguis-
tic meanings, which would be serious enough, but it has also
resulted in a certain kind of blindness to the realities they correspond
to' (Arendt 1970, p. 43)
11 Arendt wrote: 'If Gandhi's enormously powerful and successful strategy of nonviolent resistance had met with a different enemy –
Stalin's Russia, Hitler's Germany, even prewar Japan, instead of England – the outcome would not have been decolonization, but massacre and submission' (Arendt 1970, p. 53).
12 Perhaps the events in Northern Ireland since the late 1960s serve to
illustrate the point. As one source argues: 'An attempt by the IRA to
renew hostilities in Ulster between 1956 and 1962 failed from a lack
of Catholic support ... The IRA were more subtle in 1967, taking
advantage of social and sectarian injustices in Ulster to exploit civil-
rights demonstrations and a successfully orchestrated series of

marches. Indeed by 1969 the violence fomented had produced a breakdown in law and order, with rioting, fire-raising and the blowing up by the IRA of public installations' (Macksey and Woodhouse 1991, pp. 167–8).

Part II

Principles and concepts of the just war

5

Legitimate authority

The criterion of legitimate authority has become the most neglected of all the criteria that have been traditionally employed in the moral assessment of war. Nowhere is this more evident than in the popular assessment of contemporary terrorism. For many the central moral issue raised by terrorism is that of non-combatant immunity. The peculiar moral vulnerability of terrorism is seen to lie in its tendency to violate this principle of just conduct. As one study of terrorism argues: 'Perhaps the main obstacle to any agreement that terrorism may in some circumstances be morally justifiable lies in the claim that it involves the violation of the rights of innocent persons' (Wilkins 1992, p. 65). To regard terrorism in this way, however, is to make an enormous, and almost always unwarranted, moral concession, since the distinction between combatants and noncombatants (or 'guilty' and 'innocent') is one that applies only to a state of war.

Terrorists themselves are quick to acknowledge the importance of this issue.[1] In defence of their special category status the IRA prisoners in the Maze were prepared to commit collective suicide. What they were affirming was their right to war, so that their acts of killing could thereby be lifted out of the criminal category of common murder and into the lawful category of acts of war. Sadly, it is not just the terrorist who is inclined to regard things in this way. Even those who profess to uphold and maintain the rule of law can acknowledge, at least implicitly, the terrorist's possession of the right to war and therefore the uncriminal nature of his activity: as in the case of Mr Justice Flood, the Irish High Court judge, who was reported to have upheld an appeal against extradition to Britain of Joseph Magee, a man wanted for the murder of an army recruiting sergeant on the streets of Derby, partly on the grounds that 'the killing was political because the general public had not been threatened when the two gunmen walked up to Sgt Newman and shot him in the back of the head' (*The Times*, 26 February 1994).

Such a perception of terrorism is extremely common, and even among those who are engaged in the fight against terrorism and who have most to gain from its defeat the tendency to distinguish terrorist attacks on military personnel from those on civilians is often evident. Yet it is not at all clear why the deaths of civilians at the hands of the terrorist should fill us with any greater moral revulsion than the deaths of soldiers or policemen. In normal circumstances a reverse reaction is discernible, the murder of policemen provoking greater not less moral outrage than the deaths of ordinary civilians (hence, perhaps, the retention in the United Kingdom of capital punishment for the murder of policemen long after its abolition for the murder of ordinary members of the public). Only if we are prepared to concede that the terrorist has belligerent status and that the soldier or police officer has lost his or her immunity from attack by virtue of acting in a state of war is the uneven reaction to the deaths of soldiers and civilians justified.[2]

It seems, therefore, that, if any criterion of war merits greater application to terrorism than any other, it is not 'noncombatant immunity' (and not 'just cause'), but the logically prior principle of legitimate authority. Yet, astonishingly, Wilkins concludes: 'This question, if it matters at all where terrorism is concerned, lies more on the periphery. ... I find it difficult to see how the question of legitimacy could have the same moral significance for terrorism that it has for the standing of regular or irregular combatants in time of war' (Wilkins 1992, p. 72). In this instance as in others, it is perhaps the narrowly legalistic interpretation of legitimate authority that accounts for its downgrading.

The contemporary neglect of the principle is in stark contrast to earlier ways of thinking, according to which legitimate authority was a matter of fundamental concern. For St Augustine (1872) it was the key to the whole process of peacemaking. 'The natural order,' he wrote in *Contra Faustum*, 'which seeks the peace of mankind, ordains that the monarch should have the power of undertaking war if he thinks it advisable' (XXII. 75).[3]

In the interests of peace the just war tradition sought to limit the recourse to war and to curb the easy resort to violence. One way of doing this was by upholding the 'public' character of war and by outlawing 'private' warfare.

The widespread occurrence of private war was an urgent problem when the tradition was still in its infancy, in a medieval Europe where power was fragmented and where, under the influence of a Germanic and militaristic culture, combat was glorified and the resort to arms encouraged;[4] and it is hardly less of a problem today given the proliferation of self-constituted revolutionary movements and the common use of armed force or terror by non-state or sub-state agencies with an ideological proclivity to violence. The increasing predominance of internal over external or interstate warfare has led some to conclude that in the future war is likely to consist in 'a fight for civilisation – against ethnic bigots, regional warlords, ideological intransigents, common pillagers and organised international criminals' (Keegan 1993, p. 392). If such prognostications are at all well founded, far from losing its force, the criterion of legitimate authority seems likely to recover its original urgency. To insist on the public monopoly of the use of force remains a fundamental step in any process of pacification, and securing that monopoly is a precondition of civilized society.

Curtailing the very incidence of violence within the civil order was and continues to be a primary consideration; but it would be mistaken to account for the principle in merely utilitarian or pragmatic terms, that is, in terms that neglect the key issue of authority. It is the prevailing modern tendency to regard the principle in this way that has led to its weakening. For many, for example, legitimate authority has become entirely subordinated to the concept of state sovereignty. As a consequence it has become a most undemanding and largely formal principle, which invests any state whose government is in effective control of its territory with the right to war. War-making, or the *competence de guerre*, is seen simply as a formal requirement or accompaniment of state sovereignty.

The ease with which the state's right to war is recognized may account for the diminishing influence of the concept of legitimate authority and its neglect in cases of resort to violence by non-state or sub-state agencies. If the state's right to war is subject to such minimal moral scrutiny, why should the claims to belligerency of less official bodies be treated with greater moral scepticism? The tendency to stress the formal rather than the substantial requirements of the principle reduces its demands and leads to greater permissiveness.

Lackey, for example, begins his discussion of the principle by adopting the more neutral and less evaluative term 'competent authority'. He argues that, despite certain 'archaic' aspects, the principle 'is still helpful for purposes of moral judgement to distinguish wars from spontaneous uprisings, and soldiers and officers from pirates and brigands' (Lackey 1989, p. 29). What *moral* purpose the distinction serves is not at all clear, however, given the neutral and formal terms in which war is subsequently defined: 'war is a controlled use of force, undertaken by persons organized in a functioning chain of command, ... directed to an identifiable political result' (p. 30). The ability of an organization to meet these formal requirements appears sufficient to warrant the recognition of belligerent status. Thus, in Vietnam, 'the NLF assassination campaign was controlled use of force directed to political ends, not a riot and not sporadic violence. It was dirty, but it was war' (p. 31). Once more the key issue, that of authority, is simply set aside.

In its earlier and traditional form the criterion of legitimate authority was a much more morally demanding principle. Aquinas, for example, insisted that 'the ruler under whom the war is to be fought must have authority to do so' and that 'a private person does not have the right to make war' (Sigmund 1988, p. 64).[5] In the just war tradition war is seen not as a lawless or extralegal activity, but as a legal instrument, part of that coercive power (*vis coactiva*) that is an indispensable part of law itself. Within the state this law-enforcing power is vested in a government on behalf of the political community over which it rules ('the power of compulsion belongs to the whole people or to the public personage whose duty it is to inflict punishment': Sigmund 1988, p. 45), and the same applies, analogically, to international relations.

Legitimate authority is not to be taken for granted. The state's *right* to war derives not from its *de facto* or 'coercive' sovereignty

– that would be to accept the realist contention that international relations constitute a state of war – but from its membership of an international community to the common good of which the state is ordered and to the law of which it is subject. This is seen to be so even though the anarchical nature of international society ensures that the task of enforcing international law and of upholding international order falls largely to the states themselves.

In the strict sense, the 'private' use of force, whether by individuals or by states, is never permissible. Though the individual's right of self-defence may be conceded (as it is by Aquinas for example), this need not amount to a recognition of a right of private 'war', or to an acknowledgement that the individual is justified in resorting to violence, that is, to the use of force *outside* the law. When the individual exercises his right of self-defence, he may be seen as acting not simply as an individual in defence of individual interests but as a representative of the community and an upholder of the law. Strictly speaking, the individual acts not in a private but in a public capacity, albeit an unofficial one, as the idea of a citizen's arrest exemplifies.

Similarly with the state: to be authoritative its act of war must retain a public and legal character, from an external as well as from an internal point of view. When states employ force in defence of their particular interests they are justified in so doing only to the extent that, at the same time, their actions can be convincingly construed as a defence of the international order and a securing of the international common good. The defence of a 'private' interest is, or ought to be, a 'public' act. In the anarchical society that is the international order the position of the state that has recourse to war is analogous to that of the private citizen exercising the right of self-defence or making a citizen's arrest in the temporary (or, in the case of international relations, permanent) absence of a public law-enforcing agent. Whereas within the state and in respect of internal relations power and authority are located normally in the same body, in the international order authority has its source in the international community, though power (the *vis coactiva*) is exercised by the state or states.

The public or representative nature of external or interstate warfare is most obvious in wars of humanitarian intervention, when intervening states act, or claim to act, on behalf of the international community, or when the intervening force is itself an internationally constituted and mandated one. However, even when an individual state acts ostensibly on its own behalf, if it acts in defence of its legitimate interests or in vindication of its rights, it acts at the same time as the agent and representative of the international community. In order to be authoritative the defence of its 'particular' right must constitute at the same time an upholding of the rule of international law and of the shared values in which the common good of the international community consists. Without such simultaneous justification the state has no right to war, though of course its power may enable it to wage 'war' regardless.

The matter, however, is very different in respect of 'internal wars', where the tyrannical nature of a regime or the divided state of the polity may make nonsense of any governmental claim to be acting with authority or on behalf of the political community. In such cases the government itself may be at war with its own people, or at least with a substantial section of the people subjected to its rule (as in the case of the Kurds and Marsh Arabs in Iraq), so that its exercise of force is wholly without public sanction or authority. Must such persecuted communities be denied the right of collective self-defence simply because, through some historical accident, they lack the formal character of states?

The criterion of legitimate authority can be so conservatively interpreted as to rule out all non-state or unofficial resort to physical force (other than by individuals in self-defence). Such an approach serves to justify all *de facto* government and leads to political quietism. It is this conservative and uncritical rendering that has sometimes brought the principle into disrepute. Thomas Merton, for example, praises those resisters to Nazism, like Franz Jägerstätter and Simone Weil, who 'refused to accept this evil and to palliate it under the guise of "legitimate authority"' (Merton 1976, p. 91). An unwavering presumption in favour of the powers that be can transform the principle into an ideological support for the very worst forms of tyranny. So interpreted, the principle has the effect of nipping in the bud the kind of moral analysis of power that just war theory is intended to promote.

A much more radical understanding of the principle is possible, and it is one that seems to be required by the just war tradition, given that the *vis coactiva* and the right of war is vested in the state as a political community and that powers are entrusted to rulers or governments as agents of that community. If that is so, the private appropriation of power by the government of a state undermines its legitimacy and establishes, at least in principle, the right of resistance.

Such misappropriation of power may take place in a variety of ways: the problem, for example, may lie in the manner in which power was acquired in the first place, that is, through usurpation, as in the case of a foreign occupation or of the internal seizure of power by a military junta. In other cases the problem of legitimacy is seen to be rooted not in the origins of power but in its abuse, as when power is exercised outside its legitimate sphere of operation or without due process, or when, while remaining formally correct in its use, it is employed in ways that are contrary to or gravely prejudicial to the common good.

Though a regime may fail *every* test of legitimacy, perhaps the most problematic cases, morally speaking, are those in which it passes one test of legitimacy but fails another, as in the frequently encountered case of a state that has its origins in conquest (which state does not?), but in which the rule of law and constitutional government have become firmly entrenched. Two broad approaches to such cases seem discernible: one 'ideological', which focuses attention exclusively on the delegitimizing aspects of governmental power; the other 'pragmatic', which focuses on the manner and effects of its present use. For the former neither the passage of time nor its preponderantly benevolent influence can do anything to diminish the foundational illegitimacy of the state in question or to erode the right of resistance.

The right of resistance has always been conceded by the just war tradition, though whether that right should be exercised has been seen as a matter of prudential judgement involving other important considerations, such as proportionality and the prospects of success. The tendency has been to subject to close scrutiny the anticipated costs of revolutionary activity itself, as well as its likely outcome and benefits. Aquinas, for example, applied a form of proportionate reasoning to his assessment of resistance: the overthrow of a tyrannical government cannot be justified, he argued, if 'it produces such disorder that the society under the tyrant suffers greater harm from the resulting disturbance than from the tyrant's rule' (Sigmund 1988, p. 65). Similarly, he suggests that it may be better to tolerate 'a mild tyranny' than to risk many worse dangers. A rebellion that fails is likely to make an existing tyranny more extreme, while one that succeeds cannot guarantee the end or even the moderation of tyranny. The deep divisions and hostilities that the act of rebellion seems likely to create within the community may take a very long time to heal, while the new ruler, mindful of the fate that befell his predecessor, may impose 'a worse slavery upon the subjects', relinquishing 'none of the oppressive measures of his predecessor but with intensified malice [inventing] new ones' (p. 23).[6]

Aquinas's approach typifies that of the just war tradition: though the idea of a just revolution cannot be ruled out, at the same time it must not be too readily ruled in. The just war tradition's cautious and restrained acceptance of the right of resistance stands in marked contrast to that enthusiastic embrace of revolution that occurs within the modern revolutionary tradition. 'Resistance' and 'revolution' are in fact very different concepts, resting as they do on quite different values and assumptions. Recognition of the difference, and even of the divergence, of the two traditions is essential if the idea of a 'just war' is to be applied correctly to the case of revolution.

The traditional assessment of the moral claims of resistance was informed by a certain scepticism regarding the prospects of change and by an assumption that the differences between one regime and another, important though they might be, were still largely a matter of degree. Such thinking had a naturally inhibiting effect so far as the exercise of the right of resistance was concerned, as the traditional insistence on last resort and calculations of proportionality and success demonstrate. The progressive and utopian assumptions that have come to inform the modern revolutionary tradition, on the other hand, undermine such pragmatic criteria. The qualitative transformation of the human condition in which the revolutionary prize is so often seen to consist so far outstrips the present benefits derived from any pre-revolutionary regime, however mild or beneficent its form of rule, that the cause of revolution can hardly fail to pass the tests of proportionality and success. Similarly, the transformative and creative powers attributed to the act of revolution itself establish it as the preferred means of change rather than the means of last resort.

The just war approach not only permits but requires the moral analyst to take account of particular circumstances as well as matters of principle, to recognize the strengths as well as the weaknesses of a particular existing regime, to discriminate between degrees of injustice (as in Aquinas's reference to 'mild' and 'extreme' tyrannies, or in his recognition of unjust states that stop short of tyranny), and to recognize the limits of the possible (not only in general but in this particular case). It would be unjust as well as imprudent to deny a regime legitimacy and to seek to subvert its rule simply on the grounds that its form of government was, say, 'undemocratic' or 'alien', when a revolution in the name of 'democracy' or of 'national self-government' is likely to result either in general anarchy or in the installation of a regime much less inclined to respect the rule of law and the rights of the citizen, particularly the rights of minorities, than its predecessor. Assessing social needs and potentialities in the light of prevailing circumstances is a fundamental part of the kind of moral assessment favoured by the just war tradition. Such a discriminating approach, however, is alien to the modern revolutionary tradition, with its universal prescriptions and its overriding assumption that a government that fails to comply with abstract principles or with an approved ideological form stands condemned, regardless of circumstances.[7]

The idea of a just war *is* applicable to the internal or revolutionary war as well as to the external or interstate war; but it must be applied to both in its entirety, not selectively. Revolutionary war should be subjected to a moral scrutiny that is at least as stringent as that applied to conventional or interstate conflict. More often than not, however, double standards are used, and a greatly abbreviated and therefore much less demanding form of just war reasoning is applied to the war of revolution.[8]

The principle of noncombatant immunity, for example, often struggles to survive the movement from conventional to revolutionary or insurgent warfare, in theory and not just in practice. The tendency among theorists sympathetic to the revolutionary cause is to relax this important criterion of just conduct. In the first place the argument from military necessity often acquires a cogency in the minds of apologists of revolutionary war that it markedly lacks in respect of conventional or state-sponsored war (including counterinsurgency war). The military inferiority of the insurgents is allowed to dictate the relaxation of moral standards: in 'the war of the weak' moral principles must be sacrificed to military needs.[9] The common strategy of insurgents of targeting civilians as well as military personnel and of deliberately provoking attacks by counterinsurgent government forces on the civilian population, by fortifying the villages in which they live, for example, is condoned, while the excesses of the counterinsurgent force are roundly condemned. Often, however, it is much more than pragmatic perceptions of military necessity that lies behind the greater permissiveness. More radically, and much more damagingly as far as the ethics of war is concerned, a systematic undermining, or at least eroding, of the distinction between combatant and noncombatant can be seen to take place.

A good example of this occurs in the work of the moral theologian Charles Curran. Curran's application of just war categories to modern warfare in its conventional form is noticeably restrictive. This is particularly so with the principle of noncombatant immunity. According to Curran, the constant violation of this principle in modern conventional war establishes a *prima facie* moral case against that form of war. Curran can envisage circumstances in which exceptions to the norm are permitted, on grounds of proportionality; but in his view their occurrence in regular or conventional war is highly unlikely (see Curran 1977, p. 124f.). His assessment of revolutionary war, however, is decidedly more forgiving and accommodating. Here the violation of noncombatant immunity is thought to be more apparent than real. This is because in true revolutionary situations the category of combatants, that is, of those who can be justifiably targeted, is much more widely drawn than in conventional war.

What lies behind this line of reasoning is the idea, frequently encountered in the literature of revolution, of 'structural violence', that is, of a form of violence that does not find expression in physical acts, but is embedded in social and economic structures and in relationships of inequality and exploitation. Not only does this concept lower the moral threshold of revolution by reclassifying seemingly peaceful (if unjust) institutions and activities as instances of violence (thereby facilitating the recourse to violent opposition by justifying it as a form of *counter*-violence), but it has the additional and crucial effect, as far as the conduct of revolutionary war is concerned, of widening the category of 'combatant'. To be 'guilty' and therefore targetable it is no longer necessary to commit or to threaten to commit violent and aggressive acts. 'Those who are functionally involved in perpetrating the grave injustices that justify revolution are also truly combatants.' As a result, 'the revolutionary or guerilla is not morally restricted by the principle of discrimination to attacking directly only soldiers and military personnel' (Curran 1973, p. 89). Attacks on 'soft' targets, already desirable on grounds of military necessity, are thereby placed on a more secure moral footing. The 'soft' target loses his or her moral immunity from attack by acquiring the status of 'combatant'.

It is in fact difficult to see how the principle of noncombatant immunity can survive a revolutionary war in its inflated modern form, given the tendency of modern revolutionary movements to think in terms of the overthrow of a *system* of oppression. Such an approach encourages its adherents to fight in an indiscriminate way and to mount an all-out assault not just on military installations or institutions, but on political, legal, administrative, social, economic and cultural institutions as well, since all may be regarded as parts of a system that needs to be overthrown. Modern revolutionary war is countervalue warfare in its purest form, a war directed against an entire society with all its attendant institutions (that is, instruments of repression and control). The likelihood of its remaining limited, therefore, is always remote, and its tendency to become total wellnigh irresistible. It is, of course, precisely that perceived characteristic of 'total war' that accounts for the strongest moral opposition to modern conventional warfare; but its presence in a revolutionary context is often viewed more leniently by the same critics.

Those who recoil in horror and disgust from conventional war may embrace the war of revolution with enthusiasm. Perhaps it is the alluring prospect of a revolutionary war to end all wars, or of a new order free of all previous imperfections, that serves to undermine all previous moral inhibitions. As a result the revolutionary war often takes on the character of a moral crusade or holy war, subject to less moral restriction by virtue of its historic grandeur and transcendent purpose. The higher the expectations, the fewer the moral demands that are made. At the end of the day, perhaps it is the perceived nobility of the cause that the revolutionaries profess that may blind them (and us) to their moral excesses.

The inclination – paradoxically, a *moral* inclination – to apply fewer or lower moral standards to the war of revolution than to conventional war needs to be resisted, and nowhere is resistance needed more than over the question of legitimate authority. Since legitimacy is precisely what is being contested in the war of revolution, the just war criterion of legitimate authority applies in a special way and with a particular urgency to this form of warfare.[10] Revolutionary war is very different in this respect from conventional interstate warfare, as Engels, one of the most famous and influential modern advocates of revolution, argued:

> Let us have no illusions about it: a real victory of insurrection over the military in street fighting, a victory as between two armies, is one of the rarest exceptions. And the insurgents counted on it just as rarely. For them it was solely a question of making the troops yield to moral influences which, in a fight between the armies of two warring countries, do not come into play at all or do so to a much smaller extent. (Marx and Engels 1975–90, Vol. 27, p. 517)[11]

The problem of applying the criterion to the case of internal or revolutionary war is an acute one, though the underlying principle seems clear enough: since it is the *private* use of force by the ruler or regime against the community that justifies resistance in the first place, the right of resistance is enjoyed only by the community or by its agents or representatives. As Aquinas observed, it would be very dangerous, for the community as well as for its rulers, if the overthrow of a tyrannical regime was left to the private judgement of individuals. To do so would be to invite social disorder and to render all states vulnerable to subversion irrespective of their merits. Therefore Aquinas concluded that 'the solution ... lies not in the private decision of the few but in proceeding through public authority' (Sigmund 1988, p. 24). The problem is that such public procedure is likely to be ruled out in the extreme circumstances which arguably alone justify revolution, and that in its absence there seems to be no certain way of knowing that it is the community that is exercising its right, or that the insurgents' claim to be acting in a public or representative capacity is in fact well founded.

Where public procedures do exist, as in liberal democracies, the question of legitimate authority *appears* to be greatly simplified. In such cases, it seems, not only do the means exist for gauging public support for the cause in question but, if that support is forthcoming, the cause itself can be advanced in a peaceful and non-violent way. The matter, however, is not nearly as straightforward as it may seem, and the power of even a liberal or constitutional democracy to resolve all problems of legitimacy is often greatly exaggerated.

For one thing the community, in which authority is ultimately seen to rest, may not be readily identifiable with the state. Even a liberal democratic state, for example, is capable of serious discrimination against a minority ethnic community, not by the withholding of civil and political rights, but by the permanent exclusion of that minority from power (and the consequent neglect of its interests) via the normal operation of the democratic process. In those circumstances, where a minority community finds itself habitually outvoted because the electorate and the party system divide along, say, ethnic lines, any opportunity to realize its legitimate and perhaps widely-held aspirations may be permanently denied it. Moreover, the problem of legitimacy may well be magnified by the fact that the state in question has its origins in conquest. In such a case it is by no means clear that the presence of liberal democratic mechanisms, and of what may amount to no more than a theoretical possibility of constitutional change, undermines any case for revolution. Crucially, however, what those mechanisms can do is to demonstrate the strength of public disaffection with the democratic process and of public sympathy for extraconstitutional action among the minority community itself. This can be of great help in assessing the claim of a revolutionary movement to legitimate authority or public authorization.[12]

Revolutionaries themselves are often loath to accept the verdict of any democracy. The fact is, of course, that much modern 'revolutionary' activity occurs in societies where public procedure *is* available. The very openness of liberal democratic states makes them more vulnerable to certain forms of subversion than other more repressive states. It is in the liberal-democratic state, for example, that terrorism flourishes. Not only would terrorists encounter swift retribution in less liberal societies; but, deprived of the publicity on which it relies for its effect, terrorism would be unlikely to occur in the first place. In a closed society, in which terror is the established form of rule, the revolutionary's act of terror has no propaganda value whatsoever, and is entirely without effect.

Even where support for a revolutionary cause is not forthcoming and where all the democratic evidence points to its widespread unpopularity, activists can continue to feel justified not only in engaging in revolutionary activity but in claiming a form of public authorization for doing so. Some form of the Jacobin or Leninist argument is frequently invoked to justify the violent acts of a revolutionary minority in the face of mass apathy and even in the teeth of mass opposition. A 'vanguard' or revolutionary élite, typically composed of or led by the intelligentsia (that is, by a group who, in a social sense at least, are often far from representative),[13] acts in the name of and on behalf of the preferred community, which itself lacks a revolutionary consciousness and will, and which therefore is presently without the power of initiative.

For a revolutionary Marxist, for example, the unpopularity or social isolation of the revolutionary élite is no bar to action. The lack of support can be attributed to a state of 'false consciousness' induced by an oppressive social system and by the cultural hegemony of the bourgeoisie, which moulds the popular consciousness in a conservative and non-revolutionary way. The possible enjoyment by all its citizens (including the proletariat) of full civil and political rights is not deemed sufficient to legitimize the liberal-democratic state or to compensate for what is seen as that capitalist state's systematic denial of more basic and important socio-economic rights or freedoms. In such circumstances an enlightened and disciplined minority is thought to be entirely justified in seizing the initiative by embarking on a course of revolutionary action without popular support. In doing so it will act as the catalyst of social revolution, disturbing the prevailing social equilibrium and enabling the proletariat to realize its own revolutionary capacity. Where the vanguard leads the proletariat, the real and ultimate makers of history, will soon follow.

The same kind of reasoning is employed by revolutionaries of every ideological persuasion to deal with the problem of authorization. For example, the revolutionary nationalist Patrick Pearse, who led the 1916 Easter Rising in Dublin, thought in similar 'vanguard' terms. It was Pearse's conception of the Irish nation and of its historic destiny that authorized the revolutionary act, an act that by its glorious example would resurrect the Irish nation and enable it to assume its historic role and to fulfil its historic destiny. An evident lack of popular support and enthusiasm for the cause of revolution (public opinion in Ireland at that time favoured constitutional methods of change) did little to diminish the zeal of Pearse and his fellow revolutionaries or to inhibit their activities. It was the strength of their conviction that what they were doing was both in the best interests of the Irish people and in accord with an historic imperative, that gave them the confidence to act even in defiance of public opinion. They accepted that the rising might well fail militarily and in the short term; but by creating the revolutionary myth and thereby awakening a dormant nation they believed that its ultimate success would be assured.

A similar approach is evident in the contemporary movement of liberation theology, in particular in the use made by Paulo Freire and others of the concept of 'conscientization'. As with the Marxist-Leninist notion of false consciousness or the Gramscian notion of hegemony, the concept assumes a state of collective or mass delusion induced by oppressive social structures (cultural as well as socio-economic), whereby the oppressed have learned to assimilate the beliefs and values of their oppressors. A people so deceived, being unaware of their own enslavement, are incapable of self-liberation. Their prime need is one of enlightenment or education, through which they might become aware of the shortfall between their present state of radical deprivation and their and

society's real potential. In that sense education – 'conscientization' – is the first and essential step on the path to their liberation.

The importance of public education in any process of social
emancipation or reform seems undeniable: a people habituated
to a life of social and economic deprivation are all too likely to
regard their condition as natural and unavoidable. The central
moral issue is the nature of that public education. For some the
most effective, if not the only effective, form is the act of revolutionary violence itself: the so-called 'propaganda of the deed'
advocated explicitly by anarchists and practised by most other
revolutionaries. Through the revolutionary activity of a dedicated and disciplined élite and above all through the counterviolence that that activity provokes the established order will lose
its legitimacy in the minds of the people, who will then be disposed to assume a more active and self-liberating role. The Brazil-
ian revolutionary Carlos Marighela reveals the thinking behind
this revolutionary strategy and behind this particular form of
practical education: 'It is necessary to turn political crisis into
armed conflict by performing violent actions that will force those
in power to transform the political situation in the country into
a military situation. That will alienate the masses who from then
on will revolt against the army and police and blame them for
this state of things' (quoted in Hook 1976, p. 148).

This school of violence is of doubtful moral value. Its essential
moral ambiguity lies in the idea of *creating* the conditions of revolution.[14] If the conditions that justify revolution need to be created, how can revolution be justified? From a just war
standpoint, a strategy like Marighela's puts the cart before the
horse: violence is used to instigate violence rather than in
defence against it (and, moreover, to instigate it against the very
people on whose behalf the revolutionaries claim to be acting).
The revolution is justified as a response to a situation that the
revolutionaries themselves have deliberately engineered and for
which they must bear large responsibility. The argument seems
damagingly and irredeemably circular.

No doubt Marighela and others would respond by arguing that
it is not a question of creating, but of uncovering the conditions
or causes of revolution. The revolutionary simply forces to the
surface the violence that is so firmly entrenched in the estab-

lished system as to be hidden from view, including the view of the oppressed. However, even where covert and systematic violence *is* present, the violence inflicted by the revolutionary remains complicitous and therefore morally flawed. This is not education, but a ruthless kind of manipulation: being externally imposed and relying on terror for its efficacy it is not designed to promote autonomy or to enable the educand – in this instance the 'people' – to realize its own inner potential.

The need for practical education – a real and urgent need in some circumstances – can be satisfied without resort to violent methods. Social experience of autonomous activity is above all what is required to counteract habits of dependency and social passivity formed over many generations (hence the emphasis in liberation theology on 'base communities' and the creation of a self-liberating culture). Such peaceful forms of social education *may* be genuinely liberating and therefore cause few, if any, moral problems. Sometimes, however, 'conscientization' seems to have as its aim the instilling of a specific, usually Marxist, revolutionary consciousness in the people, the creation of the 'subjective' conditions of revolution to match those 'objective' conditions that it is claimed are already in existence. This seems to be a very dubious moral enterprise, given that the 'objective' conditions of revolution, as well as the means of their overcoming, are themselves the subject of honest debate and very considerable disagreement. In the process of 'conscientization' the revolutionary agenda tends to be taken for granted. In other words this is often less an attempt to get the people to think critically and for themselves (thereby enabling them to define their own needs and ends) as to ensure that they think and act in the approved revolutionary manner. The élitist and authoritarian (or 'closed') form that even this peaceful form of practical education takes makes it morally suspect. There seems to be a very fine line to be drawn between 'conscientization' on the one side and 'political indoctrination' and 'subversion' on the other.[15]

The dangers of a too permissive moral assessment of revolution seem real enough. It would be just as wrong, however, to interpret revolution too restrictively as it would be to view it too permissively. Just as in the moral assessment of conventional or regular war it is essential that moral theorizing should take account of the realities of war, so in the moral assessment of revolutionary war the internal dynamics of revolution need to be recognized. In its initial stages at least the revolution is always likely to be the work of a dedicated minority. Its minority status does not in itself mean that the revolutionary group is engaged in a form of private warfare, in other words, that it is making war on society itself. It may be that the tyranny or oppression perpetrated against a people is so extreme and so extensive that to insist, as a condition of just revolution, that the people should be the *instigators* of revolution is quite unrealistic. In such circumstances the application of the criterion of *legitimate authority* is extremely difficult.

What tends to happen is that the weight of the argument is thrown on to just cause: it is the presence or absence of just cause, that is, of the 'objective' conditions of revolution, that will determine whether the acts of a revolutionary vanguard are in fact 'authorized'. The danger of such an approach is that the criterion of legitimate authority loses all its regulative force by being reduced to a form of *self*-authorization. In this watered-down version the principle acts less as a restraint on war than as a catalyst of war. On this basis any group in society, however narrow its support or however strong the opposition to it, may consider itself justified in resorting to armed force in order to advance a 'revolutionary' or 'just' cause. There is little doubt that the modern revolutionary tradition lends itself to this permissive interpretation, and that its consequences are often dire.[16] Faced with the very real threat of anarchy the norm that the principle of legitimate authority embodies needs to be very firmly upheld. As medieval thinkers realized, the key to all civilized living lies in the common acceptance of a self-denying ordinance regarding the use of force and a common recognition of its public monopoly.

Notes

1 Perhaps they grasp intuitively the view attributed to Vitoria that, 'the faculty to declare and wage war ... is the most fundamental (in that it implies all the others) of the necessary and sufficient conditions that go into the making of the republic' (Fernández-Santamaria 1977, p. 77).

2 Such a concession seems implicit in the language frequently used (by the media and by opponents and not just by sympathizers or practitioners) to describe the phenomenon of terrorism. Talk of 'active ser-

vice units', 'decommissioning of arms' and 'ceasefires', for example, lends credence to the terrorist's claim to belligerent status.

3 The identification of the ruler or government as the agent of the state or political community in the matter of just recourse relieves the individual soldier and citizen of much (though by no means of all) of the responsibility. This stems from a recognition within the just war tradition that the individual citizen is rarely in a position to make an informed and responsible judgement about the justice or injustice of the war. The knowledge and expertise required to make a rational judgement of such key criteria as last resort, proportionality and prospects of success are almost always confined to a closed élite even in a democracy. Not only would it be imprudent to allow the public at large to exercise judgement, in this area, but the publication of the sensitive material that informed decision-making would require might jeopardize the security of the state. As a result, whereas in the case of the government the moral presumption must be against war, in the case of the individual citizen the moral presumption may be for war. In either case, of course, that presumption can be (and ought to be) overcome in the face of overwhelming evidence to the contrary. Vitoria, for example, recognized different levels of responsibility depending on the individual's (or class of individuals) proximity to the seat of government. He argued that 'lesser subjects who are not invited to be heard in the councils of the prince nor in public council are not required to examine the causes of war, but may lawfully go to war trusting the judgement of their superiors'. Even so, 'there may be ... arguments and proofs of the injustice of war so powerful, that even citizens and subjects of the lower class may not use ignorance as an excuse for serving as soldiers' (Vitoria 1991, p. 308). For a contemporary statement of the position see Finnis et al. 1988, pp. 123–4.

4 Cf. Erdmann 1977 and Johnson 1981.

5 The means of securing that authority have become much more refined and complicated than in Aquinas's day. This is particularly so in the case of democratic states, where the attempt to bring the business of recourse to war under some kind of public and democratic control often gives rise to problems. In the United States, for example, the declaration of war is subject to certain constitutional constraints. In the case of the Vietnam War it was alleged that the then President, Lyndon Johnson, committed the United States to war by stealth and without the congressional approval that the constitution demanded (it was also claimed that Johnson engineered the Gulf of Tonkin incident that persuaded Congress to enlarge the war). As a result the war was seen by many as legally (and therefore in this case morally) flawed from the start. The war was seen to lack

the 'public' character proper to a just war (of course, in the opinion of its critics, this was only one of several of the war's moral deficiencies). Since the President had acted illegally or unconstitutionally his recourse to war was 'private' rather than 'public'; he had not acted in the manner required of the appointed agent of the state. Whatever the rights and wrongs of this particular case (and despite the attempts of Congress to reassert its control over war-making in the 1973 War Powers Act) the difficulties of reconciling the necessary secrecy that surrounds the recourse to war with the need for its public authorization remain. Moreover, the incremental way in which US involvement in the Vietnam War arose is not untypical. This makes any act of public authorization extremely difficult.

6 Aquinas recounts the following story: 'Thus at a time when everyone in Syracuse wished for the death of Dionysius, an old woman kept praying for his safety and continued survival. When the tyrant found out about this he asked her why she did it. She replied, "When I was a little girl we were ruled by an evil tyrant and I kept praying that he would die. When he was killed his successor was still more oppressive, and I kept wishing for his rule to end. Then we began to have a third ruler who was even worse – you. And so if you are taken from us a worse ruler will take your place"' (Sigmund 1988, p. 23).

7 Of the French revolutionaries Burke wrote famously: 'They have "the rights of men". Against these there can be no prescription; against these no agreement is binding: these admit no temperament, and no compromise: any thing withheld from their full demand is so much of fraud and injustice. Against these their rights of men let no government look for security in the length of its continuance, or in the justice and lenity of its administration. The objections of these speculatists, if its forms do not quadrate with their theories, are as valid against such an old and beneficent government as against the most violent tyranny, or the greenest usurpation. They are always at issue with governments, not on a question of abuse, but a question of competency, and a question of title' (Burke, 1969, pp. 148–9).

8 It is noticeable how some of the strongest opponents of conventional or interstate warfare – an opposition bordering on pacifism – can often be found among the most enthusiastic supporters of revolutionary warfare. Thomas Merton, for example, combines stringent criticism of the state's resort to war with sympathetic and even indulgent acceptance of the violence of the oppressed (cf. Merton 1976, pp. 25–33 and 85–93), as do the various authors cited in Weigel's Tranquillitas Ordinis, whose fierce denunciation of US military power and intervention in Vietnam and elsewhere contrasted starkly with their uncritical embrace of the cause of revolution in Central and South America (see Weigel 1987). Lewy pursues this

theme in Peace and Revolution (1988) and, with critics and supporters, in the collection of essays edited by Cromartie (1990) *Peace
Betrayed?*

9 The insurgency war is often described as 'the war of the weak'. This
is true not only in relation to military power. To begin with insurgents usually constitute a small and unrepresentative minority,
whose first priority is to engender popular support through a variety
of methods. Talbott suggests that at the start of the Battle of Algiers
the FLN's Autonomous Zone in the Casbah had a total membership
of about 5,000, most of whom were engaged in political and administrative activities like fundraising. The military branch consisted of
about 150 members. Most were gunmen who acted as the assassins
of prominent settlers, 'collaborators' and government agents. About
50 were 'bombers', including bomb-makers, transporters and
planters. According to Talbott the planters were mostly young
women from the university (Talbott 1981, p. 81).

10 This is one of the main reasons for the emphasis placed on revolutionary or internal war in this chapter. The very high incidence of
such warfare is another. As we have seen already, some experts
believe that this will be (if it has not already become) the dominant
form of warfare in the foreseeable future. If that is so, securing legitimate government and internal state security will become one of the
prime tasks of peacemaking. The prevailing cosmopolitan assumption that the state is the enemy of peace and the friend of war seems
highly questionable. In many parts of the world the greatest single
contribution to peace that could be made would be the establishment
of the legal order that is the modern state. Still, perhaps the common
prejudice against the state explains the frequent neglect of revolutionary war in the critical literature.

11 As Kissinger observes: 'A guerilla war differs from traditional military operations because its key prize is not control of territory but
control of the population' (Kissinger 1969, p. 104).

12 In assessing such claims it seems essential to recognize the widely
varying degrees of support for revolutionary groups among the communities that they claim to represent. At one end of a spectrum of
support can be found a group like the Red Army Faction in Germany
or the Red Brigades in Italy, a group that is politically and socially
isolated, that is quite unable to mobilize more than a dedicated
minority of 'bourgeois intellectuals', that finds most of its material
and moral support from abroad – and in any case from outside the
class or community that it claims to represent.

The IRA appears to fall into a different category, and the point of
difference requires us to estimate the issue of authority differently. In
discussing the movement's claim to authority attention is often

drawn to its minority status. Here attention is focused exclusively on the armed activists and on their political supporters, represented by Sinn Fein. What this ignores is the social, cultural and political environment in which the IRA operates and on which it draws for its support. At the centre of this vortex of support is the militant and active minority made up of the IRA and its political wing Sinn Fein. Ever-widening circles of association, varying in intensity of support as the movement from centre to periphery takes place, are discernible. Some give material support to the IRA through fundraising for arms, some lend political support by voting for Sinn Fein candidates in elections, some do neither but lend moral support to the IRA through their acceptance and lauding of the revolutionary tradition to which they belong. Without this large and complex web of support, both material and moral, the IRA would find it difficult to survive. This is a movement that, unlike the Red Brigades, *does* have roots in the community that it claims to represent. The nationalist community's denunciation of IRA terrorism stops well short of rejection of the 'physical force' tradition that the IRA claims, with justification, to represent. As long as this ambivalence continues any 'peace process' will struggle to get off the ground.

Compare both the Red Brigades and the IRA, however, with the series of popular revolutions that have swept Eastern Europe in recent years. These were revolutions on a mass scale, which depended for their very success on the adoption of a revolutionary standpoint and revolutionary activism throughout society, not least among the ranks of the military itself.

13 The leading role in modern revolutions is taken, more often than not, by intellectuals whose own social experience is very different from that of the community that they claim to represent. It is claimed, for example, that out of the eight leaders who made up the inner group (Angka Leu) that directed the activities of the Khmer Rouge in Cambodia 'five were teachers, one a university professor, one a civil servant and one an economist [and] all had studied in France' (P. Johnson 1988, p. 246). The Khmer Rouge is not untypical in this regard. It is striking how many of the upper echelons of revolutionary movements are drawn not only from the intelligentsia but from the ranks of the 'enemy'. Many of the leading figures or founding fathers of Irish nationalism, for example, came from the *Anglo*-Irish community, just as most leaders of the revolutionary Left have been recruited from the ranks of the bourgeoisie ('The directors of guerilla warfare,' Guevara wrote, 'are not men who have bent their backs day after day over the furrow': McLellan 1988, p. 375). So far as their leadership is concerned, at any rate, few movements appear to have their roots in the communities that they claim to rep-

resent. Perhaps this reflects the ideological origins of most modern revolutions.

14 In *Guerilla Warfare* Che Guevara wrote: 'One does not necessarily have to wait for a revolutionary situation: it can be created' (quoted in Thomas 1971, p. 1040).

15 See P. Berger, *Pyramids of Sacrifice* (1976). Freire's own insistence on the 'dialogic' nature of 'the pedagogy of the oppressed' remains very unconvincing, given his own clear assumption of a revolutionary, and more specifically Marxist, agenda (according to which, for example, 'real' education can take place only in revolutionary 'praxis'). Popular education cannot be genuinely 'critical' when these commonly contested premises are taken for granted and serve as the accepted framework of analysis (even being regarded as 'objective truths'). It is an odd concept of 'dialogical' education that leads to the identification of Mao as one of its main theorists and practitioners (Freire 1972, pp. 82–3).

16 For example, Davies writes: 'If a revolution is for a just cause, those in power are morally bound to give way; only when it is not for a just cause has the government the right to be defended. But if it is for a just cause, then the oppressors themselves are largely responsible for any violence that may ensue' (Davies 1976, p. 159). Note how, in the case of *revolutionary* war, the single criterion of *just cause* is allowed to monopolize the assessment not only of just recourse but also of just conduct.

6

Just cause

Traditionally 'just cause' was seen as the single most important moral criterion of war. In more recent times the tendency has been to downgrade this criterion (at least in respect of interstate warfare, though not in the case of revolutionary wars or of wars of humanitarian intervention, where just cause is often allowed to monopolize the moral debate). The relative neglect of the principle owes something perhaps to the spread of moral relativism and to the inordinate value attached to state sovereignty in the modern states system. Neither of these developments are reconcilable with a just war approach rooted in the natural law tradition, and neither can be regarded as a valid ground for dispensing with the principle of just cause. There are, however, more compelling reasons for circumspection, if not for scepticism, in considering this criterion. They stem from the well-founded suspicion that an undue and improper emphasis on just cause, far from inhibiting the warlike activities of states, has led to easier recourse to war and to its less restrained prosecution.[1]

A one-sided and exaggerated emphasis on just cause may generate a moral triumphalism and a moral enthusiasm for war that transform a 'just' war into a 'holy' or a crusading war, and that have more in common with the militarist tradition than they have with the just war tradition. The absolute conviction that their cause is just (and that the adversary against whom they fight is the consummation of evil) may encourage combatants to override the moral limits of war or to neglect other equally weighty moral considerations, such as the costs of war or the shedding of innocent blood. Although the idea of just cause enjoys a certain logical priority as far as the moral analysis of war is concerned (the question of just recourse cannot even arise without it), its strategic importance must not be allowed to devalue, let alone suppress, other important moral criteria. A just cause is a necessary but not a sufficient condition of just recourse: even when the cause is most certainly just it may not be serious or weighty enough to warrant such a drastic remedy as war; or there may be other means of redress short of war that have not been tried or exhausted; or the prospects of success may be so remote as to rule war out. Similarly, however just the recourse to war, combatants are not excused from the moral constraints that apply to the conduct of war. Even a war against the most unjust of adversaries must remain limited if it is to remain just.

For the sake of the moral limitation of war itself, therefore, the importance of just cause must not be exaggerated; and yet the criterion remains central to the moral analysis of war, so that its neglect seriously distorts moral reasoning about war. Its modern downgrading coincides with its bilateral interpretation (initiated perhaps by Grotius in response to the wars of religion that had ravaged Europe) according to which 'just cause' should be assumed to apply to both or all sides in a war, since in any war all belligerents will find it difficult to fight without laying claim to justice. For many critics it is the unavoidable fact of bilateral (or, in the case of more complex wars, multilateral) justice that makes 'just cause' the essential weak link in just war theory: in the face of conflicting claims to justice (and in the absence of a disinterested and impartial judge) how can war serve as an instrument of justice?

The moral scepticism to which such reflection naturally gives rise is not out of place in just war thinking itself. Scepticism about contending claims to justice can strengthen rather than weaken the moral regulation of war, provided it is kept in check. More often than not, however, it runs amok, and leads to the unwarranted dismissal of fundamental moral considerations. Even those sympathetic to just war reasoning are prone to this tendency. In the work of Paul Ramsey, for example, the recognition of bilateral justice leads to the deliberate neglect of questions of just recourse (*ius ad bellum*) and to the virtual reduction of just war theory to matters of just conduct (*ius in bello*). 'Since at least everyone seeks peace and desires justice,' Ramsey wrote, 'the *ends* for which war may be fought are not nearly so important in the theory of the just war as is the moral and political wisdom contained in its reflection upon the *conduct* or means of war' (Ramsey 1983, p. 152). As interpreted by Ramsey (and others) the just war theory seems in danger of being reduced to a morality of means.

It is essential, therefore, to establish what role, if any, the idea of 'bilateral' justice ought to play in just war thinking. As the case of Ramsey illustrates, the idea does threaten the integrity of just war theory; but does it have to have such damaging consequences? To begin with a distinction must be drawn between 'objective' and 'subjective' justice. The sixteenth-century just war theorist Vitoria alludes to the distinction in the following passage:

> Let us suppose a clear case of ignorance (whether of the facts or of the law) then it can happen that on one side there is true justice, i.e. the war is really just, while on the other side the war is only just because good faith is an excuse for sin and invincible ignorance is a complete excuse. (cited in Hamilton 1963, pp. 145–6)

'Objective' justice relates to the true or real moral state of things; 'subjective' justice to the moral perceptions or states of mind of the warring parties, both of whom can be (indeed are likely to be) convinced of the justice of their cause. In some cases at least it may be a confusion of bilateral justice in the 'subjective' sense with bilateral justice in the 'objective' sense that leads to the downgrading or neglect of the just cause principle.

'Subjective' bilateral justice seems almost universal, though its recognition by belligerents themselves does not come easily. In a television documentary commemorating the fiftieth anniversary of the D-Day landings one British veteran recalled his astonishment and genuine sense of shock when, on the belt of a dead German soldier, he found inscribed the words 'Gott mit uns'. It had never even occurred to him that the Germans might think of themselves as fighting on the side of Right.[2] Yet there seems little doubt that, whatever their retrospective judgement of the war, most German soldiers were convinced of the justice of their cause.[3] In 1940–41 the soldiers of 16 Army serving in France saw England as the unjust aggressor ('guilty of this great war') and Germany as the peacemaker and universal benefactor. The views expressed by one soldier in a letter from the front were widely shared: 'We are working on giving England the last blow and then there will be calm. Then the great peace will come for which all peoples are hoping. Fighting for that, no sacrifice is too great' (Bartov 1991, p. 151). The conviction that they were fighting for a just cause strengthened immeasurably with the outbreak of war in the East. Here again responsibility and blame for the war was laid upon the enemy, despite Germany's initiating role. 'We had been forced into the war against the Soviet Union,' wrote one soldier. 'For God have mercy on us, had we waited, or had these beasts come to us' (Bartov 1991, p. 155). The war was seen as a defence not only of Germany, but of the whole of the civilized world. 'Our duty has been to fight and free the world from the Communist disease', another soldier wrote in a letter to his mother. 'One day, many years from now, the world will thank the Germans and our beloved Führer for our victories here in Russia. Those of us who took part in this liberation battle can look back on those days with pride and infinite joy' (Bartov 1991, pp. 157–8).[4] The defence of Germany itself was just cause enough for war; but by portraying the struggle in universalist or world-historical terms even the standpoint of national interest could be transcended, thereby greatly heightening the sense of justice and the feeling of moral righteousness.

Fewer doubts are normally expressed about the presence of just cause in the war against Nazi Germany than in the case of any other modern war (witness the way in which the 'war against Hitler' has been used as a moral precedent for war on numerous subsequent occasions). The fact, therefore, that just cause in this case was (and it seems in some quarters remains) contested is an indication of how universal bilateral justice in the 'subjective' sense really is. So universal, that it seems that to insist, as a condition of just recourse, on its exclusion would render just recourse to war virtually impossible.[5] Its exclusion is not, however, necessary. As Vitoria argued, just recourse to war does not require that enemies should be acting in bad faith or that they should recognize their own unjust conduct for what it is. Their good faith does not nullify the injustice that, objectively understood, they have perpetrated, which, as such, constitutes just cause for war.

At the same time, though not in itself excluding war, the presence and the recognition of the good faith of the enemy should have an inhibiting effect on the conduct of war, promoting its greater moral regulation. Such recognition might be expected to lead to a more sober and even more sceptical assessment of one's own claim to justice, leading perhaps to its more modest or economical formulation. It should also discourage that tendency that more than any other perhaps lies behind the barbarization of war, namely, the tendency to demonize the enemy. However misguided and abhorrent their acts, objectively regarded, it is more difficult to see enemies who are acting in good faith as the incarnation of evil.

In its subjective sense bilateral justice may well be reconcilable with just war reasoning; but can the same be said of bilateral justice in its objective sense? Can there be just cause for war when justice is *truly* bilateral? Vitoria, it seems, thought that there could not. His admission of bilateral 'subjective' justice appears to rest on an assumption of *uni*lateral 'objective' justice ('on *one* side there is true justice'). In a just war both sides may be in good faith, but on one side only can that faith be well founded. If justice really is bilateral, so that both sides have, in an objective as well as subjective sense, an equal claim to justice, then there can be no just recourse to war for either party. 'If right and justice is certain on both sides,' wrote Vitoria, 'it is unlawful to fight either offensively or defensively' (Hamilton 1963, p. 145).

It would appear at first sight then that, objectively speaking, unilateral justice is the logical requirement of any coherent account of just cause and, by extension, just recourse, since without it the pursuit of justice in war would lead necessarily to the violation of rights: that is, to an act of injustice. There are, however, strong reasons for resisting this conclusion. In the first place, the assumption of unilateral justice conflicts with the realism that informs the just war tradition, its characteristic view of the inherent complexities and moral ambiguities of international relations and of the radical moral imperfections that afflict even the better states. From a just war perspective, in the imperfect world to which just war considerations apply, unilateral or absolute justice simply does not exist, just as unilateral or absolute injustice does not exist. If unilateral or absolute justice is a condition of just recourse, then there can never be a just recourse to war. Far from being an intrinsic requirement of just war thinking, the idea of unilateral justice appears fundamentally at odds with this approach.

The second reason for doubting its applicability to just war reasoning is consequential: the assumption of unilateral justice has the effect of undermining those moral limits that the tradition seeks to place on war. It is just such an assumption that lies behind the holy war in its religious and secular or ideological forms and that leads in extreme, but by no means rare, cases to a war of annihilation. Considerations of unilateral justice lead to the suppression of the rights of an adversary, the denial of moral equality, and the undermining of that juridical understanding of war that is at the centre of the just war approach. It is because belligerents are convinced that they are engaged in 'the war of Light against Darkness' that they become persuaded of the need to exterminate the Enemy. In short, it is the *unilateral* interpretation of just cause that leads to that criterion's destructive monopoly of the moral argument about war.[6]

The idea that most accords with the spirit of just war thinking is neither unilateral justice nor bilateral justice, at least in any straightforward sense. Instead, just cause is best understood in terms of a *balance* (or perhaps more accurately an imbalance) of justice and injustice. If bilateral justice means equality of justice, or a strict balance, there can be be no just recourse to war (and it is perhaps in this sense that Vitoria's proscription of war is to be understood). Bilateral justice, however, may take a form that *is* reconcilable with just recourse. Though never absolute or unilateral, there may be such a preponderance of justice on one side and of injustice on the other as to constitute just cause, and even sufficient perhaps to justify recourse to war.[7] That it is a question of the balance of justice is a recognition of the complexities and ambiguities of international relations and of the likelihood that neither justice nor injustice will be the monopoly of one side or the other.

An examination of the Gulf War of 1990–91 illustrates the complex nature of the just war criterion and the need to adopt a bilateral approach even in conflicts that appear morally unequivocal. For many the problems of just recourse in the Gulf War had more to do with proportionality and last resort than with just cause. Most critics argued that the costs of the war would be disproportionate or that the use of force was premature. About just cause itself fewer doubts were entertained.[8] President Bush himself thought that 'nothing of this moral importance [had occurred] since World War II' and frequently likened Saddam Hussein to Adolf Hitler. The Iraqi takeover of Kuwait was a clear infringement of the principle of non-aggression, a gross violation of Kuwaiti sovereignty and a serious threat to regional security and the international order as as a whole. Many agreed, even though some felt uneasy about the president's rhetoric. In the United Nations Iraqi aggression was widely and roundly condemned. It seemed that if there was ever an occasion when the unilateral conception of just cause applied this was it.

Things looked very different from the other side, however. The leaders of Iraq's Christian Churches, in Rome to meet Vatican officials when the coalition counter-offensive began, defended Iraq's actions in morally robust fashion. 'We think the cause of Iraq is a just cause', declared the Chaldean Patriarch Raphael Bidawid. He and the others argued that the 'invasion' of Kuwait was an act of self-defence by Iraq in response to the economic warfare waged by Kuwait, as well as a legitimate attempt to recover former Iraqi territory (*The Tablet*, 26 January 1991, p. 110). There seems no reason to doubt the good faith of these and other Iraqis. Nor were they, it seems, the simple victims of Saddam Hussein's propaganda machine. Their defence of Iraqi actions, however contrived it might appear, was not without some factual basis.

The popular view (one that the Hitler analogy encouraged) that the invasion of Kuwait was an expression of pure militarism, a manifestation of Saddam's megalomania and thirst for foreign adventures, borders on caricature and is certainly a very misleading oversimplification. It would be much closer to the truth to account for the invasion, partly at least, in rational–instrumental terms. Iraqi motivation appears to have been largely economic. The invasion was seen as a solution to the severe crisis into which the Iraqi economy had been plunged. The origins of the crisis owed much no doubt to internal (or self-inflicted) factors, such as governmental mismanagement and corruption and the depletion of resources brought about by the war with Iran; but external factors played a part too. The Iraqi economy was dominated by oil. In 1989, 61 per cent of its GDP and 99 per cent of its exports were oil-related (Feiler 1993, p. 260). This made the economy extremely vulnerable to fluctuations in the price of oil. According to the Iraqis the primary cause of Iraq's economic malaise was the lowering of the price of oil brought about by Kuwaiti and UAE overproduction. In addition the Iraqis accused Kuwait of the illegal extraction of oil from the Rumaila field in the border region of southern Iraq. These charges were linked with long-standing disputes about territorial boundaries and historic rights, which added greatly to the Iraqi sense of grievance. The existing borders were thought to be arbitrary and to lack legitimacy, having arisen through colonial imposition. Why should Iraq be denied access to resources to which it had at least as strong a claim as Kuwait simply because of the incompetence of colonial administrators or of the geopolitical manoeuvring of imperial powers?

Iraq's refusal to accept the simple or unilateral moral characterization of the conflict proposed by opponents arose too from a certain scepticism about the moral claims and intentions of the forces ranged against it. From an Iraqi perspective the coalition's occupation of the moral high ground was more than suspect. The 'opposition to aggression' and 'defence of human rights' seemed too selective to be convincing. Where was the coalition when the rights of the Palestinian and other Arab peoples were being violated with great regularity by the state of Israel, or when Lebanese sovereignty was being ignored by Syria? Why was Iraq's action against Kuwait opposed when its war with Iran received at least tacit support? If Iraq now posed a threat to peace, then its willingness and ability to do so stemmed in large measure from the political and diplomatic encouragement it had received in the past and from the eagerness of Western powers to provide it with the instruments of war. The record of the recent past (not just in the Middle East but elsewhere too) indicated that this was not the moral and humanitarian intervention it purported to be, but a selective intervention in defence of the economic and strategic interests of particular states: in other words, the old *realpolitik* arrayed in moral garb.

These claims and criticisms were of course contestable. The economic policies of Kuwait, damaging though they may well have been to Iraq, hardly constituted grounds for war; and if the arbitrary and somewhat questionable origins of territorial boundaries were sufficient to establish just cause, international relations would be thrown into a state of complete anarchy. Even the charge relating to the selective enforcement of international law and the failure to respond to earlier cases of apparent injustice needed to be viewed in the light of the opportunities for intervention that arose only with the end of the Cold War. Nevertheless the claims and criticisms were not without some substance. Though seemingly insufficient to establish the kind of moral parity that Vitoria saw as an insuperable obstacle to just recourse, they were important enough not to have been without some effect on the moral assessment and determination of the conflict.

Viewed bilaterally, therefore, the question of just cause appears in a different, more muted light. The recognition of the rights and interests even of an unjust aggressor, along with the acknowledgement of one's own moral fallibility and partial responsibility for war, rule out the moral triumphalism engendered by a more unilateral moral approach, as well as the ruthless prosecution of war that is its natural outcome. This essential moral blurring of the conflict underlines the need to limit severely the action taken as well as the need to define the aims of war conservatively and the terms of peace generously and sympathetically. Understood, in this way, the bilateral understanding of just cause appears not as a threat to just recourse but as an essential prerequisite.[9] The position of a just belligerent is more that of an impartial judge who seeks to do justice to both sides in a dispute than that of an accuser or plaintiff.

There in the opinion of many lies the rub so far as just cause and, by implication, just recourse as a whole is concerned: the absence of an impartial judge. 'The whole doctrine [of just war], as a pretending pattern of international justice', one critic wrote, 'was of course vitiated by a radical weakness, a stone missing from its very foundations; it neglected the fundamental premiss of effective justice, that no man can be a judge in his own cause' (Windlass in Régamey 1966, p. 17). It is true of course that the enforcement of justice in the international arena is largely the job of the states themselves; but it would be wrong to assume that this necessarily undermines justice. Of course the dangers of partiality or moral partisanship are very real; but it is not simply in the international realm that those dangers arise. In requiring the state to be a judge in its own cause just war theory is doing no more than apply the basic requirement of any system of morality. The failure of states to act impartially, like the failure of individuals, is no reason for dispensing with the relevant moral code. Of course, realistically, not everything depends on the moral conscientiousness of the decision-makers themselves. As has been argued elsewhere,[10] the decisions relating to war are not made in a moral vacuum. The decisions that are taken will inevitably be influenced by, if not always corresponding with, the prevailing moral culture, both national and international. States may well choose to violate prevailing moral norms for the sake of a national interest narrowly conceived; but given a wide enough and strong enough moral consensus they cannot continue to do so with moral or even political impunity. Sustaining and developing a moral culture of war that encourages its more limited use and conduct (and that perhaps leads to the ostracism of states that ignore moral constraints) is a prime objective of just war theory.

It is often assumed that the solution to the problem of the partial administration of justice is to hand war over to an agent of the international community like the United Nations. This is much less of a solution than it is often presumed to be, and is even not without certain added dangers. The assumption of impartiality is often just as unfounded in this case as it is in the case of the state; but the actions of the UN tend to be regarded with much less scepticism (by insiders if not by outsiders) than the actions of any state. What purports to be an expression of international solidarity and an instrument of a common purpose is often at best no more than a coalition of interests serving the particular purposes of certain dominant states. The appearance of internationalism, however, is not without effect, though it is not always a morally beneficial one. The greatest danger, perhaps, is that, armed with its international mandate, the enforcing agency will feel less rather than more moral restraint, its heightened sense of moral purpose encouraging it to throw caution to the wind.[11] The assumption of moral unilateralism is just as dangerous here as it is in more conventional interstate conflict.

The bilateral interpretation of just cause, then, is a moral ideal to which even states, despite a natural inclination to unilateralism or moral partisanship, are expected to respond; but what, *broadly speaking*, constitutes 'just cause'?[12] As the scale and destructive power of war has increased, so the understanding of what constitutes just cause for war has narrowed. War has ceased to be regarded with the kind of equanimity that led to its being seen as a normal way of regulating international affairs and an instrument resorted to in order to redress relatively minor injustices, or even to resolve questions of honour.[13] The experience of 'total' war (above all perhaps the dread of nuclear war) has weakened that juridical understanding of war associated with the just war tradition. Even in circles normally in sympathy with the tradition this weakening has been apparent. 'Men are becoming more and more convinced', wrote Pope John XXIII in his encyclical letter *Pacem in Terris*, 'that disputes which arise between States should not be resolved by recourse to arms ... this conviction is based chiefly on the terrible destructive force of modern arms ... and for this reason it is hardly possible to imagine that in the atomic era war could be used as an instrument of justice' (Pope John XXIII 1963, pp. 45–6). As the costs of war have escalated its justification (if it retains any) becomes a justification only *in extremis*, that is, in response to the gravest of injuries threatened or received. In this way considerations of just cause have yielded progressively to considerations of proportionality.

It is not simply, however, the escalating costs of war that have accounted for the narrowing of the concept. The modern tendency simply to equate the just war with a war of self-defence and the unjust war with a war of aggression owes as much, if not more, to the current dominance of the states system, with its firmly established principles of state sovereignty and non-intervention. The emergence of just war thinking preceded the modern system of international relations, and the traditional, much broader, concept of just cause reflects its greater antiquity. The earlier concept did not give the same prominence to the distinction between aggressor and defender, because it started from an assumption of a universal community of mankind transcending particular polities. The good of that community had moral primacy, and was the ultimate measure of the justice or injustice of war. 'Since one nation is a part of the whole world, and since the Christian province is a part of the whole Christian State', wrote Vitoria in a manner entirely consistent with the tradition, 'if any war should be advantageous to one province or nation but injurious to the whole or to Christendom, it is my belief that, for this very reason, that war is unjust' (quoted in Fernández-Santamaria 1977, p. 141).[14]

It is true that the idea of self-defence featured prominently in the traditional account of just war; but it did not exhaust the moral understanding of war in the way that it has tended to do latterly. Self-defence was justified not so much on its own grounds but as a vindication of the legal and moral community to which particular states or polities were thought to belong. On the one hand, a defensive war could not be justified *ipso facto*. In deciding whether a defensive war was just account needed to be taken of what it was that was being defended (and attacked). The defence of a state that habitually and systematically violated the moral law could not be justified (except perhaps on proportionate grounds of the lesser evil when faced with an unjust attacker).[15] On the other hand, if its defensive war *was* just, then in defending itself the state was at the same time defending the universal community to which it belonged. In upholding its own rights it was at the same time upholding the legal and moral system from which those rights were derived. Moreover, self-defence was not the only way of vindicating the universal community. Some forms of vindication embraced the use of war in an *offensive* role, as in the commonly received view that princes had a *prima facie* duty to protect the innocent even when the innocent in question were not their own subjects. This notion, which justified humanitarian intervention and the infringement of a state's sovereignty, was wholly in accord with the idea of a universal moral community of mankind whose members enjoyed reciprocal rights and duties, precisely as members of that universal community and not just as citizens of particular states.

It is perhaps this notion of a just *offensive* war that is most at odds with contemporary thinking. From a just war perspective, the problem with the prevalent aggressor–defender concept of war is its moral sterility: a distinction that appears to be defined primarily in *physical* or military terms is simply mixed up with the *moral* distinction between a just and an unjust war. As it stands, the distinction takes too much for granted, and the manner in which it is employed suppresses the concept of justice, the very concept 'that links the use of force with the moral order' (Murray 1960, p. 256). Aggression does not consist in the use of force *as such* (regardless of whether the use be defensive or offensive), but in the *unjust* use of force. Without further analysis and elaboration, therefore, the distinction between defender and aggressor does not provide a satisfactory basis for the moral assessment of war.

What account of the *offensive war* does the aggressor–defender concept of war yield, and is that account satisfactory? There are at least three ways in which the idea of an offensive war becomes at least partially acceptable and reconcilable with this modern approach to war. The right of self-defence, which forms the bedrock of the approach, embraces the right to resist an ongoing attack; but it also includes the right to resist an act of aggression that has already achieved its objective. The fact that in the latter case there is an interval between the act of aggression and the defensive response does not result in the moral prohibition of that response, even though the lapse of time gives it an 'offensive' appearance. For example, the seizures of the Falklands by Argentina and of Kuwait by Iraq were followed, as a matter of military necessity, by an interval of several weeks or months before attempts at expulsion and repossession could begin. Though the enforced interval between the initial act of aggression and the military response may give belligerents a chance to settle differences without resort to force, a settlement that does not reward the initial act of aggression is unlikely. In those circumstances the resort to arms can be justified, despite the lapse of time. Clearly, however, the longer the lapse of time the more difficult (though by no means impossible) it becomes to characterize the second resort to arms as 'defensive', and the harder it is not to see it as 'aggressive' as well as 'offensive'.[16]

The second way in which the offensive war may be admitted as a corollary of the right of self-defence is in the form of a preemptive strike. Here it is a question of responding not to a completed act of aggression but to an anticipated one. Does the moral norm of self-defence rule out *all* first use of armed force, or are there circumstances in which even first use becomes permissible? The reply of international law seems to be an unambiguously negative one. Article 51 of the UN Charter, for example, speaks of 'the inherent right of individual or collective self-defence *if an armed attack occurs*'.[17] Although, morally speaking, there is a *prima facie* case against first use of force, it is difficult to see how its prohibition could be absolute. To insist that it should would be incoherent, since such insistence might have the effect of undermining the basic right of self-defence. By waiting to be attacked the capacity of a state to defend itself could be certainly and fatally compromised. The classic and most frequently cited example from recent times is the Israeli initiation of hostilities in the 1967 Six Day War. With Arab armies massing on its borders Israel carried out a pre-emptive strike directed in particular against the Egyptian air force, nine-tenths of which was destroyed on the ground. The attack is thought to have been justified by some on the grounds that the aggressive intent of Syria, Jordan and Egypt was evident, that an attack on Israel's borders was imminent, and that if Israel had waited to be attacked it would have been overrun.[18]

From the moral point of view the idea of an anticipatory war of self-defence is fraught with danger, and the possibilities of abuse are obvious. As has been seen, German aggression in the Second World War, about which few doubts are normally entertained, was nevertheless portrayed, and in some cases genuinely perceived, as a form of anticipatory defence against Soviet or Communist expansion. This particular case is hardly problematic; but the line between anticipatory defence and an act of naked aggression is often very much more difficult to draw. Moral assessment needs to be informed by a realistic and objective appraisal of the relative strengths and weaknesses, as well as the actions and intentions, of potential combatants. It is with the dangers of abuse in mind that the important distinction between 'pre-emptive' and 'preventive' war is made.[19] The latter, which attempts to justify recourse to war in the absence of an immediate and direct threat, appears far too permissive: a mere growth in the power of a state for example, without clear evidence of aggressive intent, could be

regarded as a justification for war on the grounds that it disrupts
the balance of power or that it seems likely to lead to escalation
and thereby imperils the existing international order. The boundaries of 'pre-emptive' war need to be much more narrowly and
strictly drawn. Despite the dangers, however, the fact remains
that, since effective defence may require offensive and pre-emptive
action, the first use of force cannot be absolutely prohibited once
the right of self-defence has been conceded.[20]

The third way in which the offensive war finds partial acceptance within the defender–aggressor approach to war is through
the extension of the right of self-defence from an individual state
to a collection or alliance of states. The right of collective self-
defence or collective security is enshrined in the Charter of the
United Nations (Article 51), and has been frequently invoked. In
the Gulf War few of the members of the coalition were directly
threatened by Iraq, and only one, Kuwait, had actually been
attacked. The collective definition of self-defence allowed those
states that had not been attacked or threatened to take offensive
action against Iraq without violating the legal and moral norm
that proscribes aggressive war: in attacking Iraq they were at the
same time exercising the right of self-defence. As a form of
counter-intervention this was an upholding rather than a violation of that central norm of the states system, the principle of
non-intervention, and the vindication of the right of self-defence,
not its infringement.

Is this aggressor–defender account of legitimate 'offensive' war
satisfactory? Not from a just war standpoint.[21] The moral primacy given to the right of self-defence in the aggressor–defender
image, whereby offensive war is justified only as an extension of
the right of self-defence, is not reproduced in the just war image.
The moral grounding of the two traditions in other words is very
different; and this may have important practical as well as theoretical repercussions. The just war approach is both more restrictive (or exclusive) and more permissive (or inclusive) than the
defender–aggressor paradigm: just as the internal logic of the
former rules out the latter's sweeping moral endorsement of
defensive war, so the same logic requires the former to go much
further than the latter in accepting the moral permissibility of
offensive war. Usually, of course, the right of self-defence will be

upheld by both traditions; but the clear dependence of that right on considerations of justice in the just war tradition means that just war theorists are much readier than their aggressor–defender counterparts to question, if not to withhold, that right. Did the Khmer Rouge enjoy that right when Vietnamese troops crossed the Cambodian border on Christmas Day 1978? Does any state that subjects its citizens to a reign of terror enjoy such a right? Just war theorists are much more inclined to moral scepticism in such cases, and much more disposed to accept the case for humanitarian intervention (that is, for an outright offensive war, a war of intervention rather than a war of *counter-intervention*) than those who give moral primacy to state sovereignty and the principle of non-intervention. Of course acceptance of a case, or of just cause, for intervention is not the same as acceptance of intervention itself. The presence of a just cause is not sufficient to warrant just recourse. The political and military complexities that apply perhaps in most cases may be such as to rule out intervention on the grounds that the prospects of success are far too slim or that intervention is likely to make the situation worse rather than better. As usual in just war reasoning, moral assessment needs to be informed by a frank and realistic appraisal of solutions and (of course) of causes.[22]

It seems clear, then, that a much less literal and more critical understanding of the aggressor–defender image of war (including a widening of the state's moral horizons and a revision of its moral status) is needed to bring it in line with just war thinking. Properly understood, however, the equation of the just war with a defensive war becomes acceptable. All just wars are, in a broader sense, defensive wars, involving the upholding of rights that have been violated or, at the very least, that are gravely threatened with violation. Without an injury, received or threatened, no war can be justified. In that sense all just wars are reactive or defensive wars, and all unjust wars are wars of aggression: that is, wars that are fought to commit a wrong rather than to right one. The linking of the defender–aggressor distinction with the concept of justice establishes a more secure and certainly more coherent basis for the moral assessment of war.

The moral efficacy of just cause is dependent upon the existence of *right intention*. The inclusion of this criterion in the moral analysis of war constitutes a recognition of the way in which belligerents are wont to use morality as a pretext or cover for something else. The appeal to just cause may be purely rhetorical; and a war that is fought ostensibly for a just purpose may have a hidden, and perhaps far from just, agenda. As Machiavelli argued, nothing benefits a ruler more than a good war: 'Therefore many judge that a wise prince must, whenever he has the occasion, foster with cunning some hostility so that in stamping it out his greatness will increase as a result' (Bondanella and Musa 1979, p. 148). The real aim of war may be the resolution of domestic instability, the unification of an otherwise divided state or the securing of a government's tenure of office. The real attraction of a 'just' war may be the opportunity that it provides to enlarge the power and sphere of influence of a state. As a consequence the moral claims made for war need to be viewed with very considerable scepticism, though not with the cynicism that leads to their instant dismissal.

At the same time 'right intention' should not be understood too puritanically. In the opinion of some critics, for example, the presence of an economic or 'oil' interest in the Gulf War undermined the moral position of the allied coalition. The fact that the West in particular was acting, at best, from mixed motives was thought to be enough to exclude just recourse. This common assumption that the only just war is a *disinterested* war is not shared by the just war tradition. Justice and interest are not mutually exclusive. The presence of an interest does not, *ipso facto*, nullify just cause. The real issue is whether the interest that is present is itself legitimate, and whether that legitimate interest is relevant to the case of war. Of course, the argument of critics of the Gulf War was that the oil interest was not only present but dominant, in other words, that *it* constituted the real cause for which the war was being fought. It may well have been that, in the absence of an economic or strategic interest, action would not have been taken; but this assumption, even if well founded, hardly warrants the critical conclusion. The most it demonstrates is that states, like individuals, are more likely to act morally when duty and inclination coincide. From a just war standpoint the systematic exclusion of such incentives seems perverse. It is also seen to have its dangers, for the 'purer' the motives with which war is fought the more likely it is to be fought without limit or restraint.[23]

The last point, underlining as it does the fundamental moral ambivalence of the idea of just cause, seems a fitting conclusion to this discussion of a concept that is, at once, the basis of all moral reasoning about war and the one that, more than any other perhaps, is responsible for the overriding of the moral limits of war.

Notes

1 The attention of the reader is drawn to Welch's *Justice and the Genesis of War* (1993), in which the author examines the role played by the justice motive in a number of different wars. All the wars examined are interstate wars. There is no analysis of revolutionary war. This might seem a surprising omission, given the overwhelming importance attached to justice in the modern revolutionary tradition; but, since the author's main purpose is to counteract realist neglect of this motive, he focuses deliberately on cases 'where we should intuitively expect the justice motive to be weakest, because *realpolitik* considerations ought to be strongest' (Welch 1993, p. 34). Still, perhaps the omission also reflects a prejudice, discernible in much of the literature, against interstate war and in favour of revolutionary war, that is of war aimed (among other things) at the abolition or overcoming of the states system.

2 The discovery had a sobering effect, and transformed the way in which he viewed the war and the spirit in which he subsequently fought it.

3 Given the skilful propaganda to which the German people had been subjected, this is perhaps hardly surprising. As Bartov points out: 'An eighteen-year old soldier in 1943 would have been only eight during the Nazi "seizure of power". Thus the fighting spearhead of the Third Reich was composed of men who had spent the formative years of their youth under National Socialism ... [and in many cases] within the ranks of the *Hitlerjugend* and the *Arbeitsdienst*' (Bartov 1991, pp. 108–9). Even those who left no doubt about their ability to think independently and conscientiously about the war were receptive, at least for a time, to the notion that Germany had just cause for war. Franz Jäggerstätter spent many days pondering this question in a German prison before arriving at the conclusion that it had not – a view he paid for with his life (cf. Zahn 1964).

4 The prediction of future validation is not as fanciful or far-fetched as it may seem. See Bartov's discussion in *Hitler's Army* (1991) of 'the new revisionism' expounded by contemporary historians like Michael Stürmer, Ernst Nolte and Andreas Hillgruber. For example,

Bartov attributes the following conclusion to Hillgruber: 'The ultimate defeat of the Wehrmacht [in the East] inevitably spelled the defeat of Europe, whose heart was torn out and whose body was left at the mercy of the superpowers in the periphery. Put differently, both in the "elementary sense" of fighting for their own and the civilian population's survival in the face of a barbaric invasion, and in the politico-strategic sense of defending Europe from the domination of non-European powers, the troops of the *Ostheer* were, as Nazi propaganda had claimed all along, fighting for a just cause' (Bartov 1991, p. 143).

5 It is doubtful whether *any* modern war, given its nature and demands, can be fought in bad faith. Even a predatory war, to be effective, needs to be portrayed by the leaders, and understood by the people involved, as a just war.

6 It seems that the insistence on unilateral justice has a doubly distorting effect on the moral assessment of war, ruling out war in cases where bilateral justice (or injustice) is seen to exist, while unleashing war in those cases to which unilateral justice is thought to apply.

7 As one influential source of recent just war thinking argues: '[It is a question of] the comparative justice of the positions of respective adversaries or enemies. In essence: Which side is sufficiently "right" in a dispute, and are the values at stake critical enough to override the presumption against war ... comparative justice stresses that no state should act on the basis that it has "absolute justice" on its side. Every party to a conflict should acknowledge the limits of its "just cause" and the consequent requirement to use *only* limited means in pursuit of its objectives. Far from legitimizing a crusade mentality, comparative justice is designed to relativize absolute claims and to restrain the use of force even in a "justified" conflict' (National Conference of US Catholic Bishops 1983, p. 27).

8 According to James Turner Johnson, 'this was as clear and unambiguous a case as one could hope to find in the real world' (Johnson and Weigel 1991, p. 22).

9 Welch writes: 'If national leaders were more attentive to the normative claims of others – and more circumspect about their own – they could better anticipate and manage conflicts, and in some cases avoid them altogether' (Welch 1993, p. 2).

10 See the discussion of realism in Chapter 4.

11 The encounter with failure does little to diminish the ardour with which a solution to some of the most intractable problems of international relations is sought. Far from leading to the more modest definition of objectives, failure is attributed to the timidity or lack of commitment of the intervening states, so that a solution is sought in more extreme measures.

12 The qualification is of course essential. What constitutes just cause in a specific sense owes more to political and military judgement than it does to moral theory. The moral theorist, for example, may argue the legitimacy of a pre-emptive strike (see within); but whether a particular offensive is accurately described in this way is more a matter for political and military intelligence than moral theory.

13 According to Vattel in the eighteenth century '[a prince] has a right to demand, even by force of arms, the reparation of an insult' (cited in Walzer 1992, p. 340). Of course more may have been at stake than meets the eye (especially the *modern* eye). The 'reparation of an insult' could well have been an attempt to resolve a challenge to public authority fundamental enough to warrant a military response.

14 To avoid possible confusion and misunderstanding it should perhaps be underlined that Vitoria did not regard 'the whole world' as coterminous with 'the whole Christian State' in a normative sense. The foundation of his political thought in natural law required him to distinguish clearly between the two, just as it required him to recognize the legitimacy of non-Christian 'states' such as those encountered by the Spaniards in the New World.

15 The position of the Soviet Union under Stalin illustrates both points. Given its tyrannical nature, it is doubtful whether the regime would have enjoyed a right of self-defence against an invading force intent upon unseating the government and restoring the rights of the people subject to its tyrannical rule (whether such an intervention would have been prudent or justified on grounds of its proportionality is of course another matter). Defence against the Nazi invasion was of a different order. That attack was a clear case of unjust aggression. Far from being humanitarian, its purpose was genocidal or annihilatory. Against such an adversary even an unjust regime enjoys the right of self-defence and acquires a kind of temporary legitimacy.

16 Among those who seek to justify offensive action despite the lapse of time (Argentina's claim to the Falklands/Malvinas Islands was based on an alleged illegal seizure by the British one hundred and fifty years earlier, a foundational illegitimacy that was thought to undermine the right of self-defence) considerations of justice become more explicit and, rightly or wrongly, even take precedence over the right of self-defence. Those for whom the aggressor–defender image of war is paradigmatic are strongly inclined to resist this shifting of the moral ground. Michael Walzer, for instance, whose own rather eccentric or non-traditional version of just war theory owes much to the aggressor–defender image, writes in relation to the Arab–Israeli

conflict: 'self-defense seems the primary and indisputable right of any political community, merely because it is *there* and whatever the circumstances under which it achieved statehood' (Walzer 1992, p. 82).

17 Added emphasis. For a discussion of the legal position compare Akenhurst 1987, pp. 261f.

18 Cf. the analysis of this case in Walzer 1992, pp. 82–5 and in Cohen 1989, pp.74–5.

19 Cf. Walzer 1992, Ch. 5.

20 For a critical and highly sceptical appraisal of the distinction see Tucker 1960, pp. 142ff.

21 Critics sometimes assume that it is. This is usually because they accept Michael Walzer's version of just war theory as definitive (see for example Norman 1995, Ch. 4).

22 In respect of the latter the need for a bilateral analysis is just as great in the case of humanitarian intervention as it is in conventional interstate warfare. The need is, if anything, greater, since the moral impulse (generated by the assumption if not always the reality of disinterestedness) is likely to be stronger and the temptation to simplify just cause, by interpreting it unilaterally, much more difficult to resist. In the case of the conflict in Bosnia, for example, the more enthusiastic interventionists often seem inclined to suppress the moral complexities of the conflict by focusing on the moral transgressions of the Bosnian Serbs while largely ignoring those of their Croat and Muslim neighbours.

23 For a fuller discussion of these issues see Coates 1996.

7

Proportionality
and the recourse to war

'No war is just,' wrote Vitoria, 'the conduct of which is manifestly more harmful to the State than it is good and advantageous; and this is true regardless of other claims or reasons advanced to make of it a just war' (quoted in Fernández-Santamaria 1977, p. 139). The existence of a just cause, even when allied with legitimate authority, does not in itself justify recourse to war. The criterion of proportionality requires potential combatants to consider whether or not war is a fitting or proportionate response to the injury that has been threatened or received. In this respect moral reasoning about war is seen to be no different from any other form of moral reasoning, since *some* notion of proportionality seems inherent in all moral judgement of situations of conflict, where one value cannot be promoted without damage to some other competing value.

In such moral dilemmas the preservation of a certain symmetry between the proposed course of action and the end that it serves is a key (though not necessarily the sole) moral concern. It is when that moral symmetry is missing, when the 'negativity' of the means is seen to be greater than the 'positivity' of the ends that they serve, that moral doubts commonly arise. Someone, for example, who regards abortion as justified when carried out in order to preserve the life of the mother (and the concomitant good of her family), but unjustified when performed for personal or economic reasons (such as enhancing the mother's career prospects or maintaining a higher standard of living) is applying a form of proportionate reasoning. One case seems symmetrical, the other does not. The mother's career prospects and sense of personal or vocational fulfilment, or the material prosperity of the family, are considered to be important goods, but not ones that are substantial enough to compensate for the evil that abortion is seen to constitute. In such a case the lack of proportionality may be thought to transform the 'physical' evil of abortion into a *moral* evil, thereby leading to its moral proscription: arguably, to accept proportionality in this case (unlike the other) would be to turn against the basic value attached to human life in most moral codes.[1] A similar form of reasoning is applied to the case of war.[2]

Put in its simplest form the question that the criterion of proportionality is intended to raise is this: Is this just cause *worth* a war? The simplicity of the question is of course wholly misleading, and finding a satisfactory answer to it is fraught with difficulty. Little wonder, therefore, that the criterion has become perhaps the most contentious of all just war criteria (though the specific disagreement often appears symptomatic of a much more fundamental dispute about the nature of moral reasoning itself and about the status of moral norms). The basic requirements of the principle, however, are not difficult to define. O'Brien's list of those requirements, though fuller and more detailed than most, would find common acceptance among just war theorists:

> There must be a just cause of sufficient importance to warrant its defense by recourse to armed coercion.
> The probable good to be achieved by successful recourse to armed coercion in pursuit of the just cause must outweigh the probable evil that the war will produce.
> The calculation of proportionality between probable good and evil must be made with respect to all belligerents, affected neutrals, and the international community as a whole.
> These calculations must be made in the light of realistic estimates of the probability of success. (O'Brien 1981, pp. 27–8)

The problems of interpreting or applying the criterion of proportionality stem largely from the number of variable elements that it contains. The idea of what constitutes a *sufficient cause* for war is one such variable. 'Sufficiency' is a relative concept, which varies in accordance with time and circumstance. A medieval monarch, for example, who chose to fight a war over a matter of 'honour' was not necessarily guilty of moral overreaction or of a disproportionate recourse to war, though that may be how things seem viewed from a modern standpoint. The public insult to which war, in this case, was a response may have been a deliberate challenge to an emerging and still far from secure ruling authority, a challenge that, once ignored, might have led to the rapid undermining of authority and ensuing social anarchy. The often 'symbolic' appearance of past wars is not necessarily a sign of their moral, much less their political, redundancy. The war of 'honour' may have been the medieval or renaissance equivalent of the war of non-appeasement of more modern times: a war fought to redress relatively minor injuries in the hope of preventing major ones.[3]

A similar relativity applies to the case of *war*. War is a variable, the 'fitness' of which cannot be assessed without reference to circumstances of time and place. It is not a question of comparing just cause with war in some abstract sense. It is impossible to say that this particular wrong is a 'war-justifying' cause without considering the kind of war that righting the wrong would require. A just cause, in other words, might be proportionate with some wars but not with others, a particular cause being grave enough to justify a 'small' war but insufficient to justify a 'big' one (in which case of course those having recourse to war need to be confident that the war will not escalate). There is no necessary or natural proportion between 'just cause' and 'war', and there can be no injury or threat that is grave enough to *guarantee* the proportionality of war whatever its nature and magnitude. A war that is unavoidably 'total', for example, can never be anything other than disproportionate, when judged in accordance with just war criteria. Its deliberate and wholesale violation of the moral limits of war would make its employment as an instrument of justice incoherent and morally disproportionate: it is not possible to right an injustice unjustly.

The judgement that war in its modern form *is* unavoidably total has led many to conclude that war has ceased to be a proportionate response to virtually *any* just cause. Even a grave and imminent threat to the survival of a state (or even an alliance of states), or of its way of life and fundamental values, is thought insufficient to justify the use of weaponry as destructive in its power and indiscriminate in its effects as that contained in a modern nuclear arsenal. A weapon capable of destroying all life on earth is seen to be naturally disproportionate. The dread of nuclear war during a period of superpower rivalry inspired a widespread moral suspicion not just of nuclear but also of conventional war. Some, while prepared to accept the potential and theoretical moral proportionality of conventional war, and even of nuclear war, when limited to the use of tactical and battlefield weapons, or of strategic weapons in a discriminate and counter-force role, ruled out both because of the dangers of escalation. The risk of an all-out nuclear war, with all that that would entail, rendered both a limited nuclear war and even a conventional war disproportionate. Others have argued that, leaving aside the dangers of escalation, the nature of twentieth-century conventional war itself (and still more so-called 'limited' nuclear war) is such as to exclude the proportionate use of armed force.

Though it is difficult, in just war terms, to contest the internal logic of such argumentation, its factual basis is eminently contestable. To a considerable extent, it seems, the argument rests on the confusion of a temporary with a permanent state of affairs. It was not just the presence of nuclear weapons that created the climate of fear that undermined war's moral acceptability, but the possession of those weapons by superpower rivals in a bipolar and conflictual world. It is noticeable how the end of that rivalry has led to the partial moral rehabilitation of armed force (including the widespread acceptance of its use as an instrument of justice in an emerging 'new world order') and to renewed debate about the morality of war, and in particular, the morality of *conventional* war.[4] Moreover, the alleged inevitability of total war, both nuclear and conventional, seems more assumption than fact; though crucially, as far as moral strategy is concerned, it is an assumption that, if left uncontested, may well *become* a fact. It appears that armed force, even in the late twentieth century and even against an unprincipled opponent, can continue to be effective without becoming inherently disproportionate and indiscriminate. The experience of the Gulf War suggests that the capacity (as distinct from the will) to fight a war proportionately and discriminately has in fact improved since the Second World War – an improvement that might be expected to continue with technological advances (like the development of non-lethal weaponry).

As O'Brien's second requirement makes clear, assessing the proportionality of recourse to war involves an estimation and comparison of the probable good and evil that it seems likely to produce, and it is this requirement more than any other that accounts for the problems encountered in applying this criterion and the controversies to which it gives rise. The difficulties and disagreements have to do with the form the estimation takes and with the amount of weight, morally speaking, placed on it. The assurance with which some moral theorists have tackled these problems contrasts starkly with the scepticism displayed by many just war theorists, particularly by those of a more traditional and absolutist persuasion.[5] Prominent among the former, for example, is the utilitarian philosopher Jeremy Bentham, who felt confident enough in his ability to determine the relative value of the consequences of any act to base his entire moral theory of utility on such a calculation. What inspired that confidence, of course, was Bentham's rationalist and pseudoscientific belief that it was possible not only to predict the consequences of an act with certainty, but to measure them exactly. Both assumptions seem highly dubious – dubious enough in the eyes of critics to undermine the entire moral project.

In the first place, the kind of moral consequentialism that Bentham advocated calls for a predictive knowledge that is simply not attainable. It is difficult enough in the relatively simple arena of interpersonal action to foresee the likely and lasting consequences of an act. At best it is often only retrospectively, when all the dust has long since settled, that the real consequences emerge, and even then only in the faintest outline. How much more difficult, then, to apply this predictive understanding to the complex and altogether more uncertain domain of international politics and war. To determine with any degree of exactitude the overall and long-term costs and benefits of a war that is yet to be fought is the tallest of tall orders. Comparisons of the probable state of affairs to be brought about as the result of war with the probable state of affairs produced if no military action were to be taken are inevitably highly speculative. Such calculations, on their own at least, hardly provide a solid base for the moral judgement of war. More often than not they are simply a covert and indirect way of advancing moral preferences that, in fact, are grounded independently and in advance of the consideration of consequences. To make such comprehensive knowledge of the future a condition of moral action is (or at least *ought* to be, though it often is not because of the rationalist assumptions that tend to inform this moral consequentialism) a recipe for inaction.

Proportionality in this inflated, consequentialist, form is simply unworkable. Taken seriously and understood realistically it would reduce decision-makers to a state of moral paralysis:

> How difficult to be wise, except after the event, and how every leap is a leap in the dark! ... To leap in the dark requires strong muscles, steady nerves, a taste for adventure, *and not too great a fear of the consequences.* 'I am not responsible for the consequences' Salisbury used to say, and he meant that having acted to the best of his knowledge and judgement, he could not but let the events take their course as the fates in their caprice decreed ... *in politics one is always acting in a fog.* (Kedourie 1984, p. 135, added emphasis)

How very much greater is the 'fog of war'. As Kedourie intimates, the overall and long-term consequences of an act or policy are not only unknowable in advance but uncontrollable by the agents themselves, being as much the product of chance and circumstance as of deliberate design. In effect, and in its more extreme and rationalist forms at least, moral consequentialism requires of the moral agent the kind of knowledge that theologians like St Augustine attributed to divine providence and philosophers like Hegel attributed to the 'cunning of reason': in short, the kind of knowledge that is beyond any moral agent.

The capacity for moral action is dependent, therefore, upon the exercise of a certain humility and upon a restraint of the moral imagination: clearly not on indifference to the consequences of one's act – that *would be* an abdication of moral responsibility – but on a recognition that the consequences are largely unforeseeable and not of one's own making. What providence or history will make of it all is anyone's *guess* (and even historians with the benefit of hindsight will argue interminably about that); the horizons of political (and moral) judgement are necessarily more limited or more narrowly circumscribed. 'Since when we act,' Hannah Arendt wrote, 'we never know with any certainty the eventual consequences of what we are doing, violence can remain rational only if it pursues short-term goals' (Arendt 1970, p. 79). Proportionality should be 'proximate' rather than 'remote' in its moral application. The moral agent, and not just the statesman, must learn to live with uncertainty about the remoter consequences of his or her acts and with the unavoidable risk that accompanies all moral action.

Even if certain knowledge of the consequences were attainable it would be insufficient, on its own, to deliver the decisive moral verdict expected or required of it. The second difficulty that, in the view of critics, fatally afflicts moral consequentialism of the kind favoured by Bentham and other utilitarians, is the so-called problem of *incommensurability*. It is argued by those who raise this difficulty that the moral calculation that a consequentialist reading of the principle of proportionality entails cannot in fact be made because the diverse effects are not *exactly* commensurable one with another, there being no unit of value in terms of which they might be measured and compared. As recent critics of this approach have argued: 'Cost–benefit analysis ... cannot settle the moral issue ... The relevant values and disvalues ... are diverse in kind. They are not quantifiable ... And none of the ends sought is independent of all features of the means used other than their efficiency, measurable costs, and benefits' (Finnis *et al.* 1988, p. 252).

The problem raised here has long bedevilled moral philosophy of a consequentialist or utilitarian persuasion. It was this that inspired Bentham's attempt to produce a unit of measurement in his 'felicific calculus', which would simplify moral judgement and moral practice by enabling the moral agent to choose among alternative courses of action on the basis of the quantifiable amounts of happiness (understood as units of pleasure) to which they seemed likely to give rise. Predictably, in the view of critics, the ambitions of Bentham and his more extreme utilitarian successors have not been realized. This is because the moral project itself – the aim of reducing morality to a quantitative or arithmetic form of reasoning – was ill-conceived right from the start.

Michael Walzer's reflections on Britain's decision to declare war on Germany in 1939 illustrate the nature of the difficulty:

Suppose that Nazism had triumphed unresisted in Europe and that its 'rule of violence' had resulted in twenty million deaths before an internal coup had produced a 'moderate' military regime and ended the reign of terror. But thirty million people (including some but not all of the first twenty million) died in the course of World War II. Foreknowledge of these outcomes would still not provide a sufficient reason for avoiding the war, because the human losses involved in a Nazi victory are not losses of life alone, and the gains of war or peace cannot be measured simply in lives saved ... Here it is not possible simply to count. One relies on moral intuitions which can be defended and articulated, it seems to me, only in terms of a theory of evil. (Cohen *et al.* 1974, pp. 91–2)

The moral judgement that this (and any) recourse to war engaged was not arithmetic. Even if those involved could have been certain that fewer deaths would be caused by a policy of appeasement than by a policy of war, this would not have been sufficient to establish the case for appeasement, since there was always much more at stake than the probable loss of life. The choice between good and evil was not exhausted by the choice between physical survival and violent death. It never is, since the price of survival may be too high.

The temptation to equate the process of moral reasoning with a process of quantification is a real and strong one, since it holds out the prospect of an easy and swift solution to moral difficulties and dilemmas. Moral phenomena, however, are not quantifiable. The attempt to quantify the unquantifiable, therefore, has a thoroughly distorting effect on moral judgement. It involves a form of moral reductionism, whereby the exclusive moral focus is on those aspects of the moral phenomena in question that *are* quantifiable to the neglect or relative downgrading of those that are not. This selective application of proportionality was evident, for example, in moral assessments of the Falklands War of 1982 between Britain and Argentina.

The moral reservations that many entertained about the justice of recourse to war over the Falklands were based very largely on the judgement that war would be a disproportionate response in this case. This was a conclusion drawn even by those who entertained few doubts about the justice of the cause. The cause, though considered just and certain, was not thought grave enough to warrant war. In arriving at this conclusion much was made of the small number of inhabitants of the islands (less than two thousand) at the time of the Argentine invasion. This would be a war in which potential British (let alone Argentine) fatalities might very quickly exceed the number of islanders in defence of whose rights the war was ostensibly to be fought. Additionally, attention was focused on the material and economic costs not only of the war itself but of the subsequent defence of the islands if Britain's attempt at their recapture proved successful (not to mention the loss of trade as a result of the severing of relations with Argentina and her South American allies). Britain had neither an economic nor a strategic interest in the Falkland Islands. For all these reasons the likely costs of war were thought greatly to exceed the likely benefits: the Falklands were simply not worth a war. To many there seemed to be a *natural* disproportion about the use of armed force to recover islands eight thousand miles distant, of no strategic or economic worth to Britain, and inhabited by less than two thousand people.

The case against the proportionality of the war was reinforced by the deliberate neglect and disparagement of alternative, particularly 'non-material', moral arguments and considerations. The islanders being so few, their rights of self-determination and territorial and communal integrity were thought to be without great moral substance or importance, while the appeal to moral and legal principle, so prominent in the government's defence of the recourse to war, was seen as empty rhetoric.[6] The moral image of the war was simply not taken seriously, dismissed as mere jingoism, a pathetic harking back to the morally disreputable days of empire and of gunboat diplomacy. The misplaced moral enthusiasm for war of a gullible public was being whipped up by a cunning and unprincipled government that, not unlike its Argentine counterpart, saw in war the means of its own political salvation.

An alternative, perhaps less cynical, view was available. Of course, it is true that neither Britain's economic interest nor certainly her physical survival was at stake in this war. Her moral identity, on the other hand, arguably was. It is easy to be dismissive of something so intangible or immaterial; but the existence of a political community is as much moral as physical. A community unprepared to defend those values that are fundamental to its moral, if not to its physical, survival has already ceased to be a political community in the fullest sense. Arguably, it was not jingoism or a false and inflated national pride that dictated the use of armed force in defence of the Falklands, but the recognition that too much was at stake not to respond in this way. The moral costs of acquiescence in the face of the invasion and occupation of a territory that, however marginal to the interests of the United Kingdom, remained its legal and moral responsibility, would have been immense. In brief, there was enough at stake here in the way of the defence of fundamental values, if not of material interests, to justify a war.

Whatever the merits of this particular case, the principle of proportionality is not vindicated but undermined by the common, and perhaps prevailing, tendency to interpret it simply as a calculation of material or physical gain and loss. Proportionality is about the comparison of *moral* goods or values, and not physical or material harms and benefits as such. As the American just war theorist, John Courtney Murray, argued:

> [Comparison is] between realities of the moral order and not sheerly between the two sets of material damage and loss ... The question of proportion must be evaluated ... from the viewpoint of the hierarchy of strictly moral values ... There are greater evils than the physical death and destruction wrought in war. And there are human goods of so high an order that immense sacrifices may have to be borne in their defense. (Murray 1960, p. 261)[7]

Reluctance to pay the material costs of war *may* be a sign not of moral probity and communal vigour, but of a society where moral and community values are in retreat in the face of advancing materialism. An observation of this kind informed Hegel's discussion, in the *Philosophy of Right* and elsewhere, of the 'ethical' nature of war.[8] The orderly and prosperous existence that citizens enjoy during periods of prolonged peace may leave them ill equipped to respond to the moral demands of war and vulnerable to the fate of those peoples whose 'freedom has died from the fear of dying' (Hegel 1991, p. 362). In such cases the dominance of bourgeois and material values among the citizens makes a nonsense of war: how can war, in which the soldier-citizen must be prepared to sacrifice his or her life, be seen to serve the privacy and security to which 'bourgeois' citizens have learnt to attach supreme and overriding value?[9]

Hegel argued that the purely instrumental value that such 'citizens' have learnt to give to the state fails to do justice to the true relation between state and citizen. The political community is more than an association entered into for the mutual convenience of its members, and finding validity only in its capacity to maximize their private satisfaction. The defence of the community and of the values that are vital to its continued existence is a duty falling upon all citizens, and one that may require 'the sacrifice of personal actuality'. In this respect (though certainly not in others) the Hegelian view is in line with a just war tradition indebted to Thomist and Aristotelian principles. 'The common good,' Suarez wrote, 'must take precedence over the private good, and a man is bound to lose his life for the sake of the common good' (quoted in Hamilton 1963, p. 57). The readiness of citizens to pay that price, not exultantly or enthusiastically, but deliberately and willingly nevertheless, is the moral high point of war, just as the avoidance of war for the sake of private and materialist values is the low point in the life of any political community, the point at which 'mere life' has triumphed over the 'good life', the point that marks the moral demise of that community. The problem for the citizenry, perhaps, lies in identifying the moment when ultimate human values are genuinely at stake, and not just some worthless or disproportionate cause, to which a spurious moral value is being attached and for the sake of which men, on both sides, are being required to die pointlessly.

The allusion in the previous sentence to bilateral suffering underlines the 'total' context in relation to which proportionality is to be applied. It is not, in the just war tradition at least, simply a matter of assessing the overall costs and benefits to the particular state having recourse to war that is in question (nor even the combined costs to all belligerents). The proportionality of the war needs to be viewed in relation to the international community as a whole. Nothing less will do, given the universalist principles of just war thinking, according to which the moral context of war is always a global one embracing the community of mankind with a common good that transcends and takes precedence over the goods of particular states.

The international bearing of the principle has been greatly accentuated by changes that have taken place in more recent times. For one thing, the ideological nature of much of modern warfare gives it a universalist dimension that was missing from previous wars, with the possible exception of the wars of religion. The ideological character of war, with its universal aims and aspirations, makes any such war a matter of very particular interest to the members of the international community, whether or not they are directly involved in the war in question (though the ideological nature of the conflict makes their involvement more rather than less likely, ideological war being naturally contagious). Other developments have meant that there are now fewer 'parochial' wars of material interest only to the participants themselves. The increasing interdependence of states, particularly economic, as well as the huge growth in the destructive power of modern weapons, has meant that war is no longer as containable as it once was. The effects of many modern wars reverberate throughout the world, bringing benefit or harm not just to the warring communities but to states that are in no way a party to the conflict. Their distance from the conflict does not mean that their interests can be overlooked in considering the proportionality of recourse to war.

The international context and ramifications of a potential war have at times been crucial to determining its proportionality. The Soviet invasion of Hungary in 1956 was an obvious infringement of the principle of non-aggression and a clear violation of Hungarian sovereignty and of the Hungarian people's right of self-determination. Without the military assistance of the international community it was clear that the territorial and political integrity of Hungary would not be preserved or restored. The plight of Hungary in 1956 was not unlike that of Kuwait in 1991. In both cases a just cause for counter-intervention by the international community appeared to exist. In 1991 coalition forces intervened successfully; in 1956 the rest of the world stood by while Soviet tanks crushed the resistance of Hungarian freedom-fighters. The key difference, which allowed intervention in

1991 and ruled it out in 1956, is that in 1991 the nuclear super-powers were on the same side, more or less. In 1991 the Cold War had come to an end; in 1956 it was at its height. The potential costs of counter-intervention in Hungary included the very real possibility of a Third World War and a nuclear conflict from which no part of the globe could emerge unscathed. In the light of such devastating potential costs the defence of Hungarian independence was almost bound to seem disproportionate: the cause was just, but it was not worth a war in the circumstances that prevailed at the time. On this occasion, perhaps, the rights of a member state needed to be sacrificed to the greater good of the international community.

The *prospects of success* (O'Brien's fourth requirement) are sometimes regarded as an independent criterion of just recourse. It seems more logical, however, to consider them as part of proportionality. Since war is resorted to in order to right a wrong or injury that is threatened or received, if the prospects of military success are extremely slim or remote, then the justification of war appears to fall. The harm that war inflicts will then, it seems, not only outweigh the good to be obtained, but will be wholly without the moral compensation afforded by a potential benefit. The interlocking of the two criteria was evident in moral assessments of the Falklands War.

The reservations that many had about the proportionality of the war were greatly reinforced by perceptions of the very considerable risk of failure. Johnson's view that 'the ability to project force over long distances gave the British government confidence of its success' (Johnson 1984, p. 49) is not supported by the facts. The weight of the advice given to the Prime Minister appears to have been that the military recovery of the Islands was a very risky venture. Following the advice of his departmental officials, John Nott, the Minister of Defence, appears to have been against it. So too, apparently, were the Army and Air Force Chiefs of Staff.[10] Advice from the Navy was mixed, and it is not clear to what extent Admiral Leach's enthusiasm for the use of force was shared by his colleagues. The Cabinet's decision to dispatch a task force was taken reluctantly, and even then was based on the shaky and, as it turned out, false assumption that it would not need to be used.

Doubts about the feasibility of a military response were well founded. The strategic problems confronting the task force were immense. They included the logistical nightmare of fighting a war in which communication and supply lines stretched over eight thousand miles, the lack of airborne early warning and adequate air cover (Argentine land-based combat aircraft outnumbered the carrier-based Sea Harriers by more than five to one), the vulnerability of surface ships to air and submarine attack, and the hazards of mounting a seaborne landing without air superiority and without a favourable attacker–defender ratio. It would have taken relatively little to go wrong to upset an already precarious military balance.

Calculating the prospects of success should involve an estimation of the relative strengths and weaknesses of the potential belligerents. It seems clear, however, that the decision to send the task force was taken with very little knowledge of the military capacity of the enemy.[11] The result was that 'Mrs Thatcher sent the task force with full awareness that she was taking a gamble, but without knowledge of the true odds against success' (Hastings and Jenkins 1983, p. 338). War in the South Atlantic had not been anticipated, and a war of the kind that the task force would be required to fight had not been part of contingency planning. The task force departed without a clear military strategy or plan: 'It had become a matter of acting first and asking questions later' (Dillon 1989, p. 171; Hastings and Jenkins 1983, p. 317).[12] The strategy that emerged as the task force proceeded southwards was necessarily flawed and vulnerable. The successful outcome owed much to good fortune and even more to the Argentine failure to exploit the strategic weaknesses of the task force.[13] If Argentina had used its enormous logistical advantage and its military superiority in key areas to better effect, a major military defeat might well have followed. Hundreds, perhaps thousands, of soldiers' lives would have been lost, and the Falklands would have remained even more firmly in Argentine hands.

Considerations like these lead some, as they led many at the time, to conclude that this was a reckless recourse to war. That the decision to send the task force (in effect to take military action, since Argentina's evacuation of the islands was improbable without the use of the task force) was taken without serious or adequate examination of the prospects of success seems clear from the evidence. Far from being confident of success, as Johnson suggests, the government had every reason to be fearful of the outcome. Nevertheless, the decision to commit British troops was taken. The reasons for this have to do with the state of military unpreparedness in which the British government found itself as well as the extreme urgency of the situation. The longer the delay the riskier the military operation became and the more remote the prospects of success. The predominant reason, however, was the government's apparent certainty about the proportionality of a military response. It was almost as if the government, under Mrs Thatcher's leadership, felt that it had little political or moral option but to have recourse to war, given the importance of the cause.[14] Even though the attempt to retake the islands risked military defeat and failure, it still seemed worthwhile: better to have tried and failed than not to have tried at all.

This phenomenon whereby the moral weight attached to the cause overcomes even the most serious doubts and fears about the prospects of success is a common enough one. Lackey cites the case of Belgium in August 1914. On the second of August a German ultimatum demanding free passage for German armies intent upon the seizure of Paris and the Channel ports was handed to the Belgian government. The government refused, and Belgium prepared to face the might of the German army in what was at best a delaying operation and at worst a useless sacrifice not just of the armed forces but also of civilians (given the German policy of *Schrecklichkeit*, that is, its campaign of terror against the civilian population). Though the justice of the Belgian cause was certain, considerations of proportionality suggest to Lackey that 'a decision not to fight would not have been immoral' (Lackey 1989, p. 41). This cautious and curiously inverted conclusion deliberately leaves open the question of whether to fight in the face of overwhelmingly superior force and certain defeat was morally justified. Though defeat seemed certain, it is not clear that Belgian resistance served no military purpose so far as the strategic balance of the war as a whole was concerned. The delayed advance that Belgian resistance caused prevented the realization of Germany's strategic objectives and, arguably, played a key role in the ultimate defeat of Germany. It seems that in this case, though the short-term prospects of success were bleak, to say the least, the long-term prospects might have been regarded as hopeful enough to tip the scales in favour of military resistance. The suspicion remains, however, that military considerations of this kind were not the prime motivation in the Belgian decision to resist. In the end it came down to certain moral values being judged important enough to be defended whatever the cost.[15]

In practice it seems that determining the prospects of success is simply one aspect of the general assessment of a war's worth or proportionality, rather than a limiting criterion that rules out recourse to war whenever the expectations of military success are low enough. In theory, too, the criterion can be seen to yield the moral ground. Even in the extreme case, when military failure or defeat seems certain, just recourse to war is not thereby excluded.[16] There may be a victory of a moral kind to be had that transcends military defeat. A war that is fought to defend fundamental human values can be successful even though it ends, *predictably*, in defeat. The reason for this is that the defence of values is not a material defence. There may be moral goods the defence of which outweighs the certainty of defeat. In such a case war is thought to be worthwhile precisely as a vindication of values – a vindication that does not require victory in a military sense, a vindication that may in fact be more complete the greater the certainty of military defeat. To resist in such circumstances would be to witness to a hierarchy of values in which death is not the greatest evil, while not to resist would be to pay obeisance to death, to avoid which no moral price or surrender of values is thought too high to pay. This idea of war as a form of moral witness, while acceptable in theory, is a dangerous notion in practice, particularly in a nuclear age, when a state that chose to give such witness might end up making martyrs of us all.

It seems, therefore, that in its several aspects the principle of proportionality is marked by ambiguity. Given the uncertainties that the application of the principle consequently entails, caution and moderation in its use seem prudent. Such a restrained use of the principle, however, is far from being the norm. In fact the application of the principle in an exaggerated and uncritical way is commonplace. It seemed much in evidence, for example, among critics of the Gulf War, who chose to employ it in such an inflated and one-sided way as to raise the moral threshold of war beyond the point at which any just recourse to war could remain conceivable.

As with the opposition to the Falklands War, two tactics were employed to convince doubters that the restoration of Kuwaiti independence was not worth a war. In the first place, the negative effects of the war were exaggerated, and the very worst outcome everywhere assumed: the war itself would be an attritional war involving massive casualties on both sides; it would be a total war, in which the death-toll among noncombatants might well exceed that among the military; the ecological damage caused by the firing of oil wells would have long-term effects not only on the ecology of the region but on the global environment; economies, particularly of the poorer states in the Third World, would be devastated by the rise in the price of oil as a result of the war, and mass starvation would ensue. Concomitantly, little was made of the harm being done to the state of Kuwait and to its citizens by the Iraqi occupation, of the threat to regional stability and world peace posed by Iraqi expansion, and by Iraq's development of a nuclear, biological and chemical arsenal, of the flagrant violation of the principle of non-aggression and of the threat to the international rule of law that such a violation posed, and of the damage done to the UN at a decisive moment in its history if no effective action were taken. Secondly, the motives of the American-led coalition were systematically impugned: this was a war about oil, not human rights or the rule of law, a war fought to protect a privileged (and arguably unjust) Western standard of living, not to right a wrong done to a member of the international community; the moral worth of the Kuwaiti state itself (and, by implication, of its sovereignty and independence) was doubtful; the West was Iraq's accomplice by virtue of the military and diplomatic support that it had given to Iraq in the past; the Western powers were morally duplicitous and quite unprincipled in the instances of unjust aggression that they chose to oppose (as distinct from those that they chose to defend); the war was fought to boost the Bush administration's political fortunes and finally dispose of the 'Vietnam syndrome'.[17]

Some of these fears and accusations were not without foundation; but the one-sided way in which proportionality was examined appeared tendentious and designed to tilt the balance against war right from the start. It was difficult to believe that this was a judgement or process of reasoning that was genuinely open to the moral possibility of war (in this or, perhaps, in any other case). Rather, it seemed a way of rationalizing and defending preconceived moral choices arrived at quite independently of any process of proportionate reasoning. A comparison of the negative moral analysis of the Gulf War with the much more sympathetic reception given to the case for a war of intervention in Bosnia strengthens this suspicion: the latter is typically free of the preoccupation with the proportionate *costs* of war; here matters of justice are paramount, and the costs are not even considered, let alone discounted. There seems to be a real danger of proportionality being applied unevenly and selectively, and of the moral analysis simply exaggerating the costs of those wars of which the analyst approves and minimizing the costs of those wars of which he or she disapproves. The application of the principle in this uncritical form would contribute little to the moral analysis of war, and seems likely to do much more harm than good. Proportionality, applied inclusively and evenly, however, is a key element in the moral assessment of war; though, like other moral criteria, it should not be expected to carry the entire weight of the moral argument about war, just as it should not be reduced to any crude calculation of its consequences.

Notes

1 This illustration is not meant to imply that the abortion issue can be settled simply by considerations of proportionality. Some moral theorists would see the line of reasoning described here as excessively 'proportionalist' and virtually indistinguishable from a 'morality of consequences' (the view that the moral status of any act is derived solely from a calculation of its good and bad consequences, a preponderance of good consequences being thought sufficient to justify *any* act). According to such critics (many of whom are active also in the just war field) a *direct* abortion is an intrinsically evil act (morally and not just 'physically') that no calculation of consequences or of proportionality can possibly justify. The direct and intentional killing of the foetus is *always* an attack on a basic human value. The same

is thought to apply to war, in the sense that the direct and intentional killing of the enemy (whether combatant or noncombatant) can never be morally justified. According to Finnis and his co-authors, for example: 'Deadly deeds can be chosen, not with the precise object of killing those who are using force to back their challenge to just order, but to thwart that challenge. If the social act is limited to the use of only that force necessary to accomplish its appropriate purpose, the side-effect of the death of those challenging the society's just order can rightly be accepted' (Finnis *et al.* 1987, pp. 313–14). The moral significance attached to direct–indirect killing in this passage is disputed by 'proportionalists'. For an example of the criticisms levelled at 'moral consequentialism' and 'proportionalism' by 'absolutists' see Finnis *et al.* 1987, and for arguments from both sides see McCormick and Ramsey 1985.

2 From a moral point of view, the cases of abortion and war are similar in some respects, but very different in others. One major difference perhaps is that the concept of an 'unjust aggressor', which is central to the moral assessment of war, is inapplicable in the case of abortion. The foetus is not an 'unjust aggressor', even though its presence in the womb may threaten the life (or some other good) of the mother. This view has been disputed by some: Sanchez, for example, described the foetus as a 'quasi aggressor', while Raynaud regarded it as a 'material unjust aggressor' because, even though without intent, it threatens life (see Keenan 1993, p. 314).

3 Even the 'symbolic' war itself is not a thing of the past. The present dispute between Greece and Macedonia, which has already given rise to a Greek blockade and which has at least threatened war, is ostensibly and precisely a dispute about national symbols, such as the use of the 'Star of Vergina' in the Macedonian flag and the name Macedonia itself, which Greece interprets as a challenge to its authority and a serious threat to its national and political integrity. In the modern age nationalism has proved a fertile ground for such 'symbolic' conflict.

4 This was a development partly foreseen by the American just war theorist Paul Ramsey when, in an address delivered in 1963, he argued that, 'to dismantle the balance of terror would have the effect of making just wars of liberation ... possible again, and on all sides ... Remove these weapons with their terrifying destructive force, and the nations would again be able to imagine, indeed it might become sensible for them to imagine, that war can be invoked for the purpose of repairing injustice' (Ramsey 1983, p. 210).

5 For example, see Finnis *et al.* 1988.

6 As one critic has argued: 'The Falklands War was a classic example of a situation where a formal concern with sovereignty had little to

do with any substantial threat to a way of life worth defending' (Norman 1995, p. 158). Norman's criticism also leans heavily on the assumption that an acceptable diplomatic solution was available, one which would have conceded sovereignty but preserved the interests of the islanders.

7 'What is the evil in war?' St Augustine (1872) asks in *Contra Faustum*. 'Is it the death of some who will soon die in any case, that others may live in peaceful subjection? This is mere cowardly dislike, not any religious feeling' (XXII.74).

8 See, for example, Hegel 1991, p. 360f.

9 In *The Story of a Coin* Primo Levi considers the moral plight of Chaim Rumkowski, the Jewish businessman who accepted the post of President of the Lodz ghetto (the longest-lived of all the Nazi ghettos and the largest after Warsaw with a population of 160,000). His way of defending his people and its values, and of course himself, was the way of collaboration. His story, Levi suggests, 'is the regrettable and disquieting story of the Kapos ... those who shake their heads in denial but consent, those who say "if I didn't do this, somebody worse than I would"' (Levi 1987, p. 171). As Levi argues, in the end it is a question of values and of the strength of moral conviction, 'one needs a very solid moral framework' to resist. Resistance, for any of us, does not come easily: 'Like Rumkowski, we too are so dazzled by power and money as to forget our essential fragility, forget that all of us are in the ghetto, that the ghetto is fenced in, that beyond the fence stand the lords of death, and not far away the train is waiting' (p. 172).

10 Hastings and Jenkins 1983, p. 69. Admiral Woodward, who commanded the task force, recalls 'that there were several entirely competent organizations [he lists the US Navy, the Ministry of Defence, the Army, the Royal Air Force, the Secretary of State for Defence] which initially suspected the whole operation was doomed' (Woodward and Robinson 1992, p. xvii).

11 Cf. Freedman and Gamba-Stonehouse 1990, p. 130.

12 On 5 April, *en route* to Ascension Island, the task force commander called a staff meeting 'to formulate a plan as to precisely what we would do if and when we reached the Falkland Islands'. 'Our meeting', he recalls, 'was conducted in an atmosphere of moderate disbelief, combined with a mounting realization of our very considerable ignorance ... We really knew nothing of detail about the enemy we might be asked to attack, nor of the surroundings in which we might find him ... The fact was we were nowhere near to completing our own picture of what to do if and when battle commenced' (Woodward and Robinson 1992, pp. 78–9).

13 Cf. Freedman and Gamba-Stonehouse 1990, pp. 416–17 and Dillon

1989, p. 173. This has been acknowledged by Admiral Woodward: 'In general terms the British victory would have to be judged anyway as a *fairly* close run thing in matters of timing, land forces and air forces. There was also the inescapable truth that the Argentinian commanders failed inexplicably to realize that if they had hit *Hermes* [the command ship and one of the two carriers accompanying the task force], the British would have been finished. They never really came after the one target that would surely have given them victory. As it was, we fought our way along a knife-edge ... one major mishap, a mine, an explosion, a fire, whatever, in either of our two aircraft carriers, would almost certainly have proved fatal to the whole operation' (Woodward and Robinson 1992, p. xviii). Elsewhere Woodward reveals how, before the commencement of hostilities, it had been agreed 'between Northwood [the overall command centre] and myself that major damage to *Hermes* or to *Invincible* (our vital 'second deck') would probably cause us to abandon the entire Falkland Islands operation' (p. 5). Later he draws attention to the 'crucial mistake' of the Argentine air force, during the British landings in San Carlos Bay, 'of going for our frigates and destroyers, rather than the amphibious ships and troop carriers, which were there for the taking, not to mention the three-thousand-odd men they carried' (pp. 262–3; see also pp. 243–5).

14 It was a view shared by Michael Foot, the Leader of the Opposition, who in a key parliamentary debate sought to stiffen government resolve: 'There is no question in the Falkland Islands of any colonial dependence or anything of the sort. It is a question of people who wish to be associated with this country and who have built their whole lives on the basis of association with this country. We have a moral duty, a political duty and every other kind of duty to ensure that is sustained. The people of the Falklands have the absolute right to look to us at this moment of their desperate plight, just as they have looked to us over the past 150 years' (*House of Commons Parliamentary Debates*, Vol. 21, Col. 638–9, 3 April 1982).

15 Such a calculation formed the basis of a warning delivered by Saddam Hussein to the US Ambassador, April Glaspie, a week before the invasion of Kuwait: 'You can come to Iraq with aircraft and missiles but do not push us to the point where we cease to care. And when we feel that you want to injure our pride and take the Iraqis' chance of a high standard of living, then we will cease to care and death will be the choice for us. Then we would not care if you fired one hundred missiles for each missile we fired. Because without pride, life would have no value' (Bulloch and Morris 1991, p. 11).

16 The US bishops in their Peace Pastoral appear to acknowledge this

in their brief outline of just war criteria. The section on the 'Probability of Success' reads: 'This is a difficult criterion to apply, but its purpose is to prevent irrational resort to force or hopeless resistance when the outcome of either will clearly be disproportionate or futile. *The determination includes a recognition that at times the defence of key values, even against great odds, may be a "proportionate" witness*' (National Conference of US Catholic Bishops 1983, pp. 28–9, added emphasis).

17 See for example McMahan and McKim 1993. These authors also argue that it was not just critics of the war who feared the worst. The decisionmakers themselves expected things to turn out much worse than they did but this did not prevent them from going ahead. Hence the conclusion that 'when viewed from the point of view of its planners prior to its initiation, the Gulf War violated proportionality' (McMahan and McKim 1993, p. 523).

8

Last resort

The criterion of last resort underlines the primacy of peace over war in just war thinking. Recognition of the potential moral instrumentality of war is not to be confused with moral enthusiasm for war. There are those for whom war, far from being a regrettable necessity, is in fact the preferred option, either because the prospects of material and political gain are greater in war or because war itself is seen to exercise a compelling attraction and to possess a unique and intrinsic value.[1] For those who regard it in this way war is more a matter of *first* than of last resort.

Such ready acceptance of war is foreign to the just war approach. Given the horrors of war, moral as well as physical, a just recourse to war should be marked by extreme reluctance and a sense of moral tragedy and foreboding. A hasty recourse to war is an unjust recourse to war. The move to war is to be justified only when all other means short of war have been exhausted. What the criterion of last resort entails above all is a genuine and serious commitment to the process of peacemaking, a process that should be conducted, where circumstances and considerations of justice permit, in a spirit of compromise and reconciliation, and never in one of intransigence, provocation and escalation.

It may be, of course, that, in a given situation, the process of peacemaking is not well served by acts of accommodation. The obligation to pursue peace refers not simply to the choice of ends, but to the discerning use of means. Here as elsewhere, moral considerations go hand in hand with political and military ones, and the moral judgement needs to be informed by a certain realism. Deciding when diplomatic and other non-bellicose means of securing peace have been *effectively* exhausted, or deciding when a conciliatory approach has become counterproductive, is largely a matter of political and military judgement.

It is clear that last resort must not be understood too literally. To cling too fast and too rigidly to the idea may be to do peace – the ultimate aim in just war theory – a disservice. Many have argued, for example, that Britain's policy of 'appeasement' during the 1930s did much more to undermine than it did to secure peace. By adopting such a policy the prospects for peace were damaged irreparably, and by attempting to avoid war at all costs Britain simply encouraged German aggression. In the words of the fiercest and most consistent of such critics: 'conditions were swiftly created by the victorious Allies which, in the name of peace, cleared the way for the renewal of war' (Churchill 1985, Vol. I, p. 13). In Churchill's view, events between the wars demonstrate 'how easily the tragedy of the Second World War could have been prevented, [if] the malice of the wicked [had not been] reinforced by the weakness of the virtuous' (p. 16). The cause of peace would have been better served if Britain and its allies had adopted a more bellicose posture and resisted German aggression much earlier. Then, by risking a little war, a great war might have been avoided. As it was the resort to arms, or at least the clear and unambiguous threat of such resort, was delayed too long.

It is perhaps a criticism that, in this particular case, owes too much to hindsight. In the light of subsequent German aggression, and the horrors that followed in its wake, a preventive war on the occasion of German rearmament or of the remilitarization of the Rhineland seems entirely justified. However, at the time, military action by Britain could well have been portrayed as an aggressive and escalatory act rather than as a form of peace-keeping. The British foreign secretary, Anthony Eden, suggested as much when he informed the Cabinet that a military response to the occupation of the Rhineland would be 'out of proportion to what Germany has done' (Lamb 1989, p. 179).

Ignorant of what lay ahead, many found the idea of a preventive war less than compelling. Halifax, for example, argued against 'any course of action that might plunge Europe into war now to avert what might be a war later on' (quoted in Taylor

1979, p. 981). Such reluctance was widely felt; and it is understandable in view of that society's recent past. Even if the government had been convinced of the need to oppose Hitler earlier rather than later, it is doubtful whether the British public, or even the French, could have been persuaded of the virtues of such a policy. Memories of the First World War were still too fresh and too painful to permit a course of action that might lead to an even worse conflagration[2] in response to something about which people had mixed feelings anyway. One of Baldwin's advisers, Thomas Jones, appears to have expressed the prevailing sentiment about the Rhineland occupation, when he informed the prime minister that, 'England would not dream of going to war because German troops had marched into their own territories' (Lamb 1989, p. 173). Sympathy for Germany was not inconsiderable, not least in Britain. Many regarded the terms of the Versailles Treaty as unjust or too harsh, and blamed the French for creating unnecessary tensions. It was only when the true nature of the Nazi state and the real threat that it posed came into clear view that the need for a military response was reluctantly conceded.

If Britain had gone to war over either issue it is not clear that the moral judgement of that action at the time would have been, or perhaps even ought to have been, a favourable one. But critics, like Churchill, have argued that the risks of war were minimal, if firm action had been taken from the start. Prior to German rearmament (and British disarmament) the military imbalance meant that the risk of war was non-existent; and even later, in March 1936 or in September 1938, a German climbdown would have been the likely result of Allied firmness. Some of these judgements, though made by Churchill at the time, appear conclusive only in the light of information that was not then available. It is a point that Churchill himself seems to concede. Of events in the Rhineland, for example, he wrote: 'We *now* know of the conflicts of opinion which arose at the time between Hitler and the German High Command. If the French Government had mobilised the French Army... *there is no doubt* that Hitler would have been compelled by his own General Staff to withdraw, and a check would have been given to his pretensions which might well have proved fatal to his rule' (Churchill 1985,

Vol. I, p. 175, added emphasis). Of course subsequent disclosures and events lend enormous weight to Churchill's arguments; but at the time they must have seemed much less convincing, and even to some a form of warmongering.

Whether the specific criticism is justified or not, the concept of appeasement is instructive so far as the criterion of last resort is concerned: interpret that criterion too literally, and the cause of peace, which the criterion is intended to promote, can be gravely impaired. Churchill's indictment of British foreign policy between the wars brings to mind the classical dictum: 'If you seek peace, prepare for war,' As a hard and fast rule its validity must be in serious doubt; but in certain situations its relevance can become acute. Churchill himself favoured such a pragmatic approach: 'no case of this kind can be judged apart from its circumstances'. While the earlier threat or use of force would have been the sounder and more pacific policy in respect of Germany, in different circumstances a more conciliatory approach might be the more practical, and therefore the more moral, option. 'How many wars', he wrote, 'have been precipitated by firebrands! How many misunderstandings which led to wars could have been removed by temporising!' (Churchill 1985, Vol. I, p. 287).

In the case of the Gulf War the most frequently voiced criticism was not that of appeasement, but that of the precipitate use of force, even though the occasion of war in this case, the invasion and pillaging of a sovereign state, was a much clearer and more serious violation of international law and morality than the occupation of the Rhineland. Many have argued that this particular resort to arms violated the principle of last resort.

The main political focus of such opposition at the time was the US Congress and, in particular, the Senate Armed Services Committee, chaired by Senator Nunn, and the Senate Foreign Relations Committee. That opposition reached a new intensity with President Bush's announcement in November 1990 of an 'offensive military option', involving the doubling of US forces committed to the Gulf from approximately 200,000 to 400,000. It was sustained right up to the last moment. In the congressional debate on war authorization, a few days before the initiation of military operations, Senator Nunn and others 'urged President Bush to give economic sanctions more time to work to force Iraq from Kuwait peacefully' (*The Times*, 14 January 1991, p. 9). In the end the Senate approved the war authority by a margin of five votes, the narrowest war vote in the Senate's history.[3]

Among those appearing before the Senate Foreign Relations Committee in early December was Archbishop Roach, who, as its chairman, presented testimony on behalf of the United States Catholic Conference International Policy Committee. Archbishop Roach began by invoking the just war tradition and by drawing the Committee's attention to 'the moral imperative of persistent pursuit of non-violent international pressure to halt and reverse Iraq's aggression without resort to war' (Johnson and Weigel 1991, p. 119). The principle of last resort, he went on to argue, was particularly relevant to the case before the Committee. Its purpose was 'to insist that a nation must fully and faithfully pursue (not just try, but fully pursue) all reasonable political, diplomatic and economic means to resist aggression, vindicate rights and secure justice' (p.125). The Archbishop noted the view of experts (like the former National Security Advisor Zbigniew Brzezinski, the former Defense Secretary James Schlesinger, and former chairmen of the joint chiefs of staff Admiral William Crowe and David Jones) 'that non-military options should be given a much longer time to work', and he came to the following conclusion:

> The ethical restraint on war requires a nation to try all means short of war. The embargo needs time to work. If appropriate time is not allowed for it to work, it is not accurate to say it has been tried and failed. Last resort requires that the embargo not be dismissed before it has had the time needed to achieve the legitimate objectives for which it was designed. Before war can be justified, all peaceful means must be fully pursued. Thus far, I do not believe the principle of last resort has been met. (p. 126)

This was a criticism of the war that survived its cessation, a criticism that was sustained even though many of the anticipated horrors of war had not been realized. This is, of course, as it should be: if the war really did constitute a violation of 'last resort', it would remain so despite its 'successful' outcome. There was after all nothing 'phoney' about the Gulf War, and the suffering that it inflicted, while perhaps less than anticipated, was

still very considerable. To have caused such suffering unneces-
sarily would have been to commit an injustice of the most
extreme kind. In June 1991, in an article entitled 'An Infamous
Victory', Gordon Zahn argued along these lines:

> It is the failure – actually the *refusal!* – of President Bush and his
> advisors to give priority to seeking other solutions short of war
> that should be enough to clinch the case against the Gulf War.
> The unwillingness to allow a reasonable time for international
> sanctions already in place *and having effect* to succeed, coupled
> with the adamant refusal to even consider negotiations or sup-
> port the efforts of coalition partners seeking a diplomatic solution,
> constitutes an explicit violation of the requirement that war be a
> last resort, that all other means must have been tried and failed.
> (Zahn 1991, p. 367)

In Zahn's view 'presidential intransigence and impatience'
resulted in 'the rush to war'.[4]

What is to be made of such criticism? To begin with, its prove-
nance might be questioned. Though a writer like Zahn employs
all the relevant criteria, his 'just war' criticism of the Gulf War is
most unconvincing since, on his own admission, he employs the
theory wholly without conviction and as a way of disproving the
theory itself: 'Though I do not accept the validity of the "just-
war" tradition as a source of Christian moral guidance, I feel
obliged to play the rhetorical game ... *it is a game*. Were the conditions of the "just war" ever honestly applied to an actual war,
they would lead to behavioral conclusions identical to those
required by the pacifism to which I personally subscribe' (Zahn
1991, p. 366). Clearly it is impossible to rest the principle of last
resort on a pacifist premiss. The principle is only engaged in the
first place on the assumption that a legitimate resort to war is
conceivable. For the pacifist it is impossible ever to arrive at a
point of last resort, that is, at a point at which the use of force
can seem not just morally permissible but even morally obligatory. Yet Zahn's approach is not uncommon. It seems that for
many critics of the war the charge of precipitate force was simply
a smokescreen that concealed a more fundamental moral objection either to war in general or to this particular war on other
grounds. For critics of this ilk it is difficult to see how the point

of last resort could ever have been reached: the criterion was being used simply as a way of postponing war indefinitely.[5]

Secondly, it is questionable whether the principle of last resort should even be applied to the *coalition's* use of force. Winters, for example, has argued that the criterion articulates 'an obligation on the party who *initiates* war', and that it does not apply, strictly speaking, to situations like that which confronted the coalition, where an act of aggressive war had already been perpetrated: 'Once Kuwait was invaded by Saddam Hussein in violation of the criterion of last resort, just-war theory accorded an *immediate* right of armed resistance to Kuwait and whatever allies it could speedily gather' (Winters 1991, p. 221). Michael Walzer appears to arrive at a similar conclusion: 'the doctrine of last resort doesn't seem to play any important role here' (Walzer 1992, p. xiv). It is only because of the unavoidable lapse of time between the initial hostile act and the defensive response that last resort *seems* to apply.[6]

It is evident that psychologically at least the lapse of time can become very significant in such cases. It has the effect of turning a defensive act into an offensive, or even an aggressive, one in the minds of many. As time passes it begins to seem as if the injured party is the initiator of hostilities and the disturber of the peace. What is progressively ignored is the fact that a state of war *already* exists. This psychological transformation can have a distorting effect on the moral judgement.

But what is the real moral significance of the time-lapse? Technically, it seems that Winter has a point: the criterion of last resort applies to the initiation of hostilities rather than to the defensive reply or reaction. A version of last resort remains applicable, however, to a case like this, in which an immediate and effective response is not possible. The interval may provide an opportunity to end the war without the resumption of hostilities, and it would seem that there is a moral obligation on the injured party to make the best possible use of that opportunity, though without prejudice to considerations of justice. Did the leaders of the coalition fulfil that obligation?

Two methods were employed (in addition to the threat of force) in an attempt to bring about a non-military resolution of the conflict: economic sanctions and diplomacy. The efficacy of a trade embargo as a means of resolving international conflict is much disputed. Scepticism is rife, and appears to have been justified in this case. This is not to say that sanctions served no purpose or that they played little part in the termination of the conflict. Among other things they helped to sustain the international coalition at a time when a more effective response was not feasible and, politically and psychologically, they prepared the ground for later military action. What they seemed incapable of achieving on their own and without resort to war was the withdrawal of Iraq from Kuwait.

It has often been observed that the imposition of sanctions as a means of lowering enemy morale and the will to resist is counterproductive, and that the effects of such a policy are to stiffen the resolve of the state on which they are imposed. Though this may not always be the case, there were good reasons for thinking that it was in the case of Iraq. Far from weakening Saddam's position, sanctions gave the regime an alibi: the economic plight of Iraq, grave at the best of times, could now be laid at the door of the UN. Even if the Iraqi people did pin the blame for economic distress on their own government, in an autocratic and repressive state like Iraq the opportunity to bring public opinion and pressure to bear was severely limited.

Moreover, the impact of sanctions was diminished, at least in the short term, by a number of factors. Firstly, although with the passing of UN Resolution 665 on 25 August a naval blockade of Iraq was set in place, the coalition remained unable or unwilling to interdict supplies by land, and it seemed likely that the problem of enforcement would grow rather than diminish with the passage of time. Secondly, the invasion of Kuwait itself helped to make up the shortfall in resources. Thirdly, the readiness of the government to ignore the needs of large sections of the Iraqi population (the Kurds and the Marsh Arabs, for instance) increased its ability to withstand the effects of sanctions. Fourthly, after an eight-year war with Iran, Iraq was well accustomed to the rigours of a siege economy. Finally, the effect of sanctions on Iraq's military capability would become significant only *after* the commencement of hostilities.

The subsequent record of the embargo against Iraq suggests that trade sanctions have a limited impact on Iraqi decision-making. In the postwar period Iraqi compliance with UN resolutions has been less than complete, despite the continued embargo. Even in the longer term, therefore, sanctions would have been unlikely to force an Iraqi withdrawal from Kuwait, and what would have happened in the meantime to Kuwait and to the Kuwaitis, who throughout the period of occupation were subjected to a rule of terror? Time would have been on the side of Iraq: the longer its occupation of Kuwait the more likely international acquiescence. As with the Chinese takeover of Tibet, the process of assimilation would have been strengthened by delay, with the international community turning its attention to other and more pressing problems.

Above all, a sanctions campaign that forestalled military action beyond the point of military preparedness would have undermined the military option altogether through the erosion of coalition unity, public support and troop efficiency and morale. It seems clear that many intended sanctions to have this result (and therefore were not employing sanctions with a view to exhausting non-military means prior to the possible use of military force). This intention was based either on a principled and general opposition to the use of war as a means of resolving *any* conflict, or on the narrower judgement that, even if sanctions failed, it was not worth going to war over Kuwait (as in the opinion of Senator Moynihan, who described the conflict as 'a small disturbance in a distant part of the world', big enough perhaps to warrant sanctions but too small to justify war). In effect, and in some cases in intent, to argue that 'sanctions should be given more time to work' was to rule out any future use of military means. As Henry Kissinger argued, in testimony before the Senate Armed Services Committee: 'By the time it became obvious that sanctions alone cannot succeed, a credible military option probably would no longer exist' (*The Times*, 30 November 1990, p. 13).

In relation to the criterion of last resort the instrumental power of sanctions is a major concern, since what the principle enjoins is the exhaustion of *effective* alternatives to war. The obligation to employ sanctions or other non-military methods is conditional upon their efficacy. The moral problem of sanctions, however, does not turn exclusively on the question of their efficacy. In fact, it may be that the moral difficulties increase with attempts to make sanctions more effective.

The criticism that the use of military force by the coalition violated the criterion of last resort relies for much of its persuasive force on an assumed moral superiority of sanctions or blockade over war. In part this assumption rests on considerations of proportionality: it is taken for granted that the damage inflicted in war will be much greater than that which results from a blockade. In addition, a blockade is seen as a less violent, and therefore less tainted, means of redress than war, since it does not involve direct killing. Neither view is necessarily well founded. In the first place, the overall harm inflicted by a prolonged and effective blockade might well exceed the suffering inflicted by a much shorter war. Secondly, though the blockade is not a form of direct killing, it would be misleading to describe the deaths that may result from it as unintended, since there is a very clear (and intended) causal connection between the act itself and its potentially lethal consequences.

The moral superiority of sanctions is open to further question if we consider the issue of discrimination. Given the insensitivity of the Iraqi regime to the suffering of its own people and its probable channelling of scarce supplies to its own supporters and to military personnel, the harm done to the *civilian* population might well exceed that inflicted by war. In this respect a blockade may constitute a grosser violation of morality than war itself, involving as it does a systematic attack on the civilian or noncombatant sections of the community. It has often been interpreted as such. Britain's use of a naval blockade against Germany in the First World War was seen by the Germans themselves not just as an act of war but as a violation of the laws of war and as a justification for their own indiscriminate use of submarine warfare.[7] In some important respects there seems little to choose between the blockade and strategic bombing, to which historically it is related:[8] both prefer an attack on the sources of supply and civilian morale to an engagement with enemy forces, and both are for that very reason morally problematic.

Finally, the relative moral ascendancy of an embargo seems shaky because of the unilateral nature of the suffering that it inflicts. Those who resort to its exclusive use are not subject to the same discipline and hazards, and, therefore, are not required to exhibit the same virtue as those who in the pursuit of a just cause are prepared to accept as well as to inflict suffering. The self-sacrificial aspect of war, which even its pacifist opponents are ready to acknowledge and even to admire, is altogether absent here.

The assumed moral superiority of sanctions seems, therefore, at least in doubt. It may be that, by virtue of its greater proportionality and discrimination, war is a morally preferable option to an embargo that is rigorously and comprehensively enforced. Steps can, of course, be taken to redress any imbalance and to ensure non-violation of these principles, like the exclusions made to the Iraqi embargo of medicines and humanitarian food supplies. The problem is that the more effective these remedial measures (and therefore the more morally acceptable the embargo), the less likely it is to attain its overall objective.

But what about the diplomatic process with which the policy of sanctions needed to be linked? Would sanctions have been more effective if combined with a more flexible and imaginative diplomacy? Some diehard critics have argued that when military action against Iraq was taken, war was still avoidable, since there remained a real prospect of achieving the aims of war through the employment of more peaceful means. Others have accepted that at the time action was taken in January alternative means of resolving the crisis no longer existed. They have gone on to argue, however, that this situation was of the UN's own making; in other words, that the coalition, by its earlier failure to explore alternative and more creative ways of resolving the conflict, had painted itself into a corner. The point of last resort *had* been reached, but it had been reached because of a failure of peacemaking and a lack of political and moral imagination and will shown by the leaders of the UN coalition. If, at the time of the coalition's commencement of hostilities, there was nothing to suggest that an Iraqi withdrawal from Kuwait was forthcoming, this was as much a measure of coalition neglect, incompetence and obduracy as it was of Iraqi intransigence. Not enough had been done to tempt Iraq down the path of peaceful resolution.

The broad lines of such an analysis and criticism seem clear. Right from the beginning the leadership of the coalition committed itself to military intervention, and the first steps that it took ensured that, in the absence of an Iraqi withdrawal, the logic of war would ultimately prevail. Within two weeks of the invasion of Kuwait President Bush had directed 'the biggest and fastest American military build-up since Korea' ('Make My Day', *Sunday Times*, 19 August 1990, p. 9), and it was being reported that, 'The only thing holding the Americans back from war is getting enough troops into Saudi Arabia' (p. 1). A visitor to the National Military Command Centre in Washington in mid-August was struck by the enthusiasm for war displayed by the military planners: 'The fervour of a crusade grips the war rooms. ... There is talk of "waxing" (killing) Saddam, of "trashing" (destroying) Iraq, of "making the rubble bounce" (carpet bombing Iraq)' (p. 2).

Iraqi intransigence and extremism were assumed and emphasized, some might even say encouraged, from the start. Mrs Thatcher, whose influence in the crucial early days of the crisis often seemed decisive, dismissed the prospects of a negotiated settlement. To think in those terms was wholly to misunderstand the Iraqi leadership, and in particular the evil that was Saddam Hussein: 'There will be no negotiations with a man who takes over, by force, someone else's country except that he gets out completely. You are dealing with a dictator who is an absolute tyrant... [and] who has not hesitated to use chemical weapons against innocent people. This man is a despot and a tyrant and must be stopped' (*The Times*, 27 August 1990, p. 2). Both Mrs Thatcher and President Bush were quick to draw a parallel with Hitler. This time, they insisted, there must be no appeasement.

More was seen to be at stake than the restoration of Kuwaiti sovereignty. The threat that Iraq posed was said to reach far beyond Kuwait and to be one that needed to be dealt with now rather than later. The coincidence of the invasion of Kuwait with the ending of the Cold War provided the international community and particularly the UN with a historic opportunity that it would be imprudent and irresponsible to ignore. The possibility now existed for a broader intervention, aimed at securing a more lasting settlement in the region, as well as establishing new ground rules for the international order as a whole.

This early revision and expansion of the coalition's war aims meant that a negotiated and minimalist settlement, which secured Iraqi withdrawal from Kuwait but left Saddam Hussein in power (with his chemical, biological and, imminently, nuclear, as well as his conventional military, arsenal intact), came to be regarded as something more to be feared than desired. In such circumstances, sanctions and diplomacy were pursued not as more peaceful alternatives to war, but as preparations for war. Politically as well as militarily an immediate resort to war, at least with the backing of the UN and with the widespread participation of other, particularly Arab, states, was infeasible. First, other means must be shown to have been tried and to have failed. Other means *were* explored but, throughout, the presumption, and indeed the hope, was that they would fail.

What would a more imaginative and active, and perhaps more morally acceptable, diplomacy have involved? It would have been based on different assumptions and would have begun, less antagonistically and more sympathetically, with a contextual understanding of the conflict, historical as well as political and strategic, an understanding that took account, for example, both of the arbitrary way in which a colonial power had defined the existing political boundaries and of the interminable border disputes that had ensued. Instead of treating the invasion as a manifestation of Saddam Hussein's megalomania, it would have analysed it in a more rational and instrumental way, seeing it at least in part as a response to Iraq's grave economic problems and the regime's political instability and weakness, as an attempt to reduce Iraq's indebtedness, to resolve territorial and resource disputes with Kuwait, and to secure protected access to the Gulf.

A more moral diplomacy would have been conducted in a less self-righteous and more self-critical spirit, acknowledging the vagaries and inconsistencies of Western foreign policies (including the arming and support of Iraq in its war with Iran, and the toleration of Israeli occupation of Gaza and the West Bank), the mixed signals that those policies sent to Iraq, and the suspicion and widespread mistrust of Western 'imperialism' (particularly when masquerading as the guardian of a new world order) that they bred. It would have been a diplomacy conducted not in the idiom of moral absolutes but of comparative or bilateral justice, eschewing both the demonization of Saddam Hussein and the adoption of an openly bellicose or militaristic posture. In such a diplomacy the attempt would have been made to defuse the situation, and certainly to avoid any deliberate raising of the stakes, either ideologically (for example, by transforming the specific conflict into a 'cultural' war in which the forces of civilization were ranged against the forces of barbarism) or practically (as by an early and massive deployment of troops). Rather than trying to isolate Iraq, attempts would have been made to draw her back into the international community. Recognizing that the invasion might have been the result of a grave miscalculation of the probable consequences of her action, ways would have been sought of enabling Iraq to extricate herself from the impasse without too much loss of face.

The more pacific appearance and intent of such a diplomacy are evident; but would it have been well founded, or would its lack of realism have undermined its moral pretensions and peacemaking potential?

To begin with, how appropriate in this instance was the standpoint of 'comparative' or 'bilateral' justice? It seems clear that the more blurred the moral contours of the dispute, the less acceptable its military resolution. Though justice is rarely, if ever, unilateral, a just recourse to war is more likely the more unevenly justice is distributed, or the more the imbalance of justice favours one side rather than the other. Morally speaking, therefore, was justice so well balanced in this case as to rule out the military option?

Much depended on how the nature of the Iraqi regime, its actions, and its present and future intentions were assessed. Western ineptitude or worse may have contributed to the conflict, and may have helped to explain it, but did not excuse it. Even if Iraq's aims were thought to be specific and limited and not entirely without justification, they were not sufficient cause for war. Moreover, how modest were Iraqi objectives? The specific grievances that were presented as the cause of the invasion appeared to conceal more ambitious and imperial aims, while the assumption that Iraq had somehow stumbled into Kuwait and was willing to be extricated, given sufficient political or diplomatic imagination, was belied by the speed with which the annexation of Kuwait was announced. Similarly, the harsh treatment meted out to the inhabitants of Kuwait suggested little willingness to compromise and no desire for reconciliation, and was of a piece with the Iraqi government's treatment of its own ethnic minorities. The behaviour of the occupying force suggested that it was engaged more in a war of conquest and annihilation than in a limited war fought for specific aims.

The notion that the regime was deeply committed to further expansion in the region as a whole seems neither far-fetched nor the invention of a coalition leadership intent upon war. There was good reason to believe that the conquest of Kuwait marked the beginning and not the end of Iraqi aggression, and that the Iraqi leadership was quite prepared to risk war in pursuit of its wider ambitions. The threat that the Iraqi invasion and annexation of a sovereign state posed to the region as well as to the international community as a whole was real enough, and it was one that was likely to increase with the passage of time. The seriousness with which it was viewed was borne out by its almost universal condemnation. If this had been a case simply of Western or American hyperbole and special pleading, why was the United States able to marshal such widespread support, among its traditional enemies or critics as well as among its friends? In short, this may have been one of those, perhaps rare, occasions when the standpoint of comparative or bilateral justice does more to distort or undermine moral judgement than it does to guide it.

If this is so, then the moral preference for a negotiated settlement is by no means clear. In fact the opposite preference seems to apply: there should be no negotiations, since to negotiate with the unjust aggressor is to become a party to his crime. The moral bar on negotiations rests also on consequentialist grounds: to negotiate and thereby to reward aggression is to invite further acts of aggression by the state in question, as well as by its imitators. In this way international law and order are progressively undermined.

It will perhaps be argued that negotiations have this moral significance only if they comprise substantial concessions or rewards. The analogy might be drawn with the treatment of terrorists in situations in which the terrorists, along with their hostages, have been besieged by the civil police. Here, in the interests of preserving life, the use of force is retained only as a last resort. A concerted attempt is made to avoid any immediate escalation and to take steps to defuse the situation. A line of communication is established with the terrorists, and a 'negotiator' is appointed in an attempt to build a relationship of trust with the terrorists. Firmness in the face of the terrorists' 'political' demands is combined with flexibility over relatively minor and more immediate issues. Steps can be taken, for example, to improve the physical conditions of the besieged. Given time, and with much patience and forbearance on the part of the authorities, a peaceful conclusion to the incident can be achieved without making any concessions to the original demands of the terrorist. Here conflict has been resolved through a process of negotiation that does not reward the aggressor. Such a limited form of negotiation remains a morally preferable option even in the case of an unjust aggressor. Was a negotiated settlement of an equivalent kind available in the Gulf conflict in the months prior to the coalition offensive?

The evidence suggests that it was not. Diplomatic initiatives of this kind were made, and met with no positive response. The United States, perhaps the least accommodating of the members of the coalition, was prepared to make important and arguably unjustified concessions, indicating that Iraq would not be attacked if it complied with Resolution 660 by withdrawing from Kuwait, and that a withdrawal could be followed by negotiations regarding the dispute with Kuwait and by a conference to discuss the problems of the region as a whole, with particular emphasis on the Palestinian question. The UN Secretary-General, Perez de Cuellar, visited Baghdad a few days before the 15 January deadline in a last-ditch attempt at a peaceful resolution. According to informed sources the peace plan he took with him envisaged an Iraqi withdrawal monitored by UN observers and backed by an international guarantee of no attack, the replacement of US forces in the Gulf by a UN peacekeeping force, and an early convening of a Middle East conference with a resolution of the Palestinian problem high on the agenda. The plan was rejected. Commenting on the failure of his talks with Saddam Hussein, he said: 'You need two for tango. I wanted to dance but I didn't find any nice lady for dancing with.'

Iraq's own 'peace plan' linked the solution of the Kuwaiti crisis with the *prior* resolution of all other regional problems. In a tele-vized interview in mid-December Saddam Hussein stated that, 'Any Iraqi concession on Kuwait is out of the question before the Palestinian problem is solved' (*The Times*, 19 December 1990). This was less a serious negotiating position than an attempt to divide the coalition and stall any military action. It is difficult to avoid the conclusion that Iraq was simply not interested in a negotiated withdrawal from Kuwait. As an Iraqi spokesman and aide of Saddam Hussein expressed it on the day that the deadline expired: 'We are not looking for initiatives. ... Will you pull out of your own home or California? Kuwait is our own territory, our own province' (*The Times*, 16 January 1991, p. 1).

It seems likely, therefore, that a negotiated settlement (and cer-tainly one that did not involve major concessions or rewards[9]) was never really feasible. However, the pursuit of this chimera was not without effect, though it may have been the opposite effect to the one intended. Throughout the crisis two contrasting diplomatic strategies could be seen at work: one, the strategy of Russia, France and other EC states, which sought to build bridges with Iraq and to find some face-saving formula that would facili-tate Iraqi withdrawal; the other, the preferred strategy of the US and of Britain, which sought to impress upon Iraq that, if she chose not to withdraw unconditionally, force would be used against her. Arguably, both strategies had as their common aim the avoidance of war; but the means they employed in its pursuit were very different, and often seemed to work against each other.

The 'non-conciliators' (or, as they would prefer to describe themselves, 'non-appeasers') argued that the overtly pacific approach misread the situation and encouraged Iraqi intransi-gence by fuelling expectations either that force would never be used at all or that, if it were, it would not be used with sufficient intensity and persistence to deliver a crushing blow. The result-ing damage done to peace by 'active' or 'bridge-building' diplo-macy was not confined to its direct impact on Iraqi perceptions and consequent Iraqi intransigence. Of equal and obviously related importance was its effect on public opinion in the West-ern democracies. By openly advocating a policy of conciliation, political leaders risked undermining public support for the mili-tary option. Open and enthusiastic support for 'linkage' with the

Palestinian problem reinforced this tendency, implying a stand-point of comparative justice, with its emphasis on shared respon-sibilities and moral complexities. By helping to convince Saddam Hussein that the Western democracies had no stomach for war the 'peacemakers' made the occurrence of war more rather than less likely. In this respect 'active' diplomacy, however well inten-tioned, was seen to be hugely counterproductive.

Similar considerations applied to the management of the coali-tion itself. For the Americans and the British the diplomatic manoeuvring had as its principal objective the building and sus-taining of as wide a coalition as possible, and one which, at the end of the day, would be prepared for military action against Iraq. The pursuit of such an objective lent itself to the accentua-tion of differences and threats rather than to the search for common ground associated with a more conciliatory approach. The diplomatic isolation of Iraq was an essential prelude to war, or at least to making the threat of war credible. And making the threat of war credible was thought to be the only way of per-suading Iraq to evacuate Kuwait *without* a war.

In the view of the more 'hawkish' of the coalition leaders, the process of 'active' diplomacy was bound to be fruitless, because, far from giving Saddam Hussein an incentive to comply with UN resolutions, it gave him every incentive *not* to comply. The more protracted the process the less likely it became that Iraq would be forced to quit Kuwait. In time the coalition would begin to unravel, American and other domestic support for the war would crumble, coalition forces would lose their military efficiency, Iraqi defences would be strengthened, the structure of the Kuwaiti state would be transformed, the interest of the international com-munity would wane, and Iraq would be left to enjoy its ill-gotten gains. In effect, if not in intention, 'active' diplomacy was a form of appeasement.

The criticism that the Gulf War was premature or even unnec-essary appears to exaggerate the efficacy of sanctions and of diplomacy and to underestimate the costs of further delay. How-ever, at the end of the day, much depends on political and mili-tary judgements, which by their nature are uncertain, inexact and, therefore, highly contestable. Nowhere perhaps is the inter-locking of moral with political and military reasoning that characterizes just war theory as a whole more evident than in the case of the criterion of last resort. Whether or not that criterion is adjudged to have been met in the case of the Gulf War depends as much on how the military and political facts of the case are assessed as it does on more purely moral considerations. It is this more than anything that accounts for the diverse moral judgements that are encountered here as elsewhere.

Notes

1 See Chapter 2.
2 Levine has argued that throughout this period: 'The attitudes of the people at large, and their political leaders, were affected by an almost paralyzing fear of another war. In 1924, even Churchill remarked that in another war civilization would perish. This was a common view in the 1920s and 1930s, preserved for posterity in William Cameron Menzies's remarkable movie *Things to Come*. There was no need for nuclear weapons to render war "unthinkable" – that idea was already widespread in the period between the world wars. The general public, as did air power enthusiasts [like the Italian strategist Douhet], believed that in another great war cities would be obliterated by an avalanche of high explosives and poison gas' (Levine 1992, p. 6).
3 In contrast the House of Commons debate on the use of the military option resulted in a voting majority of 477 in favour of the government. Dissenting voices, however, were to be heard. More than fifty Labour MPs, including prominent frontbenchers, voted against the early use of force and, while supporting the government, the Labour leadership expressed the hope that force would not be used before sanctions and blockade had been given the maximum time to take effect. Elder statesmen and former government ministers, like Denis Healey, Michael Foot and Tony Benn, were more outspoken in their opposition. The former prime minister, Edward Heath, urged continued reliance on sanctions ('all the indications are that they are bound to be effective'), and deplored the willingness to use force: 'What is unforgivable is to say that we must go to war because we are impatient' (*House of Commons Parliamentary Debates*, Vol. 183, Col. 754–5, 15 January 1991).
4 McMahan and McKim share a similar view: 'The Gulf War was unjust primarily because it was unnecessary ... The US chose war rather than sanctions because there were several aims that it sought to achieve in addition to the just aims – aims that only war, and not sanctions, could achieve' (McMahan and McKim 1993, p. 540).
5 On this point Margaret Thatcher has observed: 'There is never any

lack of people anxious to avoid the use of force. No matter how little chance there is of negotiations succeeding – and no matter how many difficulties are created for the troops who are trying to prepare themselves for war – the case is always made for yet another piece of last-ditch diplomacy' (Thatcher 1993, p. 826).

6   Compare Winters' and Walzer's assessments with that of the pacifist Gordon Zahn: 'It mocks logic to claim that tens of thousands of bombing sorties over Baghdad and a full-scale crossing of the Saudi/Iraqi border was "defensive"' (Zahn 1991, p. 366). Zahn's judgement appears to confuse the question of whether the response was defensive or aggressive with the question of whether it was proportionate.

7   According to Walzer, 'Statistical studies carried out after the war indicate that some half million civilian deaths, directly attributable to diseases such as influenza and typhus, in fact resulted from the deprivations imposed by the British blockade' (Walzer 1992, p. 173). A similar assessment of the devastating effects of sanctions in the case of Iraq was made by Tam Dalyell, the Labour MP and an outspoken opponent of the use of force. However, more than two years after their imposition, Dalyell concluded that, 'Far from undermining Saddam Hussein sanctions have solidified support for him' (*The Times*, 24 December 1993). A study carried out on behalf of the UN Food and Agriculture Organization calculated that the sanctions policy against Iraq had been responsible for the deaths of more than 560,000 Iraqi children (*The Times*, 1 December 1995).

8   Cf. Frankland (1965), pp. 21f. According to Frankland, 'strategic bombing was in essence naval blockade writ new' (p. 26).

9   Even proposals that envisaged very substantial concessions or rewards appeared incapable of moving Iraq. On 14 October an Iraqi statement was released denying a Soviet report that Iraq would be ready to withdraw from Kuwait in return for the disputed oilfields and islands.

9

Proportionality
and the conduct of war

In the just war tradition the specific requirements of just conduct are those of proportionality and noncombatant immunity. The criterion of proportionality, first encountered in respect of just recourse, resurfaces in relation to just conduct. Here the issue is not the justification of the war as a whole and in prospect, but the justification of the specific ways in which it is prosecuted. What is involved here is the proportionality of means rather than ends. Economy or restraint is the basic imperative, and combatants are required to employ only as much force as is necessary to achieve legitimate military objectives and as is proportionate to the importance of those targets. In other words, the use of force and the consequent infliction of suffering must be neither gratuitous nor excessive.

Here as elsewhere, the just war tradition expects moral analysis to be informed by an empathic awareness of military and political realities. In applying the criterion of proportionality, therefore, military objectives are to be understood strategically and not just tactically. Though in isolation from the context of the war as a whole a particular use of force may well appear cruel and excessive, it may still be judged proportionate and therefore morally justifiable in relation to the overall objective of destroying the military capacity of the enemy and winning the war. An incident from the Falklands War may serve to illustrate the point.

In that conflict the sinking of the Argentine cruiser *General Belgrano* by the British submarine *HMS Conqueror* has been widely criticized. The large loss of life – 368 Argentine seamen died as a result of the action, making this the most costly single incident in the whole of the war – seems out of all proportion to the threat posed by the ship at the time of the attack. In forming this judge-ment much is made of certain alleged facts: that the cruiser did not initiate hostilities; that, far from demonstrating aggressive intent, it was 40 miles south-west of the exclusion zone around the Falklands, heading away from the islands and the task force; and, that it was attacked without warning in a position where it might have expected to enjoy immunity. Many are convinced that the attack was 'politically' rather than militarily motivated, its real object being to scuttle the peace process.[1] If so, the moral infamy would be compounded: not only would the action have violated the principle of proportionality (and perhaps a form of 'noncombatant' immunity), but it would have undermined that search for peace that, even in the midst of war, remains a moral imperative. Was this an instance of an excessive or dispropor-tionate use of force, dictated perhaps by political rather than by strictly military considerations? To form a balanced judgement the event must be considered from the standpoint of the decision-makers as well as that of the victims.

Given its composition and logistical problems, the task force was immensely vulnerable to attack. In the light of the subse-quent military victory it is easy to overlook a consideration that must have been uppermost in the minds of the British decision-makers, namely, the fear of a military disaster. The loss of one of the carriers or of one of the troopships would have been fatal to the whole operation. It was not just the specific threat posed by the *General Belgrano* that gave cause for concern, but the overall threat posed to the task force by the deployment of Argentine warships (and their aircraft) around the Falklands. 'What is incontrovertible,' Hastings writes, 'is that the British strategic purpose was to defeat the enemy's air and sea forces before the amphibious landing force was committed. To achieve this, it was vital to seize the earliest opportunity to remove one or more major Argentine surface threats from the battlefield' (Hastings and Jenkins 1983, p. 148).[2] Subsequent events appear to support the thinking behind the strategy: partly as a result of this action, the Argentine Navy was confined to port throughout the ensu-ing conflict, thereby severely reducing Argentina's ability to hinder the landing and supply of the ground troops. It is con-ceivable that if the navy had not been so confined (thereby allowing attack and reconnaissance aircraft a range and mobility denied to mainland-based units), Britain might have lost the war.

The *General Belgrano*, however, was not attacked simply to encourage a general naval withdrawal. Even in terms of its own military capability the cruiser posed a real threat: it outgunned every ship in the task force, its armour-plating made it resistant to aerial attack, it was equipped with Seacat anti-aircraft missiles, and its escorting destroyers were armed with Exocet missiles. Moreover, the manner of its deployment did nothing to reassure British commanders. The fact that the cruiser was well clear of the exclusion zone and heading away from the task force at the time of the attack was not sufficient either to warrant immunity or to demonstrate pacific or defensive intent. The argument that its location outside the exclusion zone should have guaranteed its immunity is difficult to sustain (although the British government's prevarication and uncertain handling of the affair did lend credence to this view and created much confusion). When the Maritime Exclusion Zone was first announced by the British government on 7 April the first units of the task force had just been dispatched. The aim of the announcement was to inhibit reinforcement of the Argentine garrison on the Falklands in the period prior to the arrival of the task force. Even so a rider made clear that the Maritime Exclusion Zone did not define the area of potential combat: 'This measure is without prejudice to the right of the United Kingdom to take whatever additional measures may be needed in exercise of its right of self-defence' (quoted in Freedman and Gamba-Stonehouse 1990, p. 248). As the task force neared the islands, the meaning of 'additional measures' was clarified in a statement issued on 23 April: 'HMG now wishes to make clear that any approach on the part of Argentinian warships, including submarines, naval auxiliaries, or military aircraft, which could amount to a threat to interfere with the mission of the British forces in the South Atlantic will encounter the appropriate response' (p. 250). This note was conveyed to the Argentine Government via the Swiss embassy in Buenos Aires.[3] As for the suggestion that the *Belgrano's* course indicated pacific intent, this is to attach inordinate importance to course direction and insufficient importance to the overall strategic situation. It is clear that the *General Belgrano* was acting in coordination with other units of the Argentine navy. The manoeuvre in which it was (or had been) engaged appeared to Woodward, the British commander, to be part of a strategy of encirclement, whereby the task force, situated to the east of the Falklands, would find itself attacked simultaneously, from the north by the battle group headed by the carrier *Veinticinco de Mayo* and from the south by the group around the *General Belgrano*.[4]

Though the ship had not fired a shot in anger, the assumption of aggressive intent was not without foundation. Argentine naval forces had been deployed on 27 April under orders to 'find and destroy the British fleet if the islands or the mainland were attacked', and the day before the attack on the *General Belgrano* Admiral Allara, the fleet commander, had issued general orders to initiate offensive operations in response to an anticipated British landing near Port Stanley (Freedman and Gamba-Stonehouse 1990, pp. 257–8). The aggressive intentions of the Argentine fleet were known to the British, who, according to Margaret Thatcher, 'had every reason to believe that a full-scale attack was developing' (Thatcher 1993, p. 214). In fact the execution of the plan was thwarted by the prevailing wind conditions, which prevented the take-off of combat aircraft from the deck of the Argentine carrier, though a major attack on British warships by the Air Force, involving about forty mainland-based aircraft, did take place (that several ships were not sunk in this attack was not for want of trying on the part of Argentine pilots). As the prospect of an immediate British landing receded, Allara ordered a tactical withdrawal 'to shallower waters to reduce the risk of falling victim to submarine attack' (Freedman and Gamba-Stonehouse 1990, p. 260). In accordance with its specific instructions, the *General Belgrano* turned away from the islands and sailed towards the coastal waters around Staten Island. The naval withdrawal was unknown to the British political and military leaders when they sanctioned the attack. Their assumption of a continuing offensive was understandable given recent events. Contact with the northerly group around the Argentine carrier had been lost prior to its course reversal, and the last signal received from *Conqueror*, the tracking submarine, before the decision to permit an attack was taken, had indicated that the *General Belgrano*, while skirting the Exclusion Zone, was moving towards the task force.[5] Accordingly, throughout the morning of 2 May, the units of the task force 'continued to search to the north and north-west for signs of an incoming attack, trusting that *Conqueror* would deal with the threat from the south' (Woodward and Robinson 1992, p. 163).

Though the decision-makers may not have known it at the time, the *General Belgrano* did not pose any immediate threat to the task force. Yet it remained a legitimate military target, for its temporary withdrawal was wholly consistent with an early resumption of offensive operations.[6] Its strategic importance was undiminished: not only would its permanent removal seriously weaken Argentine naval capability, it might also inhibit future offensive operations by the navy as a whole. In the straitened circumstances in which they found themselves, the task force commanders simply could not afford to wait to be attacked, or to pass over an opportunity that might not arise again and that might well make the difference between overall victory and defeat. Readily and understandably, the destruction of the *General Belgrano* came to be regarded as a military necessity, and its preservation as a dereliction of duty. Recalling his own state of mind, Lord Whitelaw, a member of the War Cabinet and one of the decision-makers, posed the question:

> What would our sailors, the families and the whole of the Task Force have said if it had become known that we had the chance to attack the *Belgrano* and wouldn't do it because we were waiting to see what would happen? And then if the *Belgrano* had got away from our submarine and steamed in and caused havoc in the Task Force? Just imagine what the feelings of us who were there would have been if that had been the result. It could have been, and the moment I was told that, I had no doubt we had to take the opportunity we had. (Bilton and Kosminsky 1989, p. 299)

Judged in the light of these considerations the attack on the *General Belgrano*, however terrible its consequences, seems neither gratuitous nor excessive. In short, the military case appears strong, and convincing enough to satisfy the criterion of proportionality in this instance.[7] Whether the war as a whole satisfied that criterion is of course another and larger matter. As for the notion that the ship was sunk in order to scuttle the Peruvian peace initiative, the evidence, in particular the chronology of events, does not appear to bear this out.[8] Mrs Thatcher's claims that 'The decision to sink the *Belgrano* was taken for strictly military not political reasons ... Those of us who took the decision at Chequers did not at that time know anything about the Peruvian proposals' (Thatcher 1993, p. 215) seem entirely in accordance with the known facts.[9]

It is in the economical and compassionate deployment of his own forces that a military commander first displays his respect for proportionality. In an interview during the Gulf War the allied commander General Schwarzkopf talked about the burdens of command: 'My nightmare is anything that would cause mass casualties among the troops. I don't want my troops to die. I don't want my troops to be maimed. Therefore, every waking and sleeping moment my nightmare is the fact that I will give an order that will cause countless numbers of human beings to lose their life' (Anderson and van Atta 1991, p. 160). That nightmare had been realized in an earlier conflict, which no doubt Schwarzkopf had in mind as he contemplated the timing of the ground offensive.

The battle of Loos in September 1915 was one of the costliest British engagements of the First World War. It was especially noteworthy as the first blooding of the New Army formed from civilian volunteers a year earlier. By the end of the battle British casualties totalled 60,000, while the gains in terms of strategic advantage and territorial advance were almost non-existent. Of course it can be argued in defence of any military action in which the losses incurred far outweigh the military gains that war is an uncertain business, and that no commander can guarantee a favourable loss/gain ratio. But in the case of the battle of Loos there is evidence to suggest that the British commanders ordered their men into action in anticipation that things would turn out as they did. After making a personal reconnaissance of the intended battlefield, Haig, then commander of the First Army, reported: 'The ground, for the most part bare and open, would be swept by machine-gun and rifle fire both from the German front trenches and from the numerous fortified villages immediately behind them and a rapid advance would be impossible.' Likewise, Sir Henry Rawlinson, one of the Corps commanders, expressed his misgivings: 'It will cost us dearly,' he wrote in his diary, 'and we shall not get very far' (quoted in Babington 1985, p. 46).

The decision to engage the enemy was probably taken on political rather than strictly military grounds, its object being to convince the French and Russians that Britain was committed to the war. What Britain feared most was the conclusion of an independent peace with Germany by one or both of its allies. Therefore, in order to hold the coalition together, Britain's readiness to suffer alongside its allies had to be demonstrated.[10] Prior to the action Sir John French, the British C.-in-C., had instructed Haig to attack with artillery rather than with a large force of infantry, since the result of an infantry attack against entrenched positions could only be the sacrifice of many lives (Blake 1952, p. 100). The military command was overruled by its political masters, in particular by Lord Kitchener, the War Minister. Previously Kitchener himself had favoured a policy of active defence, considering offensive operations premature; but setbacks on the Russian front brought about a change of mind. The decision was taken that 'we must act with all our energy, and do our utmost to help the French, even though, by so doing, we suffered very heavy losses indeed' (Blake 1952, p.102): The interests of the coalition dictated the deliberate sacrifice of British troops. According to the Official History: 'Under pressure from Lord Kitchener at home due to the general position of the Allies, and from Generals Joffre and Foch in France, the British Commander-in-Chief was therefore compelled to undertake operations before he was ready, over ground that was most unfavourable, against the better judgement of himself and General Haig' (quoted in Babington 1985, p. 46).[11]

In view of this the field commanders may seem exonerated so far as the change of overall strategy is concerned; but the same cannot be said about the conduct of the battle itself. This was their direct responsibility, and it seems clear that the manner in which they chose to fight betrayed a callous disregard for loss of life. Sir John French, the Commander-in-Chief, ordered his reserves to engage the enemy at a point in the battle when the

British attack had already become bogged down, and when the prospects of further success were remote in the extreme:

> by the opening of the second day all chance of using them [the reserve divisions] to advantage had gone. But this did not mean that they went unused. Late in the morning of the 26th, without aid of gas or significant artillery preparation, they were directed to advance across 1,500 yards of No-Man's-Land towards solid banks of barbed wire and well-sited machine-guns. So hopeless was their task, and so atrocious the resulting slaughter, that when at last the battered remnants abandoned the attempt and began to stumble back, numbers of German machine-gunners and riflemen stopped shooting because they had not the heart to continue the massacre. (Wilson 1986, pp. 258–9)

To pass this incident off as a failed attack or even as a military blunder does not seem to do it justice. So predictable and foreseeable were its disastrous consequences that it could not have occurred without massive indifference on the part of the high command to the fate of its own soldiers.

The battle of Loos set the pattern for what was to follow. On the first of July of the following year the great Somme offensive began. By the time it was concluded on the eighteenth of November British killed and wounded numbered 420,000, French casualties 200,000 and German casualties in excess of half a million. By the end of the infamous first day of the offensive the gains were minimal, yet British casualties totalled 57,470, the biggest loss ever suffered by the British army in a single day. The dead accounted for one-third of that figure. Haig's diary entry for the following day is revealing: '*Sunday July 2.* ... I also visited two Casualty Clearing Stations at Montigny ... The wounded were in wonderful spirits ... The A.G. reported today that the total casualties are established at over 40,000 to date. This cannot be considered severe in view of the numbers engaged, and the length of front attacked' (Blake 1952, p. 154).

Although it is true that no commander can guarantee military success, and that in the event of failure the costs of an attack are bound to appear disproportionate, it is difficult to imagine any realistically achievable military objective that would have justified casualties on this scale – unless, that is, a sufficiently low value is placed on the lives of the soldiers themselves. Though

Haig entertained hopes of a major breakthrough, the main justification for the overall offensive was attritional: not only would it force the Germans to divert resources from the southern front, and thereby relieve pressure on the French army at Verdun; it would result in German losses of men and material so substantial as to be unsustainable in the longer term. The 'success' of the Somme offensive could therefore be gauged without reference to the acquisition or even to the loss of territory. Such a broadly defined objective was bound to be costly in terms of the expenditure of human life. The Germans could be forced to divert substantial resources only by an infantry assault that threatened their reserves, something a bombardment could not do, whatever its severity. At the same time an infantry offensive on the scale envisaged and against positions as well defended as were the German positions at the Somme could not be sustained without a staggering loss of life. All this was known in advance by the British commanders. In their view it was a price worth paying. Was it?

As with Loos, doubts about the justifiability of the Somme offensive are twofold: they relate not only to the overall objective, but also to the way the battle was conducted in the light of that objective. In the first place, even if the strategic importance of Verdun (as well as the need to sustain the coalition) justified a joint British–French offensive in the Somme sector, did it have to take the form that it did? Haig's second-in-command Rawlinson favoured a less ambitious and therefore less profligate form of attack – the so-called 'bite and hold strategy' – that might still have had the desired effect of forcing the Germans to withdraw units from Verdun to reinforce the Somme defences, but not at such enormous cost (see Wilson 1986). In a Commons speech in May Winston Churchill had criticized those whose call for a British offensive was based on the grounds that 'it is our turn now'. The error of Loos, he argued, must not be repeated: any offensive must be justified on strictly military grounds (Gilbert 1971, p. 774).[12] In a memorandum dated 1 August 1916 (one month into the great battle) Churchill addressed the argument that without a Somme offensive the Germans would have been able to divert forces to Verdun or to the Eastern front:

We could have held the Germans on our front just as well by threatening an offensive as by making one. By cutting the enemy's wire, by bombardments, raiding and general activity at many unexpected points begun earlier and kept up later we could have made it impossible for him to withdraw any appreciable force.

If the French were pressed at Verdun we could have taken over more line and thus liberated reinforcements. (Gilbert 1972, p. 1538)

The British high command was not of course unmindful of the potential heavy losses. Experience at Loos and elsewhere was sufficient to convince them of the suicidal nature of an infantry assault on well-entrenched enemy positions. The military plan of attack therefore called for a massive and prolonged bombardment of the German lines: high explosives would destroy the German artillery behind the lines, the machine-gun emplacements in the line and the dug-outs in which the front-line soldiers would be sheltering during the bombardment, while shrapnel would break up the defensive screen of barbed wire. As a result the attacking British infantry would meet with relatively little opposition, and would be unlikely to sustain heavy casualties. This was fine in theory; but the practice was very different. None of the conditions for a successful infantry attack were met: German artillery, machine-guns, barbed wire and infantry all survived the British bombardment. When the British infantry were ordered to attack everything was in place for their massacre. Though evidence of the failure of the bombardment to achieve its objectives was available to the commanders, they chose to ignore it.[13]

As the battle unfolded doubts about its justifiability accumulated. In August the German attack on Verdun came to an end, and by October the French were on the offensive themselves. Thus one of the principal justifications for the Somme offensive was removed more than two months before the attack was halted. It was clear by this time, if not long before, that there was to be no great breakthrough. As one recent historian has argued:

the case for terminating the campaign seemed irresistible. The British command, nevertheless, managed to resist it. At the end of September Haig defined a further series of objectives ... For each of them there was, on narrow tactical grounds, a sort of justification. But they offered *no reward commensurate with the sufferings involved in assaulting them.* ... On 19 September Rawlinson reported Haig's Chief of Staff as saying that the C-in-C 'means to go on until we cannot possibly continue further either from the weather or want of troops'. (Wilson 1986, pp. 347–8, added emphasis)

In fairness, the difficulties of applying the criterion of proportionality must be acknowledged. Its application depends crucially on a military assessment that, however expert, is always uncertain. Military operations that in prospect seemed justifiable on grounds of proportionality can turn out so badly as to appear outrageously disproportionate in retrospect. Yet it is the judgements that were made in the course of the battle of the Somme, when the enormous loss of life was known already and yet was discounted, that seem morally flawed. At the beginning of August Haig wrote in his diary:

> Principle on which we should act, *Maintain our offensive.* Our losses in July's fighting totalled about 120,000 more than they would have been had we not attacked. They cannot be regarded as sufficient to justify any anxiety as to our ability to continue the offensive ... I expect to be able to maintain the offensive well into the Autumn. (Blake 1952, pp. 157–8)

In the end it is the suspicion not so much of military incompetence (perhaps Haig more than any other allied commander was responsible for the ultimate victory) as of callous indifference that lies behind the moral criticism of Haig's leadership: the suspicion that he was able to take the decisions he did take only because he had lost sight of their human cost.

There are those who would claim that this criticism is grossly unfair and, from a military and strategic viewpoint, naive. John Terraine, for example, has characterized such criticism as moralistic and sentimental. He has argued that even blood-letting on the scale of the Somme and later of Passchendaele was justified. The policy that Haig adopted was one of attrition. It was the only policy that could deliver victory. Germany could be defeated only by the gradual diminution of resources that occurred as a result

of these great battles. The Somme and Passchendaele were not
military blunders that condemned thousands of men to a futile
death; they were part of a well-thought-out and well-founded
strategy that prepared the ground for ultimate victory. The
charge that Haig's conduct of the war violated the principle of
proportionality ignores this overall strategic context. It ignores
the fact that there was no other alternative. It ignores the grim
realities of modern war. The slaughter was necessary, and soldiers did not die in vain (Terraine 1963).[14]

The moral permissibility of the war of attrition (not merely a
war with an attritional element, but a war in which attrition
defines the entire strategy) must be in grave doubt. Here is a
method of warfare that has as its deliberate aim the mass expenditure of men and material. It is a dehumanized view of war
according to which war is seen as an industrial and mechanical
process in which the distinction between the human and the
material element is systematically suppressed.[15] The problem
with a war of attrition is that it is difficult to see how such a war
can ever engage the criterion of proportionate *conduct* or means.
The policy of attrition serves as a blank cheque, allowing commanders to prosecute the war without regard to those considerations that the principle of proportionality is meant to uphold:
the policy is profligate and disproportionate by design. What the
policy of attrition does is to throw the weight of the moral argument on to the proportionality of *ends* rather than means: is the
cause grave enough to warrant the war of attrition?

If a war of attrition can be justified at all, it can be justified
only *in extremis*. But can it be justified even then? To say that it
can is to imply that total war is morally permissible if the end
that it serves is just enough. This is a moral approach to war that
the just war tradition has always resisted. To accept it would be
to undermine *ius in bello*. This is not to say that any war that is
hugely destructive of human life is morally unjustified. Terraine,
in his defence of British policy, makes much of the fact that casualty figures in the Second World War exceeded those in the First.
It is not the loss of life as such, however, that engenders moral
reservations, but the policy of attrition that dictated the loss of
life in the First World War. That policy appears to be morally
incoherent, since it is a policy that deliberately discounts and

devalues human life, thereby undermining the proportionality of ends that serves to justify the attritional means in the first place. How can a humanitarian purpose be achieved by resort to such manifestly anti-humanitarian means?[16]

Though the principle of proportionality applies in the first place to the economical and compassionate deployment of one's own troops, the matter does not end there. The problems of applying the principle to the conduct of war are greatly increased by its bilateral interpretation: the insistence that consideration of the costs to the *enemy* should form part of the moral assessment of military action. Such sympathy and generosity seem to conflict with military logic and the psychology of command. When General Schwarzkopf expressed his anxieties about the human costs of war, it was above all the welfare of his own troops he seemed to have had in mind. At least by implication, proportionality was to be applied unilaterally, that is, by each commander in respect of the forces under his command. While expressing sympathy for the plight of fellow-soldiers, Schwarzkopf saw the welfare of the Iraqi troops as the concern and responsibility of the Iraqi leadership. It was for Saddam Hussein, not Schwarzkopf himself, to spare *their* suffering.[17] In the mind of a military commander there can be little room for compassion towards the enemy, since compassion would yield the military advantage, put his own troops at risk, and at best prolong the war, at worst lose it. It was a calculation of that kind that lay behind the bombing offensive mounted by coalition forces in the Gulf War – the offensive that preceded the war on the ground, about which grave moral reservations were expressed at the time. Was the bombing campaign disproportionate? Did it involve the deliberate infliction of unnecessary or excessive suffering?[18]

The overall objective of the campaign was not to win the war without a ground offensive (that was deemed impossible by most, though not by all, the military planners),[19] but to ensure that when the ground offensive did take place it was as successful and economical as possible. The outcome that the coalition leadership feared most was a long and costly war on the ground that would lead to the erosion of public support and the weakening of the coalition. It was the anticipation of such an outcome that had encouraged Iraq to invade Kuwait in the first place. The superiority of the military forces that might be ranged against Iraq was acknowledged. The trump card was thought to be the Iraqi capacity to sustain and endure losses of a magnitude that far exceeded the capacity of the coalition. In a meeting one week before the invasion, Saddam Hussein warned the US ambassador, April Glaspie, that, 'Yours is a society which cannot accept 10,000 dead in one battle' (quoted in Bulloch and Morris 1991, p. 11). To win it would not be necessary to defeat or even to out-kill the enemy, but simply to inflict losses substantial enough to undermine his will to fight. What Saddam sought was a political rather than a military victory: either the US and its allies would not go to war over Kuwait in the first place or, if they did, they would not be able to sustain the war long enough to make their military superiority count. Once casualties began to mount allied opposition would crumble, and a negotiated settlement to Iraq's advantage would ensue. The Iraqi analysis of allied vulnerability was shared by the leaders of the coalition themselves, and it lay behind their decision to preface the ground war with a prolonged and intensive bombing campaign.[20]

The first objective of the campaign was to achieve air supremacy, so that strategic bombing could take place with relative impunity and so that the eventual ground attack could be executed with the support and without the threat of tactical air power. With this in mind attacks were carried out against the Iraqi air defence system and Air Force. The overwhelming success of this part of the campaign engendered moral misgivings about the bombing offensive as a whole among some observers. Even a moral analyst as sensitive to military realities and concerns as Michael Walzer has expressed anxiety about the unequal conduct of the war that resulted from the non-participation of the Iraqi airforce: 'When the world divides radically into those who bomb and those who are bombed, it becomes morally problematic, even if the bombing in this or that instance is justifiable' (Walzer 1992, p. xxi).[21] In such a one-sided air war it was easy to see the Iraqis as the victims (an impression reinforced by the sophisticated technology employed by the allies), and to overlook the very real threat posed by the Iraqi army. Militarily speaking, however, the bombing strategy proved a sound one, and it would have been contrary to the very nature of war for the allies to have ensured a level killing field by voluntarily forgoing their greatest military advantage.[22] To create a situation of one-sidedness is, militarily speaking, the essential object of war. The moral question is not whether the allies were justified in using a weapon that, for whatever reason, was not available to the other side, but whether they took advantage of their early superiority in the air to inflict wanton destruction on a defenceless adversary.

The bombing campaign, in its second phase, was an exercise in strategic warfare, the military if not the moral precedents for which were firmly established. The use of air power in a strategic and not just in a tactical role was commonplace during the Second World War. It became an accepted military principle that, in an age in which society as a whole was geared for war, targeting policy had to embrace more than purely military objectives. There is no doubt that the development of modern strategic air power puts a considerable strain on traditional moral guidelines. This is because strategic warfare is always in danger of degenerating into total warfare. For some, strategic bombing is in fact 'a concomitant of total war, where the object is to destroy the structure of the enemy's war potential which depends on his industrial production, system of communications and civil morale' (Frankland 1989, p. 208). To be reconcilable with just war principles strategic war must stop well short of total war. Did it do so in the case of the allied conduct of the Gulf War?

What were the objectives of this part of the campaign? In the first place, allied commanders sought to disrupt lines of communication and supply to the Iraqi front as well as to destroy as much war material as possible, especially the élite armoured divisions of the Republican Guard held in rear areas, the missile sites, and nuclear, biological and chemical assets (see McCausland 1993). Such a strategy was anticipated by military analysts prior to the commencement of hostilities. What took some by surprise was the extension of targeting policy to embrace the whole of Iraq and to include services on which civilian life was greatly dependent (see M. Evans 1991a). These attacks were not gratuitous in the sense that they served no (or even no important) military purpose.[23] The virtual collapse of the Iraqi electrical power grid under the allied bombing attack brought the production of NBC weapons to a halt, greatly impaired the command and control network, and impeded aircraft maintenance and refuelling (see McCausland 1993). These were considerable military gains that contributed substantially to the allied victory. The moral problem with the selection of such 'dual purpose' targets is that their destruction may cause at least as much damage to civilian life as it does to the machinery of war. Because this damage is subsequent and indirect, there is a danger that it might be either overlooked or discounted.

The evidence suggests that allied commanders went to great pains to ensure that the loss of civilian life was kept to a minimum during the bombing offensive itself. Given the delicate state of the coalition there were strong pragmatic as well as ethical reasons for such a policy. In the first place the policy guided the selection of targets. For example, though the airfield near the town of Mosul was bombed, the Mosul dam was not, because of the devastation that a breach of the dam would cause to low-lying Baghdad and much of southern Iraq (see M. Evans 1991b). Secondly, though area bombing with B52s was used in the bombardment of isolable Iraqi ground forces, strict precision bombing was the rule in the case of military targets located in noncombatant areas. This was the case even when it meant increased risks for the air crew involved. With the aid of 'smart' bombs and other advanced technology, precision bombing of a very high order was achieved and the loss of civilian life in the course of the raids was kept to a minimum. In view of this a strong claim can be made that the manner in which the bombing campaign was conducted upheld the principle of noncombatant immunity: the killing of noncombatants in the air raids was largely avoided.[24] This did not mean, however, that the Iraqi people escaped the general devastation caused by the bombing.

Though civilians were spared in the attacks themselves, the conditions of civil life were subjected to such a sustained assault that long-term damage and widespread suffering were inevitable. Whether the military gains from the strategic bombing offensive were substantial enough to offset the harm inflicted upon the Iraqi people is a moot point. The moral judgement of proportionality hinges on answers to a number of difficult factual questions: how crucial to overall military success was the destruction of 'dual purpose' targets? What would have been the effect on the course and outcome of the war if such targets had been avoided altogether or attacked with less ferocity? How great was the suffering imposed on the Iraqi people as a result of the strategic bombing offensive itself (and not as a result of other factors beyond the control of allied commanders)?[25] Even retrospectively, there are no easy answers to these questions, which is what makes judging the proportionality of means so difficult. Whatever the answers and however great the difficulties, it is important that considerations of proportionality should carry equal weight with considerations of noncombatant immunity in the minds of the decision-makers. It is the suspicion that they did not that accounts for much of the criticism of this part of the bombing campaign.

The pounding given to Iraqi ground forces during the air offensive engendered further moral misgivings. Were such misgivings warranted? The point has been made already that the only way in which the coalition could 'lose' the war was by a premature engagement of land forces without full and prior use of air power. There seems little doubt that an earlier land war would have resulted in an increase not only in allied casualties but also in Iraqi casualties. The fear of a prolonged war of attrition was a real one, and in such a war the overall level of casualties was rightly expected to be much higher. Many of the moral reservations expressed at the time arose from the assumption that Iraqi troops were being slaughtered in great numbers by the bombing offensive, and that allied commanders were simply discounting that Iraqi loss of life. Some critics even suggested that an element of racism formed part of the calculation, with Arab lives being regarded as less valuable and therefore more expendable than the lives of Westerners.[26] Given the make-up of the coalition this assessment was far-fetched. There seems little doubt, however, that the overriding concern of allied commanders was to inflict maximum damage on Iraqi ground forces with a view to smoothing the path of the coming ground offensive and minimizing allied casualties. Such a calculation is so intrinsic a part of warfare that to exclude it on moral grounds would be to subvert the activity of war itself (something that the just war approach, with its acknowledgement that war should be fought with military efficiency as well as moral probity, is not intended to do). The action was taken for sound military reasons, and not out of any wish to inflict cruel and unnecessary suffering on the Iraqi infantry. The target was a purely military one that posed a real and substantial threat and which had to be attacked if the aims of the war were to be achieved. An alternative mode of attack would have played into the hands of the Iraqi leadership, which had pinned its hopes on an early land war. Moreover, an earlier ground offensive, while equalizing the suffering inflicted by the war, would have led not to its net reduction but to its net increase. In effect what opponents of this part of the bombing strategy were doing was to require allied commanders to buy the lives of enemy soldiers with the lives of their own troops. This is an unfair as well as an unrealistic expectation. Given the probable consequences of any alternative military strategy, the bombing of the Iraqi lines does not seem disproportionate.[27] Can the same be said of the allied conduct of the ground war?

The most striking feature of the ground war was its brevity. The war lasted about one hundred hours. Iraqi losses were very substantial, though not perhaps as great as had been feared or anticipated. At the end of the conflict the official US estimate of Iraqis killed in the war as a whole was 150,000. In the light of further evidence and more careful scrutiny analysts later reduced this figure to one of 15,000.[28] Freedman estimates that 'at most ... 10,000 died during the land war' (Freedman and Karsh 1993, p. 408). It is not the absolute magnitude of this figure that is so striking, but its comparison with a coalition 'killed in action' figure of 240 (15 fewer than the number of British servicemen killed in action during the Falklands War). While the combined total of deaths suggests that the ground war did not violate the principle of proportionality (bearing in mind the size and destructive power of the forces ranged against one another), the comparative statistic suggests that it might have done. It was such a suspicion, fuelled by events at the infamous Mutla Ridge, that played a decisive part in bringing the war to what some at the time, and many more later, thought was a premature end. Was this suspicion well-grounded?

Much depends on the definition and assessment of war aims.

If the aim was restricted to the bare minimum of ensuring Iraqi withdrawal from Kuwait, then at least part of the coalition offensive might be regarded as disproportionate, since that aim was effectively secured before the cessation of hostilities. However, coalition war aims were never so economically defined. Iraqi acceptance of additional UN resolutions, framed with a view to reducing the threat that Iraqi military power posed to regional security, was regarded by coalition leaders as a condition of any ceasefire. Iraq was required not only to withdraw from Kuwait, but to accept what amounted to a curtailment of Iraqi sovereignty. This Iraq was reluctant to do without further military persuasion. For some, even these extended war aims were insufficient. It was argued that in the interests of future peace in the region coalition forces should take advantage of their military superiority to inflict as much damage as possible on the Iraqi war machine. In this context the units of the Republican Guard, which to a considerable extent had been held back by the Iraqi high command, were seen as a principal target for destruction. Some even argued for the seizure of Baghdad and the overthrow of Saddam Hussein. Discussion of the legitimacy (or practicality) of such aims is out of place here. The point is, however, that the application of the criterion of proportionality is dependent upon, because it is relative to, the definition of war aims, and what seems disproportionate in respect of one set of aims will seem entirely fitting in respect of another, more ambitious set.

In conclusion, what lies behind this criterion of proportionality – as it lies behind just war thinking as a whole – is a basic respect for life urged on all those who engage in war. It demands economy in the use of force: that commanders should not waste the lives of their own soldiers in the pursuit of unattainable or relatively unimportant military objectives, and that they should not inflict undue and unnecessary suffering on an adversary. Compassion is a military as well as a civilian virtue. What generates such compassion is the permanent recognition of the humanity of those who fight and of those who are caught up in the fighting. Conversely, what leads to the neglect of proportionality and to the profligate and cruel prosecution of war is the tendency among those who wage it to lose sight of its real human cost.

Notes

1 Cf. Dalyell 1983; Foot 1983; Belgrano Action Group 1988.

2 Cf. also Woodward and Robinson 1992, p. 93; Freedman and Gamba-Stonehouse 1990, p. 254. Woodward makes it clear that the preferred target was the Argentine carrier *Veinticinco de Mayo* (p. 127).

3 Its import was well understood by the Argentine leadership. Rear-Admiral Allara, the commander of the task force of which the *Belgrano* formed a part, is quoted as saying: 'After the message of 23 April, the entire South Atlantic was an operational theatre for both sides. We, as professionals, said it was just too bad that we lost the *Belgrano*' (Middlebrook 1990, p. 116). The captain of the *General Belgrano* confirmed this view: 'I realized from the outset that the 200-mile limit had nothing to do with the mission I had to accomplish. The limit did not exclude dangers or risks; it was all the same in or out.'

4 Woodward and Robinson 1992, pp. 147ff.

5 Freedman and Gamba-Stonehouse 1990, p. 264. *Belgrano's* change of course was reported later by *Conqueror*, but the information was not thought significant enough to be passed on (pp. 267–8).

6 As the captain of the *Belgrano* explained later: 'We were heading towards the mainland but not going *to* the mainland; we were going to a position to await further orders' (Middlebrook 1990, p. 105).

7 For a different and rather more critical assessment cf. Hastings and Jenkins (1983) and Dillon (1989). Dillon, for example, accepts that the *General Belgrano* posed a real strategic, if not an immediate, threat to the task force. At the same time he suggests an alternative, more acceptable response: the temporary withdrawal of the task force behind a submarine screen. This would have greatly reduced the task force's freedom of movement, and does not seem to take sufficient account of the need to establish air and sea mastery as quickly as possible as a prelude to the landing.

8 Cf. Freedman and Gamba-Stonehouse 1990, pp. 284f. and Dillon 1989, pp. 151f. According to Freedman, when the decision was taken, concern was expressed 'about the possible impact on international public opinion, but there was no consideration of the effect on peace negotiations as none were believed to be taking place at the time' (p. 267). Dillon too accepts that 'the proposals were received some time after the *Belgrano* had been sunk' (p. 152) but, even if they had been received earlier, their status 'could hardly have counterbalanced the dangerous and compelling circumstances then faced by the Carrier Battle Group' (p. 156).

9 There was, of course, considerable relief in military circles that the procrastination over military action caused by the pursuit of a political settlement had been brought to an end. With the approach of

winter and the progressive loss of military efficiency, any further delay might have made the recovery of the islands impossible. Admiral Woodward cites the advice given to the Cabinet by the military planners: 'To eject the Argentinians by force, we *must* be on the edge of the Exclusion Zone by 1 May. You thus have until that date to succeed in your political negotiations, because every day you slip past 1 May is one day less for us to complete the land campaign. Don't forget, it is only in the Argentinians' interest to prevaricate. *We* are already right up against the stops' (Woodward and Robinson 1992, pp. 93–4). This military reading of the circumstances is highly relevant not just to the application of the criterion of proportionality, but to that of last resort as well.

10 See French 1988.

11 See also Richard Holmes (1991, p. 128): 'Aware that he had been saved only by Joffre's support, he [French] took care not to turn down French requests for co-operation, and thus mounted a number of operations in which he had limited confidence, with the battle of Loos in September 1915 as the most terrible case in point.' Holmes throws further light on the overall context of the battle: 'At Calais on 6 July a compromise was achieved between Joffre, who wanted the heaviest possible offensive in the West, and Kitchener, who opposed such an attack. From this agreement grew the Allied offensive, planned over July and August, and fought in late September by the French in Artois and the British at Loos. French had considerable reservations about attacking into the industrial hinterland around Loos, and believed that he lacked adequate artillery ammunition. He eventually decided to co-operate fully for two main reasons. First, he felt that his own position depended on retaining Joffre's confidence. Secondly, he believed that the French had come to doubt Britain's commitment ... that the French might conclude a separate peace.

The strategic debate helped persuade French to embark upon plans which he regarded as operationally unsound' (p. 124).

12 The assumption that military considerations could be divorced from political ones was not shared by those who argued that a British offensive was necessary in order to sustain the coalition and *thereby* to defeat Germany. It was not shared by Churchill himself when in the Second World War he justified the bomber offensive against Germany largely in terms of the need to sustain the alliance with the Soviet Union.

13 Haig wrote in his diary on the eve of the battle: 'The wire has never been so well cut, nor the Artillery preparation so thorough' (Blake 1952, p. 154). Given the clear availability of evidence to the contrary this must have been a case either of wishful thinking or of culpable ignorance on Haig's part.

14 Terraine quotes approvingly Haig's own assessment in his Final
Despatch: 'If the whole operations of the present war are regarded in
correct perspective, the victories of the summer and autumn of 1918
will be seen to be as directly dependent upon the two years of stub-
born fighting that preceded them'; 'It is in the great battles of 1916
and 1917 that we have to seek for the secret of our victory in 1918'
(Terraine 1963, pp. 481–2). The source of the strategy lay in Haig's
understanding of warfare in general: 'The guiding principles are
those which have proved successful in war from time immemorial,
viz., that the first step must always be to wear down the enemy's
power of resistance and to continue to do so until he is so weakened
that he will be unable to withstand a decisive blow; then with all
one's forces to deliver the decisive blow and finally to reap the fruits
of victory' (p. 310). It was to the great misfortune of the soldiery
fighting under his command that, in view of German reluctance to
attack, Haig saw 'vigorous offensive operations' as the only way of
wearing down the enemy.

Terraine is at pains to rebut 'the charge that he [Haig] was ever
callous or insensible to the sufferings of his men'; but the evidence of Haig's compassion and sensitivity that Terraine adduces
(in a letter Haig wrote to his wife in April 1917) is less than convincing: 'As you know ... I never hesitate to find fault, but I have
myself a tremendous affection for those fine fellows who are ready
to give their lives for the Old Country at any moment. I feel quite
sad at times when I see them march past me, knowing as I do
how many must pay the full penalty before we can have peace.
It is satisfactory to hear that a much larger percentage than usual
are slight bullet wounds during this last battle' (pp. 483–4).

15 According to Crutwell: 'The great fault of the directing brains in the
West was a kind of mechanical megalomania, pinning their faith to
masses of men, masses of guns, masses of shells, masses of transport'
(quoted in Strachan 1991, p. 61).

16 The morally corrosive effects of a war of attrition were evident again
in Vietnam, even though the counterinsurgent nature of that war,
with its natural imperative of winning 'the hearts and minds' of the
people, made such a strategy even less appropriate. According to
General Harkin (Westmoreland's predecessor as commanding general), the key to winning the war lay in the '"Three M's" – men,
money, and matériel' (Sheehan 1988, p. 288). One of General Westmoreland's staff officers, DePuy, put it even more bluntly: 'The solution in Vietnam is more bombs, more shells, more napalm ... till the
other side cracks and gives up' (Sheehan 1988, p. 619). It has been
calculated that the six million tons of bombs that the US dropped on
Indo-China – 3.6m of which fell on South Vietnam – amounted to

three times the tonnage of bombs dropped by air forces in the whole of the Second World War (Seabury and Codevilla 1989, p. 281). Here was a war conceived from the start not in economical but in inflationary terms: escalation was the name of the game. The war was disproportionate by design (or, to put it another way, the policy was such as to make the disproportionality of any means inconceivable). The intent, and not just the effect, was one of 'overkill'. The aims of the policy were always too broadly or expansively defined to have any limiting effect on the conduct of war. It became impossible to measure the success of the strategy or to find it wanting. A kind of reverse logic was applied instead – one that had the effect of releasing the inhibitions that normally apply to the conduct of war. Far from engendering scepticism and suspicion of failure, the rising expenditure of men and materials was taken as evidence that the strategy was *working*. The 'performance indicators' that were used (the 'body counts', the numbers of 'search and destroy' missions mounted, of air strikes carried out, of bombs dropped, of acres of land deforested, of 'enemy' villages destroyed, of 'free fire zones' created) were crude in the extreme, and clearly encouraged combat units to employ force disproportionately and indiscriminately. The massacre at My Lai was not an anomaly, but the natural outcome of the strategy and tactics of attrition. Rejecting the more discerning and less destructive policy of 'pacification' favoured by some of his own counterinsurgency experts, General Westmoreland declared: 'We'll just go on bleeding them until Hanoi wakes up to the fact that they have bled their country to the point of national disaster for generations' (Sheehan 1988, p. 643). The surest way to defeat the Viet Cong was to destroy Vietnam. The moral absurdity of this policy is captured in Westmoreland's own words and in the words of one of his subordinates. When questioned about the large number of civilian casualties caused by the US air strikes and bombardment, General Westmoreland replied, 'Yes, Neil, it is a problem but it does deprive the enemy of the population, doesn't it?' (p. 621). In like manner, after a devastating attack on the town of Ben Tre, a US major protested famously, 'It became necessary to destroy the town to save it' (p. 719). It was the logic of the strategy of attrition that induced men to voice these terrible absurdities.

17 It is claimed that 'the thing Schwarzkopf came to loathe the most about his enemy was Saddam's total disregard for the health and welfare of his troops' (Anderson and Van Atta 1991, p. 164).

18 Finnis *et al.* write: 'The military tactician should always limit attacks to what really will help to put an end to the enemy's unjust use of force. So he may not take as his purpose the greatest possible destruction of enemy personnel (running up the body count) or the

punitive killing of the enemy to match losses incurred. Instead, he should prefer non-lethal means of neutralizing enemy forces and encouraging their surrender' (Finnis *et al.* 1987, pp. 315–16).

19 Cf. Freedman and Karsh 1993, pp. 312ff. Similar disagreements were evident in the Second World War regarding the role and potential of the strategic bombing campaign: for some it was an adjunct to a ground offensive, for others a means of winning the war on its own.

20 The lesson of Vietnam – that attrition was 'the route to defeat' – had been well absorbed. The adoption of a strategy of attrition would have played into the hands of an enemy with an apparently unlimited capacity and readiness to sustain losses.

21 The one-sidedness of combat causes anxiety in some soldiers. Regarding his participation in the bombing of Nagasaki Leonard Cheshire recalled that, 'the height we were flying at, thirty thousand feet, worried me ... over Germany, the odds were against us: out of every twenty aircraft, one was lost, on average, in every raid. Somehow this made us feel it was a fair fight. But here we were above flak and out of reach of fighters. I can't explain it, but it felt not quite right. I was decidedly uncomfortable' (Cheshire 1991, p. 63).

22 Some coalition leaders thought otherwise, including the Syrian defence minister, who expressed a preference for 'the Soviet doctrine [whereby] the General Staff would have engaged the ground units after three hours of bombing and with simultaneous air bombardment' (quoted in Freedman and Karsh 1993, p. 326).

23 This is disputed. McMahan and McKim claim that, 'Among the targets that were directly and repeatedly hit were water purification facilities and sewage systems ... What conceivable military purpose could these attacks have been supposed to serve?' (McMahan and McKim 1993, pp. 538–9). The selection of such targets, if verified, would go a long way to justifying the otherwise extravagant claim that 'in this war the US developed a sanitized mode of terror bombing ... [using] ... precision bombing to destroy the infrastructure of the civilian society' (p. 539).

24 There was one tragic exception – the bombing of the air raid shelter in Baghdad – but this was the result of faulty intelligence rather than a change in policy. Clearly the coalition had nothing to gain and everything to lose from the incidental deaths of noncombatants (let alone from their deliberate targeting).

25 It is claimed by critics of the war that at least 150,000 Iraqi civilians died either as a direct result of war or as a result of its lingering effects (McMahan and McKim 1993). Given the complex circumstances that prevailed, and that continue to prevail in Iraq, such assessments are bound to remain highly speculative. How can

one determine the relative impact of allied military action, international sanctions and the Iraqi government's habitual neglect and abuse of its own people? According to a study sponsored by the UN Food and Agriculture Organization sanctions imposed on Iraq have been responsible for more than 560,000 deaths among children (*The Times*, 1 December 1995).

26 After the bombing of the Baghdad air raid shelter, one Saudi woman expressed what were claimed to be the feelings of many: 'For the Americans, it does not seem to be a problem if anyone else dies, especially Arabs. They treat us like insects. With Western lives it is different: if one Western is just taken hostage, not even killed, the whole world is turmoil' (Walker 1991).

27 It might be argued that an earlier land war was not the only military alternative; that there was an alternative strategy, less open to moral objection and no less efficient militarily, namely, the isolation of Iraqi ground forces. By interdicting supplies to the front through the use of air power the military capacity of front-line troops – armour as well as infantry – could have been reduced by as much as, if not by more than, by direct bombing. The answer to this is that such interdiction was attempted, but that it was not sufficient on its own to achieve the desired goal. Supplies would continue to get through, and the time it would take to bring about capitulation would cause serious and perhaps terminal problems for the coalition.

28 See *The Times*, 12 October 1994, p. 13. McMahan and McKim (1993) cite the earlier and higher estimate of 125,000–150,000 killed in action. Freedman and Karsh (1993), while emphasizing the speculative nature of any estimate, suggest a total figure of 35,000 ('based largely on circumstantial evidence'), including 25,000 in the air war (p. 408).

10

Noncombatant immunity

The moral reasoning associated with the principle of civilian or, more exactly, noncombatant immunity is one of the most strongly contested areas of just war theory. Not the least contentious issue has to do with the nature and moral status of the distinction on which the principle rests. Traditionally, the distinction is seen to arise out of the moral prohibition on the taking of innocent life. But what constitutes 'innocence' in this context? Is 'innocence' to be understood, in the dominant conventional sense, as a term descriptive of the agent's interior moral state? If so, the application of the principle becomes extremely difficult.

In the first place, those who are not engaged in war-making may well be guiltier, in a personal moral sense, than those who do the fighting. A father, who lusts after war but who is too old to fight himself, may shame his pacifically inclined and more scrupulous sons to engage in an unjust and aggressive war. If moral guilt or loss of innocence engenders loss of immunity from attack, then the warmongering civilian should be considered a more legitimate target than the reluctant conscript. Similarly, if in the absence of personal or subjective moral guilt immunity is retained, it would be impossible to wage war justly against an unjust aggressor who was acting in good faith.

Secondly, and more practically, since moral guilt or innocence can be established only by reference to the intentions, state of mind and subjective disposition of an individual, the distinction could not be used as a means of discriminating between legitimate and illegitimate targets of attack. The personal moral guilt or innocence of those whom they subject to attack is something about which combatants necessarily remain ignorant. On the other hand, to think in terms of collective guilt or innocence would be to render all citizens of a state fighting an unjust war liable to attack, thereby undermining all attempts at discrimination and embracing total war.

Problems such as these point to the conclusion that the distinction is to be understood in a non-subjective moral sense. Moreover, the logic of just war theorizing points to such an understanding of 'innocence', since the use of force in the first instance is seen to be justified only in response to an attack or threatened attack. In line with its etymological derivation from the Latin *nocere* ('to harm'), 'innocent' in this context means 'harmless' rather than 'blameless'. It is the threat that an unjust aggressor poses that results in the loss or suspension of that right of immunity from attack that all human beings are thought to possess. Conversely, it is the non-threatening or harmless status, not just of civilians but also of soldiers (when the latter have surrendered and been disarmed, for example) that either preserves or (in the case of the soldiers) restores their natural immunity from attack.

The controversy surrounding the distinction is not confined to the meaning of 'innocence'. Its application, even in the more 'objective' sense, remains fraught with difficulties. In some respects the problems are extrinsic, brought about by the development of modern warfare. In earlier times, when wars were much more limited affairs, the distinction between combatants and noncombatants appeared more clear-cut and manageable. It was only when the conflict spilled over from the battlefield that problems were seen to arise. Vitoria alludes to these moral difficulties in *De iure belli*:

> It is occasionally lawful to kill the innocent not by mistake, but with full knowledge of what one is doing, if this is an accidental effect:[1] for example, during the justified storming of a fortress or city, where one knows there are many innocent people, but where it is impossible to fire artillery and other projectiles or set fire to buildings without crushing or burning the innocent along with the combatants. (Vitoria 1991, p. 315)[2]

The problems associated with siege warfare in the Renaissance period have become generalized and commonplace with the development of modern warfare. This development has made both the interpretation and the application of the principle of noncombatant immunity increasingly difficult.

In part the difficulty lies in the sheer destructive power of modern weaponry, combined with greatly improved methods of delivery that enable a force to strike far behind enemy lines, thus rendering all citizens vulnerable to attack. The traditional notion of 'lines of battle' has become outmoded in an age when war so often takes the form either of strategic or of guerilla warfare. As the parameters of combat have become blurred, so the distinction between combatants and noncombatants has become less well-defined. Technological developments have gone hand in hand with the development of new strategies in the light of which war has ceased to be seen as the affair simply of armies. To a far greater extent than in the past contemporary or 'industrial' war is dependent for its effective prosecution on the creation and maintenance of a war economy and, therefore, dependent upon the combined efforts of military and civilian personnel. The situation is further complicated by the introduction of universal military conscription, by the consequent employment of women in munitions factories, and by the creation of huge citizen armies in keeping with the democratization of states and with the recognition that war is no longer the affair of princes and their mercenary armies but of the entire citizen body.

These changes have led to the gradual erosion and, in some cases, to the total suppression of the distinction between combatant and noncombatant. For some, modern war is by its very nature 'total war', a war that systematically and necessarily overrides that distinction. Reflecting on the lessons of the First World War, Marshal Pétain was led to conclude that, 'Henceforward the object of war appears in all its amplitude and all its cruel simplicity: it has become the destruction not of an army but of a nation.' On such a view it has become impossible to wage war, effectively at least, without gross and systematic violation of the traditional but now outmoded principle of noncombatant immunity. Modern war resembles ever more closely the war of annihilation. This is a judgement shared by some just war theorists, who, as a consequence, have been led to renounce modern war and to become *de facto* pacifists.

To resist the pacifist conclusion is to argue that there remain solid grounds for distinguishing combatants from noncombatants, despite the way in which the category of combatancy has been greatly enlarged through the development of modern, strategic, warfare. If strategic war is justified (and within certain limits it seems that it is), then there exist legitimate targets of attack other than actual combat units.[3] This process of widening has blurred the distinction between the military and civilian population. Given the key role played by many civilians in the war effort, it no longer seems appropriate to speak of civilian immunity. Civilians can be combatants as well as soldiers, not in the sense that they engage in actual fighting, but in the sense that they provide the means and instruments of combat.

Up to a point the moral permissibility, and not just the military necessity or utility, of these changes can be accepted. The flexible nature of the distinction between combatant and noncombatant, and the way in which its definition responds to the changing character and circumstances of war, may be acknowledged. At the same time it is necessary to maintain *a* distinction in face of the drift towards total or limitless war. The approach here is rather like that of liberals in respect of the distinction between the state and civil society (or between a public and a private sphere of competence): though recognizing that it may be difficult to determine exactly where to draw the line, the tradition is in no doubt that a line needs to be drawn *somewhere* if liberty is to be preserved.[4]

Certain categories of the population seem readily classifiable as noncombatants: the very young, the very old, the infirm, and all those who lack the capacity to engage in war or to contribute to the running of the machinery of war. Far from aiding the war effort, such classes of the population inhibit it by requiring the diversion of scarce resources from military to civilian use. Moreover, not every occupation or work activity is classifiable as part of the enterprise of war merely because it contributes to a national economy that sustains war. For such classification to be upheld it is necessary to establish *direct* (and potentially lethal) links between the labour activity in question and the prosecution of the war.

The distinction is at best a rough and ready one, and there remain many grey areas. It is not clear, for example, why a factory producing tanks should lose its immunity, while a plant producing the steel for the tanks retains its immunity. The process of production that is modern 'industrial' war links the armoured division with the arms factory that produces the tanks, with the steel plant that supplies the raw material, with the coal mines that supply the fuel for the blast furnaces, and so on. It seems arbitrary to break into this cycle at a certain point in order to establish immunity from attack. Arguably, all those who play a part in this process of production are readily identifiable as 'combatants', given the nature of modern war. This view is reinforced by the way in which a belligerent state regards industrial labour as equivalent to military service. The problem is that in modern war the whole economy tends to be geared to war production.

An attempt may be made to deal with this difficulty by distinguishing between those who are engaged in activities that are generated by war itself and would not take place without war and those whose activities, on which society depends for its normal functioning, war has not called forth. Will this do? It seems not; not at least without modification, since what this distinction ignores is the way in which the peaceful activities of civil society become militarized in time of war. Activities that are carried on regularly outside war and are not intrinsically warlike may yet, in times of war, become crucial to the prosecution of war and occupy a key and strategic role. The production of oil is a case in point. A ready supply of oil with which to power the machinery of war was seen as a potential and fatal chink in the German armour during the Second World War. The German oil industry, therefore, quickly came to be regarded as a legitimate military target by the Allies. Perhaps the distinction needs to be modified to take account of the transformation of some civilian enterprises brought about by war (the increase in the scale of production, for example, and the diversion of output to military use) – changes which *may* establish them as military targets.

Difficulties of classification undoubtedly remain; but what needs to be emphasized is that the burden of proof of 'combatancy' lies with the attacker. The net may need to be thrown more widely than in the past; but there must still be a great many who slip through it if total war is to be avoided. As Spaight (an unlikely authority given his vigorous defence of the British bombing offensive in the Second World War and the part that he himself played in it as Principal Secretary to the Air Ministry) argues: 'It is not a question of political or moral support, or even of material support in forms that could not possibly be called warlike. What justifies the deliberate attack on the people concerned is that they are engaged on work which is akin to that done by uniformed men in the field. They are helping to pass the ammunition' (quoted in Finnis *et al.* 1987, p. 101).[5]

The problem, however, is not simply one of definition or identification. Even where noncombatants are acknowledged it seems impossible to safeguard their immunity in the face of modern war. Of course the requirements of the principle of noncombatant immunity must not be exaggerated. Such exaggeration is evident in some formulations. According to one author,

> There is an objective and a subjective version of the principle of noncombatant immunity. The *objective* version holds that if *civilians* are killed as a result of military operations, the principle is violated. The *subjective* version holds that if civilians are intentionally killed as a result of military operations, the principle is violated. ... It follows on the subjective version that if civilians are killed in the course of a military operation directed at a military target, the principle of discrimination has not been violated. (Lackey 1989, p. 60)

Neither version of the principle appears to do it justice. The first is too restrictive, while the second is too permissive (as the author acknowledges).[6] It is clear, however, that the 'objective' version is an exaggeration of the principle's requirements, which do not stipulate that in a justly conducted war there should be no noncombatant deaths. Realistically, such deaths are an inevitable part of any war, and especially of any modern war. Though an undoubted physical evil, they may not constitute a moral evil. The moral difficulty arises only when noncombatant deaths are the foreseen (or foreseeable) consequence of a proposed course of action.

In dealing with this difficulty in the past recourse has been had to the so-called 'principle of double effect'. Double effect is not itself a moral norm or principle, but an instrument of moral analysis, an aid in the application of moral principles to situations of extreme moral conflict, in which the pursuit of a legitimate and worthy objective threatens the violation of a fundamental moral norm. It is the often tragic experience of such conflict, the realization (together with the resulting moral doubt and anxiety) that no course of action is without very substantial costs, that gives point to this approach. Whether double effect is capable of resolving, or even of clarifying, these dilemmas is an open question. For many contemporary critics double effect has outlived its usefulness, and its theoretical validity has been fatally compromised.

Though it has a much wider application, in the case of war the principle surfaces, typically, in respect of those otherwise militarily desirable actions that appear to entail the violation of noncombatant immunity. As Michael Walzer puts it, 'Double Effect is a way of reconciling the absolute prohibition against attacking non-combatants with the legitimate conduct of military activity', and he adds, critically, 'the reconciliation comes too easily' (Walzer 1992, p. 153).[7] Does it? Is the principle of double effect too permissive in its application to the conduct of war? The criticism is not uncommon; but more often than not it rests on an oversimplified interpretation of the principle that singles out certain aspects while ignoring or devaluing other essential requirements.

It would, for instance, be a grave error to suggest that the principle of double effect can be reduced to the simple proposition that 'the end justifies the means'. It is true that a consideration of the consequences of an action and a weighing of its good and harmful effects form an integral part of the moral reasoning that makes up the principle; but it is a question of a part, and not the whole. According to the traditional view at least, far from being reducible to this proposition (or to mere considerations of proportionality), the principle of double effect is systematically opposed to it. Indeed the principle has point only on the assumption that it is always wrong to promote a good end through the use of immoral means, and those who employ the principle resist the moral determination of the means solely in the light of the consequences. However beneficial the consequences that may be thought to flow from it, the intentional or direct killing of noncombatants is seen as an intrinsically evil act beyond moral justification.

Secondly, it would be a gross and highly misleading simplification to equate the principle with the view that 'it is the *inten-*

tion that informs the act that counts' – as if all that was needed to render an action morally licit was for the agent to make a mental reservation regarding the evil and wholly foreseeable consequences of his or her action. A safe conscience cannot be purchased so cheaply. This is not to belittle the importance of the agent's intention. Intention is after all at the heart of moral action. But to reduce morality to a matter of intention is to suppress other essential elements to which the theory of double effect draws attention. Right intention is a necessary but not a sufficient condition, an important part but not the whole of moral action. It cannot by itself justify the performance of an act that seems to necessitate the violation of such a basic moral norm.

Double effect (like just war thinking as a whole) can be seen as an attempt to avoid the one-sidedness associated with both 'deontological' and 'consequentialist' approaches (the exclusivism of both the 'morality of intentions' and the 'morality of consequences'). The moral reductionism that both approaches exhibit, in their different ways, contrasts with this bid to uncover and to uphold a complex moral reality, no aspect of which is seen as dispensable. Though the principle of double effect is often dismissed (with justification in some instances of its use) as a kind of moral sleight of hand, nothing could be (or ought to be) further from the truth.[8] Far from leading to the evasion of moral difficulty, whatever analytical utility the principle has (and it is in those terms alone that it should be judged) it has by virtue of its capacity to complicate rather than to simplify moral judgements. What it is meant to *inhibit* is the persistent tendency to suppress key moral elements: to oversimplify, and thereby to distort, moral phenomena.

This intention is apparent in the complex structure of the principle itself, in accordance with which four key areas of moral investigation are discernible.[9]

In the first place, the act itself needs to be independently assessed – independently, that is, either of intentions or of consequences. The traditional formulation of this condition – that the act in itself must be morally good or at least indifferent, that it must not be *malum in se* – has given rise to many difficulties. For many this criterion constitutes one of the essential weaknesses of the principle (as a result, in some formulations it is

simply omitted). Critics (even sympathetic ones) argue that it
does not make sense to talk of the *intrinsic* moral quality of an
act, since its moral quality is not something that can be established by viewing the act abstractly, or on its own. It is only in
context (that is, in the light of intentions, consequences and
other relevant circumstances) that the act becomes intelligible,
morally speaking. The *physical* structure of an act must not be
confused with its *moral* structure: the same physical performance
can be interpreted, quite validly, in diverse moral ways when
account is taken of the intention that informs it and constitutes
it as an 'act' in a moral sense (the distinction between 'murder'
and 'self-defence', for example, is not a physical distinction as
such, even though the physical properties of the act in question
are germane to its moral assessment and characterization).

To an extent this objection is upheld by the principle of double
effect itself – the 'abstract' evaluation of the act is after all a part
and not the whole of its moral assessment; yet there seems little
doubt that traditional formulations of this condition owed something to a certain 'physicalism', or to the view that the physical
properties of an act were sufficient in themselves to determine its
moral status or to establish its moral intelligibility. This seems
mistaken. What the principle of double effect assumes (necessarily so, since without this assumption the principle would make
no sense) is the inviolability of absolute moral norms such as
noncombatant immunity; but what cannot be assumed is the
application of the norm to *this* 'physical' act. Whether the act
violates or upholds the norm is precisely what is to be investi-
gated, an investigation that the principle of double effect is meant
to further. The manner in which this first condition has been
interpreted in the past has often appeared to curtail rather than
advance such investigation, and has led to that blunt or mechanical application of the principle that has brought it into disrepute.

Yet this first condition, in a revised and more analytical or
investigative form, still seems indispensable. Far from discarding
it or summarily dismissing it, as many are wont to do, there
appear strong grounds for giving it renewed and added emphasis. What it can usefully do is to direct the attention of the moral
analyst to the objective structure of the act itself. This serves a
twofold purpose. In the first place, it ensures that full value or

recognition is given to the certain physical evil (and potential moral evil) that the act contains, an evil that may be too readily discounted, or simply lost sight of, through a premature or over-hasty preoccupation with good intentions and chosen conse-quences. An accurate, complete and impartial account of the physical or pre-moral structure of the act, eschewing euphemistic and tendentious description[10] and focusing clearly and exactly on its total human costs, is a precondition of sound moral judge-ment. In this way the moral threshold of the act is raised. An act the full potential horror of which has been openly confronted is less readily justified than one the physical evil of which has never been clearly recognized or acknowledged. Language plays a key role here in determining moral perceptions. Some (perhaps most) descriptions of acts of war ('carpet bombing', 'dehousing', 'col-lateral damage', for example) seem designed to obscure their human costs and to reduce their moral impact, thereby facilitat-ing their performance.[11]

The second reason for focusing on the objective structure of the act itself lies in the need for external verification of its moral defence in terms of right intention and proportionality. That struc-ture may be such as to make more difficult, if not to rule out, the act's justification on the grounds that its evil effects are 'inciden-tal' or 'indirect' (a form of justification that the principle of double effect clearly invokes). For example, the selection of an aiming-point well away from any military target and the predominant use of anti-personnel bombs would give the lie to the defence of a bombing raid on the grounds that any civilian casualties inflicted in the raid are the unintended by-product of an attack on a legit-imate and very important military target. An examination of the physical or objective properties of the act itself (including its con-text) is, therefore, seen as an indispensable part of the moral analy-sis. Objective corroboration of moral claims (especially with regard to intentionality) is an essential requirement.[12]

The second requirement, or area of moral investigation, is right intention: the evil effects of an act are tolerable (at least potentially) only on the understanding that they are the 'unin-tended' or 'incidental' consequences of the act. What informs the principle of double effect is a certain concept of intentionality according to which 'an action or aspect of an action is intentional if it is a part of the plan on which one freely acts. That is to say, what one tries to bring about in acting, whether it be the goal one seeks to realize or the means one chooses to realize that goal, is intended. Other features of one's acts are not intended' (Finnis *et al.* 1987, p. 79). Thus, one does not intend (or, perhaps less misleadingly as far as common usage is concerned, one does not intend *in the same way*) what one accepts as a side-effect of promoting a chosen object. At the same time, the principle openly acknowledges the active role of the agent in bringing about the side-effects, which are 'foreseen, accepted (and thus *voluntarily* caused)'. Though not part of the agent's plan or object, they are not brought about inadvertently or accidentally (that is, fortuitously).[13] The principle's clear recognition of the causative role of the agent is often overlooked or played down by its critics, and this is one of the main reasons for its ill repute. According to Norman, for example, the 'principle emphasizes the importance of intentions but neglects the importance of agency' (Norman 1995, p. 91). This is difficult to fathom, since it is only the perceived importance of agency that gives point to the principle in the first place.

The intention of the agent, in this restricted or technical sense, must be directed to the good and *not at all* to the evil consequences of the act. It would not be sufficient if the distinction between good and evil effects corresponded to a distinction between 'primary' and 'secondary' intentions. The admission (even the *reluctant* admission) of the evil effect into the order of intention in any form, however minor, is enough to rule the action out in a moral sense. It must not form any part of the agent's plan or design.[14] The acid test, perhaps, is whether or not the agent has anything to gain from the evil effect itself. Does that 'evil' effect in some sense constitute a 'good' in the eyes of the agent, so that it becomes an object of his or her direct willing? The intention of the agent should be such that there can be no doubt that, if it were possible to achieve the good consequences *without* the evil effects, that would be the course of action which he or she would prefer. The evil effects must not be 'intended' or 'directly' willed (the distinction between 'intentional' and 'unintentional' being equivalent to the distinction between 'direct' and 'indirect' agency), but permitted or allowed.

The third area of investigation and concern is closely related to the second in the sense that it is designed to uncover any direct but covert willing of evil effects. As such it focuses attention on the relation between the good and the evil consequences of the act. That the evil effects are not chosen for their own sake, or as ends, is insufficient to establish their unintentional or incidental status. To argue that it does would be to drive a coach and horses through a norm like noncombatant immunity. Any military leader would then be able to justify the habitual and systematic violation of the norm on the grounds of military utility, the deaths of noncombatants being regarded as 'unintentional', 'indirect' or 'incidental' simply by virtue of not being willed on their own account, but rather on account of the ulterior military purpose that they were seen to serve. As Sir Arthur Harris argued in defence of the policy of city bombing, the intention was not to kill or even to harm civilians, as such, but to win the war. Responding to the charge that the bombing offensive included 'mere acts of terror and wanton destruction', he wrote: 'Attacks on cities like any other act of war are intolerable unless they are strategically justified' (Hastings 1993, p. 370). The principle of double effect requires not only that evil effects are not chosen for their own sake, but that they must not stand in relation to the good effects as means to end. If they were to do so, their instrumental value would make them the object of choice rather than the freely accepted side-effects of the chosen (and morally acceptable) object.[15]

The last condition engages the familiar criterion of proportionality; but it is one that warrants special emphasis in view of the criticism commonly directed at the principle that it is too permissive. It is clear that the distinction at the heart of the principle between the intended and unintended consequences of an act (or between 'direct' and 'indirect' agency) implies different *kinds* of responsibility. What it does *not* imply is that the agent bears no responsibility for the unintended side-effects of his or her acts.[16] The consequences in this case are foreseen, and therefore voluntary. The agent chooses to perform the act in the full knowledge of its potential beneficial *and* harmful effects. The agent is therefore responsible for the harmful side-effects that flow (and are seen in advance to flow) from his or her act.[17] The *question* is whether the agent is justified in accepting that responsibility and in performing the act in those circumstances. Justification must not be taken for granted. Many critics of the principle seem to assume the opposite. For example, Norman (despite his acknowledgement of the requirement of proportionality) suggests that, according to the principle, the mere fact that harmful effects are unintended is sufficient to justify the performance of the act, and that the principle virtually ignores the question of agency and of responsibility for the foreseen effects of one's actions.[18] This is a serious misrepresentation of the principle. Not only does the agent retain responsibility for the unintended harmful effects of his or her act; but that responsibility may outweigh the responsibility that the agent has for intended effects.[19] This is something that the requirement of proportionality is meant to underline. Since the consequences of the act are so mixed it is permissible only for a proportionate reason. Given the moral weight attached to noncombatant immunity by just war theory, the military objective being sought would need to be of very considerable importance in order to establish even a *prima facie* case for proceeding with the action.

In accordance with the nature of the moral reality with which it deals, therefore, the principle of double effect is a complex principle that, when considered in all its complexity, appears to be much less permissive than it is judged to be by some of its critics.[20] This can be put to the test by applying the principle to British bombing policy in the Second World War. That policy can be seen to involve several different uses of air power, the moral implications of which differ enormously. It seems clear that so far as the principle of double effect is concerned some uses are defensible and some are not. Whether those that are not are therefore incapable of any moral justification remains a key issue (as does the question of whether, in those cases, it is double effect that establishes their moral unjustifiability or some other, and perhaps simpler, moral calculation).

The first and the least problematical use of air power involved tactical deployment in support of military operations on land or at sea. For example, as the British Expeditionary Force retreated in the face of the German *blitzkrieg* air power was used to stem the German advance. Here the object of attack was either the combat units themselves or their immediate sources of supply, such as fuel and ammunition dumps, and transport and communications networks. The exact location of some of these targets, in particular their proximity to urban and residential areas, could pose serious problems. On the whole, however, the militarily defined nature of these operations made them relatively simple in moral terms. So simple in many instances that the principle of double effect hardly seems relevant. Whatever moral doubts arose could probably have been dealt with by reference to the criterion of proportionality and, given the straitened circumstances in which the British army found itself, that criterion would have been relatively easy to satisfy. This tactical use of air power continued throughout the war, though naturally its frequency, in support of land forces at least, depended on Britain's ability to mount a ground offensive. In the European sector it came into its own again during the preparation and aftermath of the Normandy invasion, when the moral problems associated with its use were exacerbated by the desperate defensive measures adopted by the German army, particularly the garrisoning of cities like Caen and Le Havre.

It is with the strategic use of air power that the moral problems begin to mount. The independent role allotted to air power engages the principle of double effect in a way that purely tactical use often does not. In this case the 'military' objective has been enlarged to comprehend not only the combat and supply units, but also their sources of supply (munitions factories, shipyards, oil refineries, etc). As suggested earlier, it seems possible for a theory of just war to accommodate this widening *up to a point*.[21] Even if the workers in a munitions factory or submarine dockyard are thought to retain their immunity from attack (and it is by no means certain that they do), it is not clear that their immunity rules out the aerial bombardment of the factory or dockyard in which they work or near which they and their families live.

On the night of 3–4 March 1942, for example, the RAF carried out a raid on the Renault factory at Billancourt in the suburbs of Paris. By this stage of the war, production of trucks and armaments at the factory had become an important part of the German war effort. Two hundred and thirty-five aircraft took part in the raid, dropping four hundred and seventy tons of high explosives and many incendiaries in a low-level attack. Precision bombing of the target was certainly intended (the objective of the attack was 'to achieve the total destruction of the factory, while at the same time causing the minimum loss of life among French civilians': Webster and Frankland 1961, Vol. 1, p. 387) and to a large extent achieved. Some deaths among the French workers in the factory and among civilians who lived nearby were anticipated, but tolerated in view of the importance of the objective. According to Wragg only five out of three thousand workers on the night shift died in the raid. Levine, however, puts the total loss of civilian lives at three hundred and sixty-seven. Estimates of the military effect of the raid also vary. Some sources claim substantial damage (with an eighth of the factory destroyed and production seriously disrupted for three months: Wragg 1986, pp. 127–8 and Levine 1992, pp. 45–6); others acknowledge the temporary disruption, but argue that long-term production at Renault was actually stimulated by the bombing ('within four months output was higher than in February': Longmate 1983, p. 212).

The Billancourt raid clearly engages the principle of double effect, since its potentially lethal impact on civilian life was well understood. In itself the bombardment of the factory, given the direct and important military use to which its products were put, was not problematic. The destruction of the factory was a legitimate act of war. The moral issue is whether the act was justified in the light of its foreseen evil effects. Those effects formed no part of the military object or plan. The manner in which the raid was conceived and executed reinforces the claim to right intention. The attacking force was at pains to eradicate or to keep to a minimum the evil and unintended consequences of the bombardment, namely, the deaths of factory workers or of civilians caught in the vicinity of the raid, and rendered vulnerable by the tendency of bombs to 'creep away' from the target.[22] This was an exercise in precision bombing, not area bombing. In this case the deaths of civilians seem accurately described as the 'incidental' or unintended side-effects of the raid, wholly without value for the attacker (the reverse was true). Lastly, though the judgement here is clearly a complex one on which it would be presumptuous for the inexpert to pronounce, the claim that the target was of such strategic importance as to be able to satisfy the requirements of proportionality appears credible, though by no means overwhelming (particularly if Levine's much higher figure of civilian fatalities and Longmate's doubts about the effectiveness of the raid are weighed in the balance).

Not all raids took this form, however. Indeed, in many respects the attack on the Renault works was the exception rather than the norm, even by that stage of the war. The huge inaccuracy of bombing,[23] combined with the alarming rate of loss of aircraft and air crew from German anti-aircraft defences when precision bombing was attempted (losses that were not simply costly, but unsustainable), had already led to the adoption by Bomber Command of an indiscriminate form of bombing in which no attempt was made, or indeed could be made, to distinguish combatant from noncombatant or military from non-military targets. As far as the British were concerned 'area' bombing by night became the accepted form of strategic air war. It was either that or nothing. By devastating a large area around the target the destruction of the target itself became more likely. The fact that this area was often a predominantly residential one, the bombing of which would result in a high loss of civilian life, was seen (to begin with, perhaps) as a regrettable necessity. It was the only way of achieving the military objective.

In considering the morality of area bombing with the aid of the principle of double effect a distinction needs to be drawn first of all between a strategy of 'selective' area bombing, that is, of area bombing that has as its sole objective the destruction of an important military target (or targets) and is resorted to out of military necessity alone (that is, because of the involuntary absence of an alternative, more discriminate and therefore more acceptable, means of attack) and a strategy of 'general' area bombing that involves deliberate targeting of noncombatants and non-military installations or structures (either solely or as an accompaniment of military targeting) as a way of undermining the capacity and will of the enemy to fight. This distinction is often suppressed in moral and just war criticisms of the British bombing offensive. In so far as the strategy of 'selective' area bombing was often more hypothetical than real, this is understandable. In theory, however (and perhaps in this instance to a limited extent in practice), the distinction appears to have *some* moral significance, sufficient to establish a clear moral preference for 'selective' over 'general' area bombing. Failure to acknowledge the distinction between the two strategies leads to the neglect of some key issues in the moral assessment of strategic bombing (as well as in those instances of tactical bombing, such as the bombardment of Caen, that are akin to siege warfare).

Considered hypothetically, then, how might this less morally objectionable and 'selective' form of area bombing satisfy 'right intention'? It would be a form of bombing that, despite its crude method of attack, remained informed and guided by a clear and strong preference for *precision* bombing of a specifically defined military target, with as little harm to civilian life as possible. Its sole objective would need to be the destruction of the military target, area bombing being accepted out of necessity rather than being freely chosen as a preferred method of attack. This would rule out the acceptance by the attacker of any military or strategic benefit from the collateral harm that the raid inflicts. The proposal, for example, that 'the rationale of eroding and/or breaking the morale or will of the enemy population by aerial attacks on population centers' is permissible 'as a collateral effect of otherwise acceptable attacks on military targets' (O'Brien 1981, p. 80) is morally incoherent.[24] As the principle of double effect maintains, to accept the benefit of the 'collateral' or 'side' effect is to 'intend' that effect, thereby undermining its 'incidental' status. The evil effect – in this case the deaths of noncombatants and the damage done to the infrastructure of goods and services that sustains civilian life – must be neither a 'primary' *nor* a 'secondary' intention. 'Selective' area bombing must not become a pretext for 'general' area bombing, with its deliberate targeting of noncombatants or with its reliance on general devastation to achieve its military objective. Of course, any form of area bombing in heavily populated urban localities could only result in massive loss of noncombatant life and extensive damage to essential services. The harm that it inflicted would be foreknown with certainty. Responsibility for that harm would have to be accepted, yet it would not have to be, and clearly must not be, 'chosen' in the sense that it formed part of the military plan or objective. In so far as the destructive impact of the bombing on civilian life was seen to be entirely without military or strategic value (it might even have considerable political and military *dis*value through the opposition to the war that it might generate among allies or a domestic public, for example) it might be considered 'unintentional' in a relevant moral sense. In the order of intention, therefore, there seems to be a real and significant difference between area bombing of this kind and general area bombing, that is, area bombing by choice.[25]

Of course, there would need to be objective corroboration of right intention. The overall context and structure of the attack would need to support the claim that this is area bombing that has the destruction of a military target as its sole objective. In planning the attack, for example, the nature and location of the specific military target would dictate how the larger target area was defined, as well as how it was to be attacked. In defining that area a well-intentioned attacker would err on the side of caution, drawing its parameters conservatively rather than expansively, and with a view to restricting its destructive impact on the civilian population as much as possible. The aiming-point, the timing and the direction of the attack would be selected to maximize damage to the military target and to minimize harm to civilians living in the commercial or residential districts. Similarly the ordnance employed in the bombardment would be chosen to inflict greater damage on structures than on persons, the use of shrapnel bombs and similar weaponry of a mainly anti-personnel nature being avoided, as well as incendiary devices the effects of which are uncontrollable by design. Right intention would be evident too in the overall context of bombing policy, in the disfavour with which area bombing was viewed by strategists and policy-makers, and in the concerted attempts to make area bombing redundant by developing a precision bombing capacity as rapidly as possible.

Finally, given the scale of the suffering inevitably inflicted on the civilian population by this method of bombing, it would be resorted to only for the gravest of reasons and in the extremest of circumstances (say, to ensure the destruction of a military research and development facility that threatened to secure an enemy victory). Easy, habitual and 'normal' recourse to 'selective' area bombing would be ruled out. Given its indiscriminate nature, there could be no blanket justification of the method. Rather, in each instance of its use proportionality would need to be strictly applied, and procedures would need to be in place to ensure that it was. The presumption would be against use: a presumption that could be set aside only for the gravest of reasons. The *possible* military benefit would need to be weighed against the *certain* deaths of civilians (civilians whose lives were not devalued in the eyes of the attacker simply because they were citizens of an enemy state).

Hypothetically, therefore, there may be a distinction of some moral relevance (and practical import) between this 'selective' form of area bombing and 'general' area bombing. In the particular case of the British bombing offensive, however, the distinction does not stand up to scrutiny, and this is so even in respect of the earlier phase of the offensive, when area bombing seems to have been resorted to not for its own sake but as the nearest thing to precision bombing that was available at the time. This becomes clear if, in accordance with one of the requirements of double effect, we look for objective corroboration of right intention not just in the plan of the attack and the manner of its execution, not just in the immediate strategy that guided both, but in the overall context out of which the strategy arose.

It is clear that the justification of selective area bombing relies in large measure on some concept of 'necessity'. The method of attack was justified, its defenders argue, because it was adopted, not by choice, but as the only way of destroying legitimate and vitally important military targets. This key concept of 'necessity', however, is not as solid or compelling as it might appear at first sight.

In the first place, though it is true that at the time the method was adopted there was no alternative method of achieving the particular military objective, this begs an important question (a question with a moral as well as a military significance): Was this the only, or even the best, objective? As some have argued, the area bombing campaign (even in its 'general' and most destructive phase) was of limited strategic value, and the resources that were deployed in its execution could have been used more effectively elsewhere (for instance, in the development of a precision bombing capacity and of a long-range fighter escort that would have allowed that capacity to be used effectively,[26] in the diversion of part of the existing bomber force to other arenas of conflict where it might have been used with equal or greater effect, in the diversion of industrial output from the bomber programme to other under-resourced but more promising military programmes, and so on).[27] The military efficacy of these alternative strategies is highly debatable; but what seems incontrovertible is their moral preferability. The existence of realistic, and more moral, alternative strategies (if proven) seriously weakens the defence of 'selective' area bombing, since it undermines its basis: the 'necessity' invoked would then be, at best, only a *relative* necessity.

The 'necessity' in question appears even more suspect if the perspective is widened, and the historical context of the bombing is taken into account. The policy was the result, not of circumstances beyond the control of the agents themselves, but of much earlier policy decisions, which had their source in the experience of that savage war of attrition that was the First World War. 'Four years of trench warfare,' writes Frankland, 'produced ... the idea of strategic bombing' (Frankland 1965, p. 110). The war forced a radical rethink of military strategy, in the course of which strategists began to see the strategic air war as a means of avoiding another costly war of attrition, even perhaps a means of bringing about the end of all war (at least between states with the capacity to wage a strategic air war).[28] As early as 1917 the Smuts Report had envisaged 'absolutely no limit to the scale of its [air power's] future independent use', and had foreseen that 'the day may not be far off when aerial operations with their devastation of enemy lands and destruction of industrial and populous centres on a vast scale may become the principal operations of war' (quoted in Hastings 1993, p. 38). The idea quickly took root, particularly in the mind of Trenchard, the first Chief of Air Staff and the dominant influence within the RAF in the years between the wars. Arguing that the object of modern war was the defeat of an enemy nation, Trenchard claimed that the quickest and most effective way to achieve this was to bypass the enemy's armed forces and to subject the centres of production, transport and communication that sustained the enemy war effort to intensive aerial bombardment (see Hastings 1993, pp. 39f). Convinced that 'the moral effect of bombing stands undoubtedly to the material effect in a proportion of twenty to one', Trenchard saw the destruction of civilian morale and of the enemy's *will* to fight as the primary objective of any future air campaign. His theories were even put into practice, in a small way, in Iraq, where air power (rather than ground forces) was used to put down rebellion by bombing villages in rebel areas.[29]

What had emerged in the interwar years was a strategy aimed deliberately and systematically at the violation of noncombatant immunity. This was well understood. Baldwin, the former prime minister, summed up the thinking in blunt but accurate terms when he addressed the House of Commons on 10 November 1932: 'The only defence is in offence, which means that you have to kill more women and children more quickly than the enemy if you want to save yourselves' (quoted in Hastings 1993, p. 43). Defenders of the strategy accepted that in future non-combatants would be killed not 'indirectly' or 'incidentally', but 'directly' and 'intentionally'. *Non*combatants were now the prime target.

It was this concept of strategic air war that informed British armaments policy as war approached. In aircraft production British efforts, unlike those of the French and Germans, were concentrated on the development of the *heavy* bomber, which with its longer range and greater load was better equipped for strategic and independent use than the medium or fighter bomber favoured by the French and Germans, which was designed with a tactical and support role in mind (see Hastings 1993, p. 50). In short, the lack of a precision bombing capacity (on which the justification from necessity largely rests) was voluntary. The British bombing force was not designed to bomb precisely, because indiscriminate bombing was the favoured strategy. Area bombing was not something forced upon reluctant British strategists by the circumstances of war. It was a strategy of *choice*, not of necessity, and, therefore, one that ruled out 'right intention' from the start. The context of 'selective' area bombing, far from providing objective corroboration of right intention, abolishes any such pretence. Despite initial wavering, area bombing was bound to appear sooner or later in its true colours.[30]

The course that the bombing offensive subsequently took confirms this assessment. The erosion of 'selective' area bombing began with the creeping acceptance of the strategic value of so-called 'collateral' damage. Sir Richard Peirse, Harris's predecessor as C.-in-C. of Bomber Command and himself an advocate of precision bombing, came to accept that what was inevitable as a by-product of an attack on a military target was also *desirable* (see Hastings 1993, pp. 96–7). As has been argued already, such acceptance of the value of 'collateral damage' clearly undermines 'right intention', since an effect ceases to be incidental as soon as it forms part (even a minor part) of the plan or design. Such considerations soon became academic, however, when what had previously formed a subordinate part of the strategy came to dominate it entirely.

By early 1942 the destruction of the cities had become the strategy's main purpose. In February an Air Ministry directive to Bomber Command made explicit a policy that had already begun to shape practice: 'the primary object of your operations should now be focussed on the morale of the enemy civil population and in particular, of the industrial workers' (Webster and Frankland 1961, Vol. IV, p. 144). Harris, the new C.-in-C. of Bomber Command, embraced the policy enthusiastically and singlemindedly. By sustained attacks from the air enough German cities could be reduced to rubble to destroy German morale and to bring war production to a virtual standstill. The aim was not the destruction of specific industries of a militarily essential nature, such as the aircraft industry, but rather the general and widespread devastation of civilian life. It was a strategy that deliberately bypassed the legitimate military target and put the civilian or noncombatant population in the front line.[31] The policy quickly bore fruit. In March Lübeck (described by Harris as 'built more like a firelighter than a human habitation') was set alight, and in May Cologne was subjected to the first 'thousand-bomber raid'. Between March and July of the following year the bombing offensive reached a new intensity with the Battle of the Ruhr, when the cities of the Ruhr valley, and Essen in particular, were bombed repeatedly and indiscriminately. Worse was to follow.

The Battle of Hamburg, codenamed revealingly 'Operation Gomorrah', took place in the summer of 1943. It was a joint operation involving a series of coordinated attacks by British and American forces, Bomber Command attacking by night and the US Eighth Air Force by day. This cooperation was a result of the policy agreed by Churchill and Roosevelt at the Casablanca Conference earlier that year. At that conference the aim of the Allied air offensive was described as follows: 'Your primary object will be the progressive destruction and dislocation of the German military, industrial and economic system, and the undermining of the morale of the German people to a point where their capacity for armed resistance is fatally weakened' (Webster and Frankland 1961, Vol. II, p. 12).

This joint declaration concealed important differences of strategy and tactics. From the start the Americans favoured the operational method of high-level precision bombing by day, having neither the will nor the capacity to engage in area bombing by night. American strategists believed that the key to the strategic air war – and perhaps to the war as a whole – lay in the targeting of selected industries on which the German war effort was vitally dependent. Harris scathingly dismissed these targets as 'panacea' targets, which were at best a distraction and at worst a threat to the real, that is, 'general', area offensive. With the support of Churchill he resisted attempts by the Americans and by at least some of the Air Staff to move British policy away from general to a more selective form of area bombing (as envisaged in the Pointblank directive, which proposed daylight, precision bombing of strategic targets by the Eighth USAAF, followed by Bomber Command's night and area bombing of the cities in which those targets were located).[32]

These strategic differences were evident in the raids on Hamburg. Unlike the four raids carried out by Bomber Command, the two American raids were not exercises in area or saturation bombing, but attempts to precision bomb the Blohm & Voss U-boat yard and the Klöckner aero-engine factory, situated on the south bank of the River Elbe opposite the main residential areas. Neither raid was particularly successful in achieving its stated objectives, and neither was very costly in terms of civilian casualties. According to one estimate, less than two hundred people died in Hamburg as a result of the American raids (Middlebrook 1980, Chs 11 and 13).

The plan and the effects of Bomber Command's operations were very different. The intention of the attack was stated uncompromisingly in the official Operations Order: 'To destroy Hamburg' (Musgrove 1981, p. vii). This was to be achieved by burning the city to the ground. The precise method was that used in most area bombing: the aiming-point was the centre of the city, which, being more densely built-up than the suburbs, was most susceptible to area attack; the first wave of bombers dropped high-explosive general purpose bombs, which were intended to block the streets and disrupt firefighting; the main force dropped 4,000 lb high capacity bombs and a mass of incendiaries; the 4,000–pounders or 'blockbusters', which had little penetrating power but an enormous blast-effect, were intended to blow in the roofs and windows of the buildings, while the incendiaries were to set them alight (see Middlebrook 1980, pp. 29–30; Levine 1992, pp. 31–2).

The targeting policy used by Bomber Command in the Hamburg raids, particularly in relation to potential and important military targets, is revealing. There is little doubt that Hamburg was a city of great strategic importance and that there were individual targets in its environs that were classifiable as key military objectives – the shipyards, which accounted for more than a third of the U-boat production, for example, or the crude-oil refineries, which made up 28 per cent of German production (Levine 1992, p. 59). The presence of these installations provided grounds for an attack; but not for one of the kind carried out.

In formulating targeting policy the evidence indicates that so far as the British contribution to the raids was concerned the military targets were simply ignored: the direction of attack (from the north in all the raids with the exception of the fourth and last) was chosen to ensure that bombs that fell short of the aiming-point as a result of the 'creep-back' effect would not be wasted but would fall on the residential districts to the north of the Elbe rather than on the U-boat yards and other strategic industrial sites to the south of the river. The plan for the first raid envisaged that 'the bombing would spread back from the area near the Aiming Point [on the north side of the river in the city's commercial and cultural centre], across the districts of Neustadt, Rotherbaum, Harvestehude, Eimsbüttel, Eppendorf and Lokstedt.

... Every one of the districts ... was mainly residential. There were no sizeable industrial establishments anywhere in the area that it was hoped to bomb. No part of the attack was planned to fall south of the river where the U-boat yards and other major war industries were located' (Middlebrook 1980, p. 100). In the second and by far the most destructive raid the aiming-point was again the city centre, with an approach flight from the east-north-east 'so that the creep-back would develop across the densely built-up residential areas south-east of the Alster lake and north of the Elbe river' (Middlebrook 1980, p. 234). In the third raid the aiming-point remained the same, with the direction of attack ('just west of due north') chosen to ensure a hit on 'the largest part of residential Hamburg not seriously damaged in previous raids' (Middlebrook 1980, p. 283). Exceptionally, the direction of attack in the fourth and final raid was from the south. There were two aiming-points, one to the north of the river, the other to the south in the town of Harburg. Since the two points straddled the industrial area of Hamburg, some damage to that area might be expected, though the target plan left few doubts about the principal objective: 'the bombing would continue to be on densely built-up areas of a mainly residential nature' (Middlebrook 1980, p. 301).

Between the nights of 24–25 July and 2–3 August more than three thousand sorties were carried out by the British. Nearly nine thousand tons of bombs, half of which were incendiaries, were dropped on the city, mainly on its residential and commercial areas.[33] Six thousand acres or nine square miles of the city were reduced to rubble, about 60 per cent of its housing was destroyed, fifty thousand of its inhabitants were killed (roughly equivalent to the number of British civilians killed by German bombing during the entire war) and forty thousand injured. In particular, the attack on the night of July 27–28 exceeded all expectations.

On that night the intensive bombing, with its high concentration of incendiaries, combined with unusual weather conditions over the target to produce a firestorm from which there was no escape. The city was transformed into a huge furnace. Families who had taken refuge in the basements of their houses and apartment blocks were overcome by fumes, and their bodies melted down by the heat where they were not reduced to ashes by the flames. Those who took to the streets fared little better in the storm that raged outside. An eyewitness has described how she and her aunt braved the falling debris, the scorching wind and the 'rain of large sparks ... each as large as a five-mark piece' to find the relative safety of open ground:

> We got to the Löschplatz all right but couldn't go on across the Eiffestrasse because the asphalt had melted. There were people on the roadway, some already dead, some still lying alive but stuck in the asphalt. They must have rushed on to the roadway without thinking. Their feet had got stuck and then they had put out their hands to try to get out again. They were on their hands and knees screaming. (Middlebrook 1980, pp. 266–7)

More than forty thousand people are thought to have perished on that single night of terror.

The British bombing of Hamburg cannot satisfy even the most basic requirement of the principle of double effect. The killing of noncombatants and the destruction of the city were not the unintended side-effects of attacks on military targets, but the primary purpose of the raids. This was openly acknowledged by the military planners, who laid no claim to 'right intention' in the double effect sense.[34] That being so, the requirement of objective corroboration of right intention is redundant, though corroboration of *wrong* intention is plain enough in the design and execution of the plan of battle. The defence of the bombing owes nothing to the distinction between direct and indirect agency or intended and incidental effects. Instead it focuses exclusively on the end that the strategy was made to serve and on the claim that the good consequences of the bombing outweighed the bad. Those who devised the raids acted not in any vindictive spirit (no doubt they would have preferred to spare noncombatants), but from the conviction that this was the best way to defeat the enemy and to bring the war to its swiftest, and least costly, conclusion. In this defence of the Hamburg raid, and of the bombing offensive as a whole, what constitutes a part of the principle of double effect, namely proportionality, comes to monopolize moral reasoning.

In a theoretical sense, what lies behind this defence is the 'consequentialist' (or 'proportionalist') notion that the morality of an

act can only be determined in the light of its foreseeable consequences (or at least in the light of its overall harms and benefits,
which may include reference to the intrinsic value or disvalue of
the act itself). If the long-term good effects or overall benefits of
the bombing policy can be seen to outweigh its long-term evil
effects or overall harms then the act becomes morally permissible, despite its pre-moral or physical evil, and thereby the distinction between the directly and indirectly voluntary, so beloved
of double effect theorists, becomes redundant. For a sufficiently
grave or proportionate reason the direct willing of the pre-moral
evil effect as a means is justifiable. In this way acts that are
regarded as intrinsically evil (in a moral sense) and therefore
morally prohibited by the 'absolutist' *may* receive moral justification at the hands of the consequentialist (or proportionalist).

Much just war theorizing has veered in this consequentialist
direction, and away from the moral absolutism associated with
the principle of double effect.[35] It may be, of course, that just war
theorists approaching the bombing of Hamburg from a consequentialist direction come to the same conclusion as those tradi-
tionalists who apply the principle of double effect. They may
argue, for example, that the long-term effects of a policy of city
bombing, including its destructive impact on the moral culture
of war and the fearful precedent that it set, far outweighed any
conceivable military or strategic benefit.[36] In other words, and as
'moderate' consequentialists or 'proportionalists' of a just war
persuasion are quick to point out, one can reach the same desti-
nation (the upholding of noncombatant immunity and the prohibition of the city bombing offensive) by a variety of routes, the
consequentialist or proportionalist route being preferable both
because it is considered truer to moral experience than its tradi-
tionalist or absolutist rival, and also because the absolutist position itself is often considered to be implicitly consequentialist.[37]

The implication, however, that the immunity of noncombatants is as secure in the hands of the 'consequentialists' as it is in
the hands of the 'absolutists' remains open to serious doubt. A
'virtually exceptionless norm', which is how the principle of noncombatant immunity is regarded by consequentialists, cannot be
as secure as one which is regarded as absolute or exceptionless.
Charles Curran, for example, endorses McCormick's view that the

norm is virtually exceptionless because 'any possible exceptions would ultimately lead to greater evils than the good that might possibly be achieved in the one exception' (Curran 1977, p. 124). It is not clear, however, that he is justified in doing so given the terms of his own argument, for he goes on to pose the following question: 'Could one not accept the rule – directly killing the innocent is wrong except in those cases where one is forced into a situation in which there is certitude that this is the only way a far greater number of innocent persons can be saved?' Curran's own advocacy of this rule rests on the dubious assumption that there will be very few cases to which it might apply, and none at all in time of war. The certitude that the rule requires is thought to be impossible 'in the complex situation of warfare and the direct killing of noncombatants' (p. 126). But is it, bearing in mind that the certitude that the rule requires can only be a relative certitude anyway?

Clearly, there are many who would wholly endorse Curran's rule, but who would reject his claim about its inapplicability to warfare. Those who justified the bombing of Hiroshima did so in large measure because they were convinced that the use of the bomb saved many more lives than it took. Curran might argue that it was only allied intransigence that tipped the scales in favour of the bombing, and that there was an alternative, namely, a negotiated peace (or a demonstration bombing). The extent to which these were genuine alternatives remains a matter of historical controversy; but let us assume that they were not, and that the choice confronting US commanders was either to invade Japan, at an estimated cost of a million American and Japanese lives, or to drop the bomb on Hiroshima. Even if certainty about the net saving of human life was attainable, would that certainty be sufficient to justify the bombing and to remove the injustice done to the people of Hiroshima? That injustice seems to be the heart of the matter, morally speaking; but it is something about which Curran's rule is silent.[38]

Not all consequentialists share the view that the norm prohibiting the direct killing of noncombatants in wartime is virtually exceptionless. Even moderate or restrained consequentialists display a clear readiness to override what is perhaps at best a *prima facie* norm in certain 'extreme' circumstances – circumstances that are by no means rare in modern war. Michael Walzer's partial defence of the British bombing offensive falls into this category. Rejecting moral-absolutism on the grounds that it is 'not ... a plausible moral doctrine', Walzer adopts a 'utilitarianism of extremity' that 'concedes that in certain very special cases, though never as a matter of course even in just wars, the only restraints upon military action are those of usefulness and proportionality' (Walzer 1992, p. 231). Applying this approach to the case of the British bombing offensive, he argues that in its early stages at least the policy was justified because it was resorted to in a supreme emergency 'when victory was not in sight and the specter of defeat ever present ... when no other decision seemed possible if there was to be any sort of military offensive against Nazi Germany' (p. 258). By the summer of 1942 that rationale no longer applied, and, therefore, the subsequent bombing of German cities, including the bombing of Hamburg, was unjustified: 'Utilitarian calculation can force us to violate the rules of war only when we are face-to-face not merely with defeat but with a defeat likely to bring disaster to a political community. But these calculations have no similar effects when what is at stake is only the speed or the scope of victory' (p. 268).[39]

If moderate forms of consequentialism threaten the principle of noncombatant immunity, more extreme or purer forms clearly undermine it. In these cases so narrowly defined are the consequences and so monopolistic and morally decisive are those consequences seen to be, that the moral prohibition on the direct killing of noncombatants is simply set aside. The instrumental value attached to such killing – its contribution to victory – is allowed to override all other considerations. In reply to a wartime speech in the Lords by Bishop Bell, in which the bishop had criticized the area bombing policy on the grounds that 'this progressive devastation of cities is threatening the roots of civilization', Viscount Cranborne, the government spokesman, said: 'The only way to end this horror is to beat our enemies rapidly and completely ... From that aim we must not avert our eyes, however kind our hearts, however deep our sentiments' (cited in Longmate 1983, p. 377). From such a standpoint the entire war is seen as a state of extreme emergency that, as such, justifies the use of any means in its effective prosecution. The harm that is inflicted as a result is not of course gratuitous; but its military or strategic utility is seen to be its sole and sufficient justification. Of the atomic bombing of Japan General Curtis LeMay wrote: 'Anything which will achieve the desired results should be employed. If those bombs shortened the war only by days, they rendered an inestimable service' (quoted in Finnis *et al.*, p. 272).[40] Those consequentialists or proportionalists who regard the principle of noncombatant immunity as virtually exceptionless will no doubt argue that Harris's or Le May's understanding of proportionate reason is grossly deficient, and that even such a limited and restrained defence of the bombing offensive as Walzer's fails to consider all the long-term consequences and moral costs of such a policy.[41] The point, however, is that the concept of proportionate reason is such an elastic concept, open to such diverse interpretation, that it cannot be other than a very unstable foundation on which to rest the norm of noncombatant immunity.

The principle of noncombatant immunity is not some abstract and *a priori* moral norm devised by moral theorists in the teeth of moral experience. Rather, it enshrines the moral convictions and understanding of past generations. Its place in the theory of just war is central, since without it that theory loses much of its coherence. How can a theory that claims to regard war as an instrument of justice countenance the injustice involved in the systematic suppression of the rights of noncombatants? Just war theory is, therefore, committed to the defence of this important principle; and that defence seems more secure in the hands of those who regard it as an 'absolute' norm than it does in the hands of those for whom it is, at best, a 'virtually exceptionless' norm. Of course those who are committed to the defence of noncombatant immunity as an absolute norm are not committed to the defence of the principle of double effect (at least not in the same way). As has already been pointed out, the principle of double effect is not itself a moral norm, but a method of moral analysis. Whatever worth it has depends therefore on its utility in this regard; and, on balance, it seems that without some version of double effect important moral implications remain hidden, and the moral judgement of war is thereby seriously impaired. By keeping firmly in view those aspects of moral practice that a consequentialist view deliberately ignores the principle of double effect lends essential support to the fundamental moral norm of noncombatant immunity.

Notes

1 Note that by 'accidental' Vitoria does not mean 'fortuitous'. Since the agent acts 'with full knowledge of what [he] is doing' this sense is ruled out. Rather 'accidental' signifies 'not essential to the act'. For a fuller consideration of this idea see the later discussion of the principle of double effect.

2 Suarez agrees with Vitoria. The burning of a city is permissible as long as 'the death of the innocent is not sought for its own sake, but it is an incidental consequence: hence it is considered not as voluntarily inflicted but simply allowed by one who is making use of his right in time of necessity. A confirmation of this argument lies in the fact that it would be impossible through any other means to end the war' (quoted in Renick 1994). In at least one respect Suarez's formulation, as it stands, is far too permissive: the death of the innocent must not be sought at all – neither for its own sake *nor* as a means to something else. The criterion of proportionality also needs to be made explicit and to be given much greater emphasis.

3 Of course, this does not mean that warring states have an automatic right to resort to strategic warfare. Such a military response might be entirely out of proportion to the threat posed, and therefore quite unjustified. In the Falklands War, for example, Britain's attack on the manifestations of Argentine armed forces was proportionate in a way that an attack on the sources of supply might not have been. The reason for the tentative conclusion is that even here, in such a limited war, the proportionality of 'strategic' warfare cannot be ruled out. If Argentina had been able to produce its own Exocet missiles, for example, a British attack on the factory where they were being made would not have been disproportionate, given the grave threat to the task force posed by that weapon. For a fuller discussion of the criterion of *proportionality* see Chapter 9.

4 Cf. Berlin 1969.

5 Of course, a quite different moral approach to the problem might be adopted (an approach that seems implicit in the First Protocol of the Geneva Convention, 1977); one that, while recognizing the legitimacy of attacks upon an armaments factory or similar industrial enterprise, seeks to uphold the noncombatant status and immunity from direct attack of the workers themselves. Such an approach has obvious moral attractions, though it is not without difficulties of its own. The first problem is the obvious and practical one: how can the factory be attacked without attacking the workers? In most cases it

cannot. Nonetheless, this approach would require the attacker to choose an alternative and less lethal method of attack in cases where such an effective alternative exists. The device of alerting the workers by first overflying the target, for example – a device that the British used in their attack on the Gnome-Rhone aero-engine factory at Limoges (according to Leonard Cheshire who took part in the raid) – might be employed as a way of saving lives. This may be feasible without handing a military advantage to the enemy and without impairing the effectiveness of the raid or greatly increasing the risks to the attacking force. Such an interpretation would have a fundamental impact on the moral understanding of strategic warfare, the justification of any instance of which would then be possible only by invoking some version of the principle of double effect. The second and much more serious problem, however, is that the workers are likely to be seen as one of the most important elements of the production process, and therefore as posing one of the greatest threats. Plant can be replaced relatively quickly. Replacing skilled workers is not so easy. On these grounds it is argued the classification of the workers in militarily essential industrial enterprises as combatants is justified. Even, therefore, direct attacks on them in their place of work do not constitute violations of the principle of noncombatant immunity.

6 The assumption underlying the second version of the principle that the moral problem only arises with the intentional killing of noncombatants is unfounded. Even the unintentional (but foreseen) killing of noncombatants is morally problematic. Such deaths, for example, may be deemed morally impermissible without a proportionate reason. Bringing about the physical evil without such reason transforms the physical evil into a moral evil. See within.

7 Walzer does end up endorsing the principle, though in a revised form. Arguably, his revision simply makes explicit something that the principle already contains in its traditional form (see pp. 152–9). Moreover, it does not prevent him suppressing the principle (and the norm of noncombatant immunity that in this instance of its application it protects) when faced with an 'extreme emergency'.

8 Norman, for example, writes of 'the impression often created by the "double effect" principle, that it is an evasion, that it lets people off the hook' (Norman 1995, p. 89). In the light of his own criticism of the principle that impression seems more than justified; but it is a criticism that relies for its force on the suppression of key elements of the principle and its virtual reduction to a matter of intentionality alone. Holmes's criticism too appears to be based on a similarly attenuated form of the principle (Holmes 1989, p. 196).

9 On this interpretation it is the investigative nature of the principle of

double effect that is to the fore. The four criteria are intended to direct the attention of the moral analyst to aspects of the act that might otherwise be overlooked. The principle is not to be understood as a kind of moral template that provides ready-made and straightforward answers to perplexing moral problems, but as a guide to moral analysis designed to reveal the hidden complexities and ramifications of the moral situation to which it is being applied, and as an aid to independent moral judgement exercised in the light of all the moral 'facts'.

10 Of course not all tendentious description is euphemistic. Critics of an act or policy will often seek to strengthen opposition to it by employing descriptive terms that take its viciousness or moral deformity for granted ('terror bombing' instead of 'area bombing', for example). 'Hypersensitization' is as unhelpful to moral analysis and judgement as 'desensitization' or 'sanitization'. Good examples of both are evident in the contemporary debate about abortion, where selective description leads not just to a breakdown of communication among the protagonists but to the suppression of key issues or areas of moral investigation.

11 Commenting, in November 1943, on a letter sent to Churchill by the Commander-in-Chief of Bomber Command, the Assistant Chief of Air Staff (Intelligence) wrote: 'Although he [Harris] speaks of nine-tenths of German industry being nearer Norfolk than Lombardy, we are sure he really means that nine-tenths of the German population is nearer Norfolk, and in the light of our new morale paper which is about to be published, it is the population which is the joint in the German armour. The C-in-C's spear is in it, but it needs a jolt to drive it home to the heart' (quoted in Hastings 1993, p. 258). Harris was not usually so evasive.

12 This is something either overlooked or played down by critics of the principle. Norman mentions it, though it plays little part in his analysis and criticism of the principle (Norman 1995, p. 86f). Holmes appears not even to recognize the requirement. For him the principle is essentially an 'internalist' principle. Hence his wholly 'permissive' interpretation of it: 'On the assumption that we can "direct" or "aim" intentions as we please, any action whatsoever can be performed with a good intention' ... 'In fact no action whatsoever is prohibited by the principle of double effect so long as one acts from a good intention' (Holmes 1989, pp. 199 and 196). What lies behind this is Holmes's view that 'acts do not themselves include intentions' (p. 197). A contrary assumption underpins double effect, according to which intentions are seen to affect the objective structure of an act. Hence the principle's insistence on the objective corroboration of right intention: Does the structure (and the context) of the act support or cast doubt on the claim to right intention?

13 Finnis *et al.* 1987, p. 291.

14 Both O'Brien and Ramsey appear to suggest that the agent is permitted to derive benefit from 'collateral' or 'side' effects. This seems incoherent and a misuse of the principle of double effect, since in such a case the effect would cease to be 'collateral' or 'incidental' and become 'intentional', that is, part of the agent's plan or design.

15 According to the traditional view the non-instrumentality of the evil effect can be guaranteed only if the good and intended effect flows at least as immediately from the act as the evil effect. If the evil effect precedes the good effect it takes on the character of a means to an end, and thereby becomes an object of direct willing. This interpretation is disputed. It has been argued, most notably by Grisez, that instrumentality does not follow automatically from physical precedence or even from cause–effect relationship. As long as the good and evil effects form part of the same act (so that the evil effect is not the product of a separate and discrete act) then the precise sequence of events is seen to be irrelevant: 'If the unity of action is preserved and the intention specifying the action is good, whether the good or evil effect is prior in the order of nature is morally irrelevant. From the ethical point of view, all of the events in the indivisible performance of a unitary human act are equally immediate to the agent; none is prior (a means) to another.' The effect of this revision on the theory of double effect is to 'allow a limited extension of its power to justify acts hitherto regarded as evil' (Grisez 1970, pp. 89–91). According to Grisez it would not be sufficient to justify the use of strategic bombing in the Second World War. This seems clear in relation to 'general' area bombing, but less obviously so in relation to 'selective' area bombing (see the discussion within).

16 Grisez writes: 'We are responsible for more than just what we aim at and choose ... one who chooses to drink and drive foresees possible harm to the lives and property of others. Though drunken drivers do not aim at this harm or include it in the proposal they adopt, they nevertheless bear some responsibility for this foreseen side effect. An accident which is due to their condition is their fault ... Although one bears responsibility for foreseen side effects, one does not have the same sort of responsibility for them as for what one chooses ... Still, in many cases the effects one foresees and accepts have a great significance for human goods. Although in some cases one may accept effects which significantly inhibit or damage some human good, this possibility is not unlimited ... Hence, although one is not responsible for side effects one accepts in the same way one is responsible for what one does by choice, responsibility for the former can be just as grave as responsibility for the latter' (Grisez 1983, p. 239).

17 Even effects which are *not* foreseen may still be imputable to the
   agent. The fact that they are not foreseen may arise from moral indifference, negligence, or *culpable* ignorance.

18 Norman argues that 'the weakness of the doctrine is ... that it too
   easily exonerates people from responsibility for the unintended outcomes which they knowingly bring about' (Norman 1995, p. 107).
   Elsewhere, with the Allied strategic bombing campaign against Iraq
   in the Gulf War in mind, he writes: 'To describe several thousand
   civilian deaths as "unintended", even if it is true, is an evasion of
   responsibility ... It does not follow ... that we are necessarily any less
   responsible for deaths which we bring about, simply because they
   are unintended ... It seems to me that in such cases the doctrine of
   double effect puts altogether too much weight on the description of
   the agents' intentions' (Norman 1995, p. 204).

19 Norman's proposition, which he enunciates by way of *criticism* of the
   principle of double effect, is in fact thoroughly endorsed by the principle itself: 'We cannot say in a general way ... that intentional acts
   carry a greater weight than unintended consequences' (Norman
   1995, p. 108).

20 Holmes's criticism of the principle rests on an oversimplification not
   just of the principle, but of the reality to which it refers. 'Suppose',
   he writes, 'two pilots fly over a military target surrounded by
   schools, hospitals, and recreation areas. Both have orders to destroy
   the military target. But one drops his bombs intending only to
   destroy the target even though he knows that in the process he will
   kill innocent persons, the other does so intending as well to kill those
   persons. They perform virtually identical acts. But the one act,
   according to double effect, is permissible, the other impermissible'
   (Holmes 1989, p. 197). This description of the act is simply too thin
   to allow reasoned moral assessment of it. It begs the very questions
   that need to be put. The situations that give rise to the moral dilemmas to which double effect is a response are invariably more complicated than this, and it is in their complexity that their moral
   meaning is to be sought (as the subsequent analysis of bombing
   policy attempts to demonstrate).

21 In the case of any strategic air war the sticking-point is likely to
   come when the 'military' definition of the target gives way to a
   much looser 'economic' definition. 'Economic' warfare may make
   strategic sense; but its reconciliation with the just conduct of war
   seems impossible.

22 It was, however, the fear of killing *French* civilians, and not civilians
   or noncombatants as such, that informed the planning of the raid.
   This suggests that in different circumstances civilians would be
   slaughtered without scruple. Sadly, this is how things turned out.

23 The Butt Report of August 1941 concluded that with the help of a full moon two in five bombing crews got to within five miles of their target. On moonless nights the proportion dropped to one in fifteen. Navigation, rather than bomb aiming, was the fundamental problem. One crew ended up bombing England rather than a German airbase in Holland as a result of navigational error (see Hastings 1993, p. 84–5).

24 The same applies to Ramsey's suggestion that a policy of nuclear deterrence that depends for its efficacy on the potential collateral damage inflicted in a counterforce attack (so-called 'collateral deterrence') is permissible when a countervalue policy is not (Ramsey 1983, Chs 14–15).

25 Cohen argues along these lines in *Arms and Judgement* (1989).

26 This was largely achieved in the latter part of the war with the introduction of improved navigational and bomb-aiming equipment and of the American Mustang long-range fighter. Arguably this could have been achieved much earlier but for the persistence with area bombing methods.

27 See Hastings 1993, p. 125.

28 The thinking here is not unlike some of the thinking that informs the strategy of nuclear deterrence, particularly in its MAD form. A war that is too horrific to contemplate is an avoidable war.

29 Churchill (who, as prime minister, later gave such strong support to 'Bomber' Harris throughout most of the city bombing offensive) wrote an outraged letter to Trenchard: 'To fire wilfully on women and children is a disgraceful act ... By doing such things we put ourselves on the lowest level. Combatants are fair game and sometimes non combatants get injured through their proximity to fighting troops, but this seems to be a quite different matter' (quoted in Boyle 1962, pp. 389–90).

30 Even as early as July 1940 Churchill had conceived of 'an absolutely devastating, exterminating attack by very heavy bombers from this country upon the Nazi homeland' (quoted in Hastings 1993, p. 116).

31 What Harris had in mind is made plain in a letter to the Air Ministry dated 7 December 1943: 'It is not possible to dogmatize on the degree of destruction necessary to cause the enemy to capitulate but there can be little doubt that the necessary conditions would be brought about by the destruction of between 40% & 50% of the principal German towns.... By the 1st April 1944 ... we should have destroyed 35,750 acres out of a total target area of 89,000 acres (i.e. 40% of built-up areas) .... the population of the towns attacked would be over 75% of the total population of towns in Germany having a population of 50,000 inhabitants or over. ... [This would]

produce in Germany ... a state of devastation in which surrender is inevitable' (Webster and Frankland 1961, Vol. II, pp. 55–6).

32 The systematic abuse of noncombatant immunity that allied bombing policy during the Second World involved was not confined to the conduct of the air war by the British or to the European sector of the war. In Japan the policy of selective targeting and precision bombing that the Americans favoured in the war against Germany gave way to a policy of area or saturation bombing that was every bit as uninhibited as that of the British. In January 1945 Curtis le May assumed command of XXI Bomber Command and embarked on the area fire-bombing of Japan's industrial cities. In the most destructive of these raids on 9/10 March Tokyo was attacked by 325 B-29s. More than 80,000 people were killed and almost 16 square miles of the city were destroyed by the firestorm they created (cf. Frankland 1989, p. 408). On 6 August the first atomic bomb was dropped on the city of Hiroshima. Though the city was an important military and naval base, the main purpose of the raid was to convince the Japanese of the futility of further resistance. The Hiroshima attack was fire-bombing taken to its most extreme but logical conclusion: 'The fireball generated a ground temperature of 6,000 degrees C.; thermal radiation vaporized thousands of people and buildings and burnt and scorched everything within a radius of two miles. A shock wave of tremendous force increased the destruction, flattening nearly everything in its path. People still on the streets were prey to flying debris caught in the fierce winds generated by the explosion, while these same winds fanned raging fires' (Frankland 1989, p. 191). Seventy thousand people were killed in the raid itself, and a further two hundred thousand are thought to have succumbed subsequently to the effects of radiation poisoning. Three days later, with the Japanese surrender still not forthcoming, the second bomb was dropped on Nagasaki. Capitulation followed quickly. At the end of it all Le May reflected: 'We had two or three weeks of work left on the cities. ... Another six months and Japan would have been beaten back into the Dark Ages' (Duus 1988, Vol. 6, p. 381).

33 A comparison with the earlier German bombing of Coventry is revealing. In that attack on 14–15 November 1940, 550 German bombers dropped 500 tons of high explosives and 30 tons of incendiaries (see Frankland 1989, p. 109).

34 In typically forthright fashion, Harris advised the Air Ministry that 'the aim of the Combined Offensive should be unambiguously stated ... the destruction of German cities, the killing of German workers and the disruption of civilized community life throughout Germany'. When informed that his directive 'neither requires nor enjoins direct attack on German civilians as such', he replied: 'The German eco-

nomic system, which I am instructed to destroy, *includes* workers, houses and public utilities, and it is therefore meaningless to claim that the wiping out of German cities is not an end in itself but the inevitable accompaniment of all-out attack on the enemy's means and capacity to wage war' (this exchange, which took place between October and December 1943, is quoted in Longmate 1983, p. 369).

35 Proportionalists (who view 'consequentialists' rather in the way that 'rule' utilitarians view 'act' utilitarians, that is, as people whose concept of utility is too narrow and short-sighted) would not accept that what they are doing undermines moral absolutes, arguing that the absolute prohibition of unlawful killing or murder is accepted by proportionalist and double effect theorist alike. The problem, and the point of disagreement, is in determining what constitutes murder. According to the proportionalist 'murder' is any killing for which there is no proportionate reason, and such killing is always morally impermissible. Unlike the absolute norm that prohibits murder, noncombatant immunity is a second-order principle or *prima facie* norm that ought to be upheld as long as there is no proportionate reason for overriding it.

36 In another version of this argument city bombing (or any other method of conducting a war that is systematically indiscriminate) is seen to be morally incoherent, since to pursue such a policy is to turn against the basic values in defence of which a just war is being fought in the first place: a means cannot be proportionate when it destroys the moral good that it is meant to uphold.

37 McCormick, for example, argues that the norm of noncombatant immunity is 'a teleological judgement (one based on proportionate reason defined by foreseeable or suspected consequences in the broadest sense), not a deontological one. Equivalently it means that direct attacks on noncombatant civilians in wartime, however effective and important they may seem will in the long run release more violence and be more destructive to human life than the lives we might save by directly attacking noncombatants' (McCormick and Ramsey 1985, p. 31).

38 Evidently Curran himself has doubts about the moral status of his rule. Why else does he consider it 'necessary to insist on the sin-filled aspects of the situation' and to employ the innovative moral concept of 'compromise'?

39 As in the case of Curran, Walzer's justification of 'the violation of the rules of war' is very ambiguous, and it is one about which he himself seems to harbour serious moral doubts and misgivings. As a result he can write, somewhat puzzlingly and apparently incoherently, about the 'forced' violation of human rights, about rights that 'are still standing at the very moment they are overridden', and

about the decision-maker's obligation 'to accept the moral consequences and the burden of guilt that his action entails' (p. 231). How
can there be a duty or moral obligation to perform an act that car-
ries with it a 'burden of guilt'? Perhaps these signs of wavering stem
from the perception that it is one thing to recognize the frequency
with which moral norms are set aside in the extreme circumstances
of war and quite another to transform that fact into a matter of
moral principle. Providing a moral justification for such conduct
helps to create a moral climate in which such violations cease to be
regarded as abnormal (cf. the discussion of the place of realism in
just war thinking in Chapter 4).

40 For a more recent version of this utilitarian defence see Loeb 1995.
Loeb endorses the view of Henry Stimson, Truman's Secretary of
War: 'This deliberately premeditated destruction was our first abhorrent choice. The destruction of Hiroshima and Nagasaki put an end
to the Japanese war. It stopped the fireraids and the strangling blockade; it ended the ghastly specter of a clash of great land armies'
(p. 11).

41 Hehir, for example, argues that 'even from a consequentialist perspective' the bombing of Hiroshima and Nagasaki was unjustified,
for 'to lose the absolute barrier against force which civilian immunity represents is to lose morality's hold on conscience and policy in
wartime' (Hehir 1995, p. 10).

11

Peacemaking

'Make war breed peace; make peace stint war.'[1] The just war tradition upholds the primacy of peace over war. War has no intrinsic or independent value. Its moral worth is of a wholly instrumental kind and is conditional upon the subordination of war to peace. War is acceptable only as a form of peacemaking. Fundamentally, it is not the *ius ad bellum* that a just war vindicates, but the *ius ad pacem*. Peace is the goal and the measure of the just war from beginning to end. It is war's essential moral context. The primacy of peace is evident in the moral criteria applied to war: in the restrictions placed on its use by the proscription of private war and the upholding of the public monopoly of war; in the limited definition and bilateral application of just cause; in the concern that the damage inflicted by war – to the international community as well as to the belligerents – should not exceed its benefits; in the requirement that all means short of war have been tried and exhausted; in the restrictions on the excessive and indiscriminate use of force; and in the generous and non-vindictive manner in which war is concluded. All of these measures are attempts at pacification, designed to limit and contain but also to resolve conflict, and to ensure that the righting of a wrong does not lead to the accumulation of injustice. The aim of the just war is not to obstruct, but to advance, the cause of peace.

In a broad and general sense this aim is hardly unique. With the possible exception of a certain kind of extreme militarism (more hypothetical than real), for which a state of permanent and constant warfare represents the ultimate goal, every approach to war can be seen to seek peace of *some* kind. 'It is,' wrote St Augustine, with the desire for peace that wars are waged, even by those who take pleasure in exercising their warlike nature in command and battle. And hence it is obvious that peace is the end sought for by war. For every man seeks peace by waging war, but no man seeks war by making peace. For even they who intentionally interrupt the peace in which they are living have no hatred of peace, but only wish it changed into a peace that suits them better. They do not, therefore, wish to have no peace, but only one more to their mind. (Deane 1963, p. 102)

This common, if not universal, acknowledgement of the primacy of peace obscures important differences. The point of difference lies in the kind of peace that war is made to serve. The concept of 'peace' is variable and contested, and the form that it takes will determine *when* and *how* war is to be fought. Some notions of peace will yield easier and bloodier recourse to war than others; some will be more complacent in their acceptance of war than others. It is not, therefore, the mere subordination of war to peace, but its conception of the peace to which war is subordinate, that marks the just war tradition off from other approaches to war. What kind of peace a just war upholds and advances becomes clearer through consideration of the perceived strengths and weaknesses of rival conceptions of peace.

In the just war tradition 'peace' is not to be confused with the cessation of hostilities or with the mere absence of war. This minimalist concept of peace, in its most extreme form, hardly counts as a form of peace at all. As Hobbes argued, the absence of *actual* war does not preclude the presence of a *state* of war: 'in all times, Kings, and Persons of Soveraigne authority, because of their Independency, are in continuall jealousies, and in the state and posture of Gladiators; having their weapons pointing, and their eyes fixed on one another; that is, their Forts, Garrisons, and Guns upon the Frontiers of their Kingdomes; and continuall Spyes upon their neighbours; which is a posture of War' (Hobbes 1991, p. 90). The absence of overt conflict does not entail the presence of peace. Even though the Soviet and Western alliances did not engage in open and direct conflict with one another during the period of the Cold War, their relations then are more aptly described as a state of war than as a state of peace. The absence of war, particularly nuclear war, is of course a good; but when it is achieved by the threat of mutual destruction, its simple equation with peace appears to be not merely exaggerated but self-contradictory.

In Hobbesian terms the only solution to the state of war in which international relations are seen to consist would be the surrender of individual state sovereignty, with all that that entails, to a world state in which all are subject to the same sovereign. Hobbes himself seems to have regarded this surrender as unnecessary and, *therefore*, utopian. Since, by adopting 'a posture of War', rulers 'uphold thereby, the Industry of their Subjects; there does not follow from it, that misery, which accompanies the Liberty of particular men' (Hobbes 1991, p. 90). There are far fewer and much less compelling incentives for the surrender of sovereignty in the international than in the domestic or municipal arena. The misery that accompanies the liberty of states is as nothing compared with that 'which accompanies the Liberty of particular men'. It is *civil* war which is truly intolerable, not interstate warfare, and *civil* peace without which 'the life of man [is] solitary, poore, nasty, brutish, and short' (Hobbes 1991, p. 89). Since mankind has insufficient incentive to do otherwise, international relations must be left in their natural state of war.

Later realists are, for understandable reasons, less sanguine than Hobbes in their acceptance of international relations as a state of war. As a result they place much greater emphasis on the ordering of international relations and the preservation of peace. Nonetheless their understanding of 'peace' is based on similar assumptions, and remains extremely modest. As Aron writes: 'Since states have not renounced taking the law into their own hands and remaining sole judges of what their honour requires, the survival of political units depends, in the final analysis, on the balance of forces, and it is the duty of statesmen to be concerned, *first of all*, with the nation whose destiny is entrusted to them. The necessity of national egoism derives logically from what philosophers called the *state of nature* which rules among states' (Aron 1966, p. 580). The 'balance of forces' or, more conventionally, the 'balance of power' exhausts the concept of peace as many realists understand that concept.

The 'balance of power', like the concept of peace, may be

understood in a variety of ways.[2] It has as its focus the 'network' of international relations. The idea implies a certain view of international relations according to which states are seen as essentially and unavoidably interdependent. This interdependence – of a factual and non-moral kind – is often defined in regional terms (with regard to Europe or the Middle East, for example), though its global application has been increasingly emphasized as events in one part of the world are seen to have an impact on states far beyond that particular region. The result is that states are thought to have an interest in events, particularly conflicts or potential conflicts, that might previously have been considered of little real concern.

The balance of power may be understood in a deterministic way as whatever state of interdependence happens to exist. From this perspective the power of the different states waxes and wanes, so that shifts in the balance are continually occurring, yet international relations always, and quite unavoidably, end up back in balance. Because of its determinism this concept of the balance of power is without moral interest or significance. What does engage moral interest are balance of power *politics*, in which the idea is understood in a manipulative or contrived sense. The object of such a policy is to prevent the natural descent of international relations into the state of conflict and chaos by countering the emergence of a preponderant or dominant power and by maintaining international relations in a state of equilibrium. Its underlying assumption is that states are naturally antagonistic, and that the only way in which they can be prevented from coming into conflict is through the presence of countervailing force. 'International peace and order,' it is argued, 'are a function of the balance of power – that is, of an approximately equal distribution of power among several nations or a combination of nations, preventing any one of them from gaining the upper hand over the others. It is this approximate, tenuous equilibrium that provides whatever peace and order exists in the world of nation states' (Morgenthau and Thompson 1985, p. 388).

In its common articulation and general orientation, the balance of power is presented as an essentially defensive and pacific strategy designed to counteract a potential aggressor and to ensure that a state of war does not degenerate into outright conflict. Though focusing in the first place on the defence of national interest, it is not unmindful of a wider interest and obligation. The conception of peace that informs the strategy may seem unduly modest, yet its concern with the maintenance of that peace is permanent and overriding. Reviewing American foreign policy in the aftermath of the Second World War, Henry Kissinger, an advocate and exponent of the strategy, argues that the US was faced with the task of taking over from an exhausted Britain 'its historical role as the guardian of the equilibrium'. 'We were obliged to step in,' he writes, 'Like it or not, we were assuming the historical responsibility for preserving the balance of power; and we were poorly prepared for the task. In both world wars we equated victory with peace, and even in the crises of 1947 we still thought the problem of maintaining global equilibrium consisted in coping with a temporary dislocation of some natural order of things ... But the management of a balance of power is a permanent undertaking, not an exertion that has a foreseeable end' (Kissinger 1971, pp. 114–15). The balance of power, it seems, is not without a moral aspect.

The recognition of its partial and instrumental value as a mechanism of peace is not inconsistent with just war reasoning. Even this limited acceptance, however, is subject to serious doubts and reservations about the manner in which the policy is commonly applied. Its application often appears open to abuse, and the key question is whether such abuse is entailed by the strategy itself. In the first place, the commitment to the policy, for all its global pretensions, may be no more than a complex but no less exclusive concern with the protection and advancement of national interest. In one reading of the strategy, certainly, the maintenance of a state of equilibrium is little more than the defence of a status quo, aimed less at the prevention of hegemonic power than at its preservation. Arguably, both Britain and America used this policy not to protect the balance of power (and world peace) so much as the *im*balance of power brought about by their own preponderant and dominant position in the world. The moral pretensions of the policy, in other words, may rest on the confusion of an imperial order with a global or world order, and on the false equation of a national interest with a community of interest.

Secondly, in its common and perhaps typical version, the principle is an amoral or morally neutral one that, if consistently applied, requires the systematic suppression of considerations of justice and the violation of the fundamental norms of the international order. A principle, for example, that recognizes 'no permanent friends or enemies', but dictates the forging and sundering of alliances with every tilt of the balance, does little to foster relations of friendship and trust among states. For the sake of the balance the rights and interests, even the very independence, of particular states may need to be sacrificed. In some applications of the strategy, for example, the good of South Vietnam was entirely subordinate to the maintenance of the regional and, ultimately, global balance of power, in which world peace (or, less generously, the defence of US or Western interests) was seen to consist.

The pacific consequences of the policy, on the assumption of which it relies for much of its moral credibility, are themselves open to question. The strategy can be seen to instigate war at least as often as it curbs it. In the opinion of many critics, for example, it was the pursuit of this policy, rather than the neglect of it, that led to the outbreak of the First World War: the policy itself was the prime source of conflict, manufacturing causes of war and forcing its practitioners down the path to war. Maintenance of the balance can be seen to require not just pre-emptive but preventive wars, wars that are fought in response not to an act of aggression or a violation of international law but merely to the growth in power of a particular state or alliance of states. Similarly, it may dictate the tolerance and even the fomenting of a war, without regard to its justice or injustice, simply because of the beneficial effects that it seems likely to have upon the balance of power. The tacit and, in some cases, active support given to Iraq in its long and destructive war with Iran owed much to the perceived need to check Iranian power and influence in a strategically important part of the world. In such instances it is the war-making rather than the peacemaking nature of the policy that seems more prominent.

The problem with the balance of power, therefore, is that the balance in question may not be a moral balance. Operationally, it may require not simply the *tolerance* of injustice (the need for which can sometimes be accepted) but the collusion with, and even the perpetration of, injustice. A policy that is ready to support or fight an unjust war in the interests of peace is in just war terms incoherent, since justice and peace are seen to be inseparable. What makes the policy coherent are the realist premises on which it is made to rest: the conception of international relations as a state of war, and the consequent conception of peace as a state in which order always takes precedence over justice.

Viewed from a just war perspective the weakness of this approach lies in its one-sidedness rather than its falsity. It is not that peace of this limited kind is simply alien to, or of no value to, the just war tradition. That tradition is catholic enough, and in this regard realist enough, to recognize the virtues of an imperfect peace and the utility of those mechanisms whereby it is commonly achieved. Realism's attachment to order as a value and its perception of the great fragility of order in the international sphere find a sympathetic response in just war thinking. The skilful maintenance of an uneasy balance of power may form part of a peace agenda;[3] but it does not exhaust that agenda, and may itself pose serious moral dilemmas.

The realist understanding of peace is too negative judged by just war standards. Peacekeeping rather than peacemaking is seen to be the primary goal of policy. Holding the line, preventing the collapse of international relations into their natural state of war, often represent the limit of aspiration. It is a too static concept of peace; for though in one sense realism views international relations dynamically – the constant shifts of power requiring continual adjustments and realignments – it conceives of the underlying reality as permanent and unchanging. The idea of the progressive and qualitative improvement or transformation of the international order to which the just war approach is wedded is out of line with realism. The reason why this more ambitious concept of peace is entertained in one case and not in the other is that just war theory recognizes in the present state of international relations a potentiality for community (that is, something real or existent, not just a mere possibility) that realism is at pains to deny. As Suarez argued: 'no matter how many diverse peoples and kingdoms the human race may be divided into, it always has a certain unity, not merely as a species but even a sort of political and moral unity ... No matter how a sovereign state, commonwealth or kingdom may be in itself a perfect society with its own members, each one is also, in a sense, as seen from the point of view of the human race, a member of the universal community' (quoted in Hamilton 1963, pp. 108–9).

In its positive and dynamic sense peace is best understood not simply as the absence of division or conflict, but as the harmony or unity of parts. Peace *is* a form of community. The *ius ad bellum* is a *ius ad pacem* in this sense. A just war is a response to the breakdown or disruption of community, and its primary purpose is to restore a shattered harmony. 'As in every state', wrote Suarez, 'there must be some lawful power to punish crime if domestic peace is to be preserved, so in the world at large, if all countries are to live in harmony, there must exist some power to punish wrongs committed by one state against another' (Hamilton 1963, p. 144). From a just war outlook there is a real and not simply a metaphorical sense in which all wars are civil or internal wars, wars that are fought between the parts of one community. To be just, war must not permit the divisions between belligerents to obscure their common humanity and essential unity. The divisions are never understood as absolute divisions, and enmity is never total. The conduct of a just war is dependent upon the recognition of a moral bond and common good that unite even the bitterest of adversaries.[4] The goal of the just war is not the unilateral triumph of a particular state, but the vindication of the international community and of the rights of its members.

The understanding of war as the realization of community is not, however, sufficient to guarantee just recourse or just conduct. Everything turns on the kind of community that war is meant to realize. There are some conceptions of unity that far from limiting war, ensure its totality. In these cases peace is a form of unity, but a unity that is conditional upon the elimination of difference. The community that is sought requires the complete and unilateral triumph of one particular community over all the rest. In other words, the international order is understood as an imperial order. In their encounter with the indigenous peoples of the New World, for example, Europeans were inclined to discount the claims of native societies to independence in theory as well as in practice. As a pagan and non-Christian people, they had no rightful dominion. The universal authority attributed to Christianity was understood at the same time as a political authority. The basis of political community was true religion, that is, Christianity; and as a Christian power, Spain had a duty as well as a right to govern these territories. As in many instances before and since, the unity of mankind was understood as an imperial unity.

A very different assessment was argued by contemporary neo-Thomists like Vitoria and Suarez.[5] In accordance with the natural law principles of their thought they defended the natural right of the Indian peoples to dominion. Convinced though they were of the truth and universal authority of the Christian religion, they resisted the temptation to define that spiritual authority in political terms. 'The aborigines undoubtedly had true dominion in both public and private matters, just like Christians', argued Vitoria (quoted in Fernández-Santamaria 1977, p. 79). The basis of the state or political community was not grace or religion, but nature.[6] Despite their pagan character and, often, in European eyes simple or even primitive or barbaric appearance, the Indian communities were 'perfect' or 'complete', and their integrity should be respected and upheld.[7]

As Thomists and just war theorists, these Spanish thinkers employed the idea of the unity of mankind as a normative concept (regulating war), but they refused to identify that unity with the creation of a universal Christian empire or commonwealth. Rather, in true Thomistic and Aristotelian fashion, the unity was conceived as a *plurality*. Vitoria wrote of 'the world as a whole, being *in a way* one single State' (Hamilton 1963, p. 105, added emphasis). While upholding (if necessary through war) their moral and legal subordination to that 'single State', his understanding of particular states or polities as 'perfect' or 'complete' communities precluded their absorption by the greater whole. The community of Mankind was understood as an 'ecumenical' and not an imperial order, an order that 'can only stand when the individual sovereignty of its parts ... is assured' (Fernández-Santamaria 1977, p. 77).

It is in such terms that the just war concept of peace as community is to be understood. It is true that the claims made for particular states when upheld in exclusive and exaggerated fashion threaten the unity of mankind and the universal common good. A conception of international relations focused exclusively on the particular interests of sovereign states is quite incompatible with just war thinking. At the same time the universal common good must not be promoted in indifference to or at the expense of the rights and claims of particular communities.[8] It will be so promoted if the concept of the universal common good is one that assumes a necessary and unresolvable antithesis between the particularity of the parts and the universality of the whole. The assumption that the two are contradictory leads either to the kind of imperial unity already exemplified (of which there are numerous modern counterparts, 'imperialism' being neither a Christian nor for that matter a capitalist monopoly) or to an abstract cosmopolitanism. While in the first case a particular identity is used to define (rather than enrich) unity, and while in the second case all particularity is extinguished, the kind of unity that just war reasoning advocates is one that transcends particular differences without abolishing or unilaterally reducing them. The international community is understood as a differentiated unity, as a whole made up of parts, the integrity (if not the absolute sovereignty) of which demands respect.[9]

Peace in just war theory is a dynamic and creative concept. Just as in the state an excessive reliance on force or the *vis coactiva* is a sign of an immature or uncivilized state, so in the international order the frequency of war's occurrence is an indication that the universal community of mankind remains more of a potentiality than an actuality. Even a just war is neither an end in itself nor even a normal and acceptable instrument of law enforcement: the aim, if not the expectation, is to make war redundant.

That is an aim or aspiration that just war theory shares with more utopian traditions of thought; and the 'utopian' aspect of just war thinking is real enough. Without such an aspiration 'peace' would be gravely diminished. It is this aspiration that drives and informs the positive agenda of peace. At the same time the threat to peace that it sometimes poses demands recognition. As Chanteur writes:

> The utopias focusing on peace are among the most dangerous ...
> A longing for peace, for a way of living that would be truly the
> opposite of war, becomes confused with the dream ... of those
> who would transmute human nature into divine nature. A uni-
> versal and unpredictable end of history replaces the visions of
> paradise after death promised by religion. (Chanteur 1992, pp.
> 195–7)

Such utopian visions of a war to end all war may increase the
frequency and intensity of war. The identification of the underlying 'structural' causes of war, with the removal of which war
will disappear and real peace will be established, multiplies the
perceived causes and occasions of war, and threatens to make
war endemic. Some concepts of 'peace' are warmongering, in
effect if not in intention. The moral enthusiasm for war generated by the prospect of its abolition leads to the undermining of
the more modest project of its moral limitation, and to the dismissal of those mechanisms or techniques whereby peace of an
inferior but still worthwhile kind is preserved.

In just war theory the 'utopian' concept of peace is the ever-
receding moral horizon that acts as a moral pull on the efforts of
peacemakers. The idea that it might be achieved all at once, or
apocalyptically, is seen as a dangerous illusion. Its moral attraction and indispensability must not be allowed to diminish the
perceived virtues and practical imperatives of a less than perfect
peace. The concept of peace that informs just war thinking is best
understood in a dialectical way, as a synthesis of 'realist' and
'utopian' elements that are normally held apart. Neither realism
nor utopianism is judged to be without merit; but the essential
weakness of both positions is seen to lie in their exclusiveness
and one-sidedness. Peace is not to be confused with the cessation
of actual war or with the restoration of a 'state of war'; peace
needs to be understood more positively and constructively than
that, and, unless it is, war loses much of its justification.
Nonetheless, the negative and limited aim of preventing or of
curbing conflict is not only very worthwhile; it may define the
limits of present possibilities. This kind of modest peacekeeping is
a fundamental part of the wider and more ambitious peacemaking process, and one that calls for the deployment of just those
skills and techniques that more utopian visions of peace tend to

decry in the name of a spurious or misconceived morality. 'Even if one holds an affirmative view of peace', Macquarrie wrote, 'nevertheless at any given time the proximate task may be the negative one of preventing an unacceptable level of conflict ... Frequently the only possibility open may be the very humble and unexciting one of reducing hostility and violence' (Macquarrie 1973, p. 30).

This complex notion of peace points to a dual strategy: one focusing on the more immediate need to bring present conflicts to a close, the other searching for more enduring solutions to the problem of war. In genuine peacemaking the two should go together; but, under the pressures of war, short-term considerations are often allowed to undermine the longer-term prospects of peace, a process discernible, perhaps, in the case of the First World War. 'The Great War lasted so long,' wrote one of its principal architects, Lloyd George, 'because the respective war aims of the two sides were irreconcilable, and neither side was prepared to give way until it was compelled to do so' (Lloyd George 1933, p. 1930). Such intransigence was carried through into the peace process. Keynes, who attended the Peace Conference as a representative of the British Government, 'became very oppressed by [its] atmosphere of hatred, and the crude exultation in victory', so much so that he resigned his post and returned to England to mount an attack on its proceedings (Wilson 1986, p. 838).[10]

The Treaty of Versailles required Germany to cede all her colonies and much of her territory to the Allies, including Alsace and Lorraine to France, a large part of East Prussia to Poland, and smaller areas to Czechoslovakia, Lithuania, Belgium, and Denmark; the Saar region was to be administered by the League of Nations (a body established by the treaty) for a period of fifteen years, during which time the productive capacity of the region would be used to make good French and Belgian losses; the Rhineland (that part of Germany situated between the Rhine and the French and Belgian borders) was to be temporarily occupied and permanently demilitarized; Germany was to be virtually disarmed; the admission of German 'war guilt' was required;[11] and severe and punitive reparations were imposed. The terms were harsh and non-negotiable; the consequence of non-compliance was the renewal of hostilities. No account was taken either of the extreme condition to which Germany had been reduced as a result of the war in general and of the economic blockade in particular (a blockade that continued to be enforced throughout the Armistice), or of the fledgling state of German democracy.[12]

Though the terms were harsh, they were not as severe as they might have been, and certainly not as severe as the terms that Germany had imposed earlier on a defeated Russia.[13] Moreover, their severity (and efficacy in curbing future aggression) were further diminished by the subsequent reluctance of the Allies to enforce them. It was not what Versailles did to Germany, but what it was *seen* to do that wrought such havoc. As Nolte suggests: 'The fatal effect of the peace treaty in Germany arose just as much from Germany's preoccupation with its own problems as from objective circumstances' (Nolte 1969, p. 393). The German people saw Versailles as a public humiliation. Von Hindenburg called it 'a disgraceful peace'. Twenty years later Hitler's claim that Germany's representatives 'were subjected to even greater degradations than can ever have been inflicted on the chieftains of the Sioux tribes' (quoted in Shirer 1964, pp. 83 and 576) still struck a chord. The treaty was seen as a public humiliation, and the peace that it proclaimed and embodied as vengeful and vindictive: the peace was neither just nor reconciliatory, but opportunistic, allowing Germany's enemies to expand their power at her expense. Versailles did nothing to heal the wounds of war or to bring the warring parties closer together. On the contrary, the resentment and sense of injustice to which it gave rise did much to unleash the forces that would lead to the renewal of conflict. Though it did not cause Germany's problems, it made their peaceful resolution much less likely.

Realist objections to Versailles stem largely from a consideration of its consequences, and focus in particular on the failure to enforce those parts of the treaty dealing with disarmament and demilitarization. The blame for this failure is laid at the door of the 'utopians', whose search for a perfect peace led to the neglect of the balance of power. From a just war perspective this criticism has some validity, but it rests on an oversimplification (and polarization) of the peacemaking process, and neglects the part that realism itself played in its breakdown. The problem with

Versailles is not that it was 'realist' rather than 'utopian' or 'utopian' rather than 'realist', but that it was 'realist' in its conception and 'utopian' in its application. The terms of the treaty created bitter resentment and strengthened the German *will* to war, while the failure to enforce the terms facilitated the exercise of that will. In other words, the problem lay in the failure to marry 'realist' with 'utopian' elements throughout. The 'negative' aim of curbing German aggression was allowed to dictate the peace settlement itself, while the 'positive' aim of advancing international solidarity and cooperation monopolized subsequent diplomatic initiatives. If the 'negative' phase had been more 'positive' and the 'positive' phase more 'negative', then perhaps the peace would have been secured.[14]

A consequentialist understanding of peace forms part of a just war understanding: the fact that a just peace is likely to be more effective and lasting is part of its moral attraction. The preference, however, is more than consequential. A just war must end in a just peace. The idea of peace as Victory, as the triumph of one side over another, is alien to a concept of peace that has reconciliation as its fundamental aim, the restoration of community among the warring parties. What leads to the conclusion of a vindictive and triumphalist peace (when the outcome of war makes such a peace possible) is a self-righteousness whereby war and peace are judged in absolute and unilateral terms. Such extreme partisanship obstructs the process of genuine peacemaking, which just war theorists have traditionally conceived as a quasi-judicial process: 'When the war is won and finished,' wrote Vitoria,

> victory should be pursued with moderation and Christian humility; the victor ought to think of himself rather as a judge between two states (the wronged and the wrong-doer) and to deliver the judgement through which the injured state can obtain satisfaction as judge rather than as accuser, so that the aggressor state may, as far as possible, be spared the worst calamities and misfortunes, and the offending individuals be penalized only within lawful limits. (quoted in Hamilton 1963, p. 157)

The construction of a just and reconciling peace requires not only a kind of judicial impartiality, but the adoption of a bilateral or bipartisan approach that recognizes that the moral contours of war and peace are necessarily blurred, and that in war injustice is rarely the monopoly of one side. This bilateral spirit and understanding should inform the victor's overall judgement of war, since it is that judgement that will largely determine the terms of the peace and the manner of their application. Among other things, peacemaking involves a process of accounting, in the course of which the causes and the conduct of the war are reviewed and conclusions drawn. In apportioning blame and proposing solutions, a bilateral judgement would not seek to oversimplify the causes of the war, but would be prepared to acknowledge, wherever appropriate, a shared responsibility for its occurrence. Given the complexity of international relations and the moral and political failures to which *all* states are prone a shared, if not equal, responsibility seems likely to be the norm rather than the exception.

A similar readiness to acknowledge shared responsibilities and common failings would mark the assessment of the way in which the war had been conducted. If war crimes have been committed bilaterally, they ought not to be judged unilaterally. At the same time, the judgement and punishment of war crimes seem essential (though who is to be punished and what form punishment should take are subject to other, often prudential, considerations – not least the urgent need to reconcile former belligerents). 'For the sake of our country and our children', writes Solzhenitsyn,

> we have the duty to *seek them all out and bring them all to trial!* Not to put them on trial so much as their crimes. And to compel each one of them to announce loudly: "Yes, I was an executioner and a murderer." ... We have to condemn publicly the very *idea* that some people have the right to repress others. In keeping silent about evil, in burying it so deep within us that no sign of it appears on the surface, we are *implanting* it, and it will rise up a thousandfold in the future. When we neither punish nor reproach evildoers, we are not simply protecting their trivial old age, we are thereby ripping the foundations of justice from beneath new generations. (Solzhenitsyn 1978, Vol. 1, pp. 175–8)

To ignore the criminal conduct of war is to undermine the moral culture of war, the preservation of which is one of the primary objectives of just war theory. Without some form of public accounting war crimes are likely to lose their criminal status. There is a very thin line to be drawn between the refusal to proceed against criminal activity and the condoning of that activity. War crimes tribunals should have the effect of drawing the line between what is and what is not acceptable in war. Given the retrospective, and often largely symbolic and representative, nature of these judgements, their purpose is as much to influence the legal and moral climate of future wars as it is to bring war criminals to justice. Their capacity to do so, of course, is largely dependent upon the avoidance of that 'victor's justice' whereby Right is subordinated to Might: 'the guilty must be punished for their guilt, not for having been defeated' (Thibon 1954, p. 6).

Peacemaking in just war terms should be an expression of the communal and moral bond that unites adversaries even in the midst of war. A concern with the rights and interests of an unjust aggressor is an essential prerequisite, and one that is never more urgent than in the moment of victory and defeat. When military supremacy has been achieved, the physical vulnerability of the defeated is matched by the moral vulnerability of the victors. The temptation to take advantage of a military victory by exceeding the aims of war and by going beyond what strict justice dictates or permits may be very great, particularly when victory has been achieved at great cost or when an adversary has conducted the war in a particularly ruthless manner. The inherently limited nature of a just war precludes its unlimited conclusion.

It is in the light of this consideration that Kenny, who analyses nuclear war and deterrence from a just war standpoint, argues in the course of that analysis that 'the unconditional surrender of the enemy is not a legitimate objective of war' (Kenny 1985, p. 9). It is Kenny's view that such a war aim undermines the specific and limited objectives – the righting of a *particular* wrong – that are the just war's sole justification. Unconditional surrender, therefore, is ruled out from the start: 'Spelling out the particular wrong which justifies one's taking up arms *eo ipso* spells out the conditions on which one ought to be ready to accept surrender.' To insist on *unconditional* surrender is to endorse total war. This view, a common one, does not appear well founded.

In the first place it fails to take account of the complex and

dynamic nature of war itself and of the way in which the justifying cause of war can be quite transformed by the course that
the war takes. Even in 1939, righting the particular wrong that
was the proximate cause of Britain's resort to war – the German
invasion of Poland – did not define or exhaust Britain's war aims.
The aims of the war were always much more general than that,
since the takeover of Poland was not thought to constitute the
limit of Germany's ambitions. As the war progressed the causes
of war and the wrongs inflicted were multiplied, and the perception of what would be required not just to right particular
wrongs but, just as importantly, to prevent future transgressions
changed accordingly. The needs of peace itself seemed to require
more than a restoration of the *status quo ante bellum*. To limit
peace to that would have been to leave in place the conditions
that had led to war in the first place. Given the moral enormity
of what had occurred, so limited a peace was morally as well as
politically unacceptable: it would have been a disproportionate as
well as an imprudent response to events.

Kenny's proscription of unconditional surrender appears to rest
not only on a too simple and too static view of war, but on the
dual assumption that a negotiated or conditional peace is necessarily a limited peace and that a policy of unconditional surrender entails the pursuit of unlimited objectives. Neither assumption
appears justified. Any peace in circumstances where one side has
achieved clear military supremacy is likely to be a coercive or
imposed peace, which is improperly and euphemistically described
as a 'negotiated peace'. Similarly, the terms of a conditional peace
settlement may be lenient or severe, reconciliatory or vindictive.
The mere fact of conditionality does not guarantee limitation or
moderation. Churchill argued as much in defence of the Allied
policy of unconditional surrender: 'I remember several attempts
being made to draft peace conditions which would satisfy the
wrath of the conquerors against Germany. They looked so terrible when set forth on paper, *and so far exceeded what was in fact
done*, that their publication would only have stimulated German
resistance. They had in fact only to be written out to be withdrawn' (Churchill 1985, Vol. IV, p. 617; added emphasis).

Just as a conditional settlement does not, *ipso facto*, guarantee
the conclusion of a just peace, so a policy of unconditional sur-

render does not necessitate the conclusion of an unjust one. On the contrary, there may arise circumstances in which the only way of securing a just peace is through the mechanism of unconditional surrender. With some justification the Allies regarded the conclusion of a negotiated and conditional *and* just and lasting peace with Nazi Germany as an impossibility.[15] Securing the latter called for an agenda (described in the Casablanca Declaration as 'the destruction of a philosophy') that was simply unachievable without the unconditional surrender of Germany: the negative tasks of denazification and demilitarization; but also the positive tasks of political and economic reconstruction. It is at least arguable that the peace that accompanied the unconditional surrender of Germany at the end of the Second World War was more positive and constructive than the conditional peace of Versailles, which did so much to ensure future hostilities. Instead of helping to secure civilian and democratic government in Germany, Versailles helped to undermine such government and to foster extremism and military adventurism. The unconditional settlement of the Second World War did more to secure peace and harmony between Germany and her former adversaries than that conditional settlement, which, though it brought war to a close, left the belligerents in a state of war.

Though unconditional surrender necessarily involves the suspension of the right of dominion or self-government, it is a question of the temporary curtailment of the exercise of that right rather than its permanent denial. Moreover, the occupying power is itself obliged (morally if not as the result of negotiation or contract) to uphold the rights of the people subject to its rule. Power may be unchecked, but it remains subject to moral limits. In presenting the policy to the House of Commons Churchill explained: 'The term "unconditional surrender" does not mean that the German people will be enslaved or destroyed ... Unconditional surrender means that the victors have a free hand. It does not mean that they are entitled to behave in a barbarous manner, nor that they wish to blot out Germany from among the nations of Europe' (Churchill 1985, Vol. IV, p. 618). Roosevelt gave the policy a similar – positive – emphasis: 'The United Nations have no intention to enslave the German people. We wish them to have a normal chance to develop in peace, as useful and respectable members of the European family' (pp. 616–17). As events have turned out, the wish appears to have been largely fulfilled, though the part that Allied policy played in its fulfilment is of course a matter of historical debate. Whatever the merits of this particular case, however, there seems no reason in principle why a policy of unconditional surrender should rule out the conclusion of a just peace. Circumstances may be extreme enough to require the just and humanitarian enactment of such a policy.[16]

Peacemaking in the just war tradition, however, is not simply a matter of bringing particular wars to an end. Though the tradition rejects the characterization of international relations as a state of war, it recognizes the partial truth of such a characterization. The unity of mankind, the fundamental premiss of all just war thinking, remains in many respects a potentiality, a reality but not yet an actuality. Realizing that potential, civilizing the international order, making it less like a state of war, completes the agenda of peace. The utopian goal of an end to war is not alien to this tradition, for all its realism. Pursuit of that goal calls for something more than the 'negative' peace that accompanies the cessation or mere absence of conflict, and that limits its ambition to the curbing of aggression and the securing of state boundaries. Hence there is seen to arise an obligation, not just on the part of statesmen and not just in a political context, to pursue peace in a more positive and constructive way by making the international community more of a reality than it already is. Peacemaking in its fullest sense, therefore, is not a temporary response to the threat of war, but a permanent task that has as its ultimate aim not the moral limitation of war but the elimination of the will to war. In the end, what the just war tradition seeks is its own abolition or supersession.

Notes

1 William Shakespeare, *Timon of Athens*, Act V, iv, 83.
2 Cf. Bull 1977, Ch. 5.
3 The deliberations about war and international relations of the Second Vatican Council, indebted as they are to just war principles, appear to bear this out: 'Peace is not *merely* the absence of war. Nor can it be reduced *solely* to the maintenance of a balance of power' (Abbott 1966, p. 290; added emphasis).
4 Just war thinking in this respect is wholly in accord with the view

expressed by Westlake: 'the mitigation of war must depend on the parties to it feeling that they belong to a larger whole than their respective tribes or states, a whole in which the enemy too is comprised, so that duties arising out of that larger citizenship are owed even to him' (quoted in Morgenthau 1973, p. 259).

5 Cf. Hamilton 1963; Fernández-Santamaria 1977; Skinner 1978, Vol. II, Ch. 5.

6 'There is absolutely nothing to prevent there being true kings among the men of infidel nations,' Molina argued. 'For rule, jurisdiction and ownership are things common to the entire human race, being based not on faith and charity but arising directly or indirectly from the very nature of things and their first foundation' (quoted in Hamilton 1963, p. 51).

7 Vitoria rejected infidelity as a cause of war: 'War is not an argument for the truth of Christianity; the Indians cannot be made to believe by war, only to pretend to believe and to receive the Christian faith, which would be horrible and sacrilegious' (quoted in Hamilton 1963, p. 124). Even shorter shrift was given to the idea that the sinful practices of the Indians constituted a cause of war. If that were the case, he argues, 'infidel rulers could make war on Christian peoples' (p. 128). He notes: 'The extraordinary thing is that fornication is allowed to the faithful, but when pagans fornicate their lands may be invaded!' (pp. 130–1). On the other hand Vitoria does not always apply the laws of war evenly (see Vitoria 1991, p. 321).

8 Walzer writes: 'Our common humanity will never make us members of a single universal tribe. The crucial commonality of the human race is particularism' (Walzer 1994, p. 74).

9 Hence the importance attached to the principle of subsidiarity within the tradition.

10 Keynes's criticism was contained in *The Economic Consequences of the Peace*, which appeared in November 1919. Britain's wartime commander Haig had feared such an outcome. In a letter to his wife, written just before the Armistice, Haig wrote: 'I am afraid the Allied Statesmen mean to exact humiliating terms from Germany. I think this is a mistake, because it is merely laying up trouble for the future, and may encourage the wish for revenge in the future.' In his diary, he wrote: 'The French are anxious to be very strict ... We must not forget that it is to our interest to return to Peace methods at once, to have Germany a prosperous, not an impoverished country. Furthermore, we ought *not* to make Germany our enemy for many years to come' (cited in Terraine 1963, p. 479). These sentiments are all the more remarkable (much more remarkable than those of Keynes, who was inclined to pacifism) coming as they do from such a ruthless practitioner of war.

11 The treaty did not refer explicitly to 'war guilt'; but the imputation lay behind the section dealing with the need for reparations, article 231 attributing the losses of the Western powers to 'the war imposed upon them by Germany and her allies' (Wilson 1986, p. 837).

12 'Before the drafting of the Weimar Constitution was finished', wrote William Shirer, 'an inevitable event occurred which cast a spell of doom over it and the Republic which it was to establish. This was the drawing up of the Treaty of Versailles' (Shirer 1964, pp. 80–1).

13 By the terms of the Treaty of Brest-Litovsk Russia was required to surrender territory equivalent in area to Austria-Hungary and Turkey combined, with a population of 56 million, 73 per cent of her total iron ore, 89 per cent of her coal production, and more than 5,000 factories and industrial plants. In addition Germany was to be paid an indemnity of six billion marks (see Shirer 1964, p. 81).

14 If the settlement itself had been informed by a more 'positive' concept of peace, by a real will to reconciliation, then the 'negative' peace by which realism, with good reason, sets such store would have been more easily secured.

15 Later, Churchill was at pains to refute the charge (one that continues to be levelled by historians) that unconditional surrender was 'one of the great mistakes of Anglo-American war policy ... [which] prolonged the struggle and made recovery afterwards more difficult' (Churchill 1985, Vol. IV, p. 616). 'Negotiating with Hitler was impossible,' he wrote. 'He was a maniac with supreme power to play his hand out to the end, which he did; and so did we' (quoted in Gilbert 1986, p. 310). Churchill's idea of peacemaking was not always so unaccommodating. His assessment of an earlier adversary was much more generous. During the Boer War he argued: 'While we continue to prosecute the war with tireless energy ... we must also make it easy for the enemy to accept defeat. We must tempt as well as compel' (Gilbert 1981, p. 16). He even drew attention to the moral complexities of that war (something he was never inclined to do in the case of the war against Germany and Japan, where a tone of moral triumphalism and vindictiveness marked many of his pronouncements): 'Neither side has a monopoly of right or reason' (p. 21). These 'bilateral' sentiments are wholly in accord with the just war notion of peacemaking.

16 On this matter Vitoria wrote: 'there may sometimes be legitimate reasons for supplanting princes, or for taking over the government. This may be because of the number or atrocity of the injuries and harm done by the enemy, and especially when security and peace cannot otherwise be ensured, when failure to do so would cause a dangerous threat to the commonwealth' (Vitoria 1991, p. 326).

Bibliography of works cited

Abbott, W. M. (ed.) (1966), *The Documents of Vatican II*, Geoffrey Chapman, London.

Aho, A. (1981), *Religious Mythology and the Art of War*, Aldwych Press, London.

Akenhurst, M. (1987), *A Modern Introduction to International Law*, Unwin Hyman, London.

Anderson, J. and Van Atta, D. (1991), *Stormin' Norman*, Zebra Books, New York.

Anscombe, G. E. M. (1981), *Collected Philosophical Papers*, Vol. 3: *Ethics, Religion and Politics*, Blackwell, Oxford.

Arendt, H. (1970), *On Violence*, Allen Lane, London.

Aron, R. (1983), *Clausewitz, Philosopher of War*, Routledge & Kegan Paul, London.

Aron, R. (1966), *Peace and War*, Weidenfeld & Nicolson, London.

Augustine, Saint (1872), *The Works of Aurelius Augustinus*, ed. M. Dods, Vol. V, T. & T. Clark, Edinburgh.

Babington, A. (1985), *For the Sake of Example*, Paladin, London.

Bartov, O. (1991), *Hitler's Army*, Oxford University Press, Oxford.

Bartov, O. (1985), *The Eastern Front 1941–45: German Troops and the Barbarisation of Warfare*, Macmillan, London.

Barzilai, G., Klieman, A. and Shidlo, G. (eds) (1993), *The Gulf Crisis and its Global Aftermath*, Routledge, London.

Beitz, C. R. *et al.* (eds) (1985), *International Ethics*, Princeton University Press, Princeton.

Belgrano Action Group (1988), *The Unnecessary War*, Spokesman Books, Nottingham.

Benda, J. (1969), *The Treason of the Intellectuals*, Norton, New York.

Berger, P. L. (1976), *Pyramids of Sacrifice*, Allen Lane, London.

Berlin, I. (1979), *Against the Current*, Hogarth Press, London.

Berlin, I. (1969), 'Two Concepts of Liberty', in *Four Essays on Liberty*, Oxford University Press, Oxford.

Bilton, M. and Kosminsky, P. (1989), *Speaking Out*, André Deutsch, London.

Blake, E. O. (1970), 'The Formation of the Crusade Idea', *Journal of Ecclesiastical History*, 21, pp. 11–31.

Blake, R. (ed.) (1952), *The Private Papers of Douglas Haig, 1914–1919*, Eyre and Spottiswoode, London.

Bond, B. (ed.) (1991), *The First World War and British Military History*, Clarendon Press, Oxford.

Bondanella, P. and Musa, M. (eds) (1979), *The Portable Machiavelli*, Penguin, London.

Boyle, A. (1962), *Trenchard*, Collins, London.

Bull, H. (1977), *The Anarchical Society*, Macmillan, London.

Bulloch, J. and Morris, H. (1991), *Saddam's War*, Faber & Faber, London.

Burke, E. (1969), *Reflections on the Revolution in France*, Penguin, London.

Caputo, P. (1978), *A Rumor of War*, Book Club Associates, London.

Carr, E. H. (1981), *The Twenty Years Crisis, 1919–1939*, Macmillan, London.

Ceadel, M. (1989), *Thinking about Peace and War*, Oxford University Press, Oxford.

Chanteur, J. (1992), *From War To Peace*, Westview Press, Boulder, Colorado.

Cheshire, L. (1991), *Where Is God In All This?*, St Paul Publications, Slough UK.

Churchich, N. (1994), *Marxism and Morality*, James Clarke, Cambridge.

Churchill, W. S. (1985), *The Second World War, Vols I–VI*, Penguin Books, London.

Clausewitz, C. von (1982), *On War*, Penguin, London.

Coates, A. J. (1996), 'The New World Order and The Ethics of War', in B. Holden (ed.) *The Ethical Dimensions of Global Change*, Macmillan, London, pp. 205–25.

Cohen, M. *et al.* (eds) (1974), *War and Moral Responsibility*, Princeton University Press, Princeton.

Cohen, S. M. (1989), *Arms and Judgement*, Westview Press, Boulder, Colorado.

Cohn, N. (1970), *The Pursuit of the Millennium*, Paladin, London.

Conquest, R. (1986), *The Harvest of Sorrow: Soviet Collectivization and the Terror-Famine*, Hutchinson, London.

Cromartie, M. (ed.) (1990), *Peace Betrayed?*, Ethics and Public Policy Center, Washington DC.

Curran, C. (1977), *Themes in Fundamental Moral Theology*, University of Notre Dame Press, Notre Dame.

Curran, C. (1973), *Politics, Medicine and Christian Ethics*, Fortress Press, Philadelphia.

Dalyell, T. (1983), *Thatcher's Torpedo*, Cecil Woolf, London.

Davies, J. G. (1976), *Christians, Politics and Violent Revolution*, SCM, London.

Deane, H. A. (1963), *The Political and Social Ideas of St. Augustine*, Columbia University Press, New York.

Deutscher, I. (1954), *The Prophet Armed*, Oxford University Press, London.

Dillon, G. M. (1989), *The Falklands, Politics and War*, Macmillan, London.

Dostoyevsky, F. (1958), *The Brothers Karamazov*, Penguin, London.

Douglass, J. (1968), *The Non-violent Cross*, Geoffrey Chapman, London.

Dudley Edwards, R. (1977), *Patrick Pearse: The Triumph of Failure*, Victor Gollancz, London.

Duus, P. (ed.) (1988), *The Cambridge History of Japan*, Vol. VI, Cambridge University Press, Cambridge.

Erdmann, C. (1977), *The Origin of the Idea of the Crusade*, Princeton University Press, Princeton.

Evans, J. W. and Ward, L. R. (eds) (1956), *The Social and Political Philosophy of Jacques Maritain*, Geoffrey Bles, London.

Evans, M. (1991a), 'Bridge Bombing Campaign Tarnishes Allies' PR Image', *The Times*, 8 February.

Evans, M. (1991b), 'Civilian Risks Keep Strategic Sites Off Allied Target List', *The Times*, 15 February.

Fanon, F. (1967), *The Wretched of the Earth*, Penguin, London.

Feifer, G. (1992), *Tennozan: The Battle of Okinawa and the Atomic Bomb*, Ticknor and Fields, New York.

Feiler, G. (1993), 'Petroleum Prices, Politics and War' in G. Barzilai *et al.* (eds), *The Gulf Crisis and its Global Aftermath*, Routledge, London, pp. 250–63.

Fernández-Santamaria, J. A. (1977), *The State, War and Peace*, Cambridge University Press, Cambridge.

Fernández-Santamaria, J. A. (1973), 'Erasmus on the Just War', *Journal of the History of Ideas*, 34, pp. 209–25.

Fest, J. C. (1972), *The Face of the Third Reich*, Penguin, London.

Fest, J. C. (1974), *Hitler*, Weidenfeld and Nicolson, London.

Finnis, J., Boyle, J. and Grisez, G. (1987), *Nuclear Deterrence, Morality and Realism*, Oxford University Press, Oxford.

Fletcher, J. (1978), 'Situation Ethics' in W. T. Reich (ed.), *Encyclopedia of Bioethics*, Free Press, New York, Vol. I, pp. 421–4.

Foot, P. (1983), 'How the Peace Was Torpedoed', *New Statesman*, 105 (13 May).

Frankland, N. (1965), *The Bombing Offensive against Germany*, Faber & Faber, London.

Frankland, N. (ed.) (1989), *The Encyclopaedia of 20th Century War-*

fare, Mitchell Beazley, London.

Freedman, L. and Karsh, E. (1993), *The Gulf Conflict 1990–1991: Diplomacy and War in the New World Order*, Faber & Faber, London.

Freedman, L. and Gamba-Stonehouse, V. (1990), *Signals of War: The Falklands Conflict of 1982*, Faber & Faber, London.

Freire, P. (1972), *The Pedagogy of the Oppressed*, Sheed and Ward, London.

French, D. (1988), 'Allies, Rivals and Enemies: British Strategy and War Aims during the First World War', in J. Turner (ed.) *Britain and the First World War*, Unwin Hyman, London.

Fussell, P. (ed.) (1991), *The Bloody Game: An Anthology of Modern War*, Scribners, London.

Fussell, P. (1989), *Wartime: Understanding and Behaviour in the Second World War*, Oxford University Press, New York.

Garcia, E. and Eagleson, J. (eds) (1975), *My Life For My Friends: The Guerilla Journal Of Nestor Paz, Christian*, Orbis Books, New York.

Gerassi, J. (ed.) (1968), *Venceremos!: The Speeches and Writings of Ernesto Che Guevara*, Weidenfeld & Nicolson, London.

Gilbert, M. (1986), *Winston S. Churchill*, Vol. VII: 1941–1945, Heinemann, London.

Gilbert, M. (1981), *Churchill's Political Philosophy*, Oxford University Press, Oxford.

Gilbert, M. (1972),*Winston S. Churchill*, Companion Vol. III: Part Two, Heinemann, London.

Gilbert, M. (1971), *Winston S. Churchill*, Vol. III: 1914–1916, Heinemann, London.

Graves, R. (1960), *Goodbye to All That*, Penguin, London.

Grigg, J. (1990), 'Nobility and War: The Unselfish Commitment?', *Encounter*, 74:2 (March), pp. 21–7.

Grisez, G. (1983), *Christian Moral Principles*, Vol. I of *The Way of the Lord Jesus*, Franciscan Herald Press, Chicago.

Grisez, G. (1970), 'Toward a Consistent Natural-Law Ethics of Killing', *American Journal of Jurisprudence*, Vol. 15, pp. 64–96.

Hamilton, B. (1963), *Political Thought in Sixteenth-Century Spain*, Clarendon Press, Oxford.

Hampshire, S. (ed.) (1978), *Public and Private Morality*, Cambridge University Press, Cambridge.

Häring, B. (1986), *The Healing Power of Peace and Nonviolence*, St Paul Publications, Slough, UK.

Harris, A. (1990), *Bomber Offensive*, Greenhill Books, London.

Hastings, M. (1993), *Bomber Command*, Pan Macmillan, London.

Hastings, M. and Jenkins, S. (1983), *The Battle for the Falklands*, Book Club Associates, London.

Hegel, G. W. F. (1991), *Elements of the Philosophy of Right*, trans. H. B. Nisbet, Cambridge University Press, Cambridge.

Hehir, B. (1995), 'The Lessons of World War II: War Must Be Limited', *Commonweal*, 18 August, pp. 9–10.

Herf, J. (1984), *Reactionary Modernism*, Cambridge University Press, Cambridge.

Herz, J. H. (1976), *The Nation-State and the Crisis of World Politics*, David McKay, New York.

Hill, R. (ed.) (1962), *Gesta Francorum*, Nelson, London.

Hobbes, T. (1991), *Leviathan*, Cambridge University Press, Cambridge.

Holden, B. (ed.) (1996), *The Ethical Dimensions of Global Change*, Macmillan, London.

Holmes, R. (1991), 'Sir John French and Lord Kitchener', in B. Bond (ed.), *The First World War and British Military History*, Clarendon Press, Oxford, pp. 113–39.

Holmes, R. L. (1989), *On War and Morality*, Princeton University Press, Princeton.

Holmes, R. L. (ed.) (1990), *Non-Violence in Theory and Practice*, Wadsworth, Belmont, CA.

Hook, S. (1976), *Revolution, Reform, and Social Justice*, Blackwell, Oxford.

Hussain, A. (1988), *Political Terrorism and the State in the Middle East*, Mansell, London.

James, W. (1924), *Memories and Studies*, Longman Green, New York.

Johnson, J. T. (1984), *Can Modern War Be Just?*, Yale University Press, New Haven.

Johnson, J. T. (1981), *Just War Tradition and the Restraint of War*, Princeton University Press, Princeton.

Johnson, J. T. and Kelsay, J. (eds) (1990), *Cross, Crescent and Sword*, Greenwood, Westport, Conn.

Johnson, J. T. and Weigel, G. (1991), *Just War and the Gulf War*, Ethics & Public Policy Center, Washington DC.

Johnson, P. (1988), *Intellectuals*, Weidenfeld and Nicolson, London.

Kamester, M. and Vellacott, J. (eds) (1987), *Militarism versus Feminism*, Virago Press, London.

Kedourie, E. (1987), 'Political Terror in the Muslim World', *Encounter*, 68: 2 (February), pp. 12–16.

Kedourie, E. (1984), *The Crossman Confessions and Other Essays*, Mansell, London.

Kedourie, E. (1966), *Nationalism*, Hutchinson, London.

Keegan, J. (1993), *A History of Warfare*, Hutchinson, London.

Keenan, J. F. (1993), 'The Function of the Principle of Double Effect', *Theological Studies*, Vol. 54, pp. 294–315.

Kennan, G. (1984), *American Diplomacy*, University of Chicago Press, Chicago.

Kenny, A. (1985), *The Logic of Deterrence*, Waterstone, London.

Keohane, R. O. (ed.) (1986), *Neorealism and Its Critics*, Columbia University Press, New York.

Kissinger, H. A. (1991), 'America Cannot Police the World Forever', *The Times*, 12 March.

Kissinger, H. A. (1982), *Years of Upheaval*, Weidenfeld & Nicolson, London.

Kissinger, H. A. (1971), *White House Years*, Little, Brown & Co., Boston.

Kissinger, H. A. (1969), *American Foreign Policy*, Weidenfeld & Nicolson, London.

Kissinger, H. A. (1957), *Nuclear Weapons and Foreign Policy*, Harper, New York.

Lackey, D. P. (1989), *The Ethics of War and Peace*, Prentice Hall, Englewood Cliffs, New Jersey.

Lamb, R. (1989), *The Drift to War, 1922–1939*, W. H. Allen, London.

Lefever, E. W. (ed.) (1988), *Ethics and World Politics*, Ethics & Public Policy Center, Washington DC.

Lenin, V. I. (1964–70), *Collected Works*, Progress, Moscow.

Levi, P. (1987), *Moments of Reprieve*, Sphere, London.

Levine, A. J. (1992), *The Strategic Bombing of Germany, 1940 – 1945*, Praeger, Westport, Conn.

Lewy, G. (1988), *Peace and Revolution*, Eerdmans, Grand Rapids, Mich.

Li, Z. (1994), *The Private Life of Chairman Mao*, Chatto & Windus, London.

Lloyd George, D. (1933), *War Memoirs*, Odhams, London.

Loeb, B. (1995), 'Hiroshima and Nagasaki: One Necessary Evil, One Tragic Mistake', *Commonweal*, 18 August, pp. 11–18.

Longmate, N. (1983), *The Bombers*, Hutchinson, London.

Macksey, K. and Woodhouse, W. (eds) (1991), *The Penguin Encyclopedia of Modern Warfare*, Penguin Books, London.

Macquarrie, J. (1973), *The Concept of Peace*, SCM, London.

Mao Tse-tung (1967), *Selected Works*, Foreign Languages Press, Peking.

Maritain, J. (1954), *Man and the State*, Hollis and Carter, London.

Marreco, A. (1967), *The Rebel Countess*, Weidenfeld & Nicolson, London.

Marshall, C. E. (1987), 'The Future of Women in Politics', in M. Kamester and J. Vellacott (eds), *Militarism versus Feminism*, Virago Press, London, pp. 45–52.

Marx, K. and Engels, F. (1975–1990), *Collected Works*, Progress, Moscow.

McCausland, J. (1993), *The Gulf Conflict: A Military Analysis*, Brasseys, London.

McCormick, R. A. and Ramsey, P. (eds) (1985), *Doing Evil To Achieve Good*, University Press of America, New York.

McLellan, D. (ed.) (1988), *Marxism: Essential Writings*, Oxford University Press, Oxford.

McMahan, J. and McKim, R. (1993), 'The Just War and the Gulf War', *Canadian Journal of Philosophy*, Vol. 23, pp. 501–41.

Merton, T. (1976), *On Peace*, Mowbray, London.

Middlebrook, M. (1990), *The Fight for the Malvinas*, Penguin, London.

Middlebrook, M. (1980), *The Battle of Hamburg*, Allen Lane, London.

Montgomery, B. L. (1958), *Memoirs*, Collins, London.

Morgenthau, H. J. (1973), *Politics Among Nations: The Struggle for Power and Peace*, 5th edn, Alfred A. Knopf, New York.

Morgenthau, H. J. (1946), *Scientific Man vs Power Politics*, University of Chicago Press, Chicago.

Morgenthau, H. J. and Thompson, K. W. (1985), *Politics Among Nations*, 6th edn, McGraw-Hill, New York.

Mosse, G. L. (1987), *Masses and Man: Nationalist and Fascist Perceptions of Reality*, Wayne State University Press, Detroit.

Mukherjee, R. (ed.) (1993), *The Penguin Gandhi Reader*, Penguin, New Delhi.

Murnion, P. J. (ed.) (1983), *Catholics and Nuclear War*, Geoffrey Chapman, London.

Murray, J. C. (1960), *We Hold These Truths*, Sheed and Ward, London.

Musgrove, G. (1981), *Operation Gomorrah*, Janes, London.

Nardin, T. and Mapel, D. R. (1992), *Traditions of International Ethics*, Cambridge University Press, Cambridge.

National Conference of US Catholic Bishops (1983), *The Challenge of Peace: God's Promise and Our Response*, Catholic Truth Society and SPCK, London.

Nisbet, R. (1974), *The Social Philosophers*, Heinemann, London.

Nolte, E. (1969), *Three Faces of Fascism*, New American Library, New York.

Norman, R. (1995), *Ethics, Killing and War*, Cambridge University Press, Cambridge.

Oakeshott, M. (1962), *Rationalism in Politics*, Methuen, London.

O'Brien, W. V. (1981), *The Conduct of a Just and Limited War*, Praeger, New York.

O'Connell, R. L. (1989), *Of Arms And Men: A History of War, Weapons, and Aggression*, Oxford University Press, New York.

Orwell, G. (1962), *Inside The Whale And Other Essays*, Penguin, London.

O'Sullivan, N. (1983), *Fascism*, Dent, London.

Owen, W. (1983), *The Complete Poems and Fragments*, ed. J. Stallworthy. Chatto & Windus, Hogarth and Oxford University Press, London.

Pascal, B. (1995), *Pensées*, trans. H. Levi, Oxford University Press, Oxford.

Peters, E. (ed.) (1971), *The First Crusade: The Chronicle of Fulcher of Chartres and Other Source Materials*, University of Pennsylvania Press, Philadelphia.

Pope John XXIII (1963), *Pacem in Terris*, CTS, London.

Post, J. M. (1990), 'Terrorist Psycho-logic: Terrorist Behavior as a Product of Psychological Forces', in W. Reich (ed.), *Origins of Terrorism*, Cambridge University Press, Cambridge, pp. 25–40.

Prosch, H. (1965), 'Limits to the Moral Claim in Civil Disobedience', *Ethics*, 75, pp. 103–11.

Ramsey, P. (1983), *The Just War*, University Press of America, New York.

Rapoport, D. C. (1990), 'Sacred Terror: A Contemporary Example from Islam', in W. Reich (ed.), *Origins of Terrorism*, Cambridge University Press, Cambridge, pp. 103–30.

Régamey, P. (1966), *Non-Violence and the Christian Conscience*, Darton Longman & Todd, London.

Reich, W. (ed.) (1990), *The Origins Of Terrorism*, Cambridge University Press, Cambridge.

Renick, T. M. (1994), 'Charity Lost: The Secularization of the Principle of Double Effect in the Just War Tradition', *The Thomist*, Vol. 58, pp. 441–62.

Ringer, F. K. (1990), *The Decline of the German Mandarins*, University Press of New England, Hanover, New Hampshire.

Ruether, R. (1975), *Faith and Fratricide: The Theological Roots of Anti-Semitism*, Search Press, London.

Russell, B. (1978), *Autobiography*, Unwin, London.

Ryan, C. C. (1983), 'Self-Defense, Pacifism, and the Possibility of Killing', *Ethics*, 93, pp. 508–24.

Sartre, J.-P. (1976), *Critique of Dialectical Reason*, NLB, London.

Schacht, J. and Bosworth, C. E. (eds) (1974), *The Legacy of Islam*, Clarendon Press, Oxford.

Seabury, P. and Codevilla, A. (1989), *War: Ends and Means*, Basic Books, New York.

Sharp, G. (1973), *The Politics of Nonviolent Action*, Porter Sargent, Boston.

Sheehan, N. (1988), *A Bright Shining Lie*, Random House, New York.

Shirer, W. L. (1964), *The Rise and Fall of the Third Reich*, Pan, London.

Sigmund, P. E. (ed.) (1988), *St Thomas Aquinas on Politics and Ethics*, Norton, New York.

Skinner, Q. (1978), *The Foundations of Modern Political Thought*, 2 vols, Cambridge University Press, Cambridge.

Solzhenitsyn, A. (1978), *The Gulag Archipelago*, Collins, London.

Stirk, S. D. (1969), *The Prussian Spirit 1914–1940*, Kennikat Press, Port Washington, NY.

Strachan, H. (1991), '"The Real War": Liddell Hart, Cruttwell, and Falls', in B. Bond (ed.), *The First World War and British Military History*, Clarendon Press, Oxford, pp. 41–67.

Synan, E. A. (1965), *The Popes and the Jews in the Middle Ages*, Macmillan, New York.

Taheri, A. (1987), *Holy Terror*, Sphere, London.

Talbott, J. (1981), *The War Without a Name*, Faber and Faber, London.

Taylor, T. (1979), *Munich: The Price of Peace*, Doubleday, New York.

Teichman, J. (1986), *Pacifism and the Just War*, Blackwell, Oxford.

Terraine, J. (1963), *Douglas Haig: The Educated Soldier*, Hutchinson, London.

Thatcher, M. (1993) *The Downing Street Years*, HarperCollins, London.

Thibon, G. (1954), *Love and Violence*, Sheed & Ward, London.

Thomas, H. (1971), *Cuba: The Pursuit of Freedom*, Harper & Row, New York.

Tolstoy, L. (1991), *War and Peace*, Oxford University Press, Oxford.

Tolstoy, L. (1986), *The Sebastopol Sketches*, Penguin, London.

Tolstoy, L. (1894), *The Kingdom Of God Is Within You*, Walter Scott, London.

Tucker, R. W. (1960), *The Just War*, Johns Hopkins, Baltimore, MD.

Turner, J. (ed.) (1988), *Britain and the First World War*, Unwin Hyman, London.

Vann, G. (1939), *Morality and War*, Burns Oates and Washbourne, London.

Veale, F. J. P. (1968) *Advance to Barbarism*, Mitre Press, London.

Vitoria, F. de (1991), *Political Writings*, ed. and trans. A. Pagden and J. Lawrance, Cambridge University Press, Cambridge.

Walker, C. (1991), 'Misgivings Mount among Saudis as Air War Takes Ugly Turn', *The Times*, 15 February.

Waltz, K. N. (1979), *Theory of International Politics*, Addison Wesley, Reading, Mass.

Walzer, M. (1994), *Thick and Thin*, University of Notre Dame, Notre Dame.

Walzer, M. (1992), *Just and Unjust Wars*, Basic Books, New York.

Webster, C. and Frankland, N. (1961), *The Strategic Air Offensive Against Germany, 1939–45*, 4 vols, HMSO, London.

Weigel, G. (1987), *Tranquillitas Ordinis*, Oxford University Press, New York.

Welch, D. A. (1993), *Justice and the Genesis of War*, Cambridge University Press, Cambridge.

Wilkins, B. T. (1992), *Terrorism and Collective Responsibility*, Routledge, London.

Wilkinson, P. (1986), *Terrorism and the Liberal State*, Macmillan, London.

Wilson, T. (1986), *The Myriad Faces of War*, Polity Press, Cambridge.

Wink, W. (1990), 'Is There An Ethic of Violence?', *The Way*, 30:2, pp. 103–13.

Winters, F. X. (1991), 'Freedom To Resist Coercion', *Commonweal*, June 1, pp. 369–72.

Woodcock, G. (1963), *Anarchism*, Penguin, London.

Woodward, J. and Robinson, P. (1992), *One Hundred Days*, Book Club Associates, London.

Wragg, D. (1986), *The Offensive Weapon: The Strategy of Bombing*, Robert Hale, London.

Zahn, G. (1991), 'An Infamous Victory', *Commonweal*, June 1, pp. 366–8.

Zahn, G. (1983), 'Pacifism and the Just War', in P. Murnion (ed.), *Catholics and Nuclear War*, Geoffrey Chapman, London.

Zahn, G. (1964), *In Solitary Witness: The Life and Death of Franz Jägerstätter*, Holt, Rinehart & Winston, New York.

Zahn, G. (1962), *German Catholics and Hitler's Wars*, Sheed and Ward, New York.

Zolo, D. (1997), *Cosmopolis*, Polity Press, Cambridge.

Index

Note: 'n' after a page reference indicates the number of a note on that page. Numbers in **bold** indicate main references.

abortion 167–8
absolutism, moral 184n1, 242,
   260, 271n35
agency 244–6, 259
aggressor–defender distinction 5,
   156–61
   and time-lapse 158, 195
Aho, A. 71n14, 74n30
Algerian War 76n39, 92, 143n9
   see also Fanon
Allara, Rear Admiral G. 212,
   228n3
Americas, conquest 46, 280–1,
   292n7
anarchism 51, 56, 86–7, 138
Anscombe, E. 85
answering, pacifist concept of 88,
   117
appeasement 24, 115, 174, 190–2,
   200
Aquinas, St Thomas 3, 13n18
   legitimate authority 126–7
   resistance, right of 129–31,
     134–5, 142n6
Arendt, H. 118n10, n11, 172–3
Aron, R. 8, 42–3, 49–50, 53, 275
Assassins 65, 71n14
Augustine, St
   just war and law of charity 29,
     83
   legitimate authority 124
   moral primacy of peace 116,
     273–4
   personal pacifism 78
   providence, divine 172

Bakunin, M. 51, 65
balance of power 19–20, 23, 99,
   160, 275–9, 285, 291n3

Baldwin, Stanley 254
barbarization of war 62, 150 *see*
   also dehumanization,
   demonization
Bartov, O. 74n32, 148–9, 163n3,
   n4
belligerency, status of 123–45
   passim
   moral responsibility and 83–4
   terrorism and 123–4
Benda, J. 41, 64
Bentham, J. 171, 173
Berlin, I. 47
Bernard, St 108, 110
Bidawid, Patriarch R. 152
Billancourt, RAF raid (1942)
   247–9
Blake E. O. 109–10
blockade *see* sanctions
bombing
   allied offensives (WWII) 27,
     246–9, 252–64
   area (saturation) 103, 249–52
   Gulf War 103, 221–6
   precision 31, 224, 248–56
     passim, 269n23
   strategic 104, 223, 232n19,
     236, 237, 247, 249,
     264n3, 268n21
   tactical 246–7, 250
Bosnia 23, 166n22, 184
Burke, Edmund 44, 52, 142n7
Bush, President George 152, 192,
   194, 200

Caen, bombing (1944) 247, 250
Cambodia 44, 144n13, 161
Caputo, P. 28–9, 31
Carr, E. H. 17–18, 21

Casablanca Conference (1943) 256,
      290
Castro, Fidel 54
casuistry, moral 9–11, 100–1,
      165n12, 189–90, 206–7,
      209, 224–5
Ceadel, M. 8, 40–2
Chanteur, J. 282–3
Chavès, L. 56
Cheshire, L. (VC) 38n8, 93,
      232n21
Churchill, Winston S.
   balance of power, defence of 20
   bombing policy (WWII) 229n12,
      256, 269n29, n30
   critic of appeasement 7, 24,
      190–2
   democracy, view of 44
   and First World War 217–18
   and unconditional surrender
      289– 90, 293n15
   war rhetoric 47, 293n15
civilian immunity 237 *see also* non-
      combatant immunity
civilian morale, targeting 132, 250,
      254–8, 266n11, 269n31,
      270n34
Clausewitz, C. von 22–8 *passim*, 43,
      70n3, 100
Cohen, M. 113
Cohn, N. 109
Cold War 5–6, 80, 154, 200, 274
collateral damage 103, 250, 255
      see also double effect
collective security 160
common good
   particular (state) 129, 177
   universal (international) 127–8,
      156–7, 178, 282
communism 44, 47, 49, 57–8, 63,
      67, 69–70
community, universal
      (international) 99, 127–8,
      155, 177–9, 183, 200, 202,
      203, 279–82
community, war and 52–4, 66–70,
      137, 176–7
compassion 58, 64, 105, 221, 227
conscientious objection 79

'conscientization' 137–9
consequentialism, moral 36,
      113–14, 171–3, 184n1,
      259–64
counterinsurgency 31, 132
courage 33, 74n28
Coventry, bombing of (1940)
      270n33
crusades 46, 48, 50, 60–1,
      106–11
Cuellar, Perez de 204
culture, moral (of war) 84, 90–1,
      102–3, 115, 155, 271n39,
      287
Curran, Charles 132–3, 260–1,
      271n38

Dalyell, T. 208n7
Davies, J. G. 145n16
deductivism, moral 9–10
dehumanization
   of enemy 38n7, 61–3, 105,
      225, 252, 268n22
   of war 84–5, 220–1, 227
democracy
   conduct of war and 103, 141n3,
      141n5, 205–6, 236
   irresponsibility (Burke) 94n8
   and militarism 44, 47
   and revolution 135–6
demonization 62–3, 105, 110,
      150, 201 *see also*
      dehumanization
Dillon, G. M. 180, 228n7, 228n8
diplomacy 21, 26, 101, 175,
      189–92, 199–206
direct-indirect, agency 244–5, 259
discrimination *see* noncombatant
      immunity
Dostoevsky, F. 64–5
double effect, principle of
      239–64
   agency and 244–6
   bombing policy (WWII) and
      246–59
   criticism of 240–1, 242, 244,
      245, 246, 266n12,
   function 239–40, 241, 263–4,
      265n9

requirements 241–6
  proportionality 245–6
  right intention 243–5,
    267n15
  structure of act 241–3
  responsibility and 245–6,
    267n16, 268n17
double standard(s) 19–21, 131,
    142n8, 153–4, 183, 201
Douglass, J. 84–5
dualism, moral 35–7, 114

Eden, Anthony 190
embargo *see* sanctions
emergency, supreme 5, 33, 261–2
enemy, classification
  absolute 45, 57, 60, 62–3,
    151
  limited (just war) 60, 280, 288
    see also dehumanization;
    right(s)
Engels, F. 68, 134 *see also* Marx
enthusiasm, war and moral 3, 43,
    50, 105–6, 133–4, 142n8,
    146, 189, 283 *see also*
    triumphalism
Erasmus, D. 94n10
escalation 160, 170
Evans, M. 223–4
evil
  instrumentality 18
  physical and moral, distinction
    168, 242, 243, 265n6

Falklands War (1982) 158, 226,
    165n16
  proportionality of conduct
    209–14
  proportionality of recourse
    174–6
  prospects of success 179–81
false consciousness 55, 136–7
Fanon, F. 54
al-Faraj, A. 48, 52
fascism 8, 40–3, 47, 49, 53, 62–3,
    66, 69
Fernández-Santamaria, J. A. 12n4,
    94n10
Fest, J. 65, 76n38

Finnis, J. *et al.* 231n18, 243–4
first use 159–60
First World War 30, 46–8, 53, 57,
    66–7
  defence of Belgium (1914)
    181–2
  Loos, battle of (1915) 214–16,
    217, 218
  Somme, battle of (1916) 216–20
  strategy of attrition 217–21,
    230n14, n15
  Versailles Treaty 284–6
Foot, Michael 187n14
force 126
  violence and 85–6, 114–15
Frankland, N. 208n8, 223, 253,
    270n32
Freedman, L. 212, 226
Freire, P. 137, 145n15
French, Sir John 215
French Revolution 27–8, 44, 49
fundamentalism, militant
  Christian 46, 48, 50, 52, 60–1,
    106–11
  Islamic 45–6, 48, 50, 52, 57,
    70n7, 75n3

Gandhi, M. K. 88–9, 92, 95n14
Garrison, William Lloyd 86
General Belgrano, attack on 209–14
Geneva Convention 264
Gilpin, R. 34–5
Graves, R. 30
Grisez, G. 267n15, n16
Grosman, V. 63
Grotius, Hugo 147
Guevara, Che 51, 56, 73n22,
    144n13, 145n14
guilt 33–4, 133, 234–5, 271n39,
    288
Gulf War 10, 19–20, 103, 160
  and just cause 151–4
  and last resort 192–207
    diplomacy 199–206
    sanctions 195–9
  and proportionality (conduct)
    214, 221–7
    bombing offensive 221–6
    land offensive 226–7

and proportionality (recourse)
183–4
and right intention 162–3

Haig, Sir Douglas 214–20, 292n10
Halifax, E. (Lord) 190
Hamas 71n14
Hamburg, bombing (1943) 255–60
hardness, ethic of 64–5, 105
Häring, B. 89, 94n6, 95n13
Harris, Sir Arthur 27, 245, 255–6,
263, 266n11, 269n31,
270n34
Hastings, M. 180, 210
Heath, Sir Edward 207n3
Hegel, G. W. F. 52, 94n9, 172,
176–7
Hehir, B. 272n41
Hemingway, Ernest 11n2, 13n8
Himmler, Heinrich 62, 65
Hiroshima, bombing (1945) 261,
270n32, 272n40, n41
Hitler, Adolf 59, 71n12, 74n30,
152, 191, 200, 285
Hobbes, Thomas 274–5
Hoepner, General E. 71n11
Holmes, R. 229n11
Holmes, R. L. 4–5, 38n4, 104,
265n8, 266n12, 268n20
holy war 46, 50, 52, 146, 151 *see
also* crusades; jihad
human nature, war and 90–1
Hungary, Soviet invasion (1956)
93, 178–9

idealism 18, 19, 22, 23, 98 *see also*
moralism
ideology, war and 25–6, 43–5,
178
ignorance 148, 268n17
images of war, concept 7–8, 97
imperialism 42, 46, 201, 277 *see
also* mankind, unity of
incommensurability 173
India, independence 92
inductivism, moral 10–11
innocence, concept of 234–5
interest(s)
and inhibition of war 25–6

and justice 162–3, 183
national 23, 34–5, 99, 155, 277
intervention 23–4, 127–8, 146,
153–4, 157, 161, 166n22,
178–9, 278
Irish Republican Army (IRA)123,
143n12 *see also* nationalism;
Pearse; terrorism

Jäggerstätter, F. 112, 128, 163n3
James, William 70n4
Jerusalem Massacre 60–1, 110
jews, persecution of 48, 61, 63,
74n32, 108–10 *see also*
dehumanization;
demonization
jihad 46, 50, 52, 70n8 *see also*
crusades; holy war
John XXIII, Pope 156
Johnson, J. T. 164n8, 179, 181
Johnson, President Lyndon 141n5
Jones, T. 191
Jünger, E. 48, 53, 66–7
just cause **146–65** 9, 288–9
and aggressor–defender
distinction 156–61
bilateral (comparative) 147–56,
164n7
Gulf War and 151–4
objective 150–1
subjective 148–50
misuse 27, 43, 45–55, 108,
110, 146–7
narrowing (of concept) 156
and right intention 161–3
unilateral (absolute) 150–1,
155, 164n6
just conduct (*ius in bello*) 8, 24, 58,
105, 26–7, 117 *see also*
double effect; noncombatant
immunity; peacemaking;
proportionality
just recourse (*ius ad bellum*) 2, 8–9,
22–3, 26–7, 43, 45, 55,
105, 117 *see also* just cause;
last resort; legitimate
authority; proportionality
and prospects of success;
right intention

just war, image **97–119**
  and militarism 2–3, 43, 49, 50,
      60, 97, 104–11,
  and realism 4, 5, 32, 37, 49,
      50, 97–104, 113–14
  and pacifism 77, 97, 111–17
just war, principles
  interrelation 43, 147–8, 167,
      179, 182
  specification 8–9
just war, tradition
  criticism of 2–7, 37n3, 80–2,
      88, 104, 112–13, 154,
  ethics of war and 1–2

kamikaze (Divine Wind Special
      Attack Force) 59
Kedourie, E. 70n6, 172
Keegan, J. 125
Kennan, George 24, 26, 38n5
Kenny, A. 288–9
Keynes, J. M. 284
Khatayevich, M. M. 55
Khmer Rouge 144n13, 161
Khomeini, Ayatollah 46, 50
King, Martin Luther 89
Kissinger, Henry
  on balance of power 20, 277
  on Gulf War 19–20, 197
  on limited war 25
  on origins of Vietnam War
      23
Kitchener, H. (Lord) 215, 229n11
kulaks, persecution of 58, 63 *see
      also* dehumanization;
      demonization

Lackey, D. P. 126, 181, 239
language, moral impact 62, 140n2,
      243, 266n10
last resort **189–208** 41, 56–8,
      101, 130
  appeasement and 189–92
  Gulf War and 192–207
      applicability 195
      diplomacy 199–206
      sanctions policy 193, 194,
          195–9
  Second World War and 190–2

law,
      international 2, 127, 154,
          159, 203
      natural 146, 281
law enforcement, just war and
      85–6, 114–15, 126, 154–6
leadership 28, 144n13
legalism 18, 26 *see also* moralism;
      idealism
legitimate authority **123–45**, 55
  basis 126–9
  belligerent status and 123–6
  importance, contemporary
      124–5, 134, 140, 143n10
  resistance and revolution
      128–40
LeMay, General Curtis E. 263,
      270n32
Lenin, V. I. 49, 53, 54, 65, 67,
      68–9, 73n20, 136–7
Levi, P. 186n9
Levine, A. J. 207n2, 248, 249
Lewis, B. 70n8
liberation theology 137, 139
Lloyd George, David 284
Loeb, B. 272n40
Longmate, N. 248–9

Machiavelli 21, 35, 38n10, 39n12,
      118n4, 162
MacNeill, Eoin 56
Macquarrie, J. 284
mankind, unity of 60, 61, 156–7,
      177–8, 279–82, 291
  concepts of
      cosmopolitan 7, 143n10, 282
      ecumenical/plural 7, 281–2
      imperial 42, 46, 70, 277,
          280–1
Mao Tse-tung 64, 73n22, 145n15
Marighela, Carlos 138
Maritain, Jacques 34, 35, 101,
      104, 118n4
Marshall, Catherine 56
martyrdom, war and 50, 107
Marx, Karl 53–4, 57–8, 67–9,
      136
McCormick, R. A. 260–1, 271n37
Merton, Thomas 117, 128

militarism **40–76** 2, 7, 8, 97,
    104–11
  concepts and definitions 8, 40–3
  ideological 44–5, 47, 48–9,
    50–2, 53–60, 62–70, 178
  religious 44, 46, 48, 50, 52,
    60–1, 106–11, 178
  undermining of just conduct 58
    noncombatant immunity
    60–5
    proportionality 58–60
  undermining of just peace
    65–70
  undermining of just recourse 43
    just cause 45–55
    last resort 56–8
    legitimate authority 55
    proportionality 55
    prospects of success 55–6
militarization of society 66–9, 90–1
Molina, L. de 292n6
Montgomery, Field Marshal Sir B.
    29
moralism **17–39** *passim*, 83, 89,
    98, 101, 103, 106
morality, efficacy 102–3, 287–8
morality and moralism 36–7,
    103–4 *see also* moral realism
morality of states 5
moral realism 98–104, 189, 279,
    283–4,
Morgenthau, H. J. 21, 33
Mosse, G. L. 53
Moynihan, Senator Daniel 197
Murray, John Courtney 100, 158,
    176

Nagasaki, bombing (1945)
    270n32, 272n40, n41
Nagel, T. 113
National Conference of US Catholic
    Bishops 164n7, 187n16
nationalism 45–8, 57, 71n10, 137,
    143n12, 144n13
National Military Command Center
    (US) 200
necessity, military 114, 132, 213,
    237, 249, 250, 252–4
neutrality 77

Niebuhr, R. 33
Nisbet, R. 76n41
Nolte, E. 285
noncombatant immunity **234–72**
    27, 31, 58, 60–5, 80–1,
    102, 104, 123–4, 131–3,
    198, 210, 224
  bombing policy (WWII) and
    246–59
  combatant/noncombatant
    235–9, 264n5
  double effect 239–46
  innocence, meaning of
    234–5
  moral consequentialism and
    259–64
  requirements 239, 263, 265n6
non-intervention 99, 156, 160,
    161
Norman, R. 1, 3–5, 12n6, 244,
    246, 265n8, 266n12,
Nott, John 179
Nunn, Senator Sam 192

Oakeshott, M. 9–10
O'Brien, W. V. 168, 171, 179,
    250, 267n14
Okinawa, battle of (1945) 59
Orwell, George 83
Owen, Wilfred 11

pacifism **77–96** 194, 236
  and just war 77, 79–82, 88, 97,
    111–17
  non-violence, ethic of 87–8
  non-violent defence 91–3
  non-violent resistance 88–9
  pacification 90–1
  realism 89–90
  varieties 77–87
Paris Commune 54, 67
particularism, moral 7, 30–1,
    34, 41–2, 60, 95, 282,
    292n8
partisanship, moral 155, 286 *see
    also* just cause, unilateral;
    particularism
Paulus, Field Marshal F. von 59
Paz, Nestor 72n15

peace, concepts of
   just war 99, 105, 115–17,
      279–84, 286–7, 291
   militarist 41–2, 45–6, 57–8,
      65–6, 69–70, 105
   pacifist 4, 115–17, 87–8
   realist 18–19, 22, 24, 25, 99,
      274–9 *see also* mankind
peacemaking **273–93** 116–17, 189
   pacification 90–1, 102–3, 115,
      124–5, 155
   realist-utopian strategy 283–6
   and unconditional surrender
      288–91
   and war crimes tribunals 286–8
peace, moral primacy (*ius ad pacem*)
      56, 116, 189, 273, 280
Pearse, P. 50, 53, 56, 57, 72n15,
      137
Peirse, Sir Richard (C-in-C Bomber
      Command) 255
Pétain, Marshal P. 236
physical force tradition 57
Pointblank, bombing directive
      (WWII) 256
Post, J. M. 52
power 17–21, 23, 33, 91, 101,
      114–15, 128, 129
prisoners of war 31, 62–3
propaganda of the deed 56, 136,
      138
proportionalism 259–64, 271n35
proportionality (of conduct)
      209–33
   bilateral interpretation 221
   First World War 214–20
   General Belgrano, sinking of
      209–14
   Gulf War 221–7
   strategic context 209, 220 *see
      also* double effect; militarism
proportionality (of recourse)
      167–88, 55, 130–1
   consequentialism and 171–4
      incommensurability 173–4
      uncertainty 171–3
   and Falklands War 174–6,
      179–81
   and Gulf War 182–4, 188n17

and international common good
      177–9
   moral not material 176–7
   and prospects of success 179–82
Prosch, H. 116
psychology, ethics of war and 31–2
puritanism, moral 18–20, 26, 162,
      183

Quakers 88
Qutbists 75n33

Ramsey, P. 147–8, 185n4,
      267n14, 269n24
Rawlinson, General Sir Henry 215,
      217, 219
realism **17–39** 4, 5, 42–3, 49, 50,
      77, 189, 285–6
   and conduct of war 24–32
   degrees (and varieties) of 7–8,
      15–37
   limited war, concept of 24–6,
      42–3, 45, 49, 100
   moralism, criticism of 17–39
      passim
   and recourse to war 22–4
   see also balance of power; just
      war, image; pacifism; peace
realpolitik 153, 163n1 *see also*
      realism
reason of state 5 *see also* realism
reductionism, moral 140, 145n16,
      146, 147–8, 174, 182–4,
      241, 259, 262
relativism, moral 146
remorse, just war and 2–3 *see also*
      compassion; enthusiasm
resistance, right of 129–30, 134 *see
      also* revolution
responsibility, moral
   assignment of 28, 34, 64, 116,
      133, 138–9, 141n3,
      148–51, 154, 201, 286–8
   command and 28, 33–4, 213,
      214–20, 221
   consequences and 172–3
   double effect and 245–6, 250–1,
      267n16
   erosion of, in war 28–32, 83–5,

108, 109–10, 112, 128,
        133–4, 146
    levels of 28, 141n3
revolution 40–76 *passim*
    and just war 130–4
    and legitimate authority 134–40
right intention
    double effect and 240–1, 243–5,
        248, 250–1, 252–5, 259
    just recourse and 3, 9, 29,
        161–3, 183
    moral puritanism and 18–20,
        26, 42–3, 162, 183
right(s)
    of enemy 31, 60, 105, 117,
        151, 225, 280–1, 288,
        290–1
    of immunity *see* noncombatant
        immunity
    of self-determination 175,
        178–9
    of war 123–45 *passim*
    see also self defence
risk
    calculation of 31–2
    indifference to 58–9
Roach, Archbishop 193
Roosevelt, President F. D. 256,
        290–1
Russell, Bertrand 96n19

Saddam Hussein 152, 187n15,
        200–6 *passim*, 221, 222,
        227
sanctions (embargo) 193–9, 285
Sartre, J-P. 54, 64
Sassoon, Siegfried 11, 30
Schlesinger, Arthur 21, 23
Schwarzkopf, Gen. Norman 214,
        221, 231n17
Second Vatican Council 291n3
Second World War 47, 65
    allied bombing offensive 246–64
    Okinawa, battle of 59
    Russian front 47, 59, 62–3
    unconditional surrender 288–91
self-defence, right of
    collective security 160
    first use 159–60

just war and 127, 156–7,
        160–1
    preemptive/preventive war
        158–60
self-fulfilment, war and 50–2,
        71n14, 72n15, 107–8,
        109–10
self-help 127, 154–5
Senate Armed Services Committee
        192, 197
Senate Foreign Relations Committee
        192, 193
Sheehan, N. 230n16
Sherman, General William T. 27
Shirer, W. L. 293n12
Sinn Fein 143n12
situation ethics 10
Six Day War 159
Smuts Report 253
Solzhenitsyn, A. 287
Somalia, US intervention 23
Sombart, W. 48
Sorel, Georges 72n16
sovereignty 34, 99, 125, 146, 156,
        161, 275, 282
Soviet Union 44, 47, 55, 58, 67,
        165n15, 229n12
Spaight, J. M. 238–9
Stalingrad, battle (1942–43) 59
state, concepts of
    fascist 41, 42, 66–7, 69
    just war 78, 99, 126–9, 135,
        143n10, 155, 156–7, 159,
        160, 161, 166, 176–7,
        280–2
    Marxist-Leninist 67–9
    pacifist 85–8, 90–1, 112–13,
        142n8
    realist 6–7, 19, 21, 34–5, 99,
        125, 156, 162, 274–9
state of war 123–4, 195
    international relations as 19, 22,
        46, 99, 127, 274–9, 283,
        291
states-system 6–7, 19, 156, 163n1
Stimson, Henry 272n40
St Just 64
Suárez, F. 13n10, 177, 264n2,
        279–80, 281

subsidiarity 292n9
success, prospects **179–82** 9, 55–6,
    101, 130–1, 216
    Belgian defence (1914) and
        181–2
    Falklands War and 179–81
    moral witness and 182, 186n9,
        187n16
    proportionality and 179, 182
suffering, unilateral 198–9, 222,
    232n21
surrender, unconditional 38n5, 65,
    105, 288–91
Sverdlov, Y. 58

Talbott, J. 143n9
targeting 223, 224, 257–8
Terraine, J. 219–20, 230n14
terrorism 51–2, 123–5, 136,
    140n2, 143n9, n12, 203–4
Thatcher, Margaret 180, 181, 200,
    207n5, 212, 214
Thibon, G. 288
Third World 183
Tokyo, bombing (1945) 270n32
Tolstoy, L. 82–4, 94n12
training, military 29–30
Trenchard, Air Marshal Sir Hugh
    253–4
triumphalism, moral 3, 61, 105–6,
    146, 154 *see also*
    enthusiasm
Trotsky, L. 64
Tucker, R. W. 37n3
tyranny 128–31

uncertainty (of consequences)
    171–3
United Nations (UN) 155, 183,
    199, 200, 201
United Nations Charter 159, 160
United States Army Air Forces
    (USAAF) 256
universalism, moral 7, 41, 42, 46,
    99, 156–7, 177, 279–82
Urban II, Pope 106–9
utilitarianism, moral 171–3, 262
utopian(ism) 17–19, 29, 37, 54,
    55, 98, 113, 115, 130,

282–3, 285–6 *see also*
    moralism
vanguard, revolutionary 136–7,
    140
Vann, G 100
Versailles Treaty (1919) 191, 290,
    284–6
Vietnam War, 23, 28–9, 38n4, 79,
    141n5, 230n16, 278
violence,
    creative 54, 138
    force and 85–6, 114, 118n10
    spiral of 87, 116
    structural 64, 90, 132–3,
        138–9
Vitoria, F. de
    accidental effect 235, 264n1
    just cause 148–51 *passim*, 154
    peacemaking 286, 293n16
    proportionality 167
    responsibility, levels of 141n3
    rights of Indians 281, 292n7
    universal community 157,
        165n14, 281

Walzer, M. 4–5, 34, 165n16,
    173–4, 195, 222, 240, 262,
    263, 292n8
war,
    absolute 24–8, 43, 47
    apocalyptic 47–8, 60, 110
    attritional 183, 214–21, 225,
        230n16, 222, 253
    civil 47–9, 125, 140, 275, 280
    countervalue 63, 133
    cultural 47, 64, 75n33, 202
    guerilla 6, 28–9, 31, 132–3,
        143n9, 236
    industrial 66–7, 84, 236, 238
    limited 24–6, 42–3, 45, 49,
        100, 147
    missionary 44–9, 107–11
    nuclear 5–6, 80, 156, 169–70
    political (rational-instrumental)
        22, 24, 25, 42–3, 49–50,
        51, 52, 100
    pre-emptive 158–60, 278
    preventive 24, 159, 190, 278
    real and absolute, distinction 25

revolutionary 40–75 *passim*,
    130–45
siege 235, 247, 250 *see also*
    sanctions
total
    and absolute war 24–8, 43,
        100
    and dehumanization 62
    and just war 6, 156, 169,
        183
    and modern war 80–1, 84,
        170, 183, 220, 223, 236
    and revolution 133
    and unconditional surrender
        65, 288
war crimes 287–8
'war is hell' 27–32
Webster, C. and Frankland, N. 248
Weigel, G. 13n16, 142n8
Welch, D. 13n9, 163n1, 164n9
Westlake. J. 48, 291n4

Westmoreland, General William
    230n16
Whitelaw, William (Lord) 213
Wilkins, B. T. 123–4
Wilkinson, P. 71n13
Wilson, T. 216, 218–19
Wilson, President Woodrow 19
Windlass, S. 154
Wink, W. 87–8
Winters, F. X. 195
witness, war as form of 56, 72n15,
    137, 182
Woodcock, G. 51, 56, 94n12
Woodward, Admiral Sir J. 186n10,
    n12, n13, 212, 213, 228n9
Wragg, D. 248

Yeats, W. B. 72n15

Zahn, G. 112, 194, 208n6
Zolo, D. 1